DAY HIKES AROUND
Sonoma County

125 GREAT HIKES

Robert Stone
2nd EDITION

Day Hike Books, Inc.
RED LODGE, MONTANA

Published by Day Hike Books, Inc.
P.O. Box 865 · Red Lodge, Montana 59068
www.dayhikebooks.com

Distributed by National Book Network
800-243-0495 (direct order) · 800-820-2329 (fax order)

Cover photograph by John W. Wall
http://ptreyesblog.blogspot.com

Back cover photo by Kathy Barnhart

Layout/maps by Paula Doherty

The author has made every attempt to provide accurate information in this book. However, trail routes and features may change—please use common sense and forethought, and be mindful of your own capabilities. Let this book guide you, but be aware that each hiker assumes responsibility for their own safety. The author and publisher do not assume any responsibility for loss, damage, or injury caused through the use of this book.

Copyright © 2016 by Day Hike Books, Inc.
2nd Edition
ISBN: 978-1-57342-072-3

Library of Congress Control Number: 2015911439

Cover photo:
Goat Rock, near Bodega Bay, Hike 30

Back cover photo:
Bodega Head, Hike 34

Awards for Day Hikes Around Sonoma County

Best Guidebook Award
Outdoor Writers of California

Best Guidebook Award
Northwest Outdoor Writers Association

Best Guidebook Award
Rocky Mountain Outdoor Writers and Photographers

I wish to thank
Meda Freeman, Karen Davis-Brown, and Jeff Taylor
from the Sonoma County Regional Parks who generously shared
their time and knowledge about the area's hiking trails.

Table of Contents

The Hikes

COASTAL HIKES

North Coast: Mendonoma
North Sonoma Coast—South Mendocino Coast
Point Arena to Sea Ranch

Central Coast Sonoma County
Stewarts Point to Jenner

Southern Coast
Jenner to Bodega Bay
Sonoma Coast State Park

INLAND HIKES

North Central Sonoma County
Guerneville • Forestville • Windsor • Lake Sonoma

Calistoga Area
Robert Louis Stevenson State Park
Bothe—Napa Valley State Park

Santa Rosa and vicinity
Central Sonoma County

Santa Rosa to Sonoma • Sonoma Valley
South Central Sonoma County

Southern Sonoma County
San Pablo Bay • Novato • Petaluma

Hiking Sonoma County

California's Sonoma County is known for its wineries and magnificent natural landscape—a picturesque mix of rugged coastline, steep cliffs, forested hillsides, and verdant agricultural valleys. The cities, towns, and villages are as diverse as the geography. In addition to the nearly 200 wineries, the county has thousands of acres of parkland, including 11 state parks and more than 40 regional parks.

Sonoma County is located 35 miles north of San Francisco via the Golden Gate Bridge. The county lies between the Pacific Ocean and the Mayacamas Mountains, the range that separates Sonoma and Napa counties. The wide variety of landscapes and microclimates can be attributed to Sonoma County's unique location between the ocean and the mountains.

This collection of 125 day hikes provides access to both well known and out-of-the-way greenspace throughout Sonoma County. Hikes are found along the Pacific, across the coastal ridges, into the wide valleys, and through thick forests. The first third of the hikes are on the coastline, accessed by Highway 1. Many coastal entry points from the highway are clearly described. The remaining hikes explore the inland mountains, hillsides, and valleys through the county's state parks and undeveloped public lands.

The Coastal Hikes

The spectacular Sonoma coast stretches 58 miles, from Bodega Bay at the southern end to the town of Gualala at the northern Sonoma—Mendocino county line. Vertiginous Highway 1 connects the coastal towns as it snakes along the dramatic oceanfront cliffs and bluffs. There are breath-taking panoramas of the crashing surf, offshore rocks, and steep forested hills.

The coastal hikes are divided into north, central, and southern sections. Hikes 1—11 are found along the Mendonoma Coast, where Mondocino County meets Sonoma County. The hikes start at the rugged Point Arena headlands and travel southwards to a series of beaches and bluffs by Gualala. Hikes 12—25 explore the majestic Salt Point State Park and Fort Ross State Historic Park. Both parks encompass thousands of acres of coastline. Rocky outcroppings, coves, beaches, and tidepools are backdropped by rolling hills and forested canyons. Hikes 26—37 continue south along Highway 1 from Jenner to Bodega Bay. Sonoma Coast State Park stretches along the coast for nearly the entire length, from Vista Trail at the north end to Bodega Head at the south. The state park is an interconnected series of beaches and bluffs.

Access to all of the coastal hikes is from Highway 1. The serpentine road passes old logging and fishing communities, offering some of the best coastal vistas in California.

The Inland Hikes

The inland hikes begin at the north end of Sonoma County and wind southward, roughly following the direction of Highway 101. The hikes are divided into north, central, and southern sections, as well as a Calistoga section, which borders the Sonoma—Napa county line.

The rich inland valleys are perfectly suited for vineyards and farms, which stretch across the county's rolling hills. The Russian River basin nourishes the area, winding through the county from Cloverdale to the ocean at Jenner. The river's meandering course flows from valleys to forests to the dramatic coastline. The Mayacamas Mountains run through the county east of Highway 101, where many of the hikes are located.

Hikes 38—48 are located at the north end of the county, where the population declines and there is more opportunity for secluded hiking. Lake Sonoma, Armstrong-Redwoods, and Austin Creek Recreation Areas are included in this section of hikes.

Hikes 49—60 are found along the northeast Sonoma—Napa county line around the Calistoga area. Two large state parks are located here—Robert Louis Stevenson State Park and Bothe-Napa Valley State Park—as well as the highest peak in Sonoma County, Mount Saint Helena. These hikes travel along mountain corridors through forests and across open slopes, with panoramic views and fantastic rock formations. Other highlights include historic sites and a forest of petrified trees.

Hikes 61–78 are located in and around Santa Rosa, the largest city in Sonoma County. The city's central location offers easy access to many of the hikes in the book. The hikes in this section are located in regional parks around Santa Rosa and the nearby communities. Several of the trails link to Santa Rosa along converted rails-to-trails routes. The trails provide access to the large number of creeks that flow across the Santa Rosa plain. Landscape features include marshlands, vineyards, and oak-dotted hills. Taylor Mountain, adjacent to the city limits, offers panoramic views from the valley to the coastal ranges. There are ample opportunities for dog walking and bird watching.

Sonoma Valley lies between the cities of Santa Rosa and Sonoma. Sonoma Creek and Highway 12 run through the valley, flanked by mountains on either side. Highway 12 is the central access road for Hikes 79–110. These hikes are located in four major state parks in central Sonoma County—Annadel, Hood Mountain, Sugarloaf Ridge, and Jack London State Parks—as well as in and around the town of Sonoma. Trails can be found along the wooded canyons and slopes of Sonoma Mountain (along the west side of Highway 12) and the southern end of the Mayacamas (along the east side of the highway). Peppered throughout the valley are vineyards and charming towns.

The mouths of Sonoma Creek, the Napa River, and the Petaluma River emerge just miles from each other at their south ends, draining into the massive marshes and tidal wetlands of San Pablo Bay. The huge watershed area offers excellent opportunities for bird and wildlife observation along the sloughs, wildlife corridors, and grasslands. Hikes 111–125 explore the watershed and rolling foothills that back-drop the marshlands.

The main access roads to all of the hikes are Highway 101 and Highway 1. Highway 101 is the major north-south freeway through the center of the county, connecting San Francisco to Mendocino County. Highway 1, also running north and south, follows the California coast-line from Los Angeles to the northern end of the state. Other key roads within the county are Highway 12 (through Sonoma Valley) and Highway 116 (from Highway 101 to the coast).

A quick glance at the hike summaries will allow you to choose a trail that is appropriate to your ability and preference. An overall map on the next page identifies the general locations of the hikes and major roads. There is a map for each hike to provide the essential details, as well as many broader regional maps (listed below). Relevant maps are listed in the statistics to aid in exploring each hike setting.

When hiking, bring the basic necessities to help ensure an optimum outing. Wear supportive, comfortable hiking shoes and layered clothing. Take along hats, sunscreen, sunglasses, water, snacks, and appropriate outerwear. Be aware that ticks and poison oak may be present. Use good judgement about your capabilities, and allow extra time to enjoy this beautiful area of California.

Major Regional Maps
All Hikes .... Sonoma County and Vicinity
Hikes 1–11 .... North Coast: Mendonoma (Sonoma–Mendocino counties)
Hikes 12–25 .... Central Coast
Hikes 12–19 .... Salt Point State Park
Hikes 22–25 .... Fort Ross State Historic Park
Hikes 26–37 .... Southern Coast
Hikes 34–37 .... Bodega Head
Hikes 38–48 .... North Sonoma County
Hikes 39–43 .... Lake Sonoma Recreation Area
Hikes 45–48 .... Armstrong Redwoods • Austin Creek
Hikes 49–60. .... Calistoga Area
Hikes 50–55 .... Robert Louis Stevenson State Park
Hikes 56–60 .... Bothe–Napa Valley State Park
Hikes 61–78 .... Central Sonoma County: Santa Rosa Area
Hikes 79–110 .... Santa Rosa to Sonoma • Sonoma Valley
Hikes 79–85 .... Annadel State Park
Hikes 86–90 .... Hood Mountain Regional Park
Hikes 91–96 .... Sugarloaf Ridge State Park
Hikes 97–103 .... Jack London State Historic Park
Hikes 111–125 .... Southern Sonoma County
Hikes 111–115 .... Napa–Sonoma Marshes Wildlife Area
Hikes 121–125 .... Novato Area

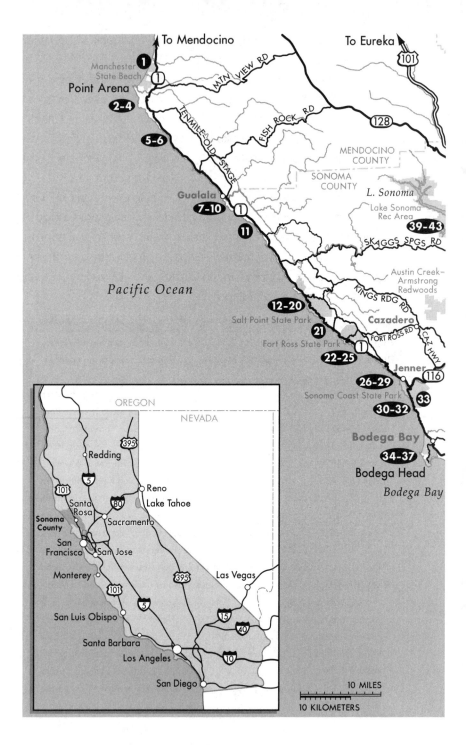

To Mendocino

To Eureka

101

Manchester State Beach

1

Point Arena

2-4

MTN VIEW RD

FISH ROCK RD

128

5-6

1

TENMILE-OLD STAGE

MENDOCINO COUNTY

SONOMA COUNTY

L. Sonoma

Lake Sonoma Rec Area

Gualala

7-10

1

39-43

SKAGGS SPGS RD

11

Austin Creek–Armstrong Redwoods

KINGS RDG RD

Pacific Ocean

12-20

Salt Point State Park

Cazadero

21

FORT ROSS RD

CAZ HWY

Fort Ross State Park

1

22-25

Jenner

116

26-29

Sonoma Coast State Park

33

30-32

Bodega Bay

34-37

Bodega Head

Bodega Bay

OREGON

NEVADA

395

Redding

5

101

Reno

Santa Rosa

80

Lake Tahoe

Sonoma County

Sacramento

San Francisco

San Jose

Monterey

395

Las Vegas

101

5

San Luis Obispo

15

40

Santa Barbara

Los Angeles

10

San Diego

10 MILES

10 KILOMETERS

MAP of the HIKES
SONOMA COUNTY and VICINITY

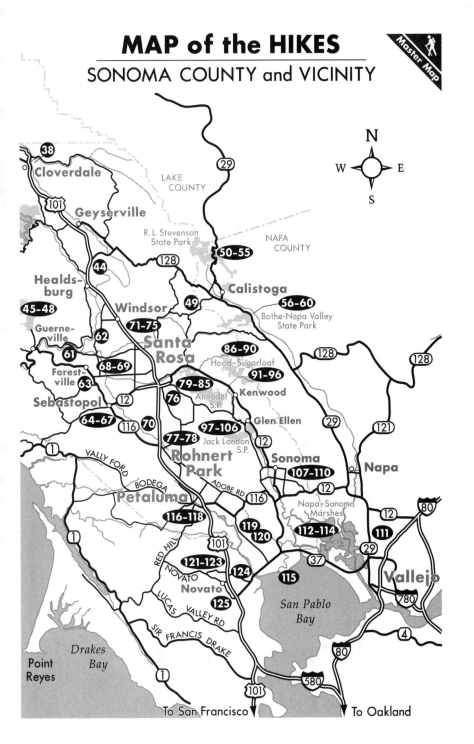

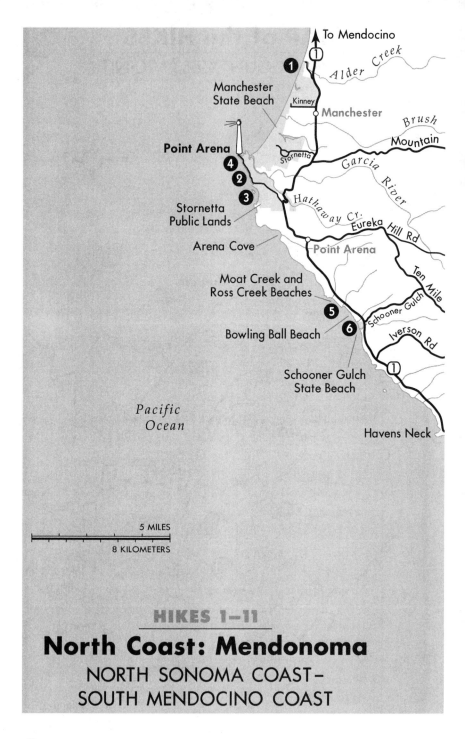

To Mendocino

① ➊

Alder Creek

Manchester
State Beach   Kinney

Manchester

Brush
Mountain

Point Arena   ➍
➋

Stornetta

Garcia River

➌

Hathaway Cr.

Stornetta
Public Lands

Eureka Hill Rd

Arena Cove

Point Arena

Ten Mile

Moat Creek and
Ross Creek Beaches

➎

Schooner Gulch

Iverson Rd

➏

Bowling Ball Beach

①

Schooner Gulch
State Beach

*Pacific
Ocean*

Havens Neck

5 MILES

8 KILOMETERS

HIKES 1–11

North Coast: Mendonoma
NORTH SONOMA COAST–
SOUTH MENDOCINO COAST

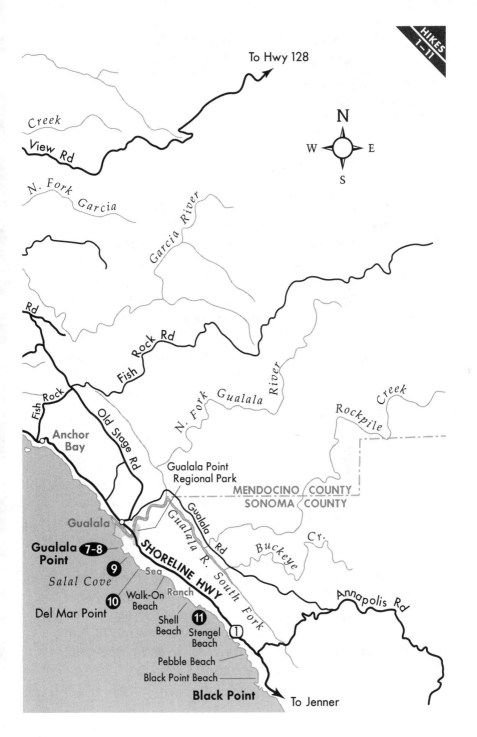

To Hwy 128

N
W · E
S

Creek

View Rd

N. Fork Garcia

Garcia River

Rd

Fish Rock Rd

Fish Rock

N. Fork Gualala River

Rockpile Creek

Anchor Bay

Old Stage Rd

Gualala Point Regional Park

MENDOCINO COUNTY
SONOMA COUNTY

Gualala

Gualala R. South Fork

Gualala Rd

Buckeye Cr.

Gualala Point 7-8

Salal Cove

9

Sea Ranch

Annapolis Rd

Walk-On Beach

Del Mar Point

10

Shell Beach

Stengel Beach

11

1

SHORELINE HWY

Pebble Beach

Black Point Beach

Black Point

To Jenner

1. Manchester State Beach
ALDER CREEK to KINNEY ROAD

Hiking distance: 2.5 miles round trip
Hiking time: 1.5 hours
Configuration: out-and-back
Elevation gain: 50 feet
Difficulty: easy
Exposure: exposed oceanfront
Dogs: allowed
Maps: U.S.G.S. Point Arena and Mallo Pass Creek

Manchester State Beach is between Point Arena and the town of Manchester in Mendocino County, just north of Sonoma County. The large beach encompasses 1,400 acres with ponds, bluffs, grass-covered dunes, and five miles of dramatic sandy coastline. It is the closest point to Hawaii on North America. Alder Creek borders the state beach to the north, where the San Andreas Fault runs into the Pacific Ocean. At the mouth of the creek is a freshwater lagoon inhabited by migratory waterfowl. The Garcia River flows into the sea at the southern border. This hike begins at Alder Creek and strolls south along the isolated dune-backed beach scattered with giant driftwood logs.

To the trailhead

17502 ALDER CREEK BEACH RD · MANCHESTER   39.003986, −123.694091

From Gualala, just north of the Sonoma County line, drive 21 miles north on Highway 1 (Shoreline Highway) to posted Alder Creek Beach Road at mile marker 22.48. The turnoff is located 7 miles north of Point Arena and 2 miles north of Manchester. Turn left and drive 0.7 miles to the trailhead at the end of the road.

Two additional roads access the state beach. The southern access is on Stoneboro Road at mile marker 19.65. Turn left and drive 1.6 miles to the parking area at the end of the road.

The central access is on Kinney Road at mile marker 21.48. Turn left and drive 1.1 miles to the trailhead at the end of the road. En route, the road passes the Manchester Beach KOA.

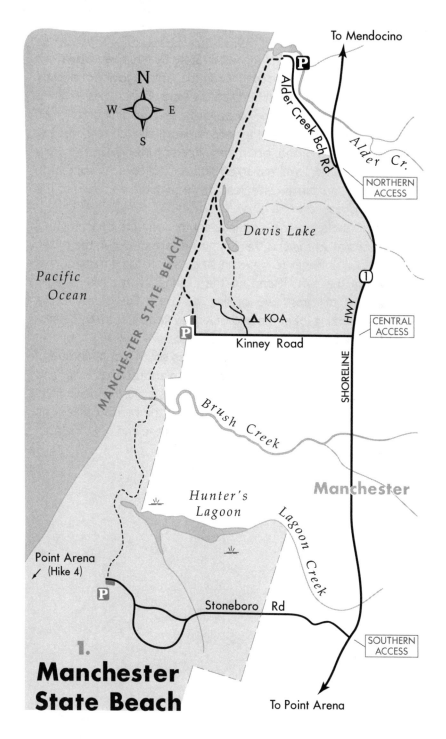

To Mendocino

P

Alder Creek Bch Rd

Alder Cr.

NORTHERN
ACCESS

Davis Lake

Pacific
Ocean

MANCHESTER STATE BEACH

1

▲ KOA

P

Kinney Road

CENTRAL
ACCESS

SHORELINE

HWY

Brush Creek

Manchester

Hunter's
Lagoon

Lagoon Creek

Point Arena
(Hike 4)

P

Stoneboro Rd

SOUTHERN
ACCESS

To Point Arena

1.

Manchester
State Beach

The hike

From the north end of Manchester State Beach, head down the dunes and toward the ocean along the large lagoon formed by Alder Creek. Curve south (left) on the sandy beach, passing piles of driftwood beneath the steep cliffs. The eroding cliffs begin to fade into low dunes along this isolated stretch of coastline. At 0.6 miles is a broad, open draw heading inland. Up the draw 150 yards is Davis Lake. A marked side trail follows the south side of the long and narrow lake, leading through the wetlands to the KOA campground.

Back at the shoreline, continue south along the beach, with a view of Point Arena and the lighthouse farther down the coast. As the dunes begin to grow in size, watch for a distinct trail channel in the cliffs. Head up the channel to the bluffs. Walk through the tall grass overlooking the coast. Curve east to the trailhead parking lot at the end of Kinney Road. Return by retracing your steps.

To extend the hike, the trail continues south along the coastal dunes. The mouth of Brush Creek is in another half mile, and Hunter's Lagoon, tucked into the dunes, is at just under a mile. Ascend the 80-foot dunes for a view of the narrow, mile-long lagoon. The trail leads to the parking area at the end of Stoneboro Road at 1.5 miles. ■

2. Northern Bluffs and the Garcia River
STORNETTA PUBLIC LANDS

Hiking distance: 2.5 miles round trip
Hiking time: 1.5 hours
Configuration: loop (with return on access road)
Elevation gain: 50 feet
Difficulty: easy
Exposure: open coastal bluffs
Dogs: allowed
Maps: U.S.G.S. Point Arena
       Bureau of Land Management Stornetta Public Lands map

The Stornetta Public Lands encompass 1,132 acres on the southern Mendocino County coast, north of the town of Point Arena. The land, with two miles of picturesque, jagged coastline, lies adjacent to the Point Arena Lighthouse and Manchester State Beach. The Garcia River (named for Rafael Garcia who built a mill here in 1869) flows through the property and enters the ocean just north of the lighthouse peninsula. The river runs along the San Andreas Fault zone and forms an estuary in the valley. It is a wintering habitat for tundra swans. The estuary also supports silver salmon and steelhead trout.

This hike follows the bluffs between the river and the lighthouse to the oceanfront. At the turbulent sea, the weather-carved bluffs form a series of narrow, finger-like peninsulas and pocket coves.

To the trailhead

45500 LIGHTHOUSE RD · POINT ARENA   38.940387, -123.729867

From Gualala, just north of the Sonoma County line, drive 16 miles north on Highway 1 (Shoreline Highway) to Lighthouse Road on the left at mile marker 17.00. Lighthouse Road is located 2 miles north of Point Arena and 3.5 miles south of Manchester. Turn left and drive 1.4 miles to the posted pullout on the left at the far end of the grove of cypress trees.

The hike

Walk a quarter mile back up the Lighthouse Road to the gated dirt road on the left (north). Pass through the trailhead gate, and head north on the two-track road. Stroll through the old corral and loading chute site. Veer left, crossing the pastureland to the west end of a cypress grove. Continue past the grove to the bluffs above the Garcia River. Follow the edge of the bluffs, overlooking the river basin. Near the ocean, the Garcia River forms a huge lagoon bounded by a sandbar covered in downfall logs. A channel on the southwest side of the arroyo is open to the sea. Follow the bluffs to the dramatic oceanfront cliffs. Pass the narrow, projecting peninsulas and pocket coves toward the Point Arena Lighthouse. Weave along the chiseled terrain, dotted with offshore rocks, while marveling at the seascape. Return by retracing the same route or by following Lighthouse Road 0.8 miles to the trailhead.

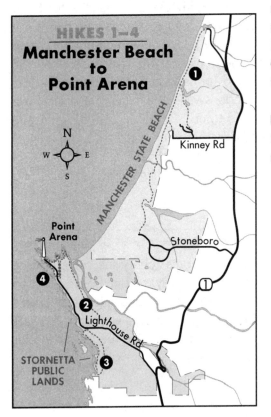

Hike 4 explores Point Arena, circling the peninsula on a nature trail. ■

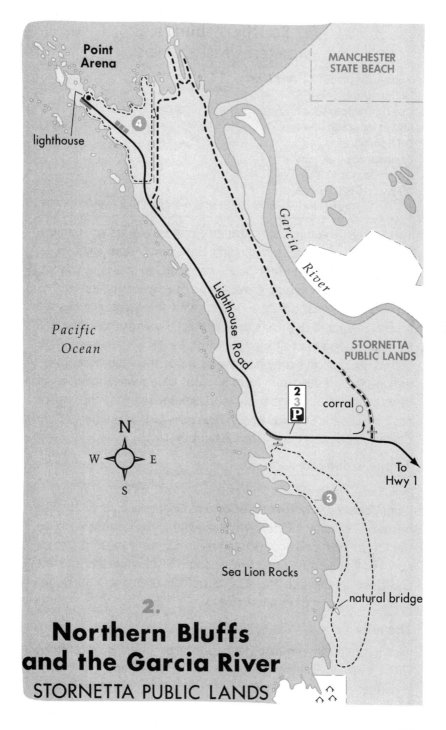

Point Arena

lighthouse

4

MANCHESTER STATE BEACH

Garcia River

Pacific Ocean

Lighthouse Road

STORNETTA PUBLIC LANDS

2 3 P

corral

To Hwy 1

3

N
W · E
S

Sea Lion Rocks

natural bridge

2.
Northern Bluffs and the Garcia River
STORNETTA PUBLIC LANDS

3. Southern Bluffs
STORNETTA PUBLIC LANDS

Hiking distance: 1.6-mile loop
Hiking time: 1 hour
Configuration: loop
Elevation gain: level
Difficulty: easy
Exposure: open coastal bluffs
Dogs: allowed
Maps: U.S.G.S. Point Arena
Bureau of Land Management Stornetta Public Lands map

The Stornetta Public Lands stretch along two miles of stunning, weathered coastline surrounding the Point Arena Lighthouse. The bucolic land includes riparian corridors, extensive wetlands, ponds, cypress and pine groves, sand dunes, and meadows. The crenulated coastal cliffs are riddled with sea caves, endless sea stacks, natural rock arches, embayments, a blow-hole, the Sea Lion Rocks, and the historic lighthouse.

This hike follows the coastline south of the lighthouse, overlooking the crashing surf from 80-foot bluffs. Many species of birds inhabit the rugged shoreline. Look for sea lions and harbor seals amidst the Sea Lion Rocks. The rocky islands are part of the California Coastal National Monument system.

To the trailhead

45500 LIGHTHOUSE RD · POINT ARENA   38.940387, -123.729867

From Gualala, just north of the Sonoma County line, drive 16 miles north on Highway 1 (Shoreline Highway) to Lighthouse Road on the left at mile marker 17.00. Lighthouse Road is located 2 miles north of Point Arena and 3.5 miles south of Manchester. Turn left and drive 1.4 miles to the posted pullout on the left at the far end of the grove of cypress trees.

The hike

Pass through the entrance gate to the south-facing oceanfront cliffs. Walk out on the peninsula to the west, and cross over a natural arch, passing tidepools along the shoreline below.

Curve along the bluffs, overlooking the caves and the flat, grassy plateau of Sea Lion Rocks. Pass old pier pilings and follow the vertical cliffs to stunning sea stacks and a natural bridge spanning the ocean. The public land ends a short distance ahead by a fenceline and a group of homes. Return along the bluffs or follow one of the less-traveled inland routes, forming a loop. ■

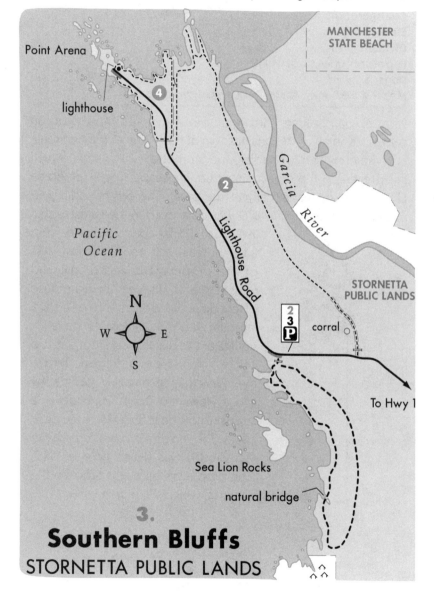

MANCHESTER
STATE BEACH

Point Arena

lighthouse

Garcia River

Pacific
Ocean

Lighthouse Road

N
W ─◇─ E
S

STORNETTA
PUBLIC LANDS

corral ○

To Hwy 1

Sea Lion Rocks

natural bridge

3.
Southern Bluffs
STORNETTA PUBLIC LANDS

4. Point Arena

Point Arena Lighthouse
STORNETTA PUBLIC LANDS

Hiking distance: 0.7-mile loop
Hiking time: 30 minutes
Configuration: loop
Elevation gain: level
Difficulty: easy
Exposure: open coastal bluffs
Dogs: allowed
Maps: U.S.G.S. Point Arena · Point Arena Lighthouse map

Point Arena is a long, narrow peninsula that juts into the ocean two miles north of the quaint town of Point Arena. The peninsula is completely surrounded by the Stornetta Public Lands, which has preserved the rugged, isolated landscape. The Point Arena Lighthouse sits majestically at the point. The original brick and mortar lighthouse from 1870 was destroyed in the catastrophic

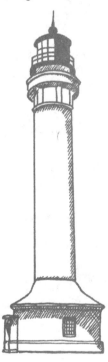

1906 San Francisco earthquake. (The San Andreas Fault zone runs just east of the property.) It was rebuilt and now stands at 115 feet. The lighthouse offers docent-led tours and has a small museum. The tour climbs 145 stairs, an equivalent to six stories. From the top of the lighthouse is a dramatic bird's-eye view of the amazing geography and a view into Devil's Punchbowl, a huge sinkhole near the end of the peninsula. The movie *Forever Young* with Mel Gibson was filmed here in 1992. The producers built a gazebo on the bluffs, which still remains.

Point Arena Lighthouse on the Mendonoma coast

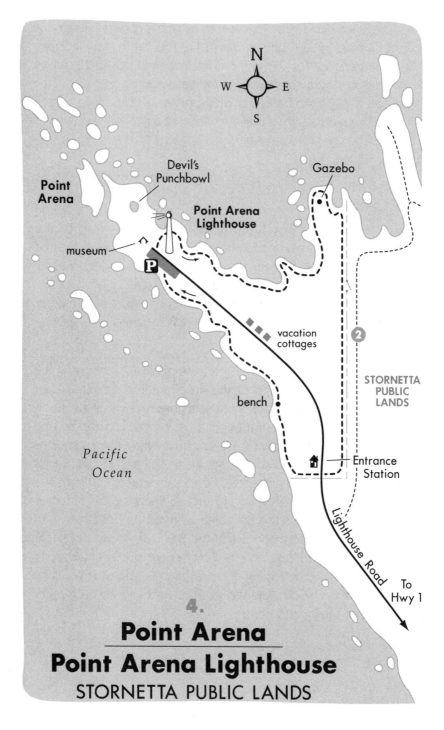

Point Arena

Devil's Punchbowl

Gazebo

Point Arena Lighthouse

museum

P

vacation cottages

STORNETTA PUBLIC LANDS

bench

Pacific Ocean

Entrance Station

Lighthouse Road

To Hwy 1

4.

Point Arena
Point Arena Lighthouse
STORNETTA PUBLIC LANDS

This hike circles the perimeter of the property atop the coastal terrace surrounding the point. The nature trail includes several benches for viewing the landscape and wildlife, which includes cormorants, sea lions, and harbor seals that are often sighted along the coast and offshore rocks just south of the point. This is also a great place to observe migrating gray whales from December through April.

To the trailhead

45500 LIGHTHOUSE RD · POINT ARENA   38.953371, -123.738729

From Gualala, just north of the Sonoma County line, drive 16 miles north on Highway 1 (the Shoreline Highway) to Lighthouse Road on the left at mile marker 17.00. Lighthouse Road is located 2 miles north of Point Arena and 3.5 miles south of Manchester. Turn left and drive 2.2 miles to the Point Arena Lighthouse entrance. Continue 0.2 miles to the parking area on the left, adjacent to the lighthouse. An entrance fee is required.

The hike

Take the path on the north edge of the peninsula, following the white fence on the edge of the eroding cliffs. Continue past deep coves and overlooks of the offshore rocks to the gazebo at the northeast corner of the lighthouse property. Loop around the finger of land, with great views of the lighthouse and northern coastal vistas. Follow the edge of the Stornetta Public Lands (Hike 2). Pass a gated entrance to the open space, and continue across the flat grasslands to Lighthouse Road by the entrance station. Cross the road to the south edge of the peninsula, with endless offshore formations and the Sea Lion Rocks. Bear right and follow the scalloped bluffs. Benches are interspersed along the trail to enjoy the steadily changing vistas. Look for sea lions on the offshore rocks. Pass the vacation cottages and complete the loop at the lighthouse. ■

5. Moat Creek Beach
Ross Creek Beach
BLUFF TOP LOOP

Hiking distance: 1.2-mile loop
Hiking time: 45 minutes
Configuration: loop
Elevation gain: 90 feet
Difficulty: easy
Exposure: open coastal meadows
Dogs: not allowed
Maps: U.S.G.S. Point Arena

Perennial Moat Creek and Ross Creek flow from the coastal hills into the ocean between Point Arena and Anchor Bay. Oceanfront bluffs separate the two sandy beach coves. Atop the 90-foot bluffs is a little known community trail that is maintained by volunteers. The loop trail circles the perimeter of the bluffs, connecting the two sheltered beach coves. En route, the trail passes a cormorant rookery. The blufftop meadow is also the site of the defunct Whiskey Shoals subdivision. This hike begins at Moat Creek Beach and follows the oceanfront cliffs to Ross Creek Beach.

To the trailhead

27310 SHORELINE HWY · POINT ARENA   38.882736, -123.673602

From Gualala, just north of the Sonoma County line, drive 12 miles north on Highway 1 (Shoreline Highway) to the posted Moat Creek turnoff on the left at mile marker 12.88. The turnoff is located 8.5 miles north of Anchor Bay and 2 miles south of Point Arena. Turn left and park in the large dirt lot.

The hike

The trail at the far southwest end of the parking lot leads 200 yards to Moat Creek Beach, a popular surfing and tidepooling beach in a sheltered cove. From the east side of the parking lot, take the posted trail and begin the loop on the right fork, hiking counter-clockwise. Climb the hillside to the grass-covered bluffs and the edge of a 90-foot bluff that overlooks Moat Creek Beach. Head southeast, with amazing vistas across the scalloped coastline, the grassy coastal terraces, and the forested hills. Curve around a deep, vertical-walled cove, passing the cormorant rookery on the left. At the southeast end of the bluffs is a junction overlooking Ross Creek Beach. The left fork stays atop the bluffs to a picnic site in a pine forest and a paved road from the abandoned subdivision. Continue straight on the right fork, and descend steps into the gulch and a junction. Detour on the right fork to Ross Creek Beach. (During low tide, Bowling Ball Beach—Hike 6—can be reached by following the sandy beach beneath the bluffs for a half mile south.)

Return and continue on the north fork, weaving through a pine grove on the spongy needle-covered path. Curve north and parallel Highway 1, completing the loop back at Moat Creek. ∎

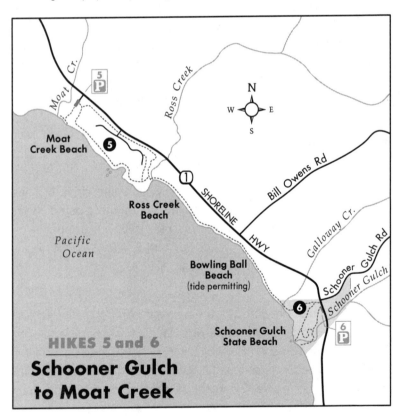

HIKES 5 and 6
Schooner Gulch
to Moat Creek

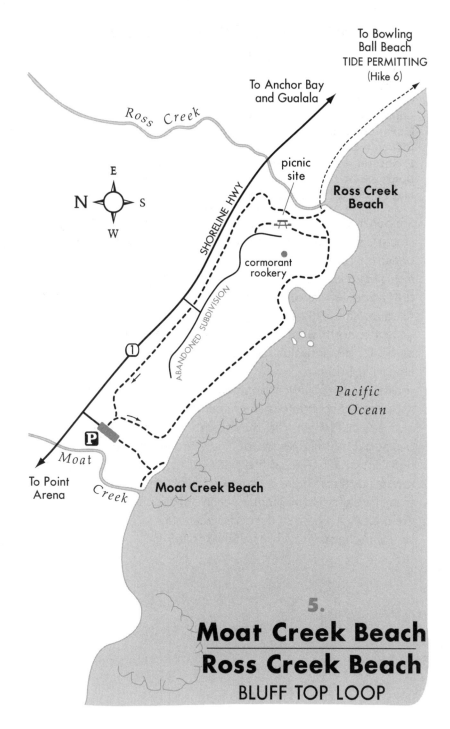

To Bowling
Ball Beach
TIDE PERMITTING
(Hike 6)

To Anchor Bay
and Gualala

Ross Creek

SHORELINE HWY

picnic
site

Ross Creek
Beach

N E S W

cormorant
rookery

ABANDONED SUBDIVISION

1

*Pacific
Ocean*

P

Moat

Moat Creek Beach

Creek

To Point
Arena

5.
Moat Creek Beach
Ross Creek Beach
BLUFF TOP LOOP

6. Schooner Gulch State Beach and Bowling Ball Beach

Hiking distance: 1 mile round trip
Hiking time: 40 minutes
Configuration: out-and-back with central loop
Elevation gain: 80 feet
Difficulty: easy
Exposure: mostly exposed with shaded ravine
Dogs: allowed
Maps: U.S.G.S. Saunders Reef and Point Arena

Schooner Gulch State Beach covers 53 acres of undeveloped state park land between Point Arena and Anchor Bay. The state beach is a protected cove tucked between towering cliffs, with a small creek, tidepools, wave-carved formations, and piles of driftwood. A quarter-mile trail descends through a redwood-filled ravine to Schooner Gulch Beach.

To the north, another trail crosses the 80-foot windswept bluffs to overlooks of Schooner Gulch and continues north along the beach to Bowling Ball Beach. The beach was named for its smooth spherical boulders. The embedded sedimentary rocks, called concretions, formed in concentric layers along the exposed cliffs. Eventually they fell from the eroding cliffs to the beach below. This garden of finely ground geological formations sits at the base of the cliffs but can only be seen during low, minus tides. There is no direct access to Bowling Ball Beach from the bluffs. However, the beach can be accessed from Moat Creek along the base of the cliffs, located 1.4 miles north (Hike 5), or from Schooner Gulch, a half mile south.

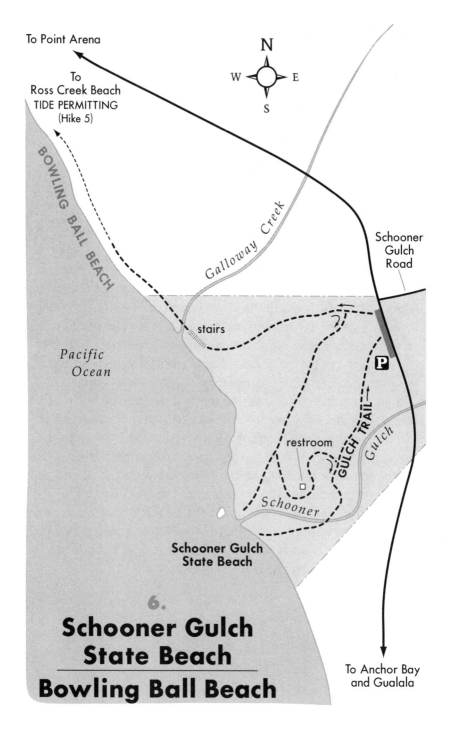

To Point Arena

To
Ross Creek Beach
TIDE PERMITTING
(Hike 5)

N
W   E
S

BOWLING BALL BEACH

Galloway Creek

Schooner
Gulch
Road

stairs

Pacific
Ocean

P

GULCH TRAIL

Gulch

restroom

Schooner

Schooner Gulch
State Beach

To Anchor Bay
and Gualala

6.
**Schooner Gulch
State Beach**
Bowling Ball Beach

To the trailhead

28500 SHORELINE HWY · POINT ARENA   38.868885, –123.653455

From Gualala, just north of the Sonoma County line, drive 10.6 miles north on Highway 1 (Shoreline Highway) to Schooner Gulch, directly opposite Schooner Gulch Road at mile marker 11.41. The parking pullout is on the west (ocean) side of the road just north of the concrete bridge crossing over the gulch. The pullout is located 7 miles north of Anchor Bay and 3.4 miles south of Point Arena.

The hike

Begin the hike on the north trail atop the pine-dotted bluffs just north of Schooner Gulch. At the Y-fork, take the right fork to the oceanfront cliffs. Descend to the right on a wooden staircase to a jumble of rocks and driftwood at the mouth of Galloway Creek. Cross the rocks to the sandy beach, and head north along the base of the 80-foot striated cliffs. Bowling Ball Beach, with the prehistoric-looking spherical boulders, resides a quarter mile ahead, but the boulders are only visible during minus tides.

After exploring the orb-like rocks in the parallel grooves and ridges along the cliffs, return to the first junction near the trailhead. Take the right (south) fork and cross the grassy bluffs to a Y-fork overlooking Schooner Gulch Beach. The right fork stays atop the grassy bluffs to the headland that protects the beach. Descend on the left fork, which weaves down to the Gulch Trail. Bear right and descend to the mouth of the creek and the sandy beach cove. The creek spills onto the beach strand and enters the sea at the base of the northern cliffs. Return a quarter mile up the Gulch Trail in a shaded redwood forest with an understory of ferns, completing the loop at Highway 1. ■

7. Gualala River Trail
GUALALA POINT REGIONAL PARK

Hiking distance: 2.4 miles round trip
Hiking time: 1 hour
Configuration: out-and-back
Elevation gain: 80 feet
Difficulty: easy
Exposure: shaded forest and open meadows
Dogs: allowed
Maps: U.S.G.S. Gualala · Gualala Point Regional Park map

The mouth of the Gualala River lies on the Mendocino-Sonoma county line. The river flows north and south, parallel to the coast, along the San Andreas fault line. Just to the north of the river is the town of Gualala, a former logging town. On the south side of the river mouth is Gualala Point Regional Park. *Gualala* (pronounced *wa-LA-la*) is the Pomo Indian word for "where the waters meet."

This hike follows the elbow of the river on the Sonoma County side. The trail begins in the Gualala Point Campground and weaves through a shady forest with redwoods, bay laurels, alders, rhododendrons, and sword ferns. The path skirts the protected estuary, a prime bird habitat, as it leads to overlooks of Gualala, the mountains, and the river. The hike ends on the extensive driftwood-strewn sandy beach and sandspit, where the river empties into the ocean.

To the trailhead

42401 COAST HWY 1 · GUALALA   38.762421, -123.514700

From Gualala, just north of the Sonoma County line, drive one mile south on Highway 1, crossing over the Gualala River, to the posted Gualala Point Regional Park turnoff on the right at mile marker 58.20. Turn left (inland)—directly across from the park entrance—and drive 0.7 miles to the Gualala Point Campground. Park in the day use parking spaces on the right by the map kiosk. A parking fee is required.

The turnoff is located 7.6 miles north of the Sea Ranch Lodge.

The hike

Walk to the south end of the campground road under a dense redwood forest to the signed trail. Skirt the edge of the Gualala River through the lush forest with gnarled bay laurel. Cross a bridge over a water channel, and emerge in a grassy clearing with tall brush. Walk under Highway 1, following the course of the river in an open meadow. Leave the grassy river flat and traverse the hillside, climbing to the blufftop and overlook. Savor the picture-perfect view of the river flowing out of the forested mountains and along the town of Gualala. The trail soon joins the park road at a picnic area. Continue along the road a short distance to the park visitor center.

From the visitor center, a paved path crosses the grassy bluffs to the beach. Instead, take the signed grassy path to the right. Descend and pass a short trail on the right that leads through laurel trees to a picnic area on the shore of the Gualala River. Follow the north edge of the bluffs, overlooking the river and the town of Gualala. Merge with the paved path and stay to the right. The paved path ends a short distance ahead and continues as a sand path to the oceanfront and the mouth of the Gualala River. After enjoying the beach, return to the campground and parking lot along the same route. ■

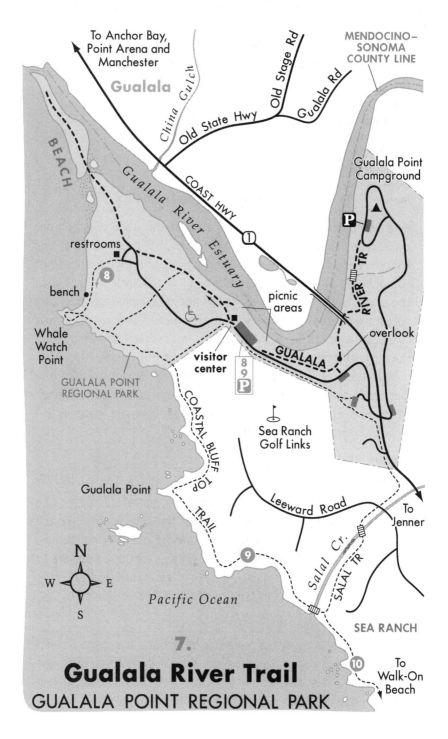

To Anchor Bay, Point Arena and Manchester

Gualala

China Gulch

Old Stage Rd

Old State Hwy

Gualala Rd

MENDOCINO–SONOMA COUNTY LINE

Gualala River Estuary

COAST HWY

BEACH

restrooms

bench

8

Whale Watch Point

GUALALA POINT REGIONAL PARK

Gualala Point

Gualala Point Campground

P

RIVER TR

overlook

picnic areas

visitor center

8 9 P

GUALALA

COASTAL BLUFF TOP TRAIL

Sea Ranch Golf Links

Leeward Road

To Jenner

Salal Cr.

SALAL TR

9

SEA RANCH

N
W · E
S

Pacific Ocean

10

To Walk-On Beach

7.

Gualala River Trail
GUALALA POINT REGIONAL PARK

8. Whale Watch Point
GUALALA POINT REGIONAL PARK

Hiking distance: 2-mile loop
Hiking time: 1 hour
Configuration: loop with spur trail along sand spit
Elevation gain: level
Difficulty: easy
Exposure: open meadows and forested pockets
Dogs: allowed
Maps: U.S.G.S. Gualala · Gualala Point Regional Park map

Gualala Point Regional Park is located at the northwest corner of Sonoma County between the town of Gualala and the Sea Ranch residential community. The oceanfront park encompasses 103 acres along the southern banks of the Gualala River. Within the park's boundary are a variety of habitats, including redwood forests, a protected estuary, oceanfront bluffs, a marine terrace with old Monterey cypress groves, a freshwater marsh, sand dunes, and a sandy beach at the mouth of the Gualala River.

This hike circles the peninsula that extends between the Gualala River and the Pacific Ocean. Grass and dirt paths branch off the paved path to blufftop overlooks at Whale Watch Point, a rocky, windswept promontory.

To the trailhead

42401 COAST HWY 1 · GUALALA   38.758924, -123.522939

From Gualala, just north of the Sonoma County line, drive one mile south on Highway 1, crossing over the Gualala River, to the posted Gualala Point Regional Park turnoff on the right at mile marker 58.20. Turn right and drive 0.6 miles through the park to the visitor center parking lot. A parking fee is required.

The turnoff is located 7.6 miles north of the Sea Ranch Lodge.

The hike

From the visitor center, a paved path crosses the grassy bluffs to the beach. Instead, take the signed grassy path to the right. Descend and pass a short trail on the right that leads through laurel trees to a picnic area on the shore of the Gualala River. Follow

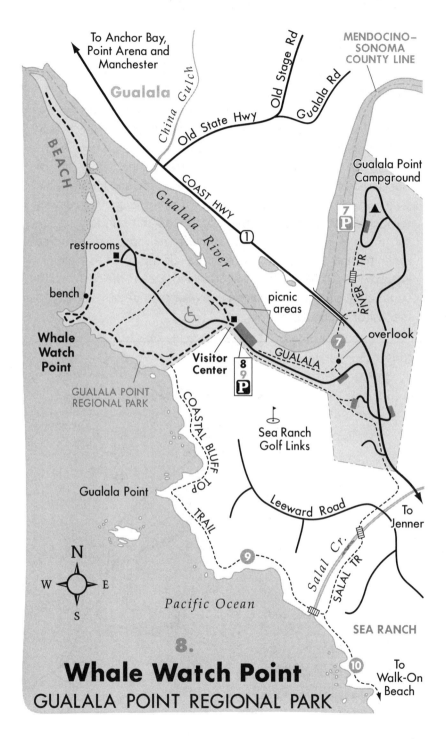

To Anchor Bay, Point Arena and Manchester

Gualala

China Gulch

Old Stage Rd

Old State Hwy

Gualala Rd

MENDOCINO–SONOMA COUNTY LINE

COAST HWY

Gualala River

1

Gualala Point Campground

7 P

RIVER TR

restrooms

bench

picnic areas

GUALALA

7

overlook

Whale Watch Point

Visitor Center

8 9 P

GUALALA POINT REGIONAL PARK

Sea Ranch Golf Links

COASTAL BLUFF TOP TRAIL

Gualala Point

Leeward Road

To Jenner

Salal Cr.

SALAL TR

9

N
W E
S

Pacific Ocean

SEA RANCH

8.
Whale Watch Point
GUALALA POINT REGIONAL PARK

10

To Walk-On Beach

the north edge of the bluffs, overlooking the river and the town of Gualala. Merge with the paved path and stay to the right. The paved path ends a short distance ahead and continues as a sand path to the oceanfront and the mouth of the Gualala River.

Return to the junction and continue 50 yards south on the paved path. At the restrooms, veer right and take the grassy path along the oceanfront bluffs, with viewing benches of Whale Watch Point. Pass through a cypress tree tunnel to a vista of Gualala Point and a junction. Detour to the right and circle Whale Watch Point, the rocky promontory. Continue south, weaving through a shaded cypress grove to the north boundary of Sea Ranch and a junction. The Coastal Bluff Trail continues into Sea Ranch to Salal Cove (Hike 9), then parallels the coast to Walk-On Beach (Hike 10). Bear left and head inland. Stay in the park on the south edge of a meadow along a row of pine trees, returning to the visitor center. ∎

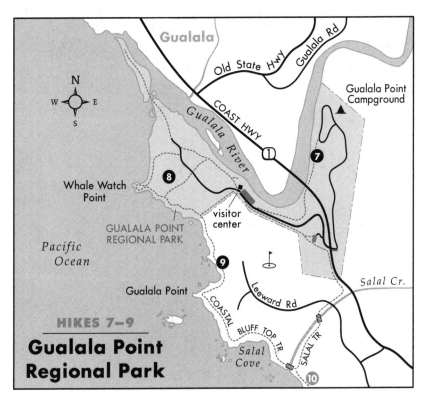

9. Coastal Bluff Top Trail
Salal Cove
GUALALA POINT REGIONAL PARK · SEA RANCH

Hiking distance: 2.8-mile loop
Hiking time: 1.5 hours
Configuration: loop
Elevation gain: 100 feet
Difficulty: easy
Exposure: mostly open coastal bluffs with a few shaded ravines
Dogs: allowed
Maps: U.S.G.S. Gualala and Stewarts Point · The Sea Ranch Trails Map

The Salal Trail was a seasonal route of the Pomo Indians from their inland camps to a sheltered ocean site near Salal Cove. Gorgeous sculpted rock formations surround the deep U-shaped cove. The Salal Trail follows a heavily vegetated stream-fed ravine to the cove and coastal bluffs. The trail weaves through the lush shaded glen with bishop pines, Monterey cypress, redwoods, red alders, and Pacific wax myrtle. Along the way is a rotunda of redwoods with a waterfall and pool. This hike begins in Gualala Point Regional Park and forms a loop along the coastline with the Sea Ranch public access trail.

To the trailhead

42401 COAST HWY 1 · GUALALA   38.758924, -123.522939

From Gualala, just north of the Sonoma County line, drive one mile south on Highway 1, crossing over the Gualala River, to the posted Gualala Point Regional Park turnoff on the right at mile marker 58.20. Turn right and drive 0.6 miles through the park to the visitor center parking lot. A parking fee is required.

The turnoff is located 7.6 miles north of the Sea Ranch Lodge.

The hike

From the visitor center, take the posted Beach Trail along the park's south boundary on the edge of the Sea Ranch Golf Links. Stroll through a hedgerow of towering pines on the south edge of a meadow. At a quarter mile, the grassy path reaches a posted junction at the oceanfront cliffs between Whale Watch Point and Gualala Point. The right fork leads 0.2 miles to Whale Watch Point and 0.6 miles to the beach (Hike 8). Bear left and leave the park into Sea Ranch on the Coastal Bluff Top Trail, a public access trail. The serpentine path follows the eroding bluffs through pockets of cypress trees. Loop around Gualala Point, with views of the Gualala Point Islands, and pass through a dark tunnel of cypress trees. One mile beyond the park, descend into Salal Cove. Cross a wooden bridge over Salal Creek to a T-junction. The right fork continues on the bluffs 2.2 miles to Walk-On Beach (Hike 10).

For this hike, bear left on the Salal Trail. Head inland through a lush stream-fed draw with ferns, lichen, and moss-covered rocks. Follow the south edge of the waterway, passing a natural rock-lined pool and a waterfall in a redwood-filled grotto. Cross a bridge to the north side of the stream and follow the watercourse. Cross Leeward Road and continue along the drainage. Climb steps and curve left. Walk parallel to Highway 1, and cross the Sea Ranch Golf Links road to the Gualala Point Regional Park entrance. Bear left into the park and skirt the edge of the golf course, returning to the visitor center. ■

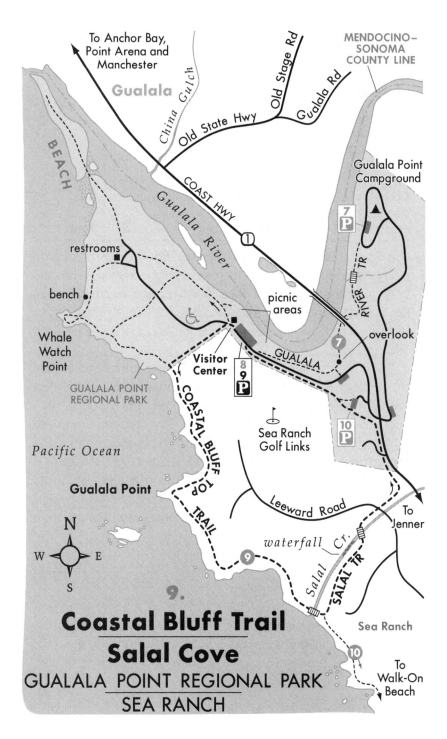

To Anchor Bay,
Point Arena and
Manchester

MENDOCINO-
SONOMA
COUNTY LINE

Gualala

China Gulch

Old Stage Rd

Gualala Rd

Old State Hwy

COAST HWY

Gualala River

①

Gualala Point
Campground

7 P

RIVER TR

restrooms

bench

picnic
areas

overlook

GUALALA

7

BEACH

Whale
Watch
Point

Visitor
Center

8
9 P

GUALALA POINT
REGIONAL PARK

10 P

Pacific Ocean

Sea Ranch
Golf Links

COASTAL BLUFF TOP TRAIL

Gualala Point

Leeward Road

To
Jenner

N
W   E
S

waterfall   Salal Cr.

SALAL TR

9.

9

Salal Cr.

Sea Ranch

Coastal Bluff Trail
Salal Cove
GUALALA POINT REGIONAL PARK
SEA RANCH

10

To
Walk-On
Beach

10. Coastal Bluff Top Trail at Sea Ranch

Salal Trail to Walk-On Beach

GUALALA POINT REGIONAL PARK to SEA RANCH

Hiking distance: 6 miles round trip
Hiking time: 3 hours
Configuration: out-and-back
Elevation gain: 100 feet
Difficulty: moderate
Exposure: mostly open coastal bluffs with a few shaded groves
Dogs: allowed
Maps: U.S.G.S. Gualala and Stewarts Point · The Sea Ranch Trails Map

The Coastal Bluff Top Trail follows scalloped sandstone bluffs along the ocean in the Sea Ranch residential community. It is the only portion of coastline on the 10-mile-long stretch of the Sea Ranch estates that allows public access. The trail is connected to Highway 1 on both ends by the Salal Trail and the Walk-On Beach Trail.

The hike begins at the entrance to Gualala Point Regional Park on the Salal Trail. The path leads through a riparian, stream-fed ravine with redwood groves, a waterfall, and pool. It connects to the Coastal Bluff Trail by Salal Cove, a deep cove with sculpted rock formations. The hike then turns southward along the serpentine Coastal Bluff Top Trail, which hugs the coastline past stands of Monterey cypress, a series of coves and points with offshore rocks, Del Mar Point, and a coastal state ecological reserve. Migrating whales are often observed offshore from November through March.

To the trailhead

42401 COAST HWY 1 · GUALALA   38.756255, –123.516717

From Gualala, just north of the Sonoma County line, drive one mile south on Highway 1, crossing over the Gualala River, to the posted Gualala Point Regional Park turnoff on the right at mile marker 58.20. Turn right and drive 0.1 mile to the entrance station, and park in the spaces on the left. Additional parking is located directly across from the park entrance. A parking fee is required.

The turnoff is located 7.6 miles north of the Sea Ranch Lodge.

The hike

Walk back towards Highway 1 and follow the mowed path, parallel to the highway. Cross the Sea Ranch Golf Links entrance road, and curve right into the stream-fed canyon. Descend steps, following the watercourse through bishop pine, Douglas fir, alder, and madrone. Cross Leeward Road and continue along the north side of the stream. Cross a bridge over to the other side of the creek. Just past the bridge is a waterfall in a lush redwood-filled grotto and a natural rock-lined pool. Continue along the south edge of the mossy, fern-lined stream to a junction with the Coastal Bluff Trail at gorgeous Salal Cove.

For a side trip to the cove, cross the footbridge over the creek to the right, and immediately bear left to the sandy, rock-walled pocket beach fronting the sea stacks. The trail leads one mile to Gualala Point Regional Park and the visitor center.

Back at the junction, continue southeast on the Coastal Bluff Top Trail. Climb steps and emerge on the oceanfront bluffs. Head south along the scalloped coastline with numerous offshore rocks. Weave along the cliffs, curving around coves and passing through dense stands of cypress trees. Cross a bridge over a stream to a stunning rock-walled cove with rounded rocks and driftwood. Pass honeycombed sandstone formations, known as *tafoni*, and a cove with sea caves. Several more rock formations lie offshore at Del Mar Point at the state ecological reserve. Curve around Del Mar Cove, leaving the reserve, and pass through a mature cypress grove. Cross three more bridges and skirt the west edge of a huge meadow to a posted junction at a cypress grove. Continue straight for 0.2 miles to Walk-On Beach. Public access to the Bluff Top Trail ends a short distance ahead. The left fork curves left and continues 0.3 miles to the Walk-On Beach trailhead at Highway 1. Return by retracing your steps. ∎

To Anchor Bay, Point Arena and Manchester

Gualala

Gualala River

Whale Watch Point

GUALALA POINT REGIONAL PARK

visitor center

START HIKE

Sea Ranch Golf Links

Gualala Point

Leeward Rd

COASTAL BLUFF TOP TR

waterfall

Salal

SALAL TR

Gualala Point Islands

Salal Cove

Gray Whale

Fish Rock

Creek

Sea Stack

COASTAL BLUFF TOP TR

Pacific Ocean

10.

Coastal Bluff Top Trail at Sea Ranch

Salal Trail to Walk-On Beach

GUALALA POINT REGIONAL PARK
to SEA RANCH

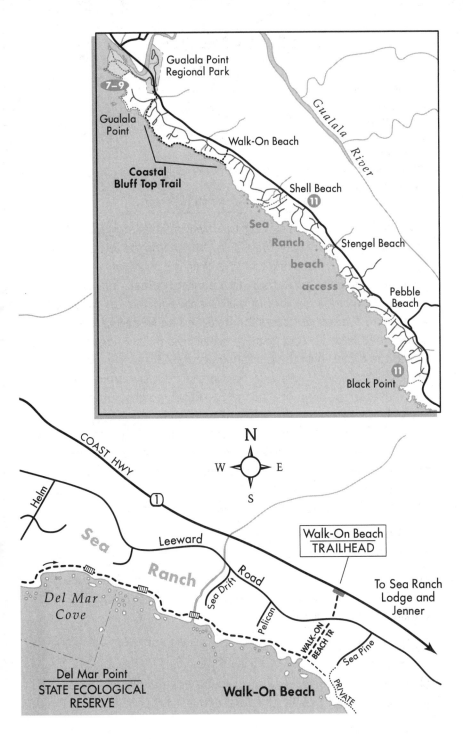

Gualala Point
Regional Park

7–9

Gualala
Point

**Coastal
Bluff Top Trail**

Walk-On Beach

Gualala River

Shell Beach

11

Sea

Ranch

Stengel Beach

beach

access

Pebble
Beach

Black Point

11

COAST HWY

Helm

Sea

1

Leeward

Ranch

N

W ← → E

S

Walk-On Beach
TRAILHEAD

To Sea Ranch
Lodge and
Jenner

Sea Drift

Road

Pelican

WALK-ON
BEACH TR

Sea Pine

*Del Mar
Cove*

PRIVATE

Del Mar Point
STATE ECOLOGICAL
RESERVE

Walk-On Beach

11. Sea Ranch Beaches
ACCESS TRAILS

Hiking distance: 0.4–1.4 miles round trip
Hiking time: 1 hour
Configuration: out-and-back
Elevation gain: nearly level
Difficulty: easy
Exposure: forested pockets and open coastal bluffs
Dogs: allowed
Maps: U.S.G.S. Stewarts Point · The Sea Ranch Trails Map

The Sea Ranch has an amazing trail system stretching over ten miles along the dramatic coastline. Within the development's 5,000 acres is a network of more than 45 miles of interconnecting trails that weave through the inland forests and coastal terrace. Unfortunately, the public is only allowed on a court-enforced 3.2 miles of coastal bluffs at the north end of the development (Hike 10) and these beach access trails. A legal battle led to the creation of the California Coastal Commission and the State Coastal Conservancy. To access the extensive trail system, you must rent or own one of the Sea Ranch homes. Otherwise, the public is allowed on just five miles of trails.

Five short beach-access trails cross the blufftop meadows from Highway 1 to the sandy beach coves. The crenulated coastline has a myriad of interesting offshore rocks. These paths to the coast range in length from 0.2 miles to 0.6 miles. Sea Ranch security will issue tickets for walking beyond these paths.

To the trailhead

42101 HWY 1 · SEA RANCH   38.740293, -123.491891

The trailheads are listed from north to south. All five trailheads are well-marked and have paved parking lots with restrooms. A parking fee is required.

WALK-ON BEACH: 1.7 miles south of Gualala Point Regional Park and 5.9 miles north of Sea Ranch Lodge at mile marker 56.53.

SHELL BEACH: 3.0 miles south of Gualala Point Regional Park and 4.6 miles north of Sea Ranch Lodge at mile marker 55.20.

STENGEL BEACH: 4.2 miles south of Gualala Point Regional Park and 3.4 miles north of Sea Ranch Lodge at mile marker 53.96. Turn west on Wild Iris and quickly turn right again into the posted parking lot.

PEBBLE BEACH: 5.9 miles south of Gualala Point Regional Park and 1.7 miles north of Sea Ranch Lodge at mile marker 52.32.

BLACK POINT: 7.35 miles south of Gualala Point Regional Park and 0.25 miles north of Sea Ranch Lodge at mile marker 50.80.

The hike

WALK-ON BEACH TRAIL (0.8 miles round trip): From the south end of the lot, descend into a dense pine, fir, and cypress forest. Cross Leeward Road and skirt the south edge of an open bluff meadow. Walk through a towering Monterey cypress grove to a T-junction with the Bluff Trail at 0.3 miles. The right fork is a public trail that leads 3 miles to Gualala Point Regional Park (Hike 10). The left fork leads 0.2 miles to Walk-On Beach.

SHELL BEACH TRAIL (1.2 miles round trip): Walk into a grove of pines and steadily descend down the trail. Cross Pacific Reach Road and continue downhill through a meadow and thickets of shrub. At 0.6 miles, the path reaches a T-junction with the Bluff Trail, overlooking massive offshore rock formations. Bear right and cross a wooden footbridge over the creek drainage at Shell Beach. Veer left and descend to the sandy beach, backed by a low bluff and endless sea rocks.

STENGEL BEACH TRAIL (0.4 miles round trip): Walk down the path lined with Monterey cypress trees. Parallel a small creek, while views of the ocean stretch out ahead. At the bluffs, curve right to an overlook. A long wooden staircase that is supported by a tilted rock formation descends from the cliffs. Walk down the stairs to the sandy pocket beach, bordered by steep cliffs and offshore rocks. The seasonal stream spills over the bluff, forming a small waterfall.

PEBBLE BEACH TRAIL (0.6 miles round trip): Head west on the grassy, tree-covered path. Slowly descend from the bishop pine forest into an open, grassy meadow, reaching the oceanfront

Bluff Trail at 0.3 miles. Bear right and cross a bridge over the lush drainage. Continue 50 yards to steep wooden steps that drop down the cliffs to the black-sand beach cove with tidepools and seastacks.

BLACK POINT TRAIL (0.6 miles round trip): The trailhead is on the northwest corner of the parking lot. Cross the grassland meadow 0.3 miles to the cliffs at the northern edge of Black Point, a huge rock knoll with twisted Monterey cypress. Descend the vertical cliff on a wooden staircase to the long, curving beach. To the south, a private Sea Ranch trail leads out onto the peninsula to an overlook and the west tip of Black Point. ■

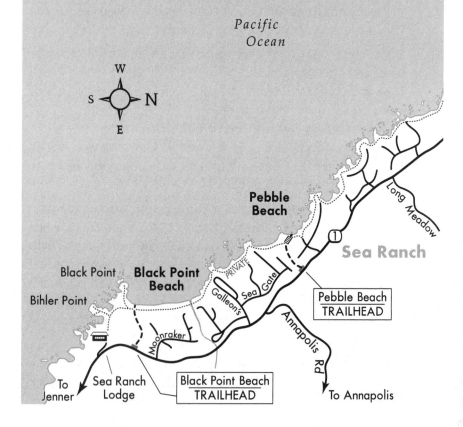

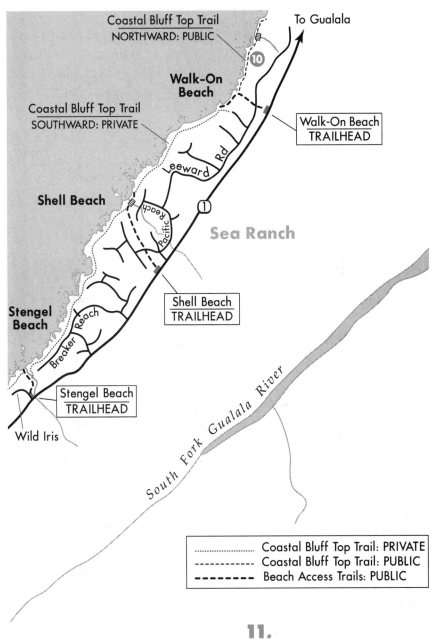

Coastal Bluff Top Trail
NORTHWARD: PUBLIC

To Gualala

⑩

Walk-On Beach

Coastal Bluff Top Trail
SOUTHWARD: PRIVATE

Walk-On Beach
TRAILHEAD

Leeward Rd

Shell Beach

Pacific Reach

① Sea Ranch

Shell Beach
TRAILHEAD

Stengel Beach

Breaker Reach

Reach

Stengel Beach
TRAILHEAD

South Fork Gualala River

Wild Iris

....	Coastal Bluff Top Trail: PRIVATE
------------	Coastal Bluff Top Trail: PUBLIC
--------	Beach Access Trails: PUBLIC

11.

Sea Ranch Beaches
ACCESS TRAILS

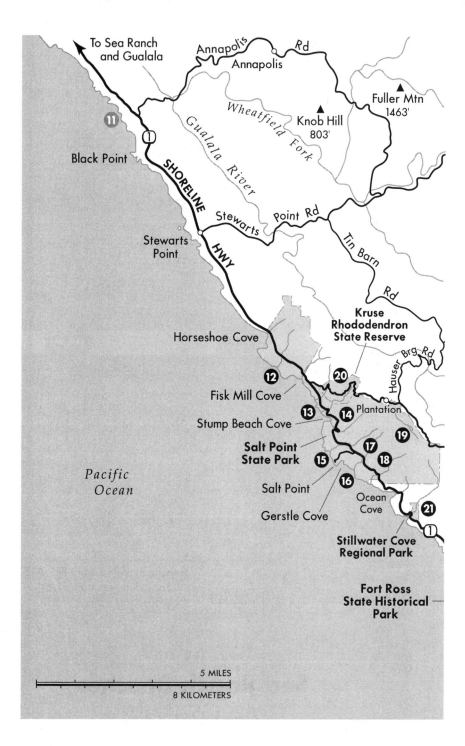

To Sea Ranch
and Gualala

Annapolis Rd

Annapolis

Wheatfield Fork

Fuller Mtn
1463'

Knob Hill
803'

Gualala River

Black Point

(11)

SHORELINE HWY

(1)

Stewarts Point Rd

Stewarts
Point

Tin Barn Rd

Kruse
Rhododendron
State Reserve

Horseshoe Cove

(12)

(20)

Hauser Brg Rd

Fisk Mill Cove

(13)

(14)

Plantation

Stump Beach Cove

Salt Point
State Park

(15)

(17)

(19)

(18)

Salt Point

(16)

Pacific
Ocean

Gerstle Cove

Ocean
Cove

(21)

(1)

Stillwater Cove
Regional Park

Fort Ross
State Historical
Park

5 MILES

8 KILOMETERS

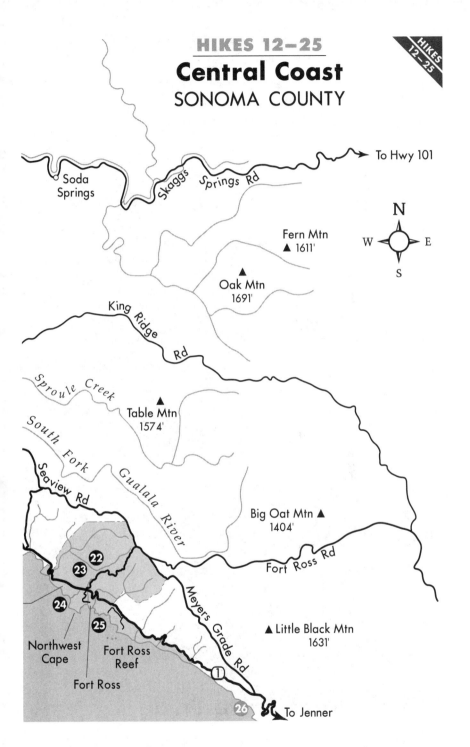

To Hwy 101

Soda Springs

Skaggs Springs Rd

Fern Mtn
▲ 1611'

N
W E
S

Oak Mtn
▲ 1691'

King Ridge Rd

Sproule Creek

Table Mtn
▲ 1574'

South Fork

Gualala River

Seaview Rd

Big Oat Mtn ▲
1404'

22
23

Fort Ross Rd

24
25

▲ Little Black Mtn
1631'

Northwest Cape

Fort Ross Reef

Meyers Grade Rd

Fort Ross

1

26 To Jenner

55

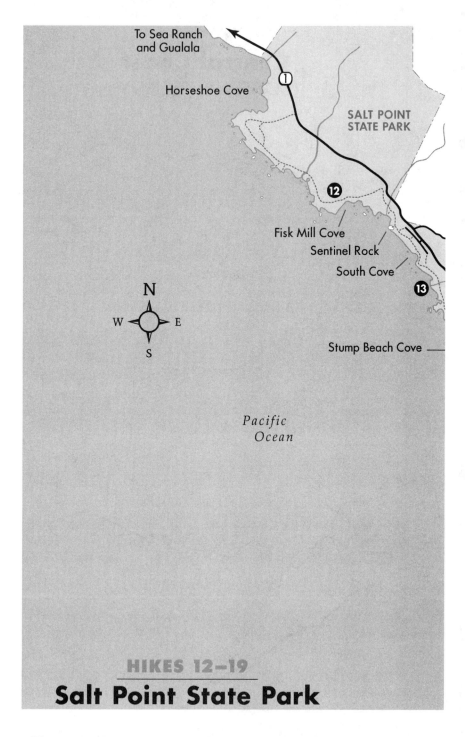

To Sea Ranch
and Gualala

Horseshoe Cove

SALT POINT
STATE PARK

Fisk Mill Cove
Sentinel Rock
South Cove

Stump Beach Cove

N
W   E
S

Pacific
Ocean

HIKES 12–19
Salt Point State Park

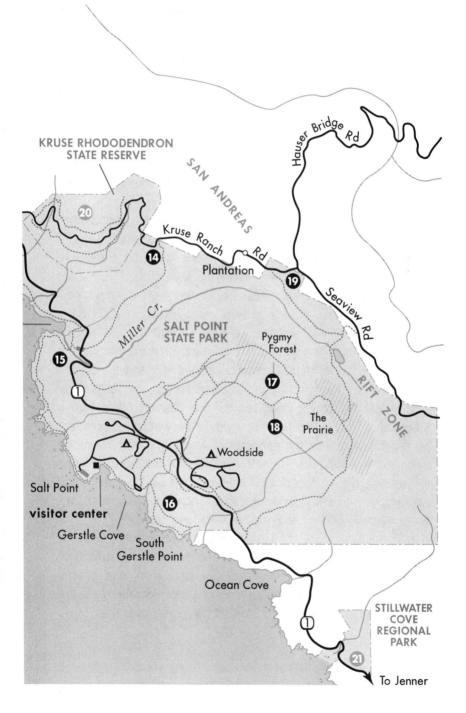

KRUSE RHODODENDRON
STATE RESERVE

20

14

Kruse Ranch Rd

Plantation

SAN ANDREAS

Hauser Bridge Rd

Seaview Rd

19

Miller Cr.

SALT POINT
STATE PARK

Pygmy
Forest

17

18

The
Prairie

RIFT ZONE

15

①

Woodside

16

Salt Point

visitor center

Gerstle Cove

South
Gerstle Point

Ocean Cove

①

STILLWATER
COVE
REGIONAL
PARK

21

To Jenner

Salt Point State Park

HIKES 12–19

25050 Coast Highway 1 · Jenner

Salt Point State Park is comprised of 6,000 acres of pristine land 90 miles north of San Francisco. The park has over six miles of incredible coastline. From the ocean, the park stretches two miles inland, rising a thousand feet to the forested coastal ridge. The area is known for its fishing, skin diving, and scuba diving, with rich, undisturbed marine life. Park amenities include two campgrounds and several picnic areas.

The park contains a wide diversity of habitats, including an expansive marine terrace, rolling hills with grassy meadows, sandy beaches, secluded coves, dramatic outcroppings, tidepools, and sheer rugged cliffs overlooking rocky points. The interior of the park has a dense forest populated with bishop pines, Douglas fir, second-growth redwoods, cypress, tanbark oaks, and madrones. The land slopes upward to 900 feet, where the San Andreas Fault runs parallel to the coast. On the upper ridge is a vast open prairie. There are sag ponds along the faultline and a pygmy forest of stunted cypress, gnarled pines, and redwoods.

The park was once inhabited by the Kashaya Pomo Native Americans. They collected salt from underwater crevices and from catch basins in the sandstone, where the water evaporated and left deposits. The salt was used for food preservation and trading. Native American village and midden sites are found throughout the park. The midden sites (ancient refuse piles) contain shell fragments of abalone, mussels, and clams.

A 20-mile network of hiking, biking, and equestrian trails lace through the park. Hikes 12–19 explore this amazing stretch of coastline. Trails runs the length of the park along the coastal headlands and marine bluffs. Several other remote trails are located along the forested ridge that backs the coastline.

12. Fisk Mill Cove to Horseshoe Point

SALT POINT STATE PARK

Hiking distance: 4 miles round trip
Hiking time: 2 hours
Configuration: out-and-back
Elevation gain: 200 feet
Difficulty: easy to slightly moderate
Exposure: shaded groves and open coastal terrace
Dogs: not allowed
Maps: U.S.G.S. Plantation · Salt Point State Park map

Fisk Mill Cove and Horseshoe Point sit on the northern coastal section of Salt Point State Park. The hike begins from the Fisk Mill Cove picnic area in a forest of bishop pine and Monterey cypress. The trail weaves through the forest to a viewing platform perched atop Sentinel Rock. From the 100-foot-high deck is a bird's-eye view into Fisk Mill Cove and far-reaching vistas of the rugged coastline. Between December and April, Sentinel Rock is a great location for observing gray whales as they migrate to Baja California. The trail continues along the uplifted coastal terrace past Fisk Mill Cove, Cannon Gulch, Deadman Gulch, and several rocky beaches to Horseshoe Point at a jutting promontory. The route circles a small knoll at the point, then returns along the picturesque coast.

To the trailhead

28650 SHORELINE HWY · JENNER   38.594058, -123.344519

From Gualala, just north of the Sonoma County line, drive 16.3 miles south on Highway 1 (Shoreline Highway) to the posted Fisk Mill Cove turnoff on the right at mile marker 42.63. The turnoff is located 20.9 miles north of Jenner and 2.7 miles north of the posted Salt Point-Gerstle Cove turnoff. Turn toward the ocean (southwest) to an immediate T-junction. Turn right and continue 0.1 mile to the signed trailhead and parking spaces on the left.

The hike

Walk 50 yards towards the ocean through the thick bishop pine forest and a posted junction. The left fork leads to South Cove and Stump Beach (Hike 13). Bear right and descend through stands of ferns and huckleberries to the edge of the weather-sculpted bluffs. Head north to a signed junction at 0.2 miles. The Bluff Trail continues on the right fork along the coastline. Detour left and climb Sentinel Rock with the aid of log steps. Atop the massive 100-foot formation is an observation platform with amazing coastal vistas above Fisk Mill Cove.

Return to the Bluff Trail and weave through the grassy pine forest, with ferns and lace lichen draped from the tree branches, to the south edge of Cannon Gulch. To the left, a path zigzags down to the rocky beach. Bear right through a grove of redwoods, then cross the stream-fed gulch. Climb to the bluffs and curve right, meandering through the grasslands near Highway 1. Bear left towards the sea, and pass through an old wood fence. Descend into a forested gulch with a junction. The left fork leads to another rocky beach. Stay to the right and follow the edge of the cliffs to a headland with rock outcroppings, sea stacks, and views of Sentinel Rock and Fisk Mill Cove. Curve around coves and rock formations. Cross stream-fed Deadman Gulch and continue on the edge of the cliffs. Side paths lead to finely etched sandstone formations on the finger-like extensions of land. Head toward forested Horseshoe Point, overlooking sea palms on the tidal rocks.

At the forested 205-foot knoll, veer right and enter the woods. Follow the old road and curve right to the ridge overlooking Horseshoe Cove and Gualala Point. This is a good turnaround point. The trail reaches Highway 1 at a roadside pullout a short distance ahead by mile marker 43.66. Return along the same route. ■

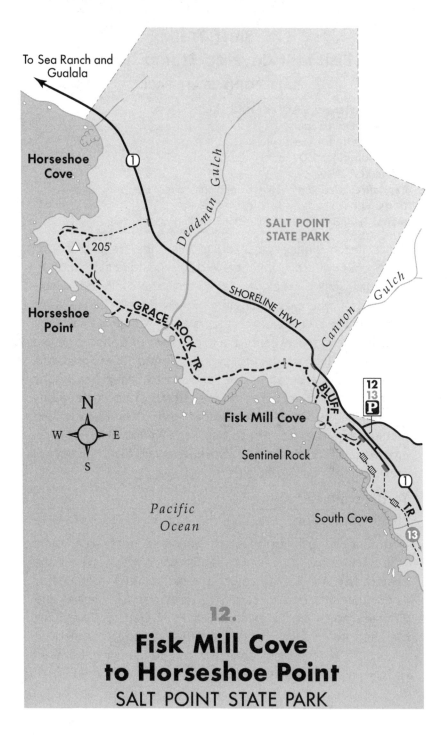

To Sea Ranch and
Gualala

Horseshoe
Cove

SALT POINT
STATE PARK

Deadman Gulch

Cannon Gulch

△ 205'

SHORELINE HWY

Horseshoe
Point

GRACE ROCK TR

BLUFF

12
13
P

Fisk Mill Cove

Sentinel Rock

TR

1

13

N
W   E
S

Pacific
Ocean

South Cove

12.

Fisk Mill Cove
to Horseshoe Point

SALT POINT STATE PARK

13. Bluff Trail:
Fisk Mill Cove to Stump Beach
SALT POINT STATE PARK

Hiking distance: 2.8 miles round trip
Hiking time: 1.5 hours
Configuration: out-and-back
Elevation gain: 150 feet
Difficulty: easy
Exposure: shaded groves and open coastal terrace
Dogs: not allowed
Maps: U.S.G.S. Plantation · Salt Point State Park map

Stump Beach (originally called Big Gulch) is a deep U-shaped sandy cove with calm water backed by sandstone cliffs and forested hills. Miller Creek weaves through the sheltered, white-sand beach, where it empties into the sea. This hike begins at the Fisk Mill Cove picnic area, on the northern section of Salt Point State Park, and snakes through a thick forest of bishop pine and Douglas fir. The path then follows the jagged 100-foot coastal bluffs through a broad grassy headland to Stump Beach, one of the few sandy beaches on this stretch of coastline. Along the way, the trail overlooks pounding surf, offshore rocks, and picturesque coves at Chinese Gulch and Phillips Gulch. The trail crosses small creeks perched above waterfalls that drop several feet from the oceanfront cliffs.

To the trailhead

28650 SHORELINE HWY · JENNER   38.594058, -123.344519

From Gualala, just north of the Sonoma County line, drive 16.3 miles south on Highway 1 (Shoreline Highway) to the posted Fisk Mill Cove turnoff on the right at mile marker 42.63. The turnoff is located 20.9 miles north of Jenner and 2.7 miles north of the posted Salt Point-Gerstle Cove turn-off. Turn toward the ocean (southwest) to an immediate T-junction. Turn right and continue 0.1 mile to the signed trailhead and parking spaces on the left.

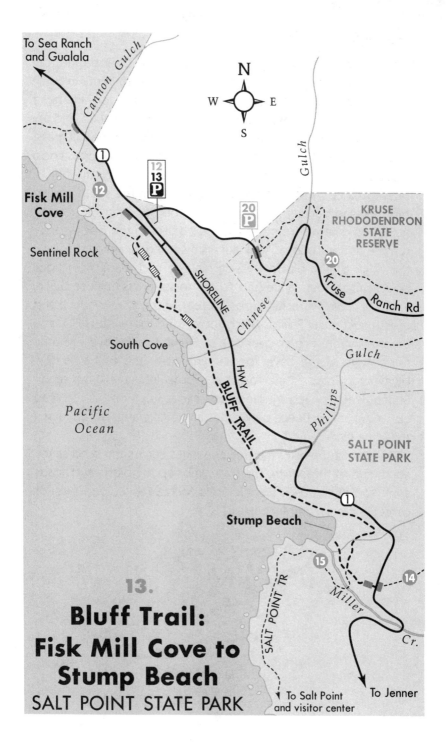

To Sea Ranch
and Gualala

Cannon Gulch

N
W   E
S

Gulch

① 12
13 P
20 P

KRUSE
RHODODENDRON
STATE
RESERVE

Fisk Mill
Cove

20

Kruse

Ranch Rd

Sentinel Rock

SHORELINE

Chinese

Gulch

South Cove

HWY

BLUFF TRAIL

Phillips

Pacific
Ocean

SALT POINT
STATE PARK

①

Stump Beach

15

SALT POINT TR

Miller

14

Cr.

To Jenner

13.
**Bluff Trail:
Fisk Mill Cove to
Stump Beach**
SALT POINT STATE PARK

To Salt Point
and visitor center

The hike

Walk 50 yards towards the ocean through the bishop pine forest and a posted junction. The right fork leads to Sentinel Rock, Fisk Mill Cove, and Horseshoe Point (Hike 12). Bear left and head through the pine forest. Cross a footbridge over a gulch and ascend steps to the oceanfront bluffs. Walk through the tall grass, and cross a second stream-fed gulch on a footbridge. Loop around a huge rock outcrop on the edge of the vertical cliffs. Descend steps and merge with the trail from the south end of the trailhead parking lot. Cross a third bridge over a fern-lined gully, and emerge from the wooded bluffs to the open grassy terrace at South Cove. Walk across a small drainage and follow the edge of the bluffs, passing massive rock slabs with tidepools and an abundance of offshore rocks. Cross Chinese Gulch, where a creek waterfall drops 50 feet to the sea. Continue and cross the creek at Phillips Gulch above a 30-foot waterfall. Climb the sloping bluff to an overlook of Stump Beach Cove. Skirt the north edge of the cove, looping around to the east side near Highway 1. Enter a pine forest and drop into a gully to sandy Stump Beach, ringed by sandstone cliffs. Steps on the left lead up to the Stump Beach parking lot and picnic area. Return along the same route.

To extend the hike, the trail continues across the sand at the south end of the beach. The trail climbs up the bluffs and heads south to Salt Point and Gerstle Cove, located at the park's visitor center and main entrance (Hike 15). ■

Rock formations such as these, known as *tafoni*, can be found along the Salt Point coastline. The cave-like holes in the rock often form a lacey pattern.

14. Stump Beach Trail
SALT POINT STATE PARK

Hiking distance: 3 miles round trip
Hiking time: 1.5 hours
Configuration: out-and-back
Elevation gain: 650 feet
Difficulty: moderate
Exposure: mostly shaded forest
Dogs: not allowed
Maps: U.S.G.S. Plantation · Salt Point State Park map

Miller Creek begins in the upper slopes of Salt Point State Park along the San Andreas Rift Zone at 800 feet. The perennial creek drains into the sea at Stump Beach. The Stump Beach Trail begins by the beach off Highway 1 and climbs the forested north wall of the Miller Creek canyon to Kruse Ranch Road. The trail is perched on the hillside and weaves through a lush forest of Douglas fir, bishop pine, tanbark oak, and towering redwood groves. The hike offers quiet solitude through a cool coastal forest.

To the trailhead

25900 SHORELINE HWY · JENNER   38.579704, -123.333072

From Gualala, just north of the Sonoma County line, drive 17.7 miles south on Highway 1 (Shoreline Highway) to the posted Stump Beach turnoff on the right at mile marker 41.20. The turn-off is located 19.5 miles north of Jenner and 1.3 miles north of the posted Salt Point—Gerstle Cove turnoff. Park in either the Stump Beach parking lot on the ocean side (west) or in the pullout on the inland side of the highway by the posted trailhead.

The hike

Walk past the log barrier and head up the forested path. Traverse the steep hillside, perched on a shelf with views into the canyon. At a half mile, cross a footbridge over a side canyon and continue uphill, passing moss-covered tree trunks and coastal redwood groves. The serpentine path steadily climbs up the north wall of the Miller Creek drainage. Near the top, descend and curve right to the end of the trail on Kruse Ranch Road, between Kruse Rhododendron State Reserve and the town of Plantation. Return along the same trail. ■

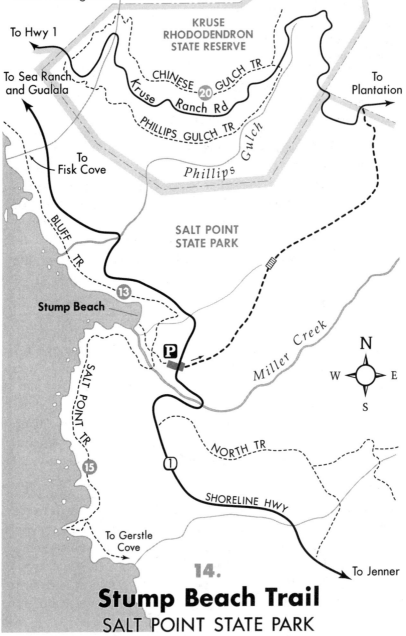

14.
Stump Beach Trail
SALT POINT STATE PARK

15. Salt Point Trail: Gerstle Cove to Stump Beach

SALT POINT STATE PARK

Hiking distance: 3.2 miles round trip
Hiking time: 1.5 hours
Configuration: out-and-back
Elevation gain: 100 feet
Difficulty: easy (with some technical sections)
Exposure: open coastal bluffs
Dogs: not allowed
Maps: U.S.G.S. Plantation · Salt Point State Park map

The Salt Point Trail is an amazing, world-class hike with a geologically unique stretch of coastal bluffs. The hike explores ancient conglomerate sandstone rocks lifted from the ocean bottom. Delicate formations are carved into the cliff faces, forming natural earth sculptures with pits, knobs, ribs, and ridges. Concretions—hard rounded rocks—sit on isolated pedestals. Natural depressions in the bedrock collect seawater, forming pools. Most dramatic are the intricate wind-carved and wave-sculpted honeycomb formations in the sandstone called tafoni. The waffle-shaped formations have a complex lacy pattern etched into the weathering sandstone.

This hike begins on Salt Point at the north end of Gerstle Cove and follows the rolling coastal bluffs north to horseshoe-shaped Stump Beach, protected by 80-foot bluffs. The trail passes sandstone outcroppings with Native American midden sites, wave-pounded rocky points, sea stacks, sea caves, and tidepools.

To the trailhead

23476 SHORELINE HWY · JENNER   38.570121, -123.323667

From Gualala, just north of the Sonoma County line, drive 19 miles south on Highway 1 (Shoreline Highway) to the posted Salt Point-Gerstle Cove turnoff on the right at mile marker 39.90. The turnoff is located 18.2 miles north of Jenner and 6.7 miles north of Fort Ross. Turn towards the ocean (west), and drive 0.7 miles to the oceanfront parking lot at Salt Point. A parking fee is required.

The hike

From the northwest corner of Gerstle Cove, take the posted Salt Point Trail along the edge of Salt Point. The paved path leads to the point, overlooking tidepools, sea stacks, sea caves, sculpted sandstone formations, sea lions, and a frequently turbulent sea. The pavement ends at the southwest tip and continues as a dirt path.

Leave the promontory and head north on the 40-foot bluffs to a Y-fork. The left fork follows the edge of the bluffs. The parallel right path meanders through a meadow with rock outcroppings and boulders. Cross over ephemeral Warren Creek, and meander through rattlesnake grass and California poppies. The two paths merge ahead at a dramatic cove with offshore sea stacks, tilted rock formations, and vertical eroding cliffs. The bluff path passes a series of rock-strewn coves and a Kashaya Pomo midden. The site is scattered with shell fragments of abalone, clams, crabs, and mussels on the leeward base of a knoll. To the left, a side path leads 50 yards on a finger of land between two coves. A short distance ahead is a fantastic, moonscape-looking rock garden with pools in the water-carved formations. Using extreme caution, explore the pock-marked tafoni formations and pools, following your own path. Return to the main trail, and continue to sandy Stump Beach in a deep cove at the mouth of Miller Creek. Descend to the beach, then cross the creek to a trail split at the canyon drainage. This is the turn-around spot.

To extend the hike, steps on the right lead up to the Stump Beach parking lot and picnic area. Across the highway is the Stump Beach Trail, which heads up the forested ridge to Kruse Ranch Road (Hike 14). The Bluff Trail climbs up the gulch to the left and crosses the stream, continuing northward along the bluffs (Hike 13). The Bluff Trail continues to South Cove, Sentinel Rock, Fisk Mill Cove, and Horseshoe Point (Hike 12). ■

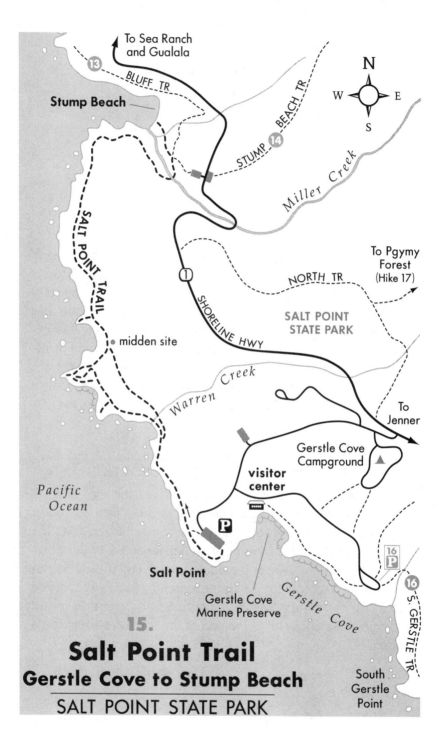

To Sea Ranch and Gualala

BLUFF TR

13

Stump Beach

STUMP BEACH TR

14

N
W E
S

Miller Creek

SALT POINT TRAIL

1

SHORELINE HWY

NORTH TR

To Pgymy Forest (Hike 17)

SALT POINT STATE PARK

• midden site

To Jenner

Warren Creek

Gerstle Cove Campground

visitor center

Pacific Ocean

P

Salt Point

Gerstle Cove Marine Preserve

Gerstle Cove

16
P

16

S. GERSTLE TR

South Gerstle Point

15.
Salt Point Trail
Gerstle Cove to Stump Beach
SALT POINT STATE PARK

16. South Gerstle Trail and the Southern Bluffs

SALT POINT STATE PARK

Hiking distance: 1 mile round trip
Hiking time: 40 minutes
Configuration: out-and-back with optional return path
Elevation gain: 50 feet
Difficulty: easy
Exposure: mostly open coastal bluffs with forested pockets
Dogs: not allowed
Maps: U.S.G.S. Plantation · Salt Point State Park map

Gerstle Cove is an underwater ecological reserve at the southern end of Salt Point State Park. The reserve supports and protects a diverse community of fish, invertebrates, and aquatic plants.

From the main entrance to the park, the South Gerstle Trail travels along the rugged bluffs above the cove. The trail explores eroding sandstone cliffs and the jagged, chiseled headland of South Gerstle Point, a rocky promontory that juts out into the ocean. The views include wave-carved caves, natural bridges, and the crashing surf, which constantly batters the offshore rocks below.

To the trailhead

23476 SHORELINE HWY · JENNER   38.570121, -123.323667

From Gualala, just north of the Sonoma County line, drive 19 miles south on Highway 1 (Shoreline Highway) to the posted Salt Point—Gerstle Cove turnoff on the right at mile marker 39.90. The turnoff is located 18.2 miles north of Jenner and 6.7 miles north of Fort Ross. Turn towards the ocean (west), and drive 0.5 miles to the signed turnoff for the visitor center. Turn left and continue 0.5 miles, passing the visitor center, to South Gerstle Cove and a picnic area parking lot at the end of the road. A parking fee is required.

The hike

From the south end of the parking lot, pass the posted trail-head gate and follow the old dirt road. Cross over Squaw Creek, where a steep path descends to the rocky beach. This trail is an access route to the cove, used by snorkelers and scuba divers. Skirt the edge of the bluffs while overlooking rock terraces, beach coves, and offshore formations. Pass through a grove of bishop pines to an open, grassy terrace covered with rock out-croppings. A faint path follows the cliffs and a two-track road crosses the terrace by South Gerstle Point. This exposed marine terrace invites exploration. Cross a small stream and follow a footpath south through a pine grove to finely etched sandstone formations. Loop around a deep, vertical-walled cove. The path ends above ephemeral Wildcat Creek and a rock-filled beach cove near the southern park boundary. Return by retracing your steps. ■

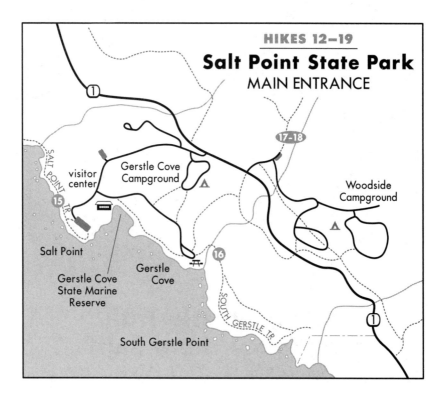

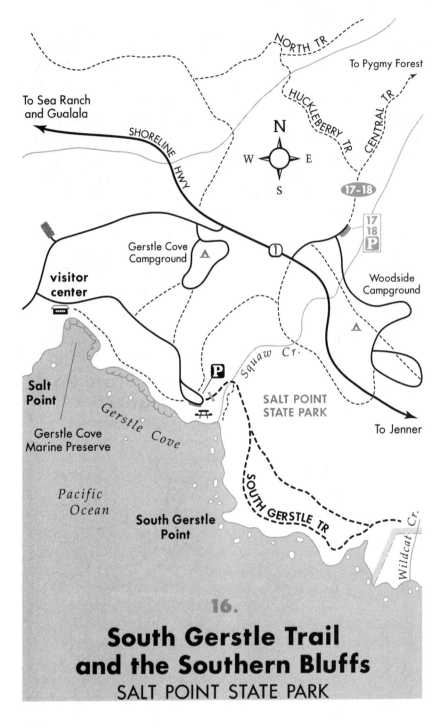

NORTH TR.

To Pygmy Forest

To Sea Ranch
and Gualala

HUCKLEBERRY TR.

CENTRAL TR.

SHORELINE HWY

N
W   E
S

17-18

17
18
P

Gerstle Cove
Campground

1

visitor
center

Woodside
Campground

Salt
Point

Gerstle Cove

P

Squaw Cr.

SALT POINT
STATE PARK

To Jenner

Gerstle Cove
Marine Preserve

*Pacific
Ocean*

South Gerstle
Point

SOUTH GERSTLE TR.

Wildcat Cr.

16.
South Gerstle Trail
and the Southern Bluffs
SALT POINT STATE PARK

17. Pygmy Forest
North Trail—Central Trail Loop
SALT POINT STATE PARK

Hiking distance: 3-mile loop
Hiking time: 1.5 hours
Configuration: out-and-back or loop
Elevation gain: 600 feet
Difficulty: moderate
Exposure: mostly shaded forest
Dogs: not allowed
Maps: U.S.G.S. Plantation · Salt Point State Park map

Salt Point State Park is known for its rocky promontories and dramatic coastline. The interior of the park, however, where the majority of the acreage lies, offers beautiful trails as well. The sloping coastal landscape is covered with a dense forest of redwoods, Douglas fir, tanbark oak, bishop pine, madrone, manzanita, trillium, ferns, and rhododendrons. Fog lifts from the pounding surf below, which often settles quietly along the forest floor.

Hikes 17—19 explore the wooded interior of the park. This area was actively logged and quarried in the mid-1800s. The land transitioned to ranchland after the 1870s. It is now covered with second-growth forests. This hike forms a loop up the coastal slope, beginning from Woodside Campground, just off Highway 1. The route follows old logging roads along two creek drainages. At the upper end of the loop is a pygmy forest. The trees grow in highly acidic, nutrient-deficient soil with a shallow hardpan surface, preventing tree roots and water to penetrate. The result is a rare grove of trees with stunted versions of bishop pines, Mendocino cypress, and coastal redwoods.

To the trailhead

23469 SHORELINE HWY · JENNER   38.569134, -123.320872

From Gualala, just north of the Sonoma County line, drive 19 miles south on Highway 1 (Shoreline Highway) to the posted Woodside Campground turnoff on the left at mile marker 39.78. The turnoff is located 0.1 mile south of the posted Salt Point—Gerstle Cove turnoff and 18.1 miles north of Jenner. Turn inland (northeast) and drive 0.1 mile to the day use parking lot. A parking fee is required.

The hike

Take the posted Central Trail past the gate, and head uphill into the dense forest. At 0.1 mile is a posted junction. Leave the Central Trail and bear left, beginning the loop on the Huckleberry Trail. Traverse the hillside and cross over Warren Creek to a signed junction with the North Trail at 0.4 miles. The left fork leads to Highway 1, just south of Stump Beach.

Go to the right and weave up the hill. Parallel the seasonal creek through a forest of coastal redwoods, bishop pines, tanbark oak, madrone, and bay laurel trees to a trail split. The right fork—the Water Tank Trail—leads 0.2 miles to the Central Trail. Stay to the left as the trail levels out. Pass the headwaters of Warren Creek, and enter the pygmy forest at just over one mile. Meander through the quiet grove for a quarter mile while viewing the interesting, stunted-growth trees. After the forest, descend on the North Trail to a T-junction with the Central Trail. The left fork leads to the The Prairie (Hike 18). Bear right and descend under the towering Douglas fir and redwood trees. Pass a row of four wooden water tanks by the connector trail to the North Trail. Continue downhill, completing the loop. ∎

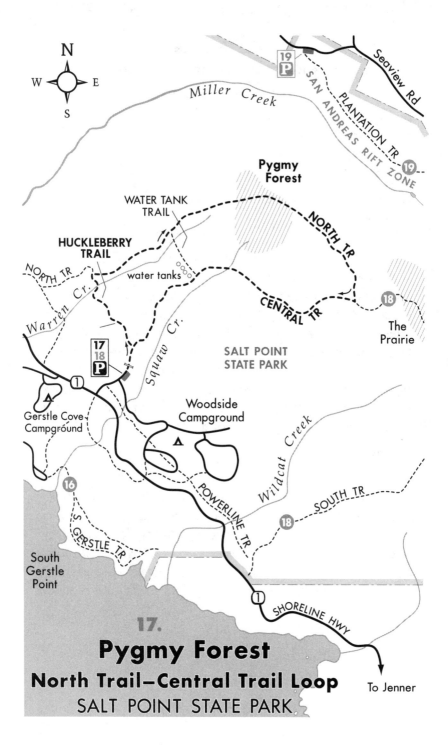

N
W E
S

Miller Creek

19 P

Seaview Rd

PLANTATION TR

SAN ANDREAS RIFT ZONE

19

Pygmy Forest

WATER TANK TRAIL

NORTH TR

HUCKLEBERRY TRAIL

NORTH TR

Warren Cr.

water tanks

Squaw Cr.

CENTRAL TR

18

The Prairie

17 18 P

SALT POINT STATE PARK

Gerstle Cove Campground

Woodside Campground

Wildcat Creek

16

S GERSTLE TR

POWERLINE TR

SOUTH TR

18

South Gerstle Point

1

SHORELINE HWY

To Jenner

17.
Pygmy Forest
North Trail–Central Trail Loop
SALT POINT STATE PARK

18. The Prairie
Central Trail—South Trail Loop
SALT POINT STATE PARK

Hiking distance: 4-mile loop
Hiking time: 2 hours
Configuration: loop
Elevation gain: 600 feet
Difficulty: moderate
Exposure: a mix of shaded forest and grassland meadow
Dogs: not allowed
Maps: U.S.G.S. Plantation · Salt Point State Park map

The Central Trail and South Trail are located in the heart of Salt Point State Park, forming a large loop through a dense conifer forest to the crest of the coastal ridge. The trails are fire roads that climb up the slope from Woodside Campground on Highway 1. At the ridge is The Prairie, a vast grassland meadow frequented by deer and hawks. The wooded, atmospheric route meanders under towering second-growth redwoods, Douglas fir, and bishop pines, with an understory of ferns, salal, huckleberry, rhododendrons, and manzanita. Early morning fog often settles in along the coastal end of the loop.

To the trailhead

23469 SHORELINE HWY · JENNER   38.569134, -123.320872

From Gualala, just north of the Sonoma County line, drive 19 miles south on Highway 1 (Shoreline Highway) to the posted Woodside Campground turnoff on the left at mile marker 39.78. The turnoff is located 0.1 mile south of the posted Salt Point-Gerstle Cove turnoff and 18.1 miles north of Jenner. Turn inland (northeast) and drive 0.1 mile to the day use parking lot. A parking fee is required.

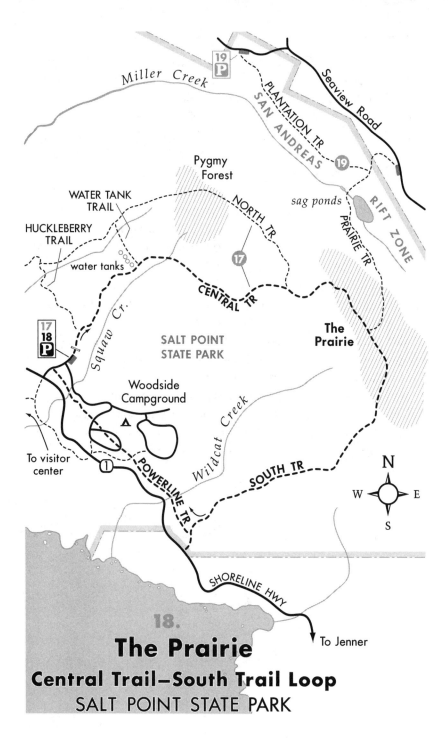

Miller Creek

Seaview Road

19 P

PLANTATION TR

SAN ANDREAS

19

RIFT ZONE

Pygmy Forest

sag ponds

WATER TANK TRAIL

NORTH TR

HUCKLEBERRY TRAIL

PRAIRIE TR

water tanks

17

CENTRAL TR

Squaw Cr.

17 **18** P

SALT POINT STATE PARK

The Prairie

Woodside Campground

Wildcat Creek

To visitor center

1

POWERLINE TR

SOUTH TR

N
W E
S

SHORELINE HWY

To Jenner

18.

The Prairie
Central Trail–South Trail Loop
SALT POINT STATE PARK

The hike

Take the posted Central Trail past the gate, and head up the fire road through the lush forest with towering Douglas fir. At 0.1 mile is a junction with the Huckleberry Trail. Stay on the Central Trail and steadily climb towards the ridge. Pass a row of four wooden water tanks on the left by the Water Tank Trail, which leads to the pygmy forest (Hike 17). Stay on the Central Trail, and curve right, climbing to a junction with the upper end of the North Trail. Stay straight and slowly descend to The Prairie, a long, open meadow that lies at about 1,000 feet above the coast. Skirt the southwest edge of the meadow to a trail split. The Prairie Trail bears left through the meadow to the sag ponds on Miller Creek along the San Andreas Fault (Hike 19).

For this hike, go straight on the South Trail and curve right, reentering the forest. Descend through the redwoods and moss-covered forest. Near the bottom of the hill, as the forest opens, watch for a trail sign on the right, located 70 yards shy of the highway. Bear right on the Powerline Trail, a footpath in a forested utility corridor. Cross Wildcat Creek and ascend the slope, walking parallel to Highway 1. Pass the campground access trail that leads to Gerstle Cove, then join the paved campground road. Either follow the road back to the trailhead or take the footpath through the campground. ■

19. Plantation and Prairie Trails
San Andreas Rift Zone
SALT POINT STATE PARK

Hiking distance: 4 miles round trip
Hiking time: 2 hours
Configuration: loop
Elevation gain: 250 feet
Difficulty: easy to slightly moderate
Exposure: a mix of shaded forest and grassland meadow
Dogs: not allowed
Maps: U.S.G.S. Plantation · Salt Point State Park map

The Plantation and Prairie Trails follow the crest of a coastal ridge along the San Andreas Rift Zone in Salt Point State Park. The two trails meander through a dense forest of towering redwoods, pine, fir, and madrones. The Prairie Trail leads to a vast, thousand-foot hilltop meadow known as The Prairie, where deer and hawks are frequently seen. En route to The Prairie, the trail passes sag ponds—water-filled depressions formed by the sinking ground along the San Andreas Fault. The quiet trails offer an away-from-the-crowds hike. This hike begins from Kruse Ranch Road at the north end of the state park.

To the trailhead

34337 KRUSE RANCH RD · CAZADERO   38.588447, -123.306797

From Gualala, just north of the Sonoma County line, drive 16.2 miles south on Highway 1 (Shoreline Highway) to the posted Kruse Ranch Road turnoff on the left at mile marker 42.75. The turnoff is located 21 miles north of Jenner and 2.8 miles north of the posted Salt Point-Gerstle Cove turnoff. Turn inland (northeast) and drive 3.7 miles up the narrow, winding road to the posted trailhead on the right. The trailhead is 0.3 miles past the community of Plantation. A parking pullout is by the trailhead.

The hike

Descend past the trailhead sign on the Plantation Trail. Traverse the hillside through the isolated forest, passing massive redwoods and moss-covered downfall. Continue descending into the forest. The path levels out and meanders through the quiet of the forest. Ascend the hillside and curve to the left to a T-junction with the Prairie Trail (also called the Seaview Trail), an old ranch road. The left fork leads 0.2 miles to another trail access along Seaview Road.

Bear right and descend on the forested dirt road along the south wall of the canyon. Cross over Miller Creek and the sag ponds on the left along the San Andreas Fault. Head uphill, weaving through the lush forest to the ridge at the massive open meadow called The Prairie. Walk through the meadow to a posted T-junction with the South Trail. Both routes lead downhill to the Woodside Campground and Highway 1. The trail to the right, which merges with the North Trail, leads to the pygmy forest. The rare grove is home to stunted versions of bishop pines, Mendocino cypress, and coastal redwoods. Return by retracing your route. ■

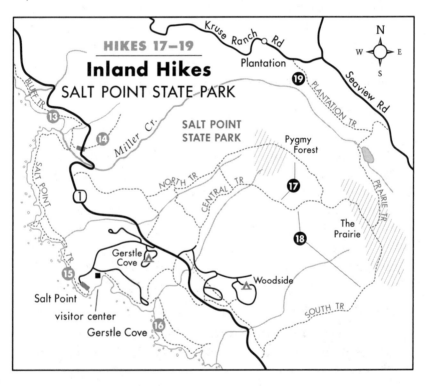

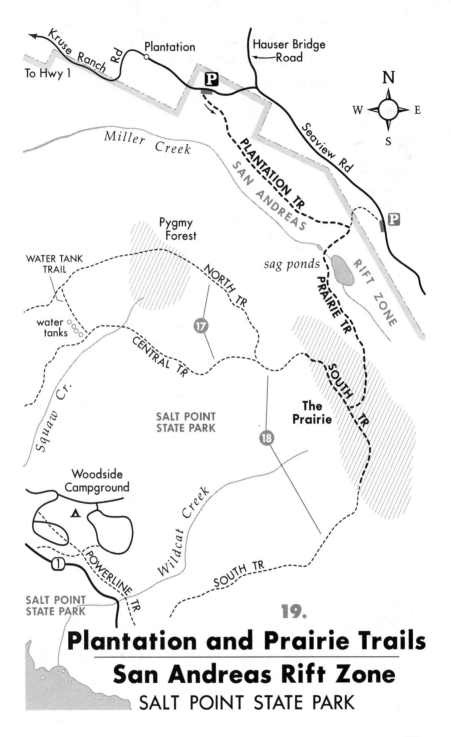

Kruse Ranch Rd

Plantation

Hauser Bridge Road

To Hwy 1

P

Seaview Rd

N
W · E
S

Miller Creek

PLANTATION TR

SAN ANDREAS

P

Pygmy Forest

WATER TANK TRAIL

sag ponds

RIFT ZONE

NORTH TR

water tanks

PRAIRIE TR

CENTRAL TR

(17)

SOUTH TR

Squaw Cr.

SALT POINT STATE PARK

The Prairie

(18)

Woodside Campground

▲

Wildcat Creek

(1)

POWERLINE TR

SOUTH TR

SALT POINT STATE PARK

19.

Plantation and Prairie Trails
San Andreas Rift Zone
SALT POINT STATE PARK

20. Kruse Rhododendron State Natural Reserve
Chinese Gulch—Phillips Gulch Loop

Hiking distance: 2.5-mile loop
Hiking time: 1.5 hours
Configuration: loop
Elevation gain: 400 feet
Difficulty: easy
Exposure: mostly shaded forest
Dogs: not allowed
Maps: U.S.G.S. Plantation · Salt Point State Park map

Kruse Rhododendron State Natural Reserve lies adjacent to the north-central end of Salt Point State Park. The reserve's 317 acres were once part of the Kruse Ranch, a sheep ranch and logging operation dating back to the 1880s. The undeveloped land was donated to the state in 1933. California rhododendrons, the namesake of the park, grow in profusion. Their brilliant pink blossoms bloom in clusters from April through June. The fast-growing rhododendrons flourished after a forest fire around 1900 removed most of the existing vegetation. The reserve is also home to a mixed forest of second-growth redwoods, Douglas fir, grand fir, tanbark oaks, madrones, manzanita, and eucalyptus.

This hike makes a loop across the reserve, from Chinese Gulch to Phillips Gulch. The fern-lined creeks flow through the reserve en route to the Salt Point coast. A total of five miles of hiking trails weave through the reserve's forested coastal hills.

To the trailhead

34899 Kruse Ranch Rd · Cazadero   38.593635, -123.339471

From Gualala, just north of the Sonoma County line, drive 16.2 miles south on Highway 1 (Shoreline Highway) to the posted Kruse Ranch Road turnoff on the left at mile marker 42.75. The turnoff is located 21 miles north of Jenner and 2.8 miles north of the posted Salt Point-Gerstle Cove turnoff. Turn inland (northeast)

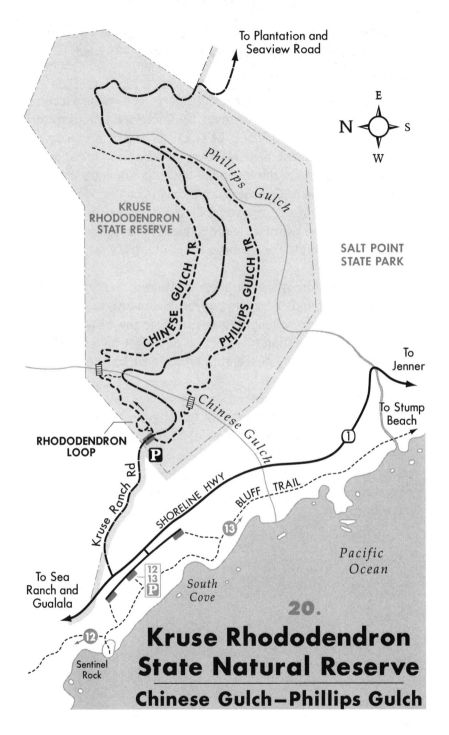

To Plantation and
Seaview Road

E
N — S
W

KRUSE
RHODODENDRON
STATE RESERVE

SALT POINT
STATE PARK

Phillips Gulch

CHINESE GULCH TR.

PHILLIPS GULCH TR.

Chinese Gulch

To Jenner

To Stump
Beach

RHODODENDRON
LOOP

P

Kruse Ranch Rd

1

SHORELINE HWY

BLUFF TRAIL

13

12
13
P

South
Cove

Pacific
Ocean

To Sea
Ranch and
Gualala

12

Sentinel
Rock

20.

Kruse Rhododendron
State Natural Reserve
Chinese Gulch–Phillips Gulch

and drive 0.45 miles up the narrow road to the posted trailhead on the left. Parking pullouts are on both sides of the road.

The hike

Begin the loop on the upper north side of the road. Ascend steps to the map kiosk. At the map, two post-lined paths form the short Rhododendron Loop. Begin on either path and weave through the lush forest, passing groves of redwoods and moss-covered tree trunks to the far end of the loop. Continue straight on the north slope of Chinese Gulch through Douglas fir, tanbark oaks, coastal redwoods, and ferns. Zigzag down to a junction in Chinese Gulch. The right fork leads 20 yards to Kruse Ranch Road at a U-shaped bend. (For a shorter loop, return 0.4 miles down the dirt road.)

Bear left and cross the wooden footbridge over the fern-lined creek. Ascend the south canyon wall and cross a small bridge. Climb two switchbacks and traverse the canyon wall, steadily gaining elevation to a junction. Bear right on the Phillips Gulch Trail, and sharply descend to Kruse Ranch Road at Phillips Gulch.

Walk 20 yards up the road to the signed trail. Descend steps and stroll through the tanbark oak forest. Veer right at a trail sign and pass a gorgeous hollow of redwoods. Switchbacks lead down the draw, returning to Chinese Gulch. Cross a wood bridge over the stream and wind up the hillside. Near the top, pass restrooms and continue 50 yards to Kruse Ranch Road at the trailhead. ■

21. Stillwater Cove Regional Park

Stockhoff Creek Loop:
Fort Ross Schoolhouse to Stillwater Cove

Hiking distance: 1.6 miles round trip
Hiking time: 1 hour
Configuration: lollipop with spur trail to coast
Elevation gain: 200 feet
Difficulty: easy
Exposure: mostly shaded forest
Dogs: allowed
Maps: U.S.G.S. Plantation · Stillwater Cove Regional Park map

Stillwater Cove Regional Park encompasses 363 acres between Salt Point State Park and Fort Ross State Park. The park sits amid pine-covered hillsides, while perennial Stockhoff Creek flows through a canyon filled with redwood, fir, and red alder. Stillwater Cove, situated at the mouth of the creek, is a gorgeous beach protected by 100-foot cliffs. The historic Fort Ross Schoolhouse sits in a tree-lined meadow in the hills above Stockhoff Creek. The one room schoolhouse was originally erected on the bluffs adjacent to the village of Fort Ross in 1885 and was active through 1920. It has since been moved to the present site and restored.

This hike explores the forested canyon, climbs to North Meadow and the schoolhouse, and returns to the scenic beach cove. Within the park is a picnic area and campground.

To the trailhead

22455 HWY 1 · JENNER   38.547540, -123.295634

From Gualala, just north of the Sonoma county line, drive 22 miles south on Highway 1 (Shoreline Highway) to the posted Stillwater Cove turnoff on the left at mile marker 37.02. It is located 2.9 miles south of the Salt Point State Park entrance. Turn inland and drive 0.2 miles to the day use parking lot on the left. A parking fee is required.

The turnoff is located 15 miles north of Jenner and 3.8 miles north of Fort Ross.

The hike

From the northwest corner of the parking lot, descend on the signed trail into the dense, dark forest on the south canyon wall. At 0.1 mile is a posted three-way junction by a bridge over Stockhoff Creek. The left fork leads 0.2 miles to Stillwater Cove across Highway 1. Straight ahead, the trail crosses the bridge over the creek—the return route.

For now, bear right and begin the loop. Follow the path along the fern-covered canyon wall through redwoods and firs. Cross a bridge over a tributary stream, following the course of the main creek. Cross two more bridges over small gullies to the signed park boundary. Cross the creek and return on the north side of Stockhoff Creek. A short distance ahead is an unsigned trail on the right. Veer right and climb the south-facing slope. Traverse the hillside to a posted junction. The left fork is the return route. Detour 50 yards straight ahead to the historic schoolhouse on the left and North Meadow on the right. After exploring the schoolhouse and the interpretive displays, return to the junction. Descend the hill to the Canyon Loop Trail. Bear right and cross the long wooden bridge, completing the loop.

To reach Stillwater Cove, follow the south side of the creek through the darkness of the dense redwood forest. The forest soon gives way to the sky and Highway 1. Cross the highway and pick up the paved path to the sandy beach pocket beneath towering rock walls and numerous offshore rocks. ∎

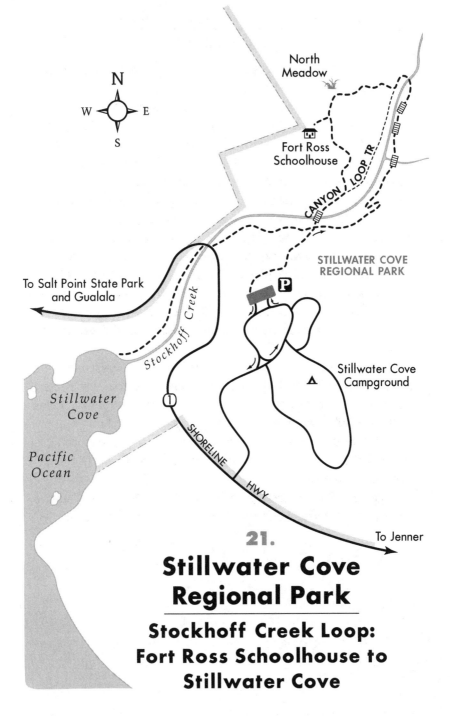

N
W E
S

North Meadow

Fort Ross Schoolhouse

CANYON LOOP TR

STILLWATER COVE REGIONAL PARK

To Salt Point State Park and Gualala

P

Stockhoff Creek

Stillwater Cove Campground

Stillwater Cove

Pacific Ocean

① SHORELINE HWY

To Jenner

21.
Stillwater Cove Regional Park
Stockhoff Creek Loop: Fort Ross Schoolhouse to Stillwater Cove

Fort Ross State Historic Park

HIKES 22 — 25

Fort Ross State Historic Park is a 3,386-acre park that is located 12 miles north of Jenner. The park was established in 1906, making it one of California's oldest parks. Kashaya Pomo Native Americans inhabited the land for over 7,000 years. In 1812, trappers followed seal and sea otter colonies down the coast from Alaska and settled the area. For almost 30 years, from 1812 to 1841, this coastal land, now located in the center of the state park, was an outpost for Russian fur traders. The settlement was abandoned in 1841. Only one of the original buildings remains, but many of the fort structures have been reconstructed, including hand-hewn log barracks, blockhouses, and a Russian Orthodox chapel. The fort sits atop the wind-washed terrace overlooking Fort Ross Cove and the Pacific Ocean. A half mile inland lies an orchard from 1814. There is a visitor center and interpretive displays that explain the geology and the historical significance of the area.

Bisecting the state park is Highway 1. To the west are high, windswept bluffs with dramatic headlands and rocky sheltered coves. To the east are the heavily forested coastal mountains with second-growth redwood groves and a mixed conifer forest of Bishop pine, Douglas fir, wax myrtle, and bay laurel. The eastern end of the park borders Seaview Road, winding 1,500 feet above the sea.

Hikes 22—25 explore the settlement structures as well as the broad marine terrace and the upland hills of this state park.

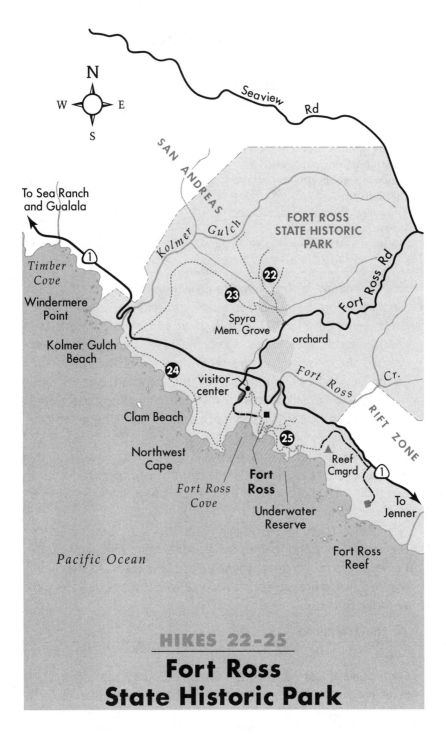

N
W   E
S

Seaview Rd

To Sea Ranch
and Gualala

SAN ANDREAS

Kolmer Gulch

FORT ROSS
STATE HISTORIC
PARK

Fort Ross Rd

Timber
Cove

1

Windermere
Point

22

23

Kolmer Gulch
Beach

Spyra
Mem. Grove

orchard

Fort Ross Cr.

24

visitor
center

RIFT ZONE

Clam Beach

Northwest
Cape

Fort Ross
Cove

25

Fort
Ross

Reef
Cmgrd

1

To
Jenner

Underwater
Reserve

Fort Ross
Reef

Pacific Ocean

HIKES 22-25

Fort Ross
State Historic Park

22. Fort Ross Orchard and Spyra Memorial Grove to Kolmer Gulch Camp

FORT ROSS STATE HISTORIC PARK

Hiking distance: 1.8 miles round trip
Hiking time: 1 hour
Configuration: out-and-back
Elevation gain: 200 feet
Difficulty: easy
Exposure: mostly shaded forest
Dogs: not allowed
Maps: U.S.G.S. Fort Ross and Plantation
Fort Ross State Historic Park map

Near the center of Fort Ross State Historic Park is the Fort Ross Orchard, a three-acre garden filled with apple, plum, and pear trees dating back to 1814. Across the road from the historic orchard is the Stanley Spyra Memorial Grove. The grove has the world's oldest known second-growth coastal redwoods.

The San Andreas Fault runs through the orchard and the memorial grove. During the infamous 1906 San Francisco earthquake, the ground suddenly shifted more than 12 feet. The grove has visible remnants of the earthquake, including offset creeks, sag ponds (water-filled depressions along the fault), escarpments, and damaged trees. The ancient redwoods had their trunks split and their tops snapped off. The branches have since grown in a deformed manner.

This hike takes an old logging road from the Stanley Spyra Memorial Grove and follows the fractured land to Kolmer Gulch Camp, an old mining camp on the edge of the creek. At the camp are benches, a fire pit, spring water, a wood shelter, and an old wooden fence.

To the trailhead

19005 FORT ROSS RD · JENNER   38.523770, –123.241040

From Gualala, just north of the Sonoma County line, drive 25.7 miles south on Highway 1 (Shoreline Highway) to the posted Fort

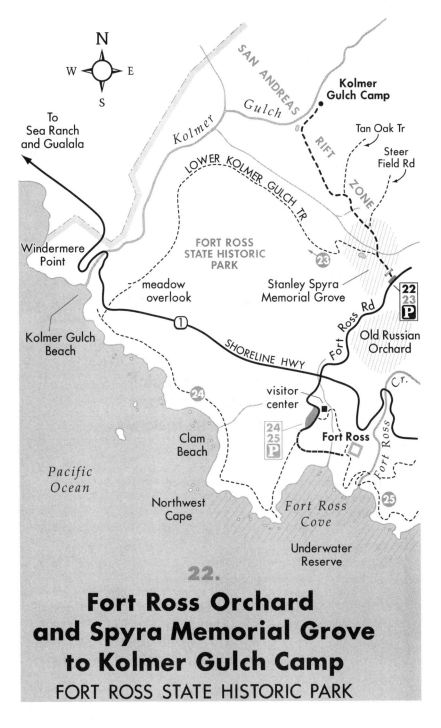

N
W   E
S

To
Sea Ranch
and Gualala

SAN ANDREAS

Kolmer
Gulch Camp

Gulch

Tan Oak Tr

Kolmer

Steer
Field Rd

RIFT ZONE

LOWER KOLMER GULCH TR

FORT ROSS
STATE HISTORIC
PARK

23

Windermere
Point

meadow
overlook

Stanley Spyra
Memorial Grove

22
23
P

Kolmer Gulch
Beach

1

Fort Ross Rd

Old Russian
Orchard

SHORELINE HWY

Fort Ross Cr.

24

visitor
center

24
25
P

Clam
Beach

Fort Ross

Pacific
Ocean

Northwest
Cape

Fort Ross
Cove

25

Underwater
Reserve

22.

Fort Ross Orchard
and Spyra Memorial Grove
to Kolmer Gulch Camp
FORT ROSS STATE HISTORIC PARK

Ross State Park turnoff on the right at mile marker 33.00. Turn left (inland) on Fort Ross Road, and drive 0.55 miles to the posted Stanley Spyra Memorial Grove on the left. Park in the pullout near the grove.

Fort Ross Road is located 11.5 miles north of Jenner.

The hike

Walk through the metal vehicle gate, and follow the old logging road into the dense redwood forest. Pass a circle of massive redwoods on the left to a signed trail split. The Lower Kolmer Gulch Trail veers left (Hike 23). Go right towards Upper Kolmer Gulch. Reenter the deep forest along a canyon on the left, passing posted Steer Field Road on the right. Cross a bridge over a seasonal tributary of Kolmer Gulch. Pass Tan Oak Trail on the right, and continue down the gradual descent. Walk past a sag pond and enter Kolmer Gulch Camp, an old logging camp on the banks of Kolmer Creek. After exploring the creekside area, return along the same route. ∎

23. Lower Kolmer Gulch to Coastal Overlook
FORT ROSS STATE HISTORIC PARK

Hiking distance: 3.4 miles round trip
Hiking time: 1.75 hours
Configuration: out-and-back (or 4-mile loop with Hike 24)
Elevation gain: 200 feet
Difficulty: easy
Exposure: mostly shaded forest (open coastal bluffs for loop option)
Dogs: not allowed
Maps: U.S.G.S. Fort Ross and Plantation
   Fort Ross State Historic Park map

The majority of the Fort Ross State Historic Park lies east of Highway 1. The undeveloped uplands rise over 1,500 feet to the coastal ridge. Old logging roads wind through the dense conifer forest with second-growth coastal redwoods and timbered meadows.

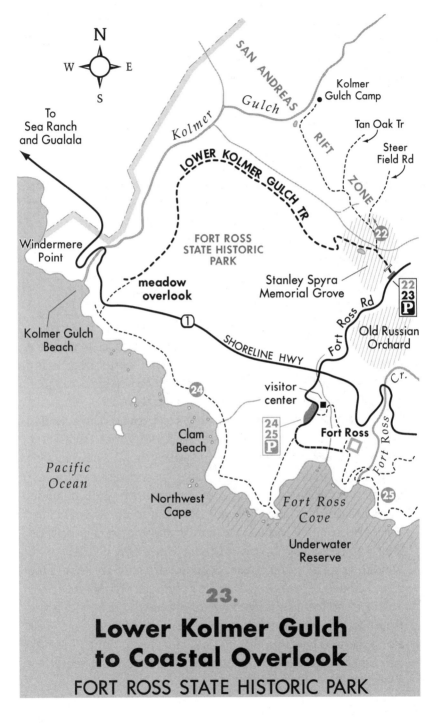

N
W E
S

To
Sea Ranch
and Gualala

SAN ANDREAS

Kolmer Gulch

Kolmer
Gulch Camp

RIFT

Tan Oak Tr

Steer
Field Rd

LOWER KOLMER GULCH TR

FORT ROSS
STATE HISTORIC
PARK

ZONE

22

Windermere
Point

meadow
overlook

Stanley Spyra
Memorial Grove

22
23
P

Kolmer Gulch
Beach

1

Fort Ross Rd

Old Russian
Orchard

SHORELINE HWY

Fort Ross Cr.

24

visitor
center

Clam
Beach

24
25
P

Fort Ross

Fort Ross

*Pacific
Ocean*

25

Northwest
Cape

*Fort Ross
Cove*

Underwater
Reserve

23.

Lower Kolmer Gulch
to Coastal Overlook
FORT ROSS STATE HISTORIC PARK

This hike weaves through the deep forest, meadows, and open grassland along the San Andreas Rift Zone to an overlook of the ocean above Windermere Point. Along the way are close-up views of fault trenches and sag ponds, formed from sinking ground along the fault zone. ■

To the trailhead

19005 FORT ROSS RD · JENNER   38.523770, -123.241040

From Gualala, just north of the Sonoma County line, drive 25.7 miles south on Highway 1 (Shoreline Highway) to the posted Fort Ross State Park turnoff on the right at mile marker 33.00. Turn left (inland) on Fort Ross Road, and drive 0.55 miles to the posted Stanley Spyra Memorial Grove on the left. Park in the pullout near the grove.

Fort Ross Road is located 11.5 miles north of Jenner.

The hike

Walk past the trailhead gate, and head down the old logging road through the Stanley Spyra Memorial Grove. Notice the redwoods that lost their tops from the 1906 earthquake. Pass a magnificent circle of redwoods on the left to a posted trail split. The right fork leads to Kolmer Gulch Camp (Hike 22).

Veer left and pass a sag pond on the left covered in reeds and cattails, another visible feature of the San Andreas Fault. Curve left on a sweeping S-curve through the meadow while enjoying a view of the ocean. Enter a Douglas fir and redwood forest on the west edge of a gulch, meandering at a near-level grade. Gradually descend and curve left along the south side of Kolmer Gulch. Head uphill and weave through the forested grasslands. Descend through Bishop pines to a huge meadow with a view of Windermere Point, the ocean, beautiful offshore rocks, and the sound of barking sea lions. This is a good turn-around spot.

To extend the hike, drop down to Highway 1 (just under a mile from the park entrance). Carefully cross the highway and walk along the oceanfront bluffs toward Northwest Cape. This hike may be combined with Hike 24 for a 4-mile loop, connected by a stretch of the park road. ■

24. Fort Ross North Headlands
FORT ROSS STATE HISTORIC PARK

Hiking distance: 2.6 miles round trip
Hiking time: 1.5 hours
Configuration: out-and-back
Elevation gain: 75 feet
Difficulty: easy
Exposure: exposed coastal bluffs
Dogs: not allowed
Maps: U.S.G.S. Fort Ross and Plantation
Fort Ross State Historic Park map

The Fort Ross North Headlands are 100-foot windswept bluffs along coastal Fort Ross State Historic Park. Along the serrated, wave-pounded cliffs are deep, stream-cut canyons and sheltered coves. The hike explores the high marine terrace from Northwest Cape (by the visitor center) to an overlook of Kolmer Gulch Beach, just shy of Windermere Point. The route does not follow a designated trail, but rather traverses the expansive, open coastal plateau along the edge of the grassy bluffs. Throughout the hike are far-reaching vistas, including Sonoma's Lost Coast and Point Reyes.

To the trailhead

19400 SHORELINE HWY · JENNER   38.518444, -123.246444

From Gualala, just north of the Sonoma County line, drive 25.7 miles south on Highway 1 (Shoreline Highway) to the posted Fort Ross State Park turnoff on the right at mile marker 33.00. Turn right (towards the ocean), and drive 0.2 miles to the parking lot at the visitor center. An entrance fee is required.

From Jenner, Fort Ross is 11.5 miles north on Highway 1.

The hike

From the far end of the parking lot, follow the dirt road southwest. As the road curves left toward the fort, veer right on a grassy path by the distinct rock outcropping. Climb the ladder over the fence, and head to the oceanfront edge of Northwest Cape at the western tip of Fort Ross Cove. Follow the edge of the grassy coastal bluff to the right, passing a series of rocky beaches along Northwest Cape. The bluffs overlook jagged offshore formations with barking sea lions. At the western tip of Northwest Cape, veer north and cross a series of small seasonal drainages. A steep side path descends to the rocky shoreline and tidepools at Clam Beach. The hike ends just shy of Windermere Point at an overlook of Kolmer Gulch Beach, where the protected sandy cove meets Highway 1. Return along the same route. ■

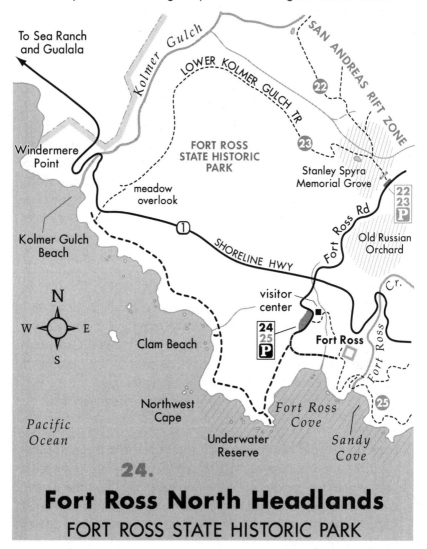

Fort Ross North Headlands
FORT ROSS STATE HISTORIC PARK

25. Fort Ross—Russian Cemetery
Fort Ross Cove—Southern Bluffs

FORT ROSS STATE HISTORIC PARK

Hiking distance: 2.8 miles round trip
Hiking time: 1.5 hours
Configuration: out-and-back
Elevation gain: 200 feet
Difficulty: easy
Exposure: mostly exposed coastal bluffs
Dogs: not allowed
Maps: U.S.G.S. Fort Ross · Fort Ross State Historic Park map

At the main entrance to Fort Ross State Historical Park sits an assembly of buildings that are representative of an early 1800s Russian settlement and the ranching era that followed. Between 1812 and 1841, Russian trappers made this coastal point into a base for their fur trading operations, hunting the sea otters that inhabited the coast. The land was also cultivated for agriculture, supplying wheat and other crops to Alaska. Fort Ross is a reconstruction of the stockade that once stood atop the cliffs in 1812. Only one of the original settlement buildings remain, but many of the buildings and structures that were once here have been reconstructed, including hand-hewn log barracks, blockhouses, and a Russian Orthodox chapel. A Russian Orthodox Cemetery sits atop a grassy knoll above the cove and across the creek-fed gulch from the fortress. The cemetery has traditional crosses marking the burial sites.

Fort Ross Cove is a protected beach below the fort. The cove was the site of the first shipyard in California. The grassy southern bluffs rise nearly 200 feet and lead to Reef Campground, with 20 primitive campsites. A visitor center and interpretive panels describe the land's natural history and its past inhabitants.

This hike begins at the visitor center and explores the historic fort, the isolated cove, and the cemetery. The trail then crosses the undulating coastal terrace, passing gullies and transient streams to the campground.

To the trailhead

19400 SHORELINE HWY · JENNER   38.518444, -123.246444

From Gualala, just north of the Sonoma County line, drive 25.7 miles south on Highway 1 (Shoreline Highway) to the posted Fort Ross State Park turnoff on the right at mile marker 33.00. Turn right (towards the ocean), and drive 0.2 miles to the parking lot at the visitor center. An entrance fee is required.

From Jenner, Fort Ross is 11.5 miles north on Highway 1.

The hike

Take the paved path along the right (south) side of the visitor center. Descend through a Monterey cypress forest, and cross a wood bridge over a transient creek. Pass the historic Call Ranch buildings on the right to the west wall of Fort Ross at 0.3 miles

After exploring the fort's structures, return to the fort's west (main) gate. Follow the dirt lane across the bluff to the edge of the cliffs. Curve left and descend into U-shaped Fort Ross Cove. At the base of the deep cove, walk toward a footbridge over Fort Ross Creek. Cross the bridge and climb the vegetated east slope of the stream-fed gulch through bay laurel, willow, and alder. Leave the forest to the open, grassy slopes and enter the historic Russian cemetery, with old wood crosses and views across the gulch of the fort and cove.

Return to Fort Ross Cove, and follow the gated dirt road to the beach. Bear left and climb the wood steps up the cliffs to the headland bluffs. Follow the open coastal terrace past rocky coves and sea stacks. Loop around the deep cove, crossing three footbridges over gullies. The trail ends at the Reef Campground. Return along the same route. ▪

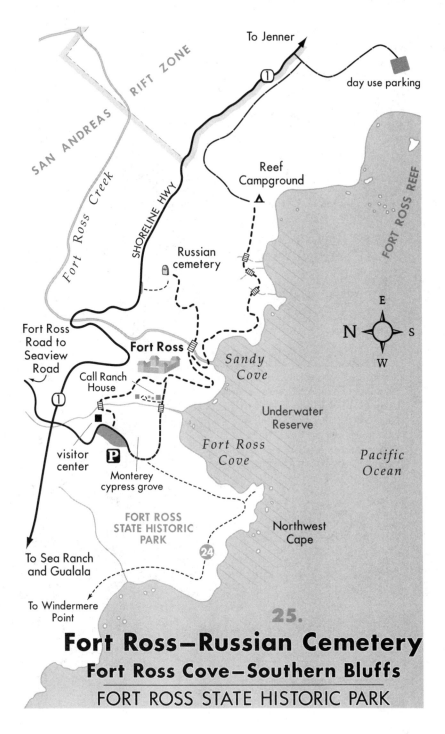

To Jenner

1

day use parking

SAN ANDREAS RIFT ZONE

Fort Ross Creek

SHORELINE HWY

Reef Campground

FORT ROSS REEF

Russian cemetery

Fort Ross Road to Seaview Road

E
N — S
W

1

Fort Ross

Call Ranch House

Sandy Cove

Underwater Reserve

Fort Ross Cove

Pacific Ocean

visitor center

P

Monterey cypress grove

FORT ROSS STATE HISTORIC PARK

24

Northwest Cape

To Sea Ranch and Gualala

To Windermere Point

25.

Fort Ross—Russian Cemetery
Fort Ross Cove—Southern Bluffs
FORT ROSS STATE HISTORIC PARK

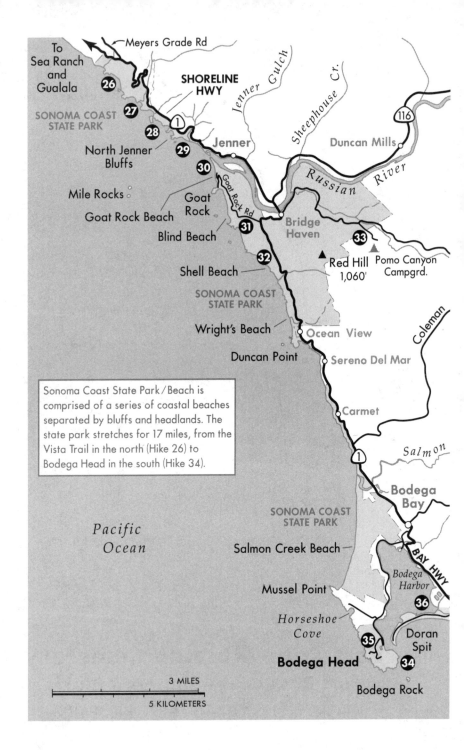

To
Sea Ranch
and
Gualala **26**

Meyers Grade Rd

**SHORELINE
HWY**

Jenner Gulch

Sheephouse Cr.

116

SONOMA COAST
STATE PARK

27

28

1

29

Jenner

Duncan Mills

North Jenner
Bluffs

30

Russian River

Goat Rock Rd

Mile Rocks

Goat
Rock

Goat Rock Beach

31

Bridge
Haven

33

Blind Beach

Red Hill
1,060'

Pomo Canyon
Campgrd.

32

Shell Beach

SONOMA COAST
STATE PARK

Wright's Beach

Ocean View

Coleman

Duncan Point

Sereno Del Mar

Sonoma Coast State Park / Beach is
comprised of a series of coastal beaches
separated by bluffs and headlands. The
state park stretches for 17 miles, from the
Vista Trail in the north (Hike 26) to
Bodega Head in the south (Hike 34).

Carmet

Salmon

1

*Pacific
Ocean*

**Bodega
Bay**

SONOMA COAST
STATE PARK

BAY HWY

Salmon Creek Beach

*Bodega
Harbor*

36

Mussel Point

*Horseshoe
Cove*

Doran
Spit

35

34

Bodega Head

Bodega Rock

3 MILES

5 KILOMETERS

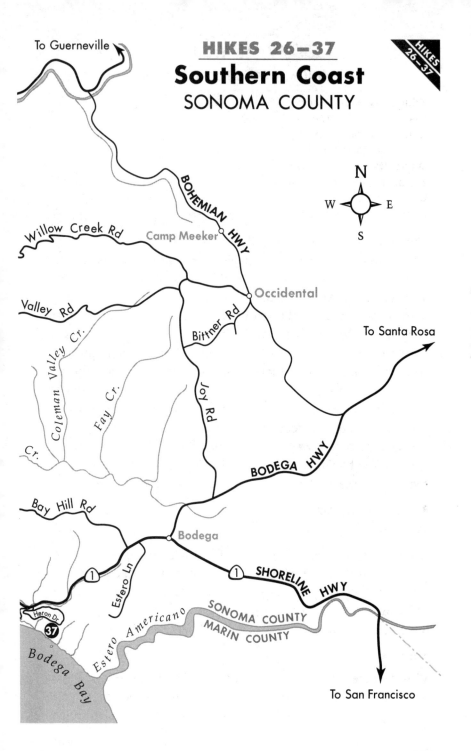

To Guerneville

BOHEMIAN HWY

Willow Creek Rd

Camp Meeker

Occidental

N
W E
S

Valley Rd

Bittner Rd

To Santa Rosa

Coleman Valley Cr.

Fay Cr.

Joy Rd

Cr.

BODEGA HWY

Bay Hill Rd

Bodega

1

Estero Ln

1 SHORELINE HWY

Heron Dr.

37

Estero Americano

SONOMA COUNTY
MARIN COUNTY

Bodega Bay

To San Francisco

26. Vista Trail
SONOMA COAST STATE PARK

Hiking distance: 1-mile loop
Hiking time: 30 minutes
Configuration: loop
Elevation gain: 50 feet
Difficulty: very easy (wheelchair accessible)
Exposure: exposed coastal bluffs
Dogs: not allowed
Maps: U.S.G.S. Arched Rock

The Vista Trail is located at the northernmost end of Sonoma Coast State Park, which is actually a series of beaches, bluffs, and headlands. The state park lands stretch along the coast for 17 miles southward to Bodega Head (with a few parcels of private land). This open, blufftop trail provides some of the most spectacular coastal vistas in California. The one-mile loop sits atop the Jenner Grade on a high plateau 600 feet above the sea. From the trail are unobstructed panoramic vistas of the chiseled coastline and jagged cliffs. The 272-acre open grassland rests at the southern base of Little Black Mountain, high above the ocean and Russian Gulch. Access to the trail is via the twisting, corkscrew route of Highway 1, cut into the edge of the rugged coastal cliffs. The blufftop trail (a wheelchair-accessible path) circles the natural area, with picnic areas and an observation deck.

To the trailhead

19226 SHORELINE HWY · JENNER   38.478709, –123.162653

From Jenner, drive 5 miles north on Highway 1 (Shoreline Highway) to the posted Vista Trail on the left at mile marker 26.30. It is at the summit, directly across from Meyers Grade Road. The turnoff is 32 miles south of Gualala and 6.5 miles south of Fort Ross State Park. Turn towards the ocean and park in the paved lot.

The hike

Walk past the trailhead kiosk on the paved path to a Y-fork. Begin the loop on the left fork, heading south. At the southern end are magnificent views into the deep, creek-fed Russian Gulch

(Hike 27). Loop around the south end of the expansive plateau to another Y-fork. The left fork leads 50 yards to a platform over-look with a bench and sweeping coastal views, including Point Reyes National Seashore, Bodega Head, Goat Rock, the Russian River, Russian Gulch, and Northwest Cape at Fort Ross. Return to the junction and continue across the grassland beneath forested Little Black Mountain, completing the loop. ■

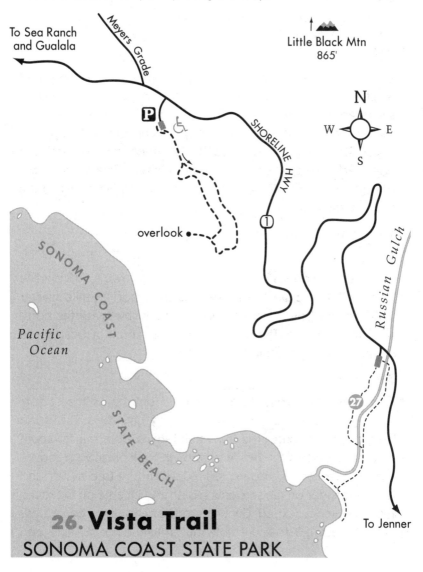

To Sea Ranch and Gualala

Meyers Grade

Little Black Mtn
865'

P

SHORELINE HWY

N
W ← → E
S

overlook

SONOMA COAST

Russian Gulch

Pacific Ocean

STATE BEACH

27

To Jenner

26. Vista Trail
SONOMA COAST STATE PARK

27. Russian Gulch
SONOMA COAST STATE PARK

Hiking distance: 0.7 miles round trip
Hiking time: 30 minutes
Configuration: out-and-back
Elevation gain: level
Difficulty: easy
Exposure: shaded forest and open coast
Dogs: not allowed
Maps: U.S.G.S. Arched Rock

Russian Gulch is a stream-fed canyon that begins in the upper reaches of Little Black Mountain. The creek flows through a sheltered valley to the sea and forms a lagoon on the crescent-shaped beach. The expansive sandy beach, part of the Sonoma Coast State Park, is bordered by 120-foot vertical cliffs and scattered offshore rocks. This trail begins on the coastal side of Highway 1 and weaves through a thick riparian forest to the scenic beach cove.

To the trailhead

18794 SHORELINE HWY · JENNER   38.471070, -123.154200

From Jenner, drive 3.2 miles north on Highway 1 (Shoreline Highway) to the posted Russian Gulch turnoff at mile marker 24.55, located on the ocean side of the highway on the north side of the bridge. The turnoff is 34 miles south of Gualala and 8.3 miles south of Fort Ross State Park.

The hike

Two trails leave from the parking lot. From the northeast corner, a gated dirt road leads to the rocky creekbed. This is the least desirable route. The main trail begins from the far south end of the parking lot. Descend through thick brush with above-ground tree roots, willows, red alders, mossy tree trunks, and ferns. Meander on the serpentine path and emerge on the rocky Russian Gulch creekbed. Continue to the huge sandy beach nestled beneath 120-foot unstable bluffs. To the north is a lagoon at the mouth of the creek, with two 25-foot-high rock formations. After exploring the beach, return along the same trail. ■

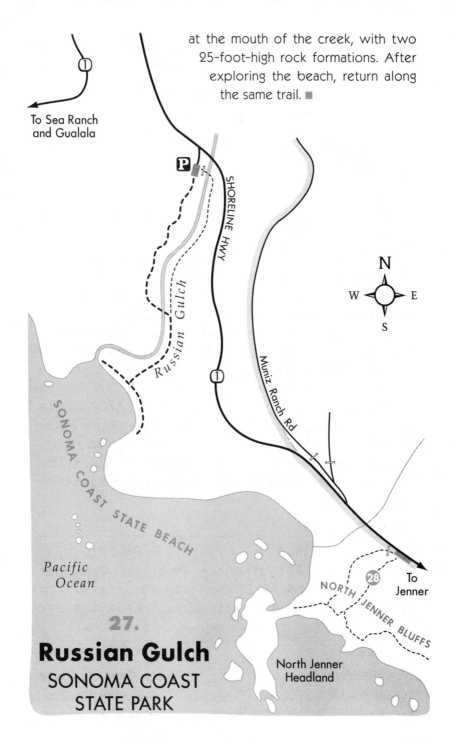

To Sea Ranch and Gualala

P

SHORELINE HWY

Russian Gulch

1

N
W   E
S

Muniz Ranch Rd

SONOMA COAST STATE BEACH

Pacific
Ocean

27.
Russian Gulch
SONOMA COAST
STATE PARK

28

NORTH JENNER BLUFFS

To Jenner

North Jenner
Headland

28. North Jenner Headland
NORTH JENNER BLUFFS
SONOMA COAST STATE PARK

Hiking distance: 1.5 miles round trip
Hiking time: 45 minutes
Configuration: out-and-back
Elevation gain: 50 feet
Difficulty: easy
Exposure: exposed coastal bluffs
Dogs: allowed
Maps: U.S.G.S. Arched Rock

North of Jenner, Highway 1 clings to the rugged, breath-taking cliffs with winding bends and steep hairpin switchbacks. This dramatic and pristine stretch of coastline offers sweeping vistas of craggy cliffs plunging into the turbulent sea and jagged offshore rocks. The North Jenner Headland sits atop the steep oceanfront bluffs between Russian Gulch and Jenner. The massive 100-foot-high monolith rises out of the ocean, connected to the mainland by a narrow ridge.

This hike crosses the marine terrace from Highway 1 to the headland. A cliff-edge trail follows the serrated bluffs across the 200-foot plateau, passing a series of secluded pocket beaches and elevated overlooks. The panoramic vistas include beach coves, sea stacks, oceanfront mountains, and sweeping coastal views.

To the trailhead

18640 SHORELINE HWY · JENNER   38.463262, -123.148852

From Jenner, drive 2.5 miles north on Highway 1 to North Jenner Headland at mile marker 23.83. The turnoff is 34.7 miles south of Gualala and 9 miles south of Fort Ross State Park. Park in the large pullout on the ocean side of the highway by a gated road.

The hike

The posted trail is just south of the metal gate. Cross the grassy oceanfront terrace to the 200-foot cliffs that front the massive North Jenner Headland. Bear right to an elevated bluff with amazing vistas of the rugged, scalloped coastline. Rocks with wave-cut arches lie offshore. The path ends at Highway 1 on the south edge of a deep stream-fed gulch.

Return and head southeast through the low, coastal scrub. A steep side path descends to a pocket beach. The blufftop trail follows the edge of the North Jenner Bluffs to a promontory. The trail continues south and connects with Hike 29. Choose your own turn-around spot. ■

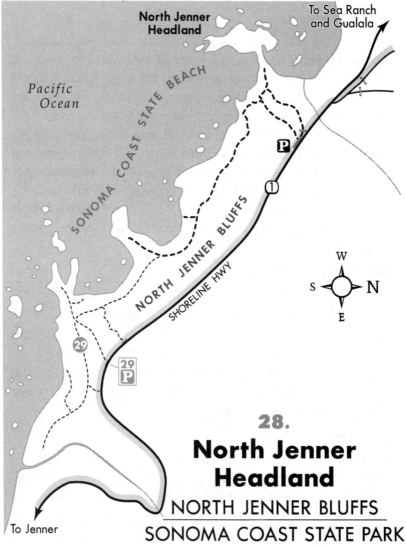

North Jenner Headland

To Sea Ranch and Gualala

Pacific Ocean

SONOMA COAST STATE BEACH

NORTH JENNER BLUFFS

SHORELINE HWY

W
S ◆ N
E

28.

North Jenner Headland

NORTH JENNER BLUFFS
SONOMA COAST STATE PARK

To Jenner

29. North Jenner Bluffs
SONOMA COAST STATE PARK

Hiking distance: 1.2 miles round trip
Hiking time: 30 minutes
Configuration: out-and-back
Elevation gain: 50 feet
Difficulty: easy
Exposure: exposed coastal bluffs
Dogs: allowed
Maps: U.S.G.S. Arched Rock

The North Jenner Bluffs sit along a three-mile stretch of coastline between the Russian River at Jenner and Russian Gulch to the north. The access road, which is now Highway 1, was originally built in the 1870s. It is perched on the rolling contours of the angular cliffs high above the sea. This area is along one of the finest coastal stretches in California. The 200-foot oceanfront bluffs stretch across a rolling marine terrace to rocky headlands and a series of beach coves. The trail includes an overlook of the crenulated coast and the Russian River as it flows into the Pacific. The offshore rock islands are isolated remnants of the former coastline.

To the trailhead

18490 SHORELINE HWY · JENNER   38.457707, -123.140892

From Jenner, drive 1.9 miles north on Highway 1 to the North Jenner Bluffs at mile marker 23.21. The turnoff is 35 miles south of Gualala and 9.6 miles south of Fort Ross State Park. Park in the narrow pullout on the oceanside edge of the highway by the trail sign. Fifty yards north is a deeper parking pullout with more off-highway breathing room.

The hike

Head west across the grassy plateau to the edge of the 200-foot cliffs. On the right is a gorgeous U-shaped bay with off-shore rocks covered in bird guano. A narrow footpath descends the cliffs to the beach cove. Walk out onto the peninsula to the narrow, razor-sharp spine. The path extends out onto the vertigo-inducing ridge. If this route is attempted, use caution and good judgement. Continue south on the main footpath, skirting the edge of the bluffs to a trail fork. The left fork returns to Highway 1 at mile marker 23.17. Stay to the right, following the bluffs to a knoll. At a trail split, the right fork descends to the beach on an easy grade. From the beach, it is possible to walk south to the Russian River at low tide. The other route on the blufftop leads to an overlook on the edge of a deep, spring-fed drainage, where there are views of offshore rocks with natural arches and the Russian River mouth. Return by retracing your route. ■

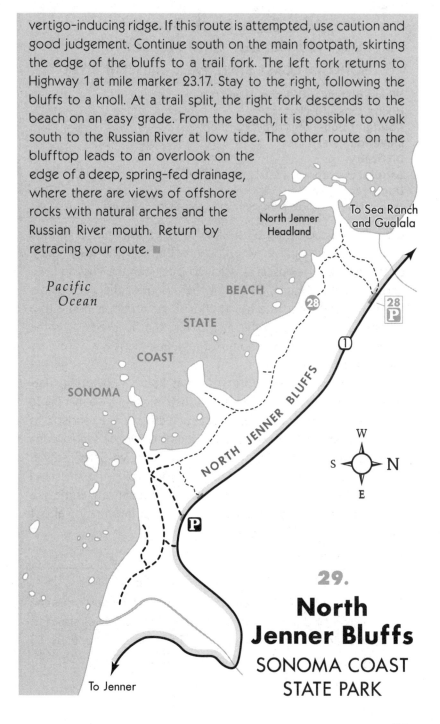

Pacific Ocean

North Jenner Headland

To Sea Ranch and Gualala

BEACH

STATE

COAST

SONOMA

NORTH JENNER BLUFFS

29.

North Jenner Bluffs

SONOMA COAST STATE PARK

To Jenner

30. Goat Rock Beach to Harbor Seal Nursery

SONOMA COAST STATE PARK · RUSSIAN RIVER

Hiking distance: 0.75 miles round trip
Hiking time: 40 minutes
Configuration: out-and-back or loop
Elevation gain: 50 feet
Difficulty: easy
Exposure: exposed coastal promontory
Dogs: not allowed
Maps: U.S.G.S. Duncan Mills · Sonoma Coast State Beach map

Goat Rock Beach is located along a sand spit that is formed where the Russian River empties into the sea. The low, north-pointing sandy peninsula is wedged between the Russian River and the Pacific Ocean, ending at the mouth of the river below the town of Jenner. The north end of the strand is home to a colony of harbor seals that number in the hundreds. It is the largest seal rookery in Sonoma County. Seal pups are born from March through June.

This hike begins just north of Goat Rock, a towering, flat-topped promontory connected to the mainland by a manmade causeway. The path to Goat Rock Beach crosses the sandspit to the harbor seal nursery, where the seals bask on the sand. During the pupping season, adult seals can be protective. Safely stay at least 50 yards from the pups to avoid disturbing the seals and their habitat. From March through August, docents are at the site with binoculars and spotting scopes to offer information about the harbor seals.

To the trailhead

GOAT ROCK ROAD · JENNER   38.445362, -123.126092

From Highway 1 and Highway 116 (just south of Jenner) cross the Russian River bridge on Highway 1, and drive 0.65 miles south to Goat Rock Road at mile marker 19.15. Turn right and continue 1.9 miles to the lower parking lot at the north end of the road.

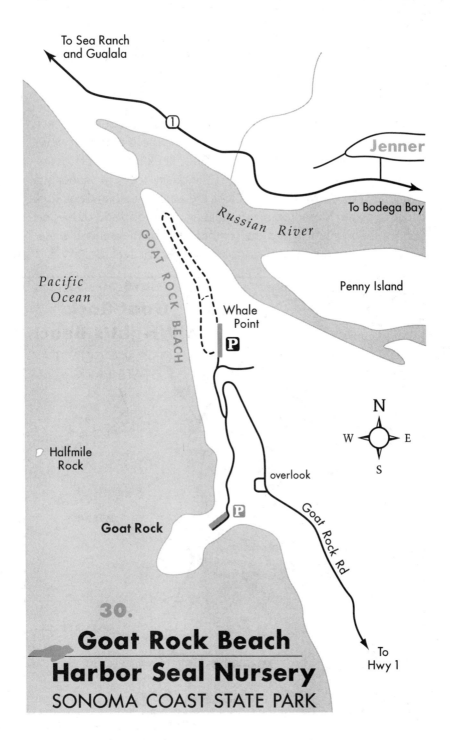

To Sea Ranch
and Gualala

Jenner

1

Russian River

To Bodega Bay

Pacific
Ocean

GOAT ROCK BEACH

Penny Island

Whale
Point

P

N

W ✦ E

S

Halfmile
Rock

overlook

Goat Rock Rd

P

Goat Rock

To
Hwy 1

30.

Goat Rock Beach
Harbor Seal Nursery
SONOMA COAST STATE PARK

From Bodega Bay, drive 8 miles north on Highway 1 to Goat Rock Road at mile marker 19.15. Turn left and continue 1.9 miles to the lower parking lot at the north end of the road.

The hike

Head north past Whale Point on the sandy peninsula between the Russian River and the Pacific Ocean. The panoramic views include Penny Island in the river, Goat Rock jutting out to sea, and picturesque off-shore rocks. The quaint town of Jenner sits on the cliffs above the river. Cross the sand spit along Goat Rock Beach on the low scrub dunes, passing driftwood and old wood pilings. Continue toward the northern end of the peninsula near the mouth of the river, overlooking the harbor seal rookery. ■

31. Kortum Trail: north end
Blind Beach to Shell Beach
SONOMA COAST STATE PARK

Hiking distance: 4.6 miles round trip
2.3-mile one-way shuttle to Shell Beach
4.0-mile one-way shuttle to Wright's Beach
Hiking time: 2.5 hours
Configuration: out-and-back (or shuttle)
Elevation gain: 300 feet
Difficulty: easy
Exposure: exposed coastal cliffs and beach
Dogs: not allowed
Maps: U.S.G.S. Duncan Mills · Sonoma Coast State Beach map

Sonoma Coast State Park stretches 17 miles, from Bodega Head (Hike 34) to the Vista Trail (Hike 26), located four miles north of Jenner. The state park is actually a series of sandy beaches that are separated by rocky 100-foot bluffs and headlands. The craggy coastline includes secluded coves, reefs, fertile tide-pools, rugged headlands, natural rock arches, sand dunes, and wildflower-covered meadows.

The Kortum Trail is a four-mile coastal trail from Goat Rock to Wright's Beach. The trail closely follows the coastal cliffs, dipping down to gullies and beaches along the rocky shoreline. Many boardwalks, bridges, and stairs have been built along the trail. Hikes 31 and 32 explore the length of the Kortum Trail, dividing it into the north section and the south section.

This hike follows the north section, from Blind Beach to Shell Beach. The trail starts from the cliffs above Blind Beach, overlooking Goat Rock just to the north. The trail heads south along the exposed coastal bluffs to Shell Beach, a sandy pocket beach surrounded by jagged offshore rocks. En route to the beach are southward views that span all the way to Point Reyes.

To the trailhead

GOAT ROCK ROAD · JENNER   38.435135, -123.120470

From Highway 1 and Highway 116 (just south of Jenner) cross the Russian River bridge on Highway 1, and drive 0.65 miles south to

Goat Rock Road at mile marker 19.15. Turn right and continue 0.75 miles to the Blind Beach parking lot on the left side of the high bluffs.

From Bodega Bay, drive 8 miles north on Highway 1 to Goat Rock Road at mile marker 19.15. Turn left and continue 0.75 miles to the Blind Beach parking lot on the left.

Shuttle car

8901 HWY 1 · JENNER   38.418837, -123.101977

TO SHELL BEACH: The turnoff is located one mile south of Goat Rock Road at mile marker 18.22 along Highway 1.

7170 HWY 1 · BODEGA BAY   38.401243, -123.094288

TO WRIGHT'S BEACH: The lot is located 1.4 miles south of the Shell Beach turnoff at mile marker 16.8 along Highway 1.

The hike

From the parking lot is a great bird's-eye view of Goat Rock and Blind Beach. A steep, rough path descends the cliffs to Blind Beach, 200 feet below. For this hike, walk 30 yards back down the road to the posted Kortum Trail on the right. Ascend the grassy slope toward prominent Peaked Hill. Climb to the saddle between the 377-foot peak on the right and the rocky outcrop on the left. From the ridge, the southern views stretch past Bodega Head to Point Reyes. Descend the southeast slope, and pass through a fence to a giant rock formation on the marine terrace. Curve right to the oceanfront cliffs and continue south. Pass dramatic formations on the grassy bluffs and offshore rocks, including Gull Rock, a nesting site for gulls and cormorants. Cross a small gully and continue atop the plateau. Cross a larger gully with the aid of stairs and a footbridge. Follow a 300-foot boardwalk over a wetland. Curve inland, walk across another 150-foot boardwalk, and return to the oceanfront cliffs. Pass through a fence and continue on a gravel path to the Shell Beach parking lot. A path on the right descends the bluffs to the beach. Return along the same route for a 4.6-mile out-and-back hike.

For a four-mile shuttle hike to Wright's Beach, continue with Hike 32. ∎

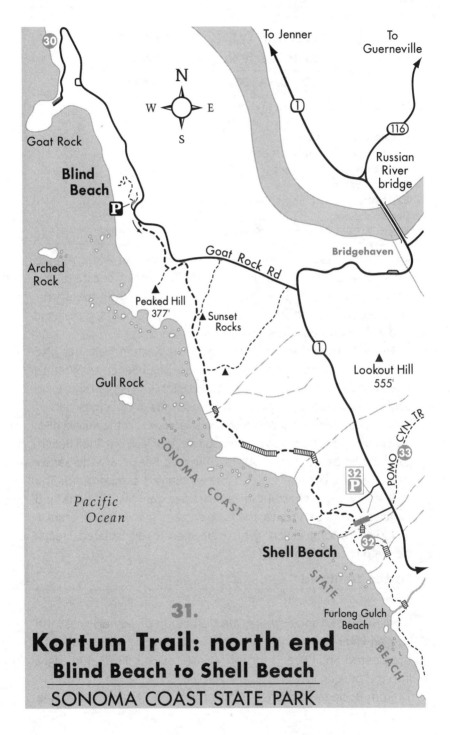

To Jenner

To Guerneville

N

W E

S

30

Goat Rock

Blind Beach

P

Russian River bridge

116

1

Bridgehaven

Goat Rock Rd

Arched Rock

Peaked Hill 377'

Sunset Rocks

1

Lookout Hill 555'

Gull Rock

POMO CYN TR

33

Pacific Ocean

SONOMA COAST

32 P

32

Shell Beach

STATE

Furlong Gulch Beach

31.

BEACH

Kortum Trail: north end
Blind Beach to Shell Beach
SONOMA COAST STATE PARK

32. Kortum Trail: south end
Shell Beach to Wright's Beach

SONOMA COAST STATE PARK

Hiking distance: 3.3 miles round trip
1.6-mile one-way shuttle to Wright's Beach
Hiking time: 1.5 hours
Configuration: out-and-back
Elevation gain: 200 feet
Difficulty: easy
Exposure: exposed coastal cliffs and beach
Dogs: allowed
Maps: U.S.G.S. Duncan Mills · Sonoma Coast State Beach map

The Kortum Trail is an excellent hike to experience the rugged oceanside bluffs of Sonoma County. The rocky coastline and crashing surf offer some of the best scenery along the north-central California coast. The trail follows open bluffs, dipping in and out of ravines across bridges and boardwalks.

Hikes 31 and 32 explore the four-mile Kortum Trail. This hike follows the south half of the trail from Shell Beach to Wright's Beach. Shell Beach is a sandy sheltered inlet with jagged shoreline rocks that support tidepools. The beach sits at the crossroad of four trails, which lead down to the shoreline, up the inland hills, and in both directions along the coastal bluffs. From Shell Beach, the hike leads 1.6 miles south to Wright's Beach, a wide sandy beach with a picnic area and tree-sheltered campground. The trail follows the coastal bluffs past abundant wildflowers and large sea stacks. En route, the path crosses five seasonal creeks, including Furlong Gulch, which empties to an isolated beach beneath the 80-foot bluffs.

To the trailhead

8901 HWY 1 · JENNER   38.418837, -123.101977

From Highway 1 and Highway 116 (just south of Jenner) cross the Russian River bridge on Highway 1, and drive 1.6 miles south to the posted Shell Beach turnoff at mile marker 18.22. Turn right into the parking lot.

From Bodega Bay, drive 7 miles north on Highway 1 to the

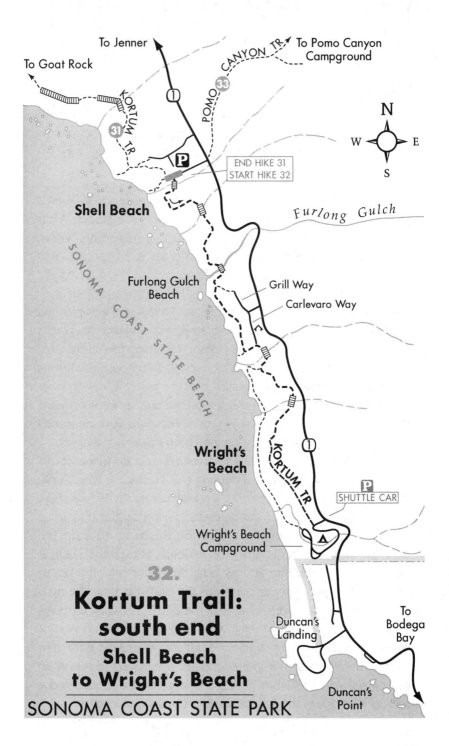

To Jenner

To Goat Rock

KORTUM TR

POMO CANYON TR

To Pomo Canyon Campground

33

1

31

P

END HIKE 31
START HIKE 32

Shell Beach

Furlong Gulch

SONOMA COAST STATE BEACH

Furlong Gulch
Beach

Grill Way

Carlevaro Way

**Wright's
Beach**

KORTUM TR

1

P
SHUTTLE CAR

Wright's Beach
Campground

32.

Kortum Trail:
south end

Duncan's
Landing

To
Bodega
Bay

Shell Beach
to Wright's Beach

Duncan's
Point

SONOMA COAST STATE PARK

N
W   E
S

posted Shell Beach turnoff at mile marker 18.22. Turn left into the parking lot.

Shuttle car

7170 HWY 1 · BODEGA BAY   38.401243, –123.094288

TO WRIGHT'S BEACH: The turnoff to Wright's Beach is located 1.4 miles south of Shell Beach at mile marker 16.8 along Highway 1.

The hike

From the west end of the parking lot, a trail descends 150 yards to scenic Shell Beach, surrounded by jagged sea stacks. After exploring the beach, take the posted Kortum Trail south. Weave down into a stream-fed drainage, and cross a footbridge over the first of five seasonal creeks. Climb out of the gully to the coastal terrace and the oceanfront cliffs at an overlook of Shell Beach and the dramatic offshore rocks. Follow the edge of the bluffs and curve inland. Drop into a second drainage and cross the bridge over the ephemeral stream. Return to the bluffs, with views of Red Hill and the sandy beach at the mouth of Furlong Gulch. Zigzag down switchbacks into the gulch. Cross another bridge over the creek and a shorter bridge over a feeder stream. After the second bridge is a junction. The right fork descends steps to Furlong Gulch Beach on the south edge of the creek.

Climb back up to the 100-foot bluffs and continue south. Atop the terrace, pass a connecting trail from Grill Way. Curve left toward the house near the end of Carlevaro Way. Before reaching the house, veer to the right, staying on the trail. Drop down and cross a bridge over the fourth stream to a posted junction. Straight ahead, the right path leads to a sandy beach at the mouth of the stream. At low tide, this route can be taken to Wright's Beach, forming a loop with the blufftop trail. The main trail curves left and weaves across the bluffs, crossing a bridge over a winter stream near Highway 1. Follow the south wall of the drainage, and return to the oceanfront, where the path joins a gravel utility road. The gravel ends at the paved access road leading down to Wright's Beach and the campground. Wind a quarter mile down the access road to the sandy beach. ■

33. Pomo Canyon Trail
Pomo Canyon Campground to Shell Beach

SONOMA COAST STATE PARK

Hiking distance: 6.6 miles round trip
3.3-mile one-way shuttle to Shell Beach
Hiking time: 3.5 hours
Configuration: out-and-back
Elevation gain: 650 feet
Difficulty: moderate
Exposure: a mix of forest and open hillsides
Dogs: allowed
Maps: U.S.G.S. Duncan Mills · Sonoma Coast State Beach map

Pomo Canyon Campground sits on the alluvial flats above broad Willow Creek canyon in a beautiful redwood grove. The Pomo Canyon Trail begins at the campground and winds across the rolling coastal hills, skirting the north slope of Red Hill. The trail follows an ancient trading route of the Pomo and Miwok people. The path weaves through lush redwood forests, oak woodlands, and open grasslands, crossing seasonal streams en route to the ocean at Shell Beach. From the trail are panoramic vistas of the lower Russian River, Willow Creek, the town of Jenner, and the serrated coastline.

To the trailhead

WILLOW CREEK RD · JENNER   38.430110, -123.070255

From Highway 1 and Highway 116 (just south of Jenner) cross the south side of the Russian River bridge on Highway 1. Immediately turn left (inland) on Willow Creek Road at mile marker 19.79. Drive 2.6 miles on the narrow road to the Pomo Canyon Campground turnoff. Park near the gated road (but not in front of it). The campground is open from April through November. During that time, drive a half mile up the campground road and park by the kiosk.

From Bodega Bay, drive 9 miles north on Highway 1 to Willow Creek Road at mile marker 19.79. The road is just before the Russian River bridge. Turn right (inland) and follow the directions above to the Pomo Canyon Campground.

Shuttle car

8901 HWY 1 · JENNER   38.418837, -123.101977

Leave the shuttle car at the Shell Beach parking lot. The turnoff is located at mile marker 18.22 along Highway 1.

The hike

From Willow Creek Road, walk past the gate and follow the unpaved campground access road. Stroll a half mile through a grassy valley between forested hills to the campground entrance. Head into the campground on the right as the road veers off to the left. Go 15 yards and bear right on the posted Dr. David Joseph Memorial Pomo Canyon Trail.

Enter the gorgeous redwood forest and stay to the right, passing two paths on the left and the campsites on each side of the main trail. Climb up the ridge through tanbark oak, bay laurel, Douglas fir, circular stands of redwoods, sword ferns, and trillium. Emerge from the forest to a Y-fork at 0.8 miles, located in a clearing with views of Jenner and the mouth of the Russian River. The left fork leads to the 1,062-foot summit of Red Hill and forms a loop with this trail—an optional return route.

Stay to the right towards Shell Beach, and traverse the hill. Cross a bridge over a seasonal creek and curve right, skirting a rock outcrop. Descend through brush to the open, rolling slopes with ocean views. Cross a small stream and reenter a fir and redwood forest. Cross a third stream and gradually descend through the thick brush. Curve left into the gulch, cross the creek, and head down the draw. Ascend the hill to a knoll with a picnic area and vista point on the right. The main trail continues straight, with a view of the serpentine Russian River. Head up another hill on the wide, grassy path to a knoll atop the 500-foot oceanfront ridge and a junction with the west end of the Red Hill Trail. Pass a trail on the right leading to Lookout Hill, then descend the slope, with views of Point Reyes, Bodega Head, Gull Rock, and Goat Rock. Drop down a partially paved utility road to the trailhead gate, across the road from the Shell Beach parking lot. ▪

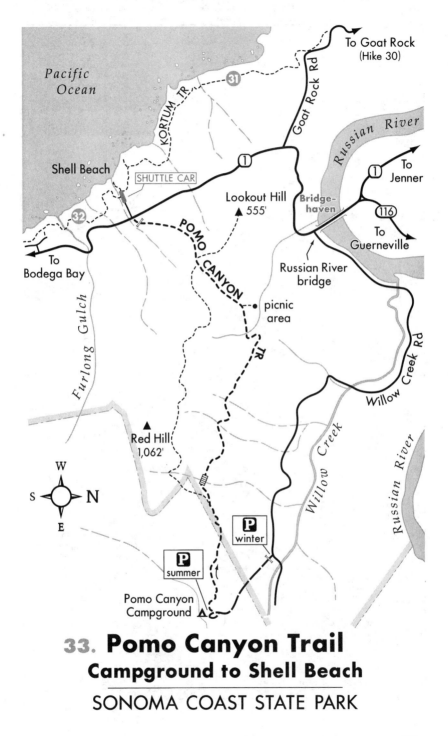

Pacific
Ocean

Shell Beach

KORTUM TR.

31

Goat Rock Rd

To Goat Rock
(Hike 30)

Russian River

SHUTTLE CAR

1

Lookout Hill
▲ 555'

Bridge-
haven

1 To
Jenner

116

To Jenner

32

To
Bodega Bay

POMO CANYON

Russian River
bridge

To
Guerneville

picnic
area

TR

Furlong Gulch

Willow Creek Rd

Red Hill
▲ 1,062'

Willow Creek

Russian River

W

S ◆ N

E

P
winter

P
summer

Pomo Canyon
Campground ▲

33. **Pomo Canyon Trail**
Campground to Shell Beach
SONOMA COAST STATE PARK

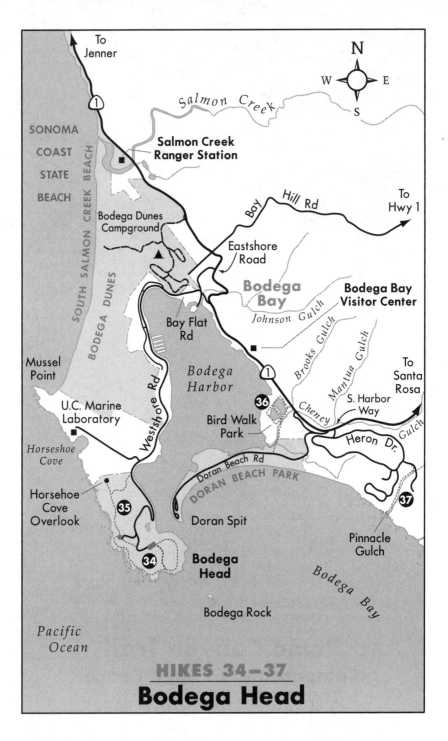

To Jenner

N
W E
S

Salmon Creek

SONOMA
COAST
STATE
BEACH

SOUTH SALMON CREEK BEACH

**Salmon Creek
Ranger Station**

Bay Hill Rd

To Hwy 1

Bodega Dunes
Campground

Eastshore
Road

**Bodega
Bay**

**Bodega Bay
Visitor Center**

Johnson Gulch

BODEGA DUNES

Bay Flat
Rd

*Bodega
Harbor*

Brooks Gulch

Mantua Gulch

To
Santa
Rosa

Mussel
Point

U.C. Marine
Laboratory

36

Cheney

S. Harbor
Way

Gulch

*Horseshoe
Cove*

Westshore Rd

Bird Walk
Park

Heron Dr.

Horsehoe
Cove
Overlook

35

Doran Beach Rd

DORAN BEACH PARK

37

Pinnacle
Gulch

34

Doran Spit

**Bodega
Head**

Bodega Bay

*Pacific
Ocean*

Bodega Rock

HIKES 34–37
Bodega Head

34. Bodega Head
SONOMA COAST STATE PARK

Hiking distance: 1.7-mile loop
Hiking time: 1 hour
Configuration: loop
Elevation gain: 200 feet
Difficulty: easy
Exposure: exposed oceanfront bluffs
Dogs: not allowed
Maps: U.S.G.S. Bodega Head · Sonoma Coast State Beach map

Bodega Head is a massive granite promontory that juts into the ocean north of Point Reyes. The promontory forms the west side of Bodega Harbor. The 800-acre harbor is almost entirely enclosed from Bodega Bay by a narrow two-mile-long sand spit known as Doran Spit.

This hike explores the exposed, southern tip of Bodega Head, circling the grassy headland 200 feet above Bodega Harbor and Doran Spit. The trail loops around to the open sea, overlooking the rocky shores, hidden caves and coves, undisturbed beaches, sea stacks, natural arches, bird-nesting cliffs, coastal bluffs, a series of eroded spires, and the open ocean. The nearly treeless landscape is covered with scrub vegetation and coastal grass.

Gray whale pods often migrate past the headland with their new calves from December through April, following a northerly route from Baja California to Alaska. The high cliffs offer an excellent vantage point for observation. Docents offer information about the whale migration every weekend from January through April.

To the trailhead

WESTSHORE ROAD · BODEGA BAY   38.302862, -123.057919

From downtown Bodega Bay, drive north on Highway 1 to East Shore Road and turn left. (The turnoff is one mile north of the Bodega Bay Visitor Center.) Continue 0.3 miles to Bay Flat Road and turn right. Drive 3.3 miles to a road fork. (En route, Bay Flat Road becomes Westshore Road.) Veer left and go 0.4 miles to the east trailhead parking area. A parking fee is required.

The hike

From the far east end of the parking lot by the restrooms, head east. The trail overlooks the sandy beach of the Doran Spit, enclosed Bodega Harbor, Bodega Bay, Point Reyes, and the ocean. Curve around to the south end of the headland. Off the steep cliffs are offshore outcroppings, the sound of barking sea lions, and Bodega Rock, less than a half mile from shore. Follow the south edge of the cliffs through scrub vegetation and coastal grassland, passing offshore rocks and a small, inaccessible pocket beach. Climb the open, grassy slope to the highest point of the hike, passing vertical rock cliffs, stunning sea stacks, and far-reaching vistas. Pass a memorial to fishermen lost at sea and a popular overlook for observing migrating whales by the west parking lot. Pick up the footpath on the left (north) side of the restroom. Traverse the sloping grassland and pass through a small grove of windswept cypress to the east parking lot access road. Walk around the vehicle gate and follow the road 0.2 miles to the right, completing the loop at the trailhead. ■

35. Horseshoe Cove Overlook
BODEGA HEAD
SONOMA COAST STATE PARK

Hiking distance: 1.2 miles round trip
Hiking time: 40 minutes
Configuration: out-and-back
Elevation gain: 200 feet
Difficulty: easy
Exposure: exposed oceanfront bluffs
Dogs: not allowed
Maps: U.S.G.S. Bodega Head · Sonoma Coast State Beach map

Horseshoe Cove sits on the ocean side of Bodega Head, a large promontory that extends four miles into the Pacific. The cove lies adjacent to the Bodega Marine Laboratory and Marine Reserve. The laboratory and reserve are part of the University of California Natural Reserve System. The research and teaching facility protects 362 acres of undisturbed intertidal habitat, a

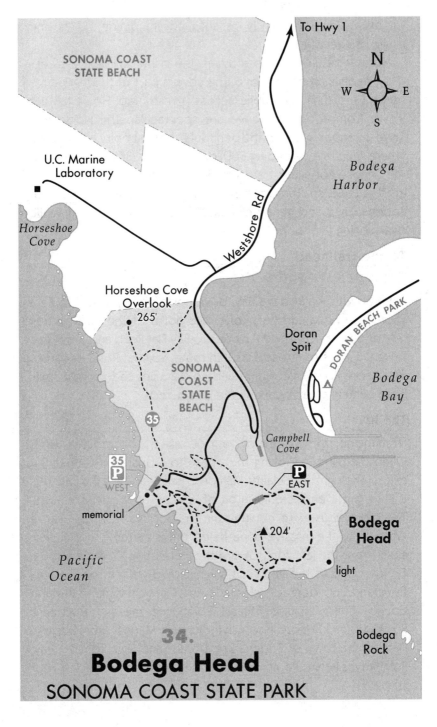

SONOMA COAST
STATE BEACH

U.C. Marine
Laboratory

*Horseshoe
Cove*

Horseshoe Cove
Overlook
● 265'

SONOMA
COAST
STATE
BEACH

35

35
P
WEST

memorial

*Pacific
Ocean*

▲ 204'

To Hwy 1

N
W ✦ E
S

*Bodega
Harbor*

Westshore Rd

DORAN BEACH PARK

Doran
Spit

*Bodega
Bay*

Campbell
Cove

P
EAST

**Bodega
Head**

● light

**Bodega
Rock**

34.
Bodega Head
SONOMA COAST STATE PARK

salt marsh, mudflats, sandy beaches, coastal prairie, dunes, and a mile of coastline.

Horseshoe Cove is exactly as the name implies, a deep, U-shaped sandy beach cove. The cove is part of the marine reserve. Unfortunately, public access is restricted. However, the views from above the cove are spectacular. The Horseshoe Cove Overlook sits atop the peninsula's highest point at 265 feet, where there are sweeping 360-degree vistas. Scattered around the windswept summit are weathered rock outcroppings covered with lichen. The trail begins from the western trailhead of Bodega Head and gently climbs 200 feet to the summit while overlooking the Pacific.

To the trailhead

WESTSHORE ROAD · BODEGA BAY   38.303872, -123.064099

From downtown Bodega Bay, drive north on Highway 1 to East Shore Road and turn left (one mile north of the Bodega Bay Visitor Center). Continue 0.3 miles to Bay Flat Road and turn right. Drive 3.3 miles to a road fork. (En route, Bay Flat Road becomes Westshore Road.) Veer right and go 0.2 miles to the west trailhead parking area. A parking fee is required.

The hike

From the north end of the parking lot, take the posted trail north. Climb the hill overlooking the ocean to a posted Y-fork at 0.4 miles. (The right fork claims Salmon Creek Beach is 2.2 miles. This is true, but it entails quite a bit of walking on Westshore Road. The old trail used to cut through the Bodega Marine Reserve en route to the massive dune fields, but is currently not accessible.) Take the left fork toward the Horseshoe Cove Overlook. Gently climb to the 265-foot summit amid granite rock formations and 360-degree vistas. Views of the Sonoma and Marin County coast include Mussel Point, the massive 900-acre Bodega Dunes, Horseshoe Cove, Bodega Marine Labs, Bodega Harbor, the town of Bodega Bay, Doran Sand Spit, Tomales Bay, Point Reyes Peninsula, and the open sea. Return by retracing your steps. ■

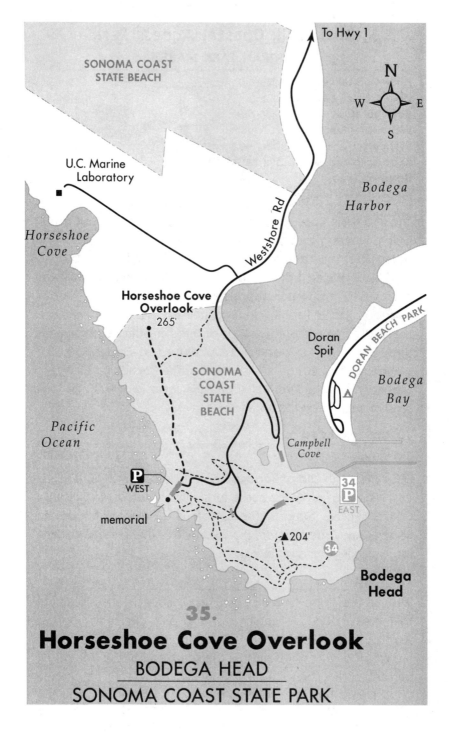

SONOMA COAST
STATE BEACH

To Hwy 1

N
W   E
S

U.C. Marine
Laboratory

*Bodega
Harbor*

Westshore Rd

*Horseshoe
Cove*

**Horseshoe Cove
Overlook**
265'

DORAN BEACH PARK

Doran
Spit

SONOMA
COAST
STATE
BEACH

*Bodega
Bay*

*Pacific
Ocean*

*Campbell
Cove*

P
WEST

memorial

34
P
EAST

▲204'

34

**Bodega
Head**

35.

Horseshoe Cove Overlook
BODEGA HEAD
SONOMA COAST STATE PARK

36. Bird Walk Coastal Access Park
DORAN PARK MARSH

Hiking distance: 0.75-mile loop
Hiking time: 30 minutes
Configuration: loop
Elevation gain: level
Difficulty: very easy (moderate accessibility)
Exposure: exposed coastal marshland
Dogs: allowed
Maps: U.S.G.S. Bodega Head

The Bird Walk Coastal Access Park lies at the mouth of Cheney Gulch, where it empties into Bodega Harbor just north of the Doran Spit. The coastal access trail follows old levees built to hold silt dredged from Bodega Harbor. The elevated walkway circles two freshwater ponds held within the levees. The trail overlooks Doran Park Marsh (a revitalized saltwater marsh) and the 800-acre harbor. Thousands of birds inhabit the marshlands throughout the year, making it a superb bird observation area for waterfowl, shorebirds, and songbirds. The Cheney Creek Bridge Trail connects the Bird Walk Coastal Access Park with the long sandy beach along the Doran Spit.

To the trailhead

355 HIGHWAY 1 · BODEGA BAY   38.321098, –123.035268

From the south end of Bodega Bay, just before Highway 1 heads eastward and leaves the coast, turn right at the posted Bird Walk Coastal Access turnoff. (The turnoff is 0.7 miles south of the Bodega Bay Visitor Center.) Drive 0.1 mile to the trailhead parking lot. A parking fee is required.

The hike

Walk up the slope on the paved, handicapped-accessible path to the east pond. A rectangular loop path circles the ponds, which can be hiked in either direction. These directions go to the left, hiking clockwise. Cross the south end of the first pond, parallel to the Cheney Gulch channel on the left. The Cheney Creek Bridge Trail forks to the left and crosses a bridge over the channel, heading south to Doran Beach. Continue on the pond loop to the far end of the second (west) pond, overlooking the expansive Doran Park Marsh, a protected mudflat. The vistas include Point Reyes in Marin County; prominent Bodega Head; and the narrow, two-mile-long arm of Doran Spit, the crescent-shaped sand spit that separates Bodega Harbor from Bodega Bay. Continue clockwise around the ponds on the well-defined trail, skirting the edge of Bodega Harbor back to the parking lot. ■

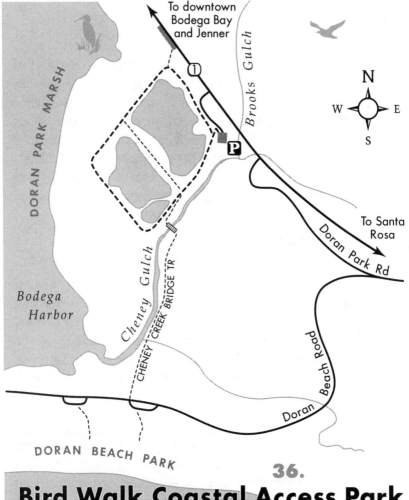

36.
Bird Walk Coastal Access Park
DORAN PARK MARSH

37. Pinnacle Gulch
BODEGA BAY

Hiking distance: 1.2 miles round trip
Hiking time: 40 minutes
Configuration: out-and-back
Elevation gain: 350 feet
Difficulty: easy
Exposure: mostly exposed
Dogs: allowed
Maps: U.S.G.S. Bodega Head
       Pinnacle Gulch-Shorttail Gulch Coastal Access map

Pinnacle Gulch drains into Bodega Bay at the far east end of Doran Beach, just south of the town of Bodega Bay. The half-mile gulch leads to Pinnacle Beach, a quiet sandy beach cove with a distinctive off-shore rock. The beach, accessed via a trail along the stream-fed gulch, is used mainly by locals . The trailhead is tucked away in a newer housing development by a golf course. The Coastal Access Trail, part of the Sonoma County Regional Parks, leads down the narrow gulch alongside a winter stream to the beach. Pinnacle Rock lies just off shore.

To the trailhead

20600 MOCKINGBIRD DR · BODEGA BAY   38.313027, -123.014703

From the south end of Bodega Bay, just after Highway 1 heads eastward and leaves the coast, turn south on South Harbor Way. (The turnoff is 1.2 miles south of the Bodega Bay Visitor Center.) Drive one block to the end of the street. Turn left on Heron Drive, and continue 0.9 miles to Mockingbird Road. Turn left and go 0.1 mile to the posted trailhead on the right. Park in the lot on the left. A parking fee is required.

The hike

Cross Mockingbird Drive to the posted trailhead. Descend through a canopy of cypress and wax myrtle. Follow the dirt path, paralleling Mockingbird Road, and curve right to the head of Pinnacle Gulch. Zigzag down five short switchbacks into the lush drainage overgrown with coastal scrub, coyote brush, and berry vines. The creekbed is lined with willows and salmonberry. Cross a footbridge on the north wall of the narrow, stream-fed canyon. Coastal scenery and homes perched on the bluffs above the gulch soon come into view. The trail hugs the canyon wall while crossing two more bridges over small water channels. Descend to the isolated quarter-mile sandy beach on Bodega Bay. Pinnacle Rock lies just offshore. The gorgeous coastal views include Tomales Bay; Point Reyes; Bodega Head; and the narrow, two-mile-long Doran Beach Park, the crescent-shaped sand spit that separates Bodega Harbor from Bodega Bay. ◼

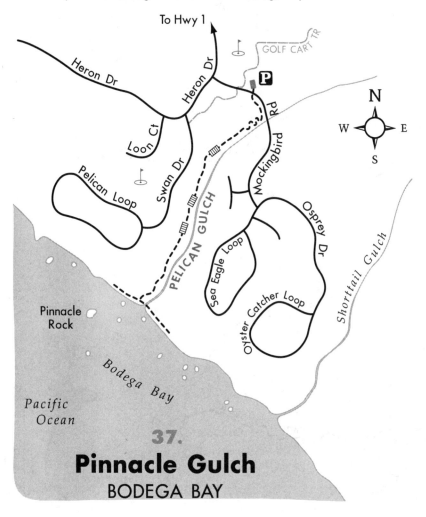

37.
Pinnacle Gulch
BODEGA BAY

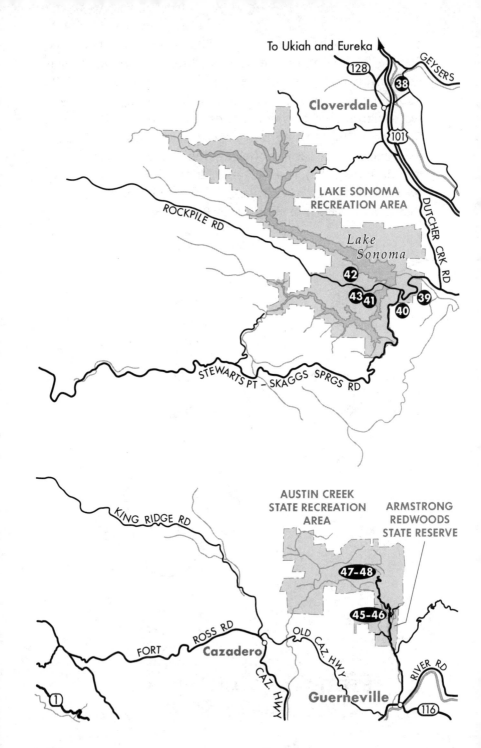

To Ukiah and Eureka

128

38

GEYSERS

Cloverdale

101

DUTCHER CRK RD

LAKE SONOMA
RECREATION AREA

ROCKPILE RD

Lake
Sonoma

42

43 41

40

39

STEWARTS PT – SKAGGS SPRGS RD

KING RIDGE RD

AUSTIN CREEK
STATE RECREATION
AREA

ARMSTRONG
REDWOODS
STATE RESERVE

47-48

45-46

FORT ROSS RD

Cazadero

OLD CAZ. HWY

CAZ. HWY

RIVER RD

Guerneville

116

1

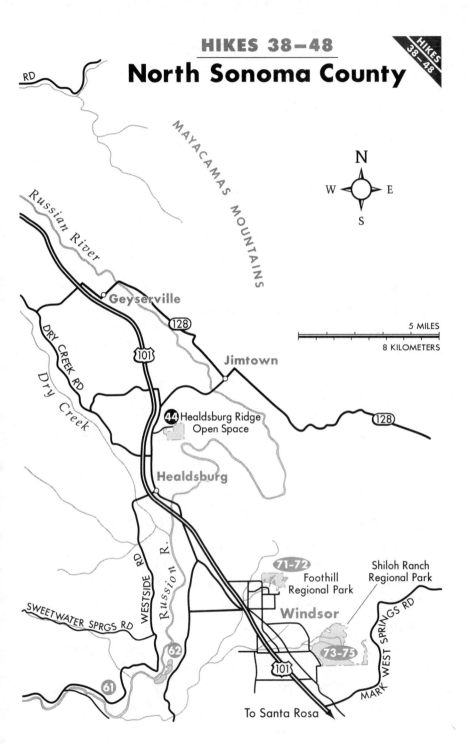

RD

Russian River

MAYACAMAS MOUNTAINS

N
W ← → E
S

Geyserville

128

DRY CREEK RD

Dry Creek

101

5 MILES
8 KILOMETERS

Jimtown

44 Healdsburg Ridge Open Space

128

Healdsburg

71-72

Foothill Regional Park

Shiloh Ranch Regional Park

WESTSIDE RD

Russion R.

SWEETWATER SPRGS RD

Windsor

73-75

MARK WEST SPRINGS RD

62

61

101

To Santa Rosa

38. Cloverdale River Park

Hiking distance: 2.2 miles round trip
Hiking time: 1 hour
Configuration: out-and-back
Elevation gain: level
Difficulty: easy
Exposure: a mix of open meadows and shaded woodlands
Dogs: allowed
Maps: U.S.G.S. Cloverdale · Cloverdale River Park map

The town of Cloverdale is tucked into the rolling hills of northern Sonoma County on the banks of the Russian River. Cloverdale River Park stretches 1.3 miles along the west bank of the river from First Street, near downtown, to McCray Road at the north end. A mile-long paved trail follows the river through the 72-acre park, passing freshwater marshes, grassland meadows, oak woodlands, riparian scrub, and riparian forest. This hike begins from the southern trailhead, but the trail can be started from either entrance.

To the trailhead

550 E. 1ST ST · CLOVERDALE   38.808198, –123.009787

SOUTH TRAILHEAD. From downtown Cloverdale on Cloverdale Boulevard, take East First Street 0.5 miles east towards the Russian River. Turn left on Crocker Road, 40 yards before the Russian River bridge, and park in the trailhead spaces on the right.

31820 MCCRAY RD · CLOVERDALE   38.823311, –123.010687

NORTH TRAILHEAD. From the north end of Cloverdale on Cloverdale Boulevard, cross under Highway 101. Continue 0.1 mile to McCray Road and turn right. Drive 0.5 miles to the posted trailhead parking lot on the left.

The hike

Walk 40 yards down East First Street to the posted trailhead by the Russian River bridge. Bear left and follow the west bank of the Russian River upstream. At the city water treatment plant, curve right on the paved path, skirting the facility to the Makahmo Trail.

Continue along the river through the riparian forest with walnut, maple, willow, buckeye, bay, and box elder trees. Weave through the woodland and cross a metal bridge over Oak Valley Creek and an interpretive panel. Meander through open grassland meadows to the northern trailhead parking lot off of McCray Road. Return along the same route. ■

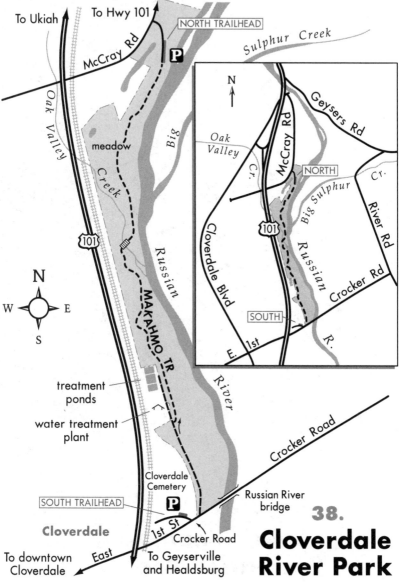

38.
Cloverdale River Park

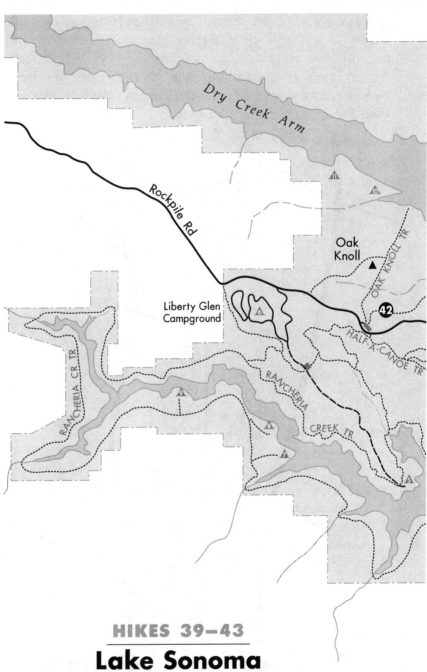

HIKES 39–43

Lake Sonoma
Recreation Area

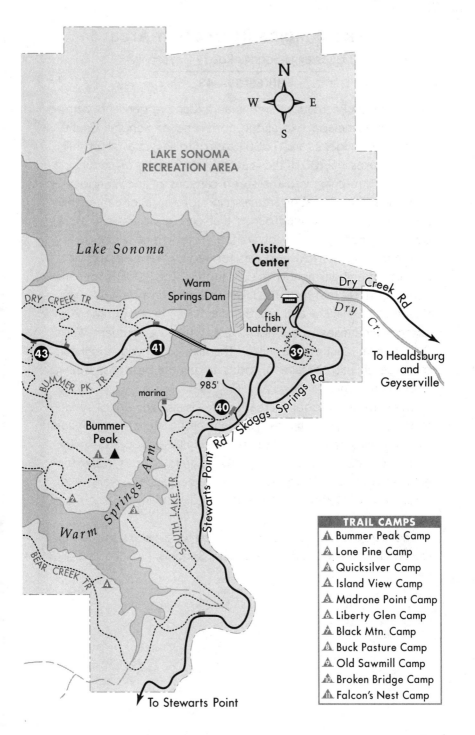

N
W · E
S

LAKE SONOMA
RECREATION AREA

Lake Sonoma

Visitor
Center

Warm
Springs Dam

fish
hatchery

Dry Creek Rd

Dry Cr.

To Healdsburg
and
Geyserville

DRY CREEK TR

43

41

39

BUMMER PK TR

marina

985'

40

Bummer
Peak

Warm

Springs Arm

SOUTH LAKE TR

Stewarts Point Rd / Skaggs Springs Rd

BEAR CREEK TR

To Stewarts Point

TRAIL CAMPS
- Bummer Peak Camp
- Lone Pine Camp
- Quicksilver Camp
- Island View Camp
- Madrone Point Camp
- Liberty Glen Camp
- Black Mtn. Camp
- Buck Pasture Camp
- Old Sawmill Camp
- Broken Bridge Camp
- Falcon's Nest Camp

Lake Sonoma Recreation Area

3333 Skaggs Springs Road · Geyserville

HIKES 39—43

Lake Sonoma Recreation Area is an expansive parkland with a sprawling manmade lake at the north end of Sonoma County. Within its boundaries are 17,600 acres of rolling, coastal foothills. The lake takes in 2,700 of these acres, with 53 miles of undulating shoreline stretching into the steep canyons of the Mendocino Highlands. The recreation area also includes a visitor center; marina; and primitive campgrounds that can be accessed via car, boat, bike, horse, or on foot. Dogs are allowed on all the trails.

The long and narrow lake was formed by Warm Springs Dam, an earthen embankment dam built in 1983. The 3,000-foot-long dam stands 319 feet high. The lake has two main arms, with many finger-shaped inlets and scores of coves. The Dry Creek Arm extends nine miles to the northwest, while the southern Warm Springs Arm reaches four miles. The lake is rich with steelhead trout, perch, catfish, salmon, and is among the best bass fishing lakes in California.

This popular outdoor recreation area is also known for swimming, picnicking, boating, camping, and hiking. More than 40 miles of hiking, equestrian, and mountain biking trails loop around the lake on the steep hills, weaving through grassy slopes, redwood groves, Douglas fir forests, and oak woodlands. A variety of trails lead to overlooks of the lake and to many backcountry camps.

The next five hikes explore the varied terrain along the shoreline and high above both arms of Lake Sonoma.

39. Woodland Ridge Trail
LAKE SONOMA RECREATION AREA

Hiking distance: 1.5-mile loop
Hiking time: 1 hour
Configuration: loop
Elevation gain: 150 feet
Difficulty: easy
Exposure: mostly forested woodlands with open hilltop
Dogs: allowed
Maps: U.S.G.S. Warm Springs Dam · Lake Sonoma map

The Woodland Ridge Trail is an easily accessible interpretive loop trail that offers an introduction to the various habitats around Lake Sonoma. The trail moderately climbs through four different plant communities: chaparral, coast redwood, Douglas fir, and oak woodland. At the ridge are sweeping vistas of Alexander Valley, the Mayacamas Mountains, Warm Springs Dam, and the lower portion of Lake Sonoma. The interpretive trail has 19 learning stations and an accompanying nature guide available at the Lake Sonoma Visitor Center. The learning stations describe how plants adapt, how the climate effects plants, the effects of fire, edible and medicinal plants, and wildlife.

To the trailhead

3216 STEWARTS POINT—SKAGGS SPRINGS RD · GEYSERVILLE
38.715791, -122.999990

HEALDSBURG. From Highway 101, head 10.3 miles northwest on Dry Creek Road to the base of Warm Springs Dam and Lake Sonoma Visitor Center on the right. (Dry Creek Road becomes Skaggs Springs Road in the park.)

GEYSERVILLE. Geyserville is located 8 miles south of Cloverdale and 8 miles north of Healdsburg. Exit Highway 101 on Canyon Road. Drive 2.1 miles west to a T-junction with Dry Creek Road. Turn right and continue 3.2 miles to the base of Warm Springs Dam and the Lake Sonoma Visitor Center on the right.

FROM THE VISITOR CENTER. Continue 0.2 miles to the parking area on the right by the trailhead.

The hike

Cross the wood footbridge and begin the loop to the left. Enter a grove of towering redwoods, and climb a long series of wood steps. Traverse the hillside through bay laurel trees high above Skaggs Springs Road. Climb another set of steps, and zigzag up to the ridge through a mixed forest of Douglas fir, madrone, and a variety of oaks. From the bald ridge are views of Dry Creek Valley, Alexander Valley, and the Mayacamas Mountains, rising above Sonoma Valley and Napa Valley. Follow the ridge through live oaks and black oaks, cresting the ridge. A short path on the left leads through a brushy canyon to a vista point with an over-look of Warm Springs Dam and the lower portion of Lake Sonoma.

Return to the main loop and descend on wood steps, winding down a stream-fed draw shaded by madrones. Continue down to the base of the hill, cross a wood bridge, and complete the loop at the trailhead bridge. ∎

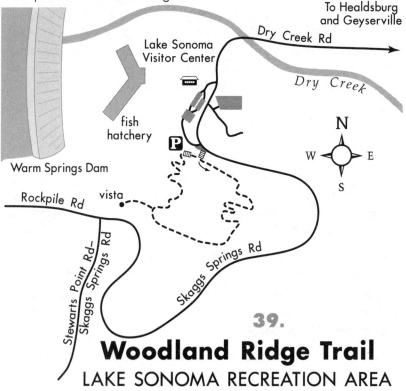

39.
Woodland Ridge Trail
LAKE SONOMA RECREATION AREA

40. South Lake Trail to Skaggs Springs Vista

LAKE SONOMA RECREATION AREA

Hiking distance: 3.8 shuttle or 7.6 miles round trip
Hiking time: 2 hours (shuttle) or 4 hours (round trip)
Configuration: out-and-back
Elevation gain: 500 feet
Difficulty: moderate
Exposure: forested woodlands and rolling grasslands
Dogs: allowed
Maps: U.S.G.S. Warm Springs Dam · Lake Sonoma map

The South Lake Trail traverses the steep, upper hillside along the wooded south side of Lake Sonoma. Throughout the hike are spectacular vistas of the Warm Springs Arm of the lake, including the marina, private coves, fingers of land extending into the lake, Bummer Peak, and the rolling hills surrounding the lake. This hike begins below the observation deck and picnic area at the 985-foot overlook, high above the south end of the dam. The trail passes forested stream-fed drainages and an access path to Quicksilver Camp en route to Skaggs Springs Vista. Quicksilver Camp has eleven campsites along the oak-filled hillside and near the water.

To the trailhead

3495 Stewarts Point—Skaggs Springs Rd · Geyserville
38.707196, -123.008475

Healdsburg. From Highway 101, head 10.3 miles northwest on Dry Creek Road to the base of Warm Springs Dam and Lake Sonoma Visitor Center on the right. (Dry Creek Road becomes Skaggs Springs Road in the park.)

Geyserville. Geyserville is located 8 miles south of Cloverdale and 8 miles north of Healdsburg. Exit Highway 101 on Canyon Road. Drive 2.1 miles west to a T-junction with Dry Creek Road. Turn right and continue 3.2 miles to the base of Warm Springs Dam and the Lake Sonoma Visitor Center on the right.

FROM THE VISITOR CENTER. Continue 1.7 miles to a posted junction. Turn left on Stewarts Point/Skaggs Springs Road, and continue 0.5 miles to the Lake Sonoma Overlook turnoff. Turn right 100 yards and turn left into the posted trailhead parking lot.

Shuttle car

STEWARTS POINT—SKAGGS SPRINGS RD · GEYSERVILLE
38.686349, -123.014538

For a one-way shuttle hike, the signed Skaggs Springs Vista Trailhead is located 2.3 miles farther on Stewarts Point/Skaggs Springs Road. Turn right into the parking lot.

The hike

Pass the trailhead fence at the southwest end of the lot. Traverse the hillside overlooking Lake Sonoma, and cross the marina access road. Steadily descend through oaks, pines, and madrones high above the marina. Weave along the hillside contours. The views extend across the Warm Springs Arm of Lake Sonoma to Bummer Peak, with its rounded, oak-covered summit (Hike 41). Bummer Peak Camp can be spotted on the lower (west) knoll. Curve in and out of a series of lush drainages and grottos, and walk through a grove of moss-covered oak trees. Continue along the trail with several small dips and rises. After topping a minor ridge, drop down 50 yards to a posted junction at 2 miles. The right fork descends 0.7 miles to Quicksilver Camp at the lakeshore.

Bear left and continue traversing the hill. Descend to a stream-fed drainage at 2.7 miles, and cross the rolling grasslands. Descend to within 50 yards of the lake and a four-way junction at 3.2 miles. The right fork leads 0.1 mile to the lake. One mile straight ahead is Island View Camp at the shoreline. Bear left and climb through the forest to an open ridge. Veer left to the Skaggs Springs Vista Trailhead. Return by retracing your steps. ■

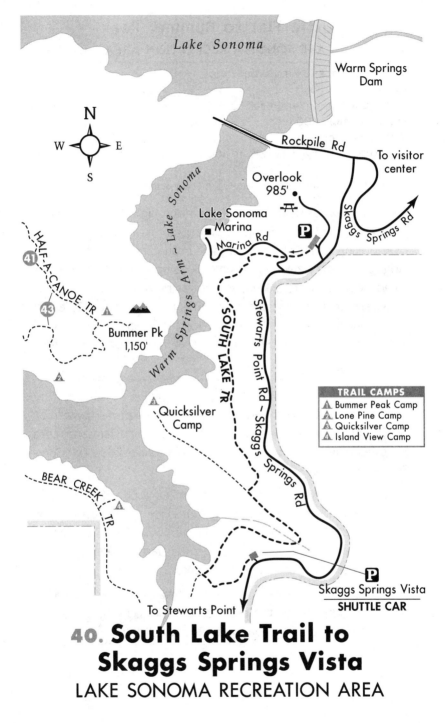

Lake Sonoma

Warm Springs Dam

N
W E
S

Rockpile Rd

To visitor center

Overlook 985'

Lake Sonoma Marina

Marina Rd

Skaggs Springs Rd

P

~ Lake Sonoma

Warm Springs Arm

HALF-A-CANOE TR

41

43

Bummer Pk
1,150'

SOUTH LAKE TR

Stewarts Point Rd ~ Skaggs Springs Rd

Quicksilver Camp

TRAIL CAMPS
🏕 Bummer Peak Camp
🏕 Lone Pine Camp
🏕 Quicksilver Camp
🏕 Island View Camp

BEAR CREEK TR

P
Skaggs Springs Vista
SHUTTLE CAR

To Stewarts Point

40. **South Lake Trail to Skaggs Springs Vista**
LAKE SONOMA RECREATION AREA

41. Little Flat to Bummer Peak
LAKE SONOMA RECREATION AREA

Hiking distance: 3.4 miles round trip
Hiking time: 2 hours
Configuration: out-and-back
Elevation gain: 600 feet
Difficulty: moderate
Exposure: rolling grasslands with pockets of woodlands; exposed ridge
Dogs: allowed
Maps: U.S.G.S. Warm Springs Dam · Lake Sonoma map

Bummer Peak lies at the end of the ridge high above the Warm Springs Arm of Lake Sonoma. The peak is a 1,150-foot knoll overlooking Lake Sonoma and the surrounding rugged foothills. Adjacent to the peak is Bummer Peak Camp, a primitive two-site camp open to hikers, bikers, and equestrians.

Several trails access the ridge. This hike begins at Little Flat on the Bummer Peak Trail. The mile-long trail climbs through oak, madrone, and redwood groves to great views along the ridge.

To the trailhead

14055 ROCKPILE RD · GEYSERVILLE   38.713557, -123.031275

HEALDSBURG. From Highway 101, head 10.3 miles northwest on Dry Creek Road to the base of Warm Springs Dam and Lake Sonoma Visitor Center on the right. (Dry Creek Road becomes Skaggs Springs Road in the park.)

GEYSERVILLE. Geyserville is located 8 miles south of Cloverdale and 8 miles north of Healdsburg. Exit Highway 101 on Canyon Road. Drive 2.1 miles west to a T-junction with Dry Creek Road. Turn right and continue 3.2 miles to the base of Warm Springs Dam and the Lake Sonoma Visitor Center on the right.

FROM THE VISITOR CENTER. Continue 2.7 miles, crossing the bridge over Lake Sonoma, to the posted Little Flat parking lot on the right. (En route, the road becomes Rockpile Road.)

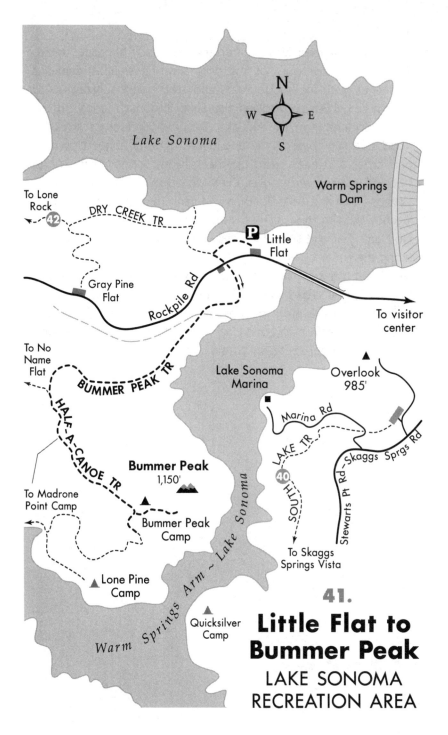

N
W E
S

Lake Sonoma

Warm Springs Dam

To Lone Rock
42
DRY CREEK TR

P Little Flat

Gray Pine Flat

Rockpile Rd

To visitor center

To No Name Flat

BUMMER PEAK TR

Lake Sonoma Marina

Overlook 985'

Marina Rd

HALF-A-CANOE TR

LAKE TR

Bummer Peak
1,150'

40

SOUTH

Stewarts Pt Rd

Skaggs Sprgs Rd

To Madrone Point Camp

Bummer Peak Camp

Warm Springs Arm ~ Lake Sonoma

To Skaggs Springs Vista

Lone Pine Camp

Quicksilver Camp

41.
Little Flat to Bummer Peak
LAKE SONOMA RECREATION AREA

The hike

From the trailhead kiosk, enter the oak and madrone forest. Traverse the contours of the hills, crossing small stream-fed drainages with mossy boulders and tree trunks. Zigzag up to the ridge while overlooking the Lake Sonoma Marina on the Warm Springs Arm of the lake. Descend and cross Rockpile Road, heading toward the lake. Curve right, continue downhill, and cross a stream. Head up the hillside, following the ridge into a grove of redwoods. Climb to an overlook of the redwood grove and Lake Sonoma, reaching the upper ridge and a T-junction with the Half-A-Canoe Loop. The right fork leads to No Name Flat and Lone Rock Flat (Hike 43). Bear left and weave along the roller coaster ridge to Bummer Peak Camp. The camp sits on an terraced, oak-covered knoll with picnic benches, fire pits, and great views of the lake. This is the turn-around spot.

To extend the hike, loop around the camp and descend a stream-fed canyon to Lone Pine Camp at the lakeshore. Return by retracing your route, or continue on the Half-A-Canoe Loop (Hike 43). ■

42. Dry Creek Trail
Lone Rock to Gray Pine Flat
LAKE SONOMA RECREATION AREA

Hiking distance: 4.6 miles round trip
Hiking time: 2.5 hours
Configuration: out-and-back (or loop along road)
Elevation gain: 400 feet
Difficulty: easy to moderate
Exposure: rolling grasslands, forested hillsides and exposed overlooks
Dogs: allowed
Maps: U.S.G.S. Warm Springs Dam · Lake Sonoma map

The Dry Creek Arm of Lake Sonoma is nine miles long and has multiple finger-like channels. The Dry Creek Trail follows the lower end of the Dry Creek Arm near Warm Springs Dam. The trail weaves through oak woodlands, redwood groves, grasslands, and wildflower-covered meadows to overlooks of the lake. This hike begins from Lone Rock, the western access of the Dry Creek Trail, and heads east to Gray Pine Flat.

To the trailhead

13300 ROCKPILE RD · GEYSERVILLE   38.715009, -123.046178

HEALDSBURG. From Highway 101, head 10.3 miles northwest on Dry Creek Road to the base of Warm Springs Dam and Lake Sonoma Visitor Center on the right. (Dry Creek Road becomes Skaggs Springs Road in the park.)

GEYSERVILLE. Geyserville is located 8 miles south of Cloverdale and 8 miles north of Healdsburg. Exit Highway 101 on Canyon Road. Drive 2.1 miles west to a T-junction with Dry Creek Road. Turn right and continue 3.2 miles to the base of Warm Springs Dam and the Lake Sonoma Visitor Center on the right.

FROM THE VISITOR CENTER. Continue 4.3 miles, crossing the bridge over Lake Sonoma, to the posted Lone Rock parking lot on the right. (En route, the road becomes Rockpile Road.)

The hike

From the trailhead map board, bear left and descend, looping clockwise around the knoll in an oak forest. Zigzag down into the lush, shady redwood grove, crossing small feeder streams. Slowly gain elevation while returning to the oak and madrone forest. Cross the rolling terrain, with views through the trees of the Dry Creek Arm of Lake Sonoma. At 1.5 miles, the Warm Springs Dam comes into view. At an unsigned Y-fork, veer right and drop into a fern-filled grotto. Cross a footbridge over the stream to a posted junction. The left fork leads to Little Flat, the lakeshore, and a boat ramp. Stay to the right toward Gray Pine Flat. Ascend the slope and wind up the hillside to the large parking lot overlooking the dam and surrounding hills. Return by retracing your steps, or follow Rockpile Road one mile to the right, completing a loop. ■

42.

Dry Creek Trail:
Lone Rock to Gray Pine Flat
LAKE SONOMA RECREATION AREA

43. Half-A-Canoe Loop
LAKE SONOMA RECREATION AREA

Hiking distance: 5.5-mile loop
Hiking time: 3 hours
Configuration: loop
Elevation gain: 1,100 feet
Difficulty: moderate to strenuous
Exposure: open ridge with pockets of woodlands
Dogs: allowed
Maps: U.S.G.S. Warm Springs Dam · Lake Sonoma map

The Half-a-Canoe Loop is a circular hiking and biking path that follows a rolling ridge between the two arms of Lake Sonoma. It is the only biking trail in the park. The trail leads to Bummer Peak Camp atop the ridge, overlooking the Warm Springs Arm of Sonoma Lake, then drops down to the lakeshore at Lone Pine Camp. The Half-a-Canoe Trail has several connector trails—from Liberty Glen Campground, Lone Rock Flat, No Name Flat, and Little Flat. This hike follows the No Name Flat Trail to the ridge through oak woodlands and grasslands.

To the trailhead

14065 ROCKPILE RD · GEYSERVILLE   38.714472, -123.035572

HEALDSBURG. From Highway 101, head 10.3 miles northwest on Dry Creek Road to the base of Warm Springs Dam and Lake Sonoma Visitor Center on the right. (Dry Creek Road becomes Skaggs Springs Road in the park.)

GEYSERVILLE. Geyserville is located 8 miles south of Cloverdale and 8 miles north of Healdsburg. Exit Highway 101 on Canyon Road. Drive 2.1 miles west to a T-junction with Dry Creek Road. Turn right and continue 3.2 miles to the base of Warm Springs Dam and the Lake Sonoma Visitor Center on the right.

FROM THE VISITOR CENTER. Continue 3.6 miles, crossing the bridge over Lake Sonoma, to the posted No Name Flat parking lot on the left. (En route, the road becomes Rockpile Road.)

The hike

From the trailhead kiosk, take the No Name Flat Trail downhill. Cross a footbridge over a small stream, and head up the oak-dotted hillside to sweeping vistas of the rolling hills. Cross a second wooden bridge to a T-junction on the ridge with the Half-A-Canoe Trail at 0.6 miles, overlooking the Warm Springs Arm of Lake Sonoma.

Begin the loop to the left, and follow the rolling ridge. Pass the Bummer Peak Trail (Hike 41) at just over a mile. Weave along the contours of the hills past rock outcroppings, over-looking the Rockpile Road bridge and the Lake Sonoma Marina en route to Bummer Peak Camp. The camp sits on a terraced, oak-covered knoll below the 1,150-foot peak. Loop around the camp and descend to the floor of a stream-fed canyon, passing moss-covered tree trunks and rocks. Continue down to the edge of the lake and a junction. The left fork leads a short distance to Lone Pine Camp in a grove of oaks.

Go to the right along the edge of the lake to the north end of the inlet. Leave the shore and wind up the hill. Head north-east, steadily gaining elevation. Pass a junction to Madrone Point Camp, the bike route on the left. Continue climbing up the creek-fed canyon to a junction. The left fork leads to Liberty Glen Campground and another access to Madrone Point Camp. Bear right, heading uphill on the north wall of the valley. Parallel Rockpile Road, passing a trail to Lone Rock on the left. Curve right to the No Name Flat Trail, completing the loop. Bear left and return 0.6 miles to the trailhead. ■

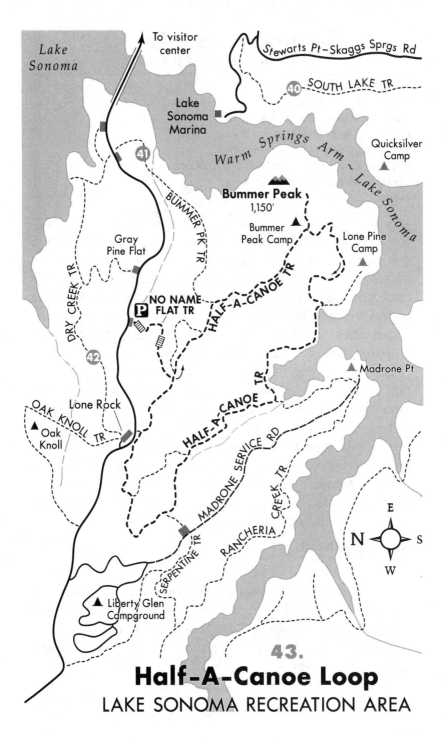

Lake Sonoma

To visitor center

Stewarts Pt–Skaggs Sprgs Rd

40 SOUTH LAKE TR

Lake Sonoma Marina

Warm Springs Arm ~ Lake Sonoma

Quicksilver Camp

41

BUMMER PK TR

Bummer Peak
1,150'

Bummer Peak Camp

Lone Pine Camp

DRY CREEK TR

Gray Pine Flat

P NO NAME FLAT TR

HALF-A-CANOE TR

Madrone Pt

42

HALF-A-CANOE TR

Lone Rock

OAK KNOLL TR

▲ Oak Knoll

MADRONE SERVICE RD

RANCHERIA CREEK TR

E

N — S

W

SERPENTINE TR

▲ Liberty Glen Campground

43.

Half-A-Canoe Loop
LAKE SONOMA RECREATION AREA

44. Healdsburg Ridge
OPEN SPACE PRESERVE

Hiking distance: 3.5-mile double loop
Hiking time: 2 hours
Configuration: double loop
Elevation gain: 200 feet
Difficulty: easy to moderate
Exposure: mix of forested hills and exposed meadows
Dogs: allowed on paved trails only
Maps: U.S.G.S. Jimtown
        Healdsburg Ridge Open Space Preserve map

Healdsburg Ridge Open Space Preserve sits on the prominent oak-dotted ridgeline at the northern end of Healdsburg. The park was opened to the public in 2008. The 161 acres of parkland contain a network of trails in scenic forested hills that lead to five beautiful overlooks. There is a wide variety of natural communities, including woodlands, open grasslands, and rocky chaparral, as well as wetlands, vernal pools, and a pond.

This double-loop trail travels through the wide array of habitats, including four of the overlooks and Fox Pond. The Russian River Overlook offers a postcard-perfect view of the river at River's Bend, framed by the surrounding vineyards. Other overlooks offer panoramas of Fitch Mountain, the Mayacamas Mountains (including Mount Saint Helena), and the coastal range. The trails weave through the oak groves and mixed evergreen forest to the overlooks. Fox Pond, a small but scenic tarn, has lily pads covering its western edge.

To the trailhead

388 BRIDLE PATH · CITY   38.640354, -122.860812

From Highway 101 in Healdsburg, exit on Dry Creek Road. Turn right (east) and go 0.2 miles to Healdsburg Avenue. Turn left and drive 0.8 miles to Parkland Farms Boulevard. Turn right and continue 0.75 miles to the end of the road at Bridle Path. Turn right and park alongside the road on Bridle Path or Arabian Way.

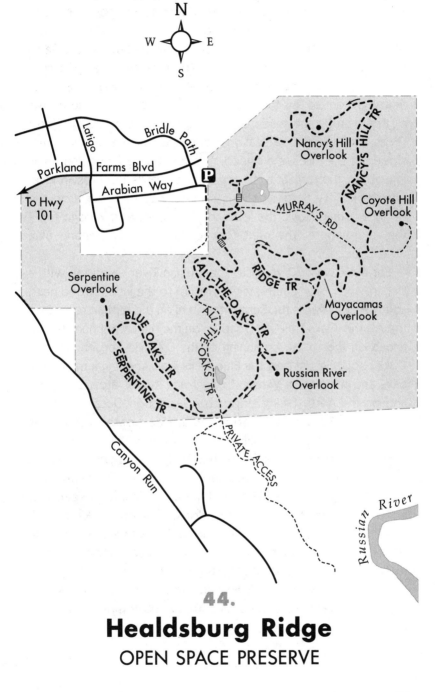

N
W · E
S

Latigo

Bridle Path

Parkland | Farms Blvd

Arabian Way

P

To Hwy 101

Nancy's Hill Overlook

NANCY'S HILL TR

Coyote Hill Overlook

MURRAY'S RD

Serpentine Overlook

ALL-THE-OAKS TR

RIDGE TR

Mayacamas Overlook

BLUE OAKS TR

ALL-THE-OAKS TR

SERPENTINE TR

Russian River Overlook

PRIVATE ACCESS

Canyon Run

Russian River

44.

Healdsburg Ridge
OPEN SPACE PRESERVE

The hike

From the far east end of Arabian Way, take the paved road to the right. At 50 yards is the trailhead map kiosk on the left. Walk 25 yards to a trail split with the Nancy's Hill Trail to the left. Begin the loop straight ahead on Murray's Road towards the ridge. Fifty yards farther is a posted junction above Fox Pond on the left. Bear right on the All-the-Oaks Trail. Wind up the hillside on the dirt path under the shade of a mixed forest dominated by oaks. Cross a bridge over a seasonal drainage, and gently climb the slope. At 0.4 miles is a signed Y-fork with the Ridge Trail veering off to the left. Stay to the right towards the Russian River Overlook. Fifty yards ahead is a three-way trail split atop the ridge by a map kiosk. The left fork leads back to the Ridge Trail—the return route. The right fork leads to the Serpentine-Blue Oaks Loop.

For now, walk 70 yards to the Russian River Overlook with a bench. After taking in the views, return to the junction and head southwest towards the Serpentine Trail on the asphalt road. Pass the All-the-Oaks Trail (Alternative) on the right. Continue straight ahead on the to the beginning of the 0.4 mile Serpentine-Blue Oaks Loop. Go right on the Blue Oaks Trail, strolling among blue oaks and madrones. Weave through the forest atop the ridge and on the north-facing slope to a T-junction. Detour right 80 yards to the Serpentine Overlook, with a view of the Mayacamas Mountains, oak-cloaked hills, and vineyards. Return to the junction and continue on the Serpentine Trail in a tree-lined meadow.

Return to the kiosk by the Russian River Overlook. Take the Ridge Trail along the semi-shaded ridge to a trail fork. Veer right 60 yards to the Mayacamas Overlook. Back on the Ridge Trail, continue winding down the hill to a junction with Nancy's Hill Trail on the right. Go right and traverse the exposed slope, crossing three footbridges. Skirt the northern edge of the open space. Walk up and over Nancy's Hill to an overlook of Fox Pond. Cross the bridge over the pond's outlet stream and complete the loop just shy of the trailhead. ∎

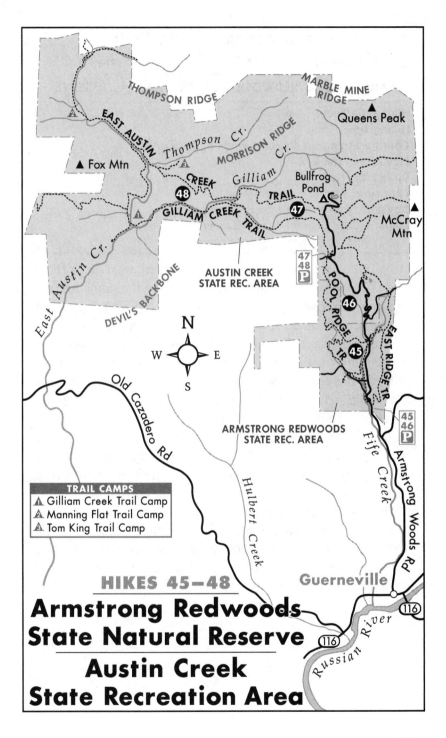

THOMPSON RIDGE

MARBLE MINE RIDGE

▲ Queens Peak

EAST AUSTIN

Thompson Cr.

MORRISON RIDGE

Gilliam Cr.

▲ Fox Mtn

CREEK

Gilliam

Bullfrog Pond

⟨48⟩

TRAIL

⟨47⟩

GILLIAM CREEK TRAIL

East Austin Cr.

⟨46⟩

POOL RIDGE TR.

▲ McCray Mtn

DEVIL'S BACKBONE

47 48 P

AUSTIN CREEK STATE REC. AREA

⟨45⟩

EAST RIDGE TR.

N
W — E
S

Old Cazadero Rd

ARMSTRONG REDWOODS STATE REC. AREA

45 46 P

Hulbert Creek

Fife Creek

Armstrong Woods Rd

TRAIL CAMPS
⚠ Gilliam Creek Trail Camp
⚠ Manning Flat Trail Camp
⚠ Tom King Trail Camp

Guerneville

116

HIKES 45–48

Armstrong Redwoods
State Natural Reserve

116

Russian River

Austin Creek
State Recreation Area

45. Armstrong Nature Trail
Pioneer Trail • Icicle Tree Trail • Discovery Trail
ARMSTRONG REDWOODS STATE NATURAL RESERVE

Hiking distance: 1.7 miles
Hiking time: 1 hour
Configuration: out-and-back with central loop
Elevation gain: level
Difficulty: easy
Exposure: shaded redwood forest
Dogs: allowed on paved roads and picnic areas
Maps: U.S.G.S. Guerneville and Cazadero
       Armstrong Redwoods State Reserve map

In the 1870s, lumberman Colonel James Armstrong, a Union officer in the Civil War, realized that if not preserved, this gorgeous area of primeval redwoods would be destroyed by logging. He set aside the land as a natural park and botanical garden. Due to this early preservation, the 805-acre reserve contains the largest remaining first-growth coast redwoods in Sonoma County. It is also the only grove of first generation redwoods open to the public in the county. This ancient grove flourishes along Fife Creek in a cool and dark valley floor at 3,316 feet. Scattered among the stately redwoods are tanbark oak, California bay laurel, and bigleaf maple. The shady forest floor, highlighted by filtered sunlight, is carpeted with redwood sorrel, trillium, fairy bells, redwood orchid, mushrooms, lichens, and mosses.

This hike strolls through the heart of the redwood cathedral under the forest canopy. The Armstrong Nature Trail and Icicle Tree Trail are self-guided nature trails with interpretive displays and a printed guide. The Discovery Trail is a Braille Trail for the visually impaired. Both trails are connected to the Pioneer Trail, leading from the visitor center to the large group picnic area.

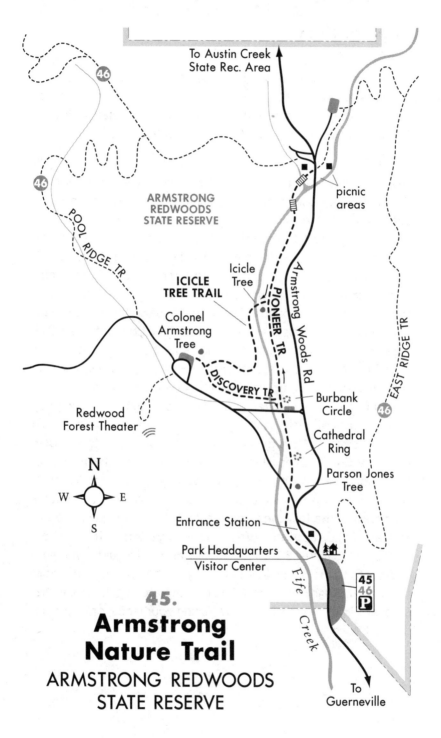

To Austin Creek State Rec. Area

ARMSTRONG REDWOODS STATE RESERVE

picnic areas

POOL RIDGE TR

Icicle Tree

ICICLE TREE TRAIL

PIONEER TR

Armstrong Woods Rd

EAST RIDGE TR

Colonel Armstrong Tree

DISCOVERY TR

Burbank Circle

Redwood Forest Theater

Cathedral Ring

Parson Jones Tree

N
W   E
S

Entrance Station

Park Headquarters Visitor Center

Fife Creek

45
46
P

45.
Armstrong Nature Trail
ARMSTRONG REDWOODS STATE RESERVE

To Guerneville

To the trailhead

17020 ARMSTRONG WOODS RD · GUERNEVILLE   38.532384, -123.002999

From downtown Guerneville on Main Street (Highway 116), drive 2.3 miles north on Armstrong Woods Road to the visitor center on the right, just before the state park entrance station. Park in the large lot on the right by the visitor center.

The hike

From the visitor center parking lot, walk up the park road past the park entrance kiosk to the posted nature trail. Bear left and parallel Fife Creek through a forest of massive redwoods. Cross the park road to the 1,300-year-old Parson Jones Tree. It is the tallest tree in the grove at 310 feet and a diameter of 13.8 feet. Stroll through the redwoods and cross another road to Burbank Circle, an enormous ring of redwood trees. Continue to a junction with the Discovery Trail. For now, stay to the right on the Pioneer Trail. Follow Fife Creek upstream to a second junction with the Icicle Tree Trail, the return route. Continue straight, crossing a bridge over Fife Creek and a second bridge over a tributary stream. At 0.75 miles, the trail reaches a road fork by the picnic area.

Return to the Icicle Tree Trail, and curve right to Icicle Tree, with clusters of icicle-shaped burl formations (nodules) growing on the side of the tree's trunk. Cross a wooden footbridge over Fife Creek. Climb steps and weave through the forest to the Colonel James Armstrong Tree near the park road. The tree is at least 1,400 years old and is the largest tree (in mass) within the reserve. The towering tree reaches 308 feet high with a diameter of 14.6 feet. Veer left on the Discovery Trail. This portion of the hike is a Braille Trail. It is equipped with a guide wire and interpretive stations in Braille and English that describe trailside features through touch and smell. Complete the loop by the Burbank Circle. Go to the right, retracing your steps, or return on the park road. ■

46. East Ridge—Pool Ridge Loop

ARMSTRONG REDWOODS STATE NATURAL RESERVE
AUSTIN CREEK STATE RECREATION AREA

Hiking distance: 5.6-mile loop
Hiking time: 4 hours
Configuration: loop
Elevation gain: 1,100 feet
Difficulty: moderate to strenuous
Exposure: shady, forested canyons and slopes; open grassy meadows
Dogs: allowed on paved roads and picnic areas
Maps: U.S.G.S. Guerneville and Cazadero
        Armstrong Redwoods State Reserve map

The East Ridge-Pool Ridge Loop circles the heart of Armstrong Redwoods State Reserve on two ridges that overlook the first-growth redwood forest deep in the Fife Creek Canyon. The hike begins and ends on the canyon floor among the magnificent giant sentinels. The East Ridge Trail climbs 1,100 feet through

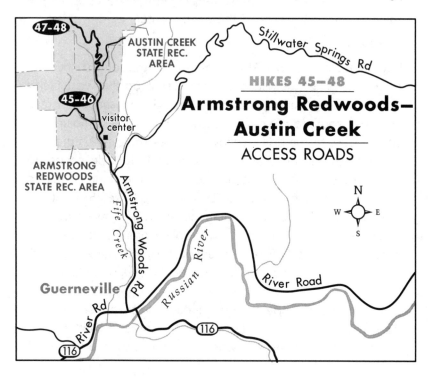

Douglas fir, tanbark oak, California bay laurel, and madrones, emerging to far-reaching views across the tops of the ancient forest. En route, the trail crosses the headwaters of Fife Creek and passes Pond Farm, which was the home, workshop, and school of well-known ceramic artist Marguerite Wildenhain from 1949 to 1980. The hike returns on the Pool Ridge Trail, which parallels the opposite side of the canyon in the Austin Creek State Recreation Area. The trail leads to the canyon floor and the Colonel Armstrong Tree, passing open grassy slopes and skirting the West Branch of Fife Creek. The trail descends through gnarled oaks, bay laurels, and Douglas fir. The two trails are also equestrian routes

To the trailhead

17020 ARMSTRONG WOODS RD · GUERNEVILLE   38.532384, -123.002999

From downtown Guerneville on Main Street (Highway 116), drive 2.3 miles north on Armstrong Woods Road to the visitor center on the right, just before the state park entrance station. Park in the large lot on the right by the visitor center.

The hike

Begin at the posted East Ridge Trailhead on the south (right) side of the visitor center. Head up the hillside on the west-facing slope, steadily gaining elevation through the shaded forest. Thick tree roots form a mosaic pattern on the trail. Climb up two switchbacks to the ridge. Follow the rises and dips on the rolling ridge to a junction at 1.2 miles. The left fork descends 0.3 miles to the picnic area at Fife Creek and the Pioneer Trail on the canyon floor for a shorter 2.2-mile loop (Hike 45). Continue straight, climbing and descending the hilly route toward McCray Mountain. Emerge from the forest to a sloping meadow with vistas of the densely forested canyon. Drop down to Fife Creek and a T-junction with Meadow Road on the park boundary at 1.8 miles.

Bear left on the unpaved service road, and cross a bridge over the creek in Austin Creek State Recreation Area. Pick up the East Ridge Trail on the right, 20 yards ahead. Climb to an overlook of

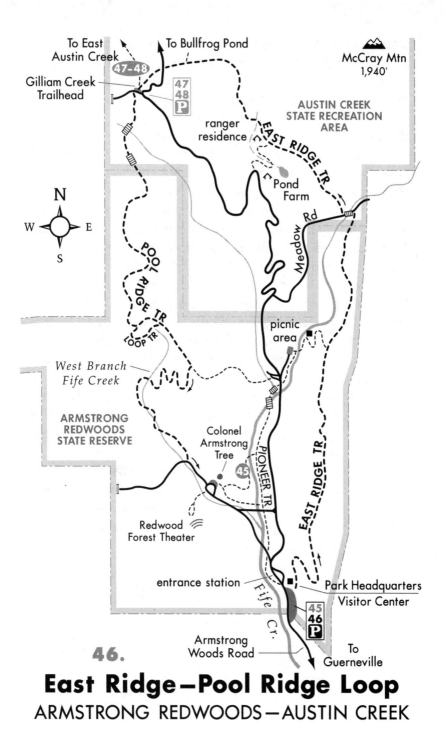

To East
Austin Creek

To Bullfrog Pond

McCray Mtn
1,940'

47-48

Gilliam Creek
Trailhead

47
48
P

ranger
residence

AUSTIN CREEK
STATE RECREATION
AREA

EAST RIDGE TR

Pond
Farm

Meadow Rd

N
W E
S

POOL RIDGE TR

LOOP TR

picnic
area

West Branch
Fife Creek

ARMSTRONG
REDWOODS
STATE RESERVE

Colonel
Armstrong
Tree

45

PIONEER TR

EAST RIDGE TR

Redwood
Forest Theater

entrance station

Fife Cr.

Park Headquarters
Visitor Center

45
46
P

Armstrong
Woods Road

To
Guerneville

46.
East Ridge—Pool Ridge Loop
ARMSTRONG REDWOODS—AUSTIN CREEK

a pond in a scenic, grassy depression. Follow the east side of the pond to a Y-fork. The left branch leads to Pond Farm and the park road. Stay to the right and continue uphill through Douglas fir, passing a ranger's residence on the left. Cross over a small stream on an S-curve, and emerge to an open slope, with vistas across the Russian River to Mount Tamalpais. Follow the slope to the ridge with a viewing bench and a junction. To the right, the East Ridge Trail continues 1.3 miles to Bullfrog Pond. Take the left fork 150 yards to the park road, with views into the East Austin Creek drainage. Cross the road, descend steps, and curve left. Enter a redwood forest and return to the road at the Gilliam Creek Trailhead. (Hikes 47 and 48 head to the north.) Follow the narrow road 85 yards to the right to the posted Pool Ridge Trail.

Bear left on the footpath and head downhill into the forest, leaving the panoramic views. Weave along the contours of the cliffs and skirt around deep ravines. Descend on three switchbacks and cross two bridges, hugging the hillside over two steep drainages through oak groves. Reenter Armstrong Redwoods State Reserve, and pass two junctions with the posted Loop Trail on the right at 4 miles. The side path leads to an abandoned apple orchard and an overlook. A short distance ahead is a trail split. The left fork (straight ahead) leads 0.6 miles to the Pioneer Trail on the valley floor.

Go to the right and descend on six switchbacks along the West Branch of Fife Creek. Cross the creek four times, following it downstream to a park road. Bear left 0.1 mile to the main road. Veer right and continue 0.4 miles through the stately redwoods, returning to the visitor center. ∎

47. Gilliam Creek Trail— East Austin Creek Trail

• EAST LOOP •

AUSTIN CREEK STATE RECREATION AREA

Hiking distance: 4.2-mile loop
Hiking time: 3 hours
Configuration: loop
Elevation gain: 1,000 feet
Difficulty: moderate to strenuous
Exposure: shady, forested canyons and slopes; open grassy meadows
Dogs: allowed on paved roads and picnic areas
Maps: U.S.G.S. Cazadero
    Austin Creek State Recreation Area map

Austin Creek State Recreation Area encompasses 5,683 acres in a largely undeveloped area in north-central Sonoma County. The isolated wilderness is adjacent to (and accessed through) Armstrong Redwoods State Reserve. The rugged topography includes rolling grassland meadows, oak-covered knolls, deep valleys, forested ridges, chaparral hillsides, oak woodlands, conifer forests, and year-round streams. There are three backcountry camps and more than 20 miles of hiking and equestrian trails.

A large nine-mile loop trail traverses the recreation area from east to west. This shorter, 4.2-mile hike explores the first half of the loop. The hike begins with vistas across the Russian River Valley from 1,100 feet. The path contours across grassy slopes and tree-lined creek ravines on the Gilliam Creek Trail. En route, the trail fords Schoolhouse Creek three times. The hike returns on the East Austin Creek Trail, an unpaved service road. The road steeply winds up the canyon through meadows along the aptly named Panorama Grade, offering spectacular vistas.

The next hike—Hike 48—includes directions for the entire nine-mile loop.

To the trailhead

17020 ARMSTRONG WOODS RD · GUERNEVILLE   38.555978, -123.011888

From downtown Guerneville on Main Street (Highway 116), drive 2.3 miles north on Armstrong Woods Road to the visitor center on the right, just before the state park entrance station. Continue 2.5 miles past the entrance station, staying to the right, to the Gilliam Creek Trailhead parking area. The last 1.7 miles winds up a narrow, paved mountain road on a 12% grade. An entrance fee is required.

The hike

From the trailhead map, head downhill on the Gilliam Creek Trail. Wind down the mountain slope, crossing two forks of Schoolhouse Creek by its headwaters. Cross Gilliam Ridge, a rolling, grassy ridge dotted with oaks, then traverse the north slope of the canyon. Walk over a few seasonal tributaries to the canyon floor and Schoolhouse Creek at just under a mile. Rock-hop over the creek, and follow the southwest wall of the canyon. Stroll through the lush, wet forest with fern-covered hills. Thick green moss covers the rocks and tree trunks. Rock-hop over Schoolhouse Creek two consecutive times to a posted junction at two miles. The trail straight ahead leads to Gilliam Creek Camp. To extend the hike for a nine-mile double loop, continue with Hike 48.

For this shorter hike, wade across Schoolhouse Creek and curve right, looping around a hill to the south bank of Gilliam Creek. Head upstream to a junction with the East Austin Creek Trail by a bridge. Veer right, staying on the south side of the creek. Head up the hill along Gilliam Creek. Curve away from the creek, and steadily climb the well-named Panorama Grade, gaining a thousand feet over 1.5 miles. Steadily climb, with barely a break, to the trail gate by the park road, where the climb mercifully ends. The left fork leads to Bullfrog Pond Campground. Bear right and follow the paved road 0.6 miles back to the trailhead. ∎

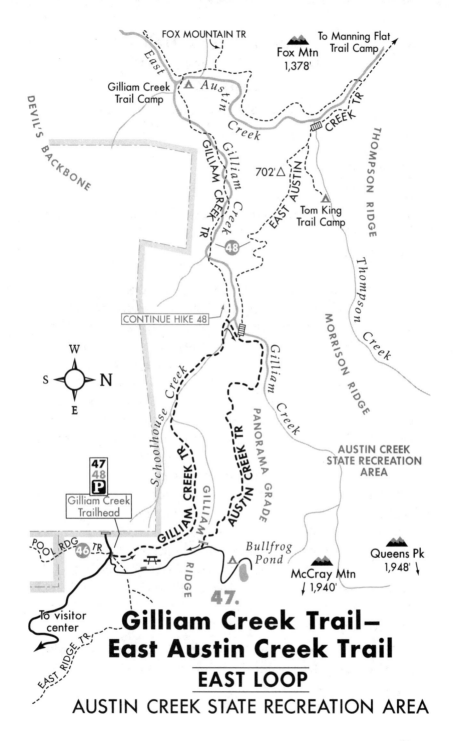

FOX MOUNTAIN TR

To Manning Flat
Trail Camp

Fox Mtn
1,378'

East

Austin

Creek

Gilliam Creek
Trail Camp

Austin
Creek

GILLIAM CREEK TR

Gilliam Creek

CREEK TR

THOMPSON RIDGE

702'△

EAST AUSTIN

Tom King
Trail Camp

Thompson Creek

DEVIL'S BACKBONE

48

CONTINUE HIKE 48

MORRISON RIDGE

Schoolhouse Creek

W
S   N
E

GILLIAM CREEK TR

AUSTIN CREEK TR

PANORAMA GRADE

Gilliam Creek

AUSTIN CREEK
STATE RECREATION
AREA

47
48
P
Gilliam Creek
Trailhead

POOL RDG TR

46

GILLIAM CREEK TR

GILLIAM RIDGE

Bullfrog
Pond

Queens Pk
1,948' ↓

McCray Mtn
↓ 1,940'

To visitor
center

EAST RIDGE TR

47.

Gilliam Creek Trail—
East Austin Creek Trail
EAST LOOP
AUSTIN CREEK STATE RECREATION AREA

48. Gilliam Creek Trail— East Austin Creek Trail
• DOUBLE LOOP •
AUSTIN CREEK STATE RECREATION AREA

Hiking distance: 9-mile double loop
Hiking time: 5.5 hours
Configuration: double loop
Elevation gain: 1,700 feet
Difficulty: very strenuous with several creek crossings
Exposure: shady, forested canyons and slopes; open grassy meadows
Dogs: allowed on paved roads and picnic areas
Maps: U.S.G.S. Cazadero
Austin Creek State Recreation Area map

This is a strenuous and secluded nine-mile loop trail that traverses the width of Austin Creek State Recreation Area, a large, undeveloped park adjacent to Armstrong Redwoods State Reserve. Hike 47 explores the first half of the loop. This hike follows the entire double loop. The route begins on the Gilliam Creek Trail. The trail contours across grassy slopes and drops down tree-lined ravines to three creeks—Schoolhouse Creek, Gilliam Creek, and East Austin Creek. The path continues parallel to Gilliam Creek in an oak-shaded woodland, crossing the creek nine times (which all require wading). The route climbs out of the creek drainage along an old dirt road to the East Austin Creek Trail, a 4.7-mile unpaved service road. The road drops from 1,200 feet to 300 feet, winding down the remote canyon through a mix of forested groves, grassy meadows, and spectacular vistas of the rugged coastal mountains and the Russian River Valley. En route, the hiking and equestrian trail passes Gilliam Creek Trail Camp (at the confluence of Gilliam Creek and East Austin Creek) and the Tom King Trail Camp (on the banks of Thompson Creek). Biking is allowed on the East Austin Creek Trail.

NOTE: During the winter, the lower Gilliam Creek Trail can be impassable due to high water. Check with the rangers at the visitor center before heading out.

To the trailhead

17020 ARMSTRONG WOODS RD · GUERNEVILLE   38.555978, -123.011888

From downtown Guerneville on Main Street (Highway 116), drive 2.3 miles north on Armstrong Woods Road to the visitor center on the right, just before the state park entrance station. Continue 2.5 miles past the entrance station, staying to the right, to the Gilliam Creek Trailhead parking area. The last 1.7 miles winds up a narrow, paved mountain road on a 12% grade. An entrance fee is required.

The hike

From the trailhead map, head downhill on the Gilliam Creek Trail. Wind down the mountain slope, crossing two forks of Schoolhouse Creek by its headwaters. Cross Gilliam Ridge, a rolling grassy ridge dotted with oaks, then traverse the north slope of the canyon. Walk over a few seasonal tributaries to the canyon floor and Schoolhouse Creek at just under a mile. Rock-hop over the creek, and follow the southwest wall of the canyon. Stroll through the lush, wet forest with fern-covered hills. Thick moss covers the rocks and tree trunks. Rock-hop over Schoolhouse Creek two consecutive times to a posted junction at 2 miles. The trail to the right (across Schoolhouse Creek) joins to the East Austin Creek Trail—the return route (Hike 47).

Continue straight along the south edge of Schoolhouse Creek, heading west. Schoolhouse Creek soon converges with Gilliam Creek. Continue west along Gilliam Creek in a lush forest with thick, mossy tree trunks and lichen-covered boulders. The East Austin Creek Trail—the return route—can be seen on the north side of the creek. Cross Gilliam Creek at a major tributary stream. This is the first of nine consecutive creek crossings that all require wading. After the ninth soaking, head up the north slope and traverse the canyon wall across minor dips and rises. At 3.8 miles, return to the creek at Gilliam Creek Trail Camp, a rustic camp at the confluence with East Austin Creek. Wade across larger East Austin Creek wherever the best passage can be found. Walk up the slope 100 yards to an old dirt road being reclaimed by nature.

Veer right above East Austin Creek and head upstream. Cross a side stream and climb through a meadow to a posted junction at 4 miles. The Fox Mountain Trail bears left. Continue straight, weaving through the forest on the dirt road while overlooking East Austin Creek. At 5.3 miles, wade across the creek for the last time to a posted junction with the East Austin Creek Trail. (For a detour, the left fork leads 0.7 miles to Manning Flat Trail Camp, perched on the west bank of the creek.)

Bear right and head downstream along the north side of East Austin Creek. Pass redwoods and cross the Thompson Creek bridge. Climb to a junction with the trail to Tom King Trail Camp on the left. Stay straight, with a view of Devil's Backbone to the south, Thompson Ridge to the north, and Morrison Ridge to the east. Steadily climb, skirting the north edge of Knoll 702. Weave back down on four sweeping bends to Gilliam Creek. Cross a bridge over Gilliam Creek to a junction with the Gilliam Creek Trail at 7 miles, completing the west end of the loop.

Head to the left on the Gilliam Creek Trail, staying on the southeast side of the creek. Continue uphill along the creek, then curve away from the creek towards the east. Steadily climb the well-named Panorama Grade, gaining a thousand feet over 1.5 miles. Steadily climb, with barely a break, to the trail gate by the park road, where the climb mercifully ends. The left fork leads to Bullfrog Pond Campground. Bear right and follow the paved road 0.6 miles back to the trailhead. ∎

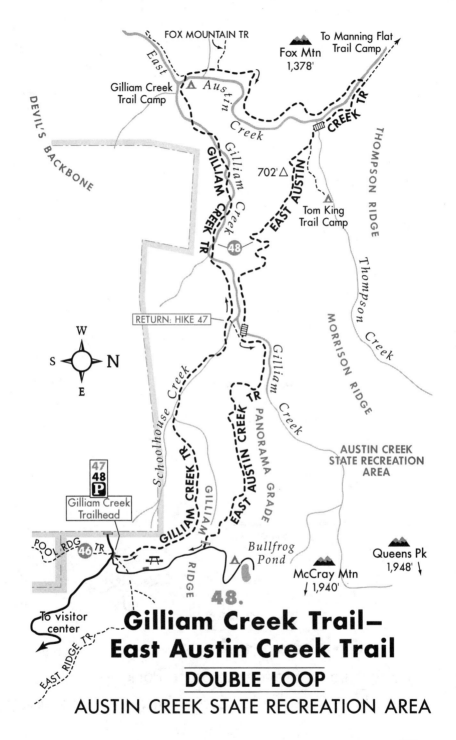

FOX MOUNTAIN TR

To Manning Flat
Trail Camp

Fox Mtn
1,378'

East

Gilliam Creek
Trail Camp

Austin

Creek

DEVIL'S BACKBONE

CREEK TR

THOMPSON RIDGE

702'

Gilliam Creek

GILLIAM CREEK TR

EAST AUSTIN

Tom King
Trail Camp

Thompson Creek

48

RETURN: HIKE 47

MORRISON RIDGE

W

N

S

E

Schoolhouse Creek

Gilliam Creek

EAST AUSTIN CREEK TR

PANORAMA GRADE

AUSTIN CREEK
STATE RECREATION
AREA

47
48
P

Gilliam Creek
Trailhead

GILLIAM CREEK TR

GILLIAM RIDGE

Bullfrog
Pond

McCray Mtn
1,940'

Queens Pk
1,948'

POOL RDG TR
46

To visitor
center

EAST RIDGE TR

48.
Gilliam Creek Trail—
East Austin Creek Trail
DOUBLE LOOP
AUSTIN CREEK STATE RECREATION AREA

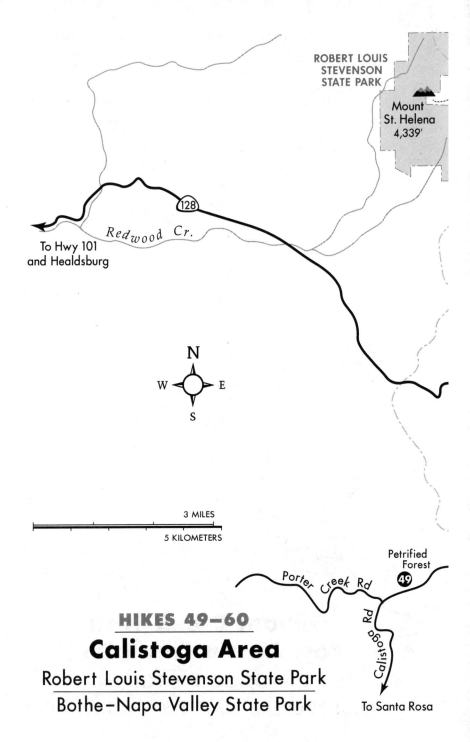

ROBERT LOUIS
STEVENSON
STATE PARK

Mount
St. Helena
4,339'

128

Redwood Cr.

To Hwy 101
and Healdsburg

N
W E
S

3 MILES

5 KILOMETERS

Petrified
Forest
49

Porter Creek Rd

Calistoga Rd

HIKES 49–60
Calistoga Area
Robert Louis Stevenson State Park
Bothe–Napa Valley State Park

To Santa Rosa

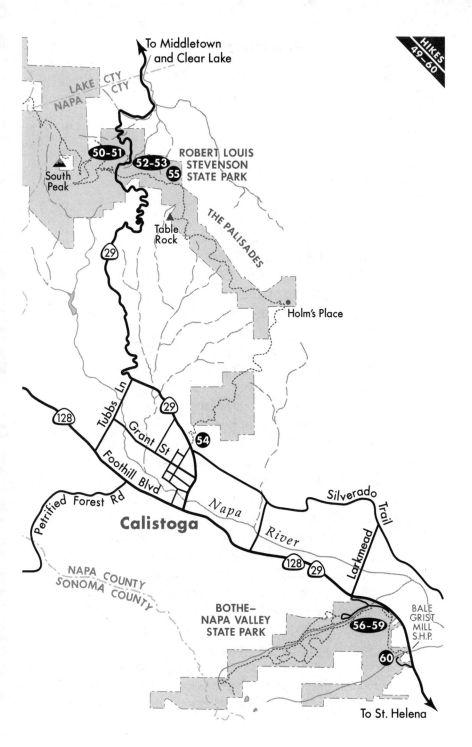

To Middletown
and Clear Lake

LAKE CTY
NAPA CTY

50-51

South
Peak

52-53
55

ROBERT LOUIS
STEVENSON
STATE PARK

THE PALISADES

Table
Rock

29

Holm's Place

Tubbs Ln

128

Grant St

29

54

Foothill Blvd

Petrified Forest Rd

Calistoga

Napa

River

Silverado Trail

Larkmead

128 29

NAPA COUNTY
SONOMA COUNTY

BOTHE–
NAPA VALLEY
STATE PARK

BALE
GRIST
MILL
S.H.P.

56-59

60

To St. Helena

49. Petrified Forest

Open Daily: Winter 9—5 · Summer 9—7 · (707) 942-6667

Hiking distance: 0.5-mile loop plus 0.5-mile spur trail
Hiking time: 40 minutes
Configuration: loop
Elevation gain: 100 feet
Difficulty: easy
Exposure: mostly forested
Dogs: allowed
Maps: U.S.G.S. Mark West Springs
　　　　The Petrified Forest trail map

The Petrified Forest is a massive forest of stone trees in the hills of eastern Sonoma County near Calistoga. Sitting at an elevation of 1,000 feet, the fossilized redwood forest resulted from volcanic ash blanketing the area 3.4 million years ago. The buried trees were saturated with water containing silica. The silica seeped into the decomposing wood fibers, slowly replacing the organic material cell by cell. It eventually led to their petrifaction, resulting in one of the best Pliocene fossil forests in the world. The trees all point in a southwest direction, but researchers cannot agree on the origin of the magma blast.

In the 1870s, Charlie Evans, a friend of Jack London and Robert Louis Stevenson, discovered the geological wonder while tending his cows. He became known as Petrified Charlie. Uplift, erosion, and excavation have exposed the giant petrified redwoods, creating the natural museum we see today. Within the spectacular fossils are deposits of minerals, crystal, obsidian, wood opal, and silica. Out of the rock trees grow oaks, Douglas firs, red-bark manzanitas, bay laurels, toyons, and madrones.

A half-mile trail loops around the natural displays of the major tree exposures. Interpretive signs describe the process of how living trees evolve into stone. On weekend mornings, a guided Meadow Walk is available. This extended hike leads to an area closed to the public. It departs from The Giant and heads northwest through a locked gate into the upper meadow. The trail visits an overlook of Mount Saint Helena and the 100-foot-high

Ash Fall. The ash fall is rich with volcanic material, including tuff, iron, obsidian, pumice, and petrified wood chunks. The walk can extend to a fern and redwood forest by a tributary of Mark West Springs. Call for tour times.

The privately owned park, declared a historical landmark in 1978, includes a museum, gift shop, and picnic areas. Leashed dogs are allowed on the trails.

To the trailhead

4100 PETRIFIED FOREST RD · CALISTOGA   38.554978, -122.638709

From Highway 12 and Calistoga Road at the north end of Sonoma Valley, drive 11.5 miles north on Calistoga Road to the signed Petrified Forest entrance on the left. (At 7 miles, the road veers right and becomes Petrified Forest Road.)

The hike

Walk through the gift shop and to the trailhead by the massive trunk of an 850-year-old coastal live oak that blew over in 2004. Veer left onto the trail, passing the 43-foot-long Pit Tree on the left, the only petrified pine in the park. Up ahead is Petrified Woodpile, a pile of broken fragments covered with moss and embedded with lichen. Stroll through the mixed evergreen forest among oak, pine, fir, and madrone. At the top of the trail, across from Petrified Charlie's Meadow, are viewing platforms that showcase a group of well-preserved petrified redwoods. Among these are The Giant, a 60-foot-long tree with deeply ribbed bark, and the Queen, with an 8-foot diameter and a giant root ball. The Queen has a live oak growing through it. Pass an area where new excavation has exposed two more fossilized trees. Walk through the 105-foot-long Monarch (Tunnel Tree) on the left, the largest known intact petrified tree in the world. Next is the Rock of Ages Tree, a double tree that is also known as Twin Trees. The last major tree on the loop is the Robert Louis Stevenson Tree, mentioned by the author in the book *The Silverado Squatters*. Descend the slope and complete the loop back at the gift shop.

The Meadow Walk meets at The Giant on weekend mornings.

With a guide, walk through the locked gate. Weave through man-zanita and madrone groves, oak-lined meadows, and past out-croppings from the ancient lava flows to a knoll. From the knoll is a great view of Mount Saint Helena. If your guide is willing, con-tinue past the knoll to an ash flow with lava, pumice, obsidian, and bits of petrified wood. Two hundred yards ahead, on the backside of the hill, are undisturbed petrified trees still in place. A nature trail continues a half mile north into the shaded forest to the fern-covered canyon floor and a stand of redwood trees by a seasonal drainage of Mark West Springs. ■

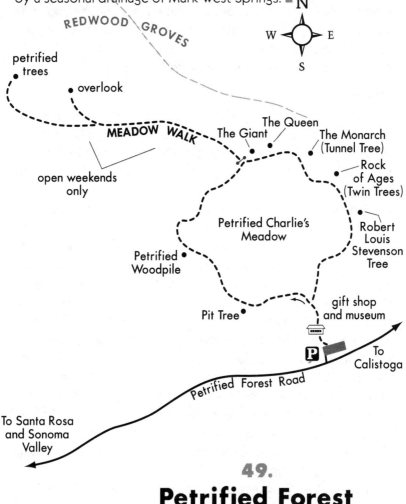

Petrified Forest

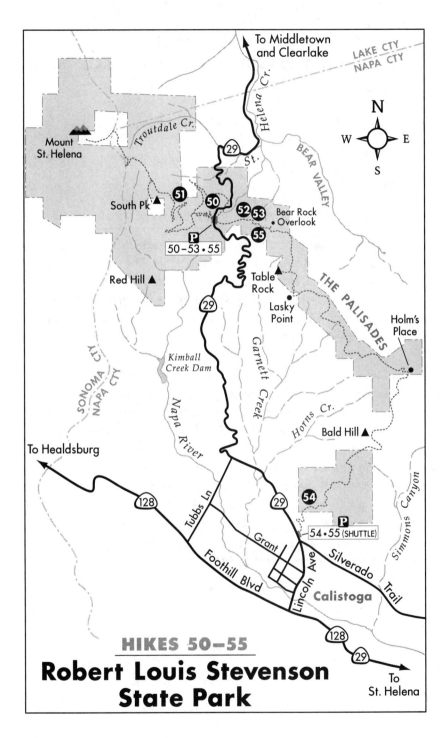

HIKES 50–55

Robert Louis Stevenson State Park

To Middletown and Clearlake

LAKE CTY
NAPA CTY

Troutdale Cr.

St. Helena Cr.

Mount St. Helena

BEAR VALLEY

29

N
W E
S

South Pk

51

50

52 53

Bear Rock Overlook

55

P
50-53 • 55

Red Hill

Table Rock

THE PALISADES

Lasky Point

Holm's Place

29

Kimball Creek Dam

Garnett Creek

SONOMA CTY
NAPA CTY

Napa River

Horns Cr.

Bald Hill

Simmons Canyon

To Healdsburg

128

Tubbs Ln

29

54

P
54 • 55 (SHUTTLE)

Grant

Silverado Trail

Foothill Blvd

Lincoln Ave

Calistoga

128

29

To St. Helena

50. Stevenson Memorial Trail
ROBERT LOUIS STEVENSON STATE PARK

Hiking distance: 1.4 miles round trip or 2.2-mile loop
Hiking time: 1 hour
Configuration: out-and-back (to memorial) or loop
Elevation gain: 500 feet
Difficulty: easy to moderate
Exposure: mostly forested
Dogs: not allowed
Maps: U.S.G.S. Detert Reservoir
　　　　 Bothe-Napa Valley and Robert Louis Stevenson State Parks map

Robert Louis Stevenson State Park encompasses 5,272 acres in the Mayacamas Mountains above Calistoga. The immense park straddles Sonoma, Napa, and Lake Counties. The centerpiece of the park is 4,339-foot Mount Saint Helena, the highest peak in Sonoma County. The state park is undeveloped. Hiking and biking are the primary activities.

This hike makes a loop along the lower portion of the trail to the Stevenson Memorial. In the summer of 1880, Robert Louis Stevenson, author of *Treasure Island* and *Kidnapped*, honeymooned for several months in an abandoned, two-story bunkhouse near the Silverado Mine. Stevenson wrote about his time here in his book *Silverado Squatters*. A memorial marker identifies the site of the abandoned mine building. The memorial, unveiled in 1911, has a quartz base and an open, book-shaped Scotch granite cap inscribed with a Stevenson poem. The short loop hike zigzags up the hillside under the shade of Douglas fir, live oak, madrone, tanbark oak, and manzanita. Hike 51 continues from the loop to the summit of Mount Saint Helena.

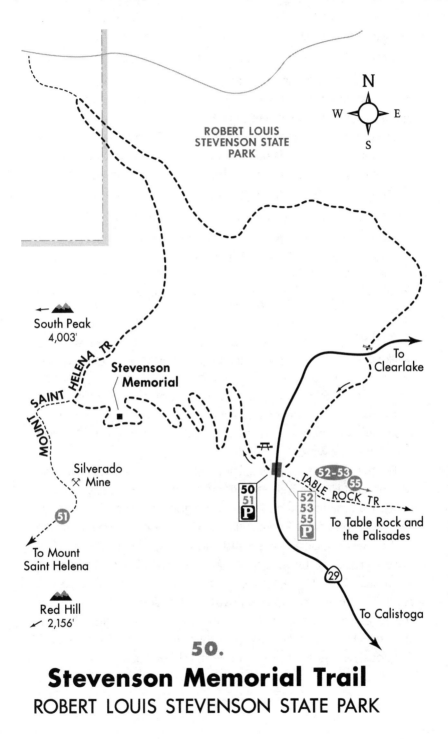

ROBERT LOUIS
STEVENSON STATE
PARK

N
W E
S

South Peak
4,003'

SAINT HELENA TR

Stevenson
Memorial

Silverado
Mine

To Clearlake

52-53
55

TABLE ROCK TR

50
51
P

52
53
55
P

To Table Rock and
the Palisades

51

To Mount
Saint Helena

Red Hill
2,156'

29

To Calistoga

50.
Stevenson Memorial Trail
ROBERT LOUIS STEVENSON STATE PARK

To the trailhead

4625 LAKE COUNTY HWY · CALISTOGA   38.652694, -122.599820

Robert Louis Stevenson State Park is located in Napa Valley, northeast of Calistoga on Highway 29. Three main routes access Napa Valley from Sonoma County.

From the north, access is via Highway 128 out of Geyserville and Healdsburg. From Santa Rosa, access is via Calistoga Road off of Highway 12 (15 miles). From the south, access is via Highway 12, south of the town of Sonoma.

CALISTOGA. From Highway 29 and Lincoln Avenue in Calistoga, drive 8.5 miles northeast on Lincoln Avenue (Highway 29), through town and up the winding mountain road.

Park in the parking area on the left at the road's summit. Additional parking is in a larger parking area directly across the road.

The hike

Walk up the steps to a flat, grassy picnic area and posted trailhead. Head up the forested hillside on the rock-embedded path. Six switchbacks zigzag up the forested mountain. In a shady flat at 0.7 miles is the Stevenson Memorial, a stone monument by a mossy rock formation. This is the turn-around point for a 1.4-mile out-and-back walk.

For the 2.2-mile loop hike, climb two more switchbacks to the Mount Saint Helena Trail—a T-junction with a service road at 0.85 miles. The trail to Mount Saint Helena goes left and climbs 1,600 feet over the next 4.5 miles (Hike 51) For this hike, go to the right and continue clockwise around the loop, steadily descending northward. Cross under power lines at a right U-bend and head southeast. Near Highway 29, pass through a metal gate to the road. Carefully cross the highway and descend 40 yards into the forest to a footpath. Bear right and climb 0.3 miles through the forest to the highway, directly across from the trailhead. Cautiously cross the road, completing the loop. ■

51. Mount Saint Helena Trail
ROBERT LOUIS STEVENSON STATE PARK

Hiking distance: 10.6 miles round trip
Hiking time: 5—6 hours
Configuration: out-and-back
Elevation gain: 2,100 feet
Difficulty: very strenuous
Exposure: mostly exposed with forested pockets
Dogs: not allowed
Maps: U.S.G.S. Detert Reservoir and Mount Saint Helena
      Bothe-Napa Valley and Robert Louis Stevenson State Parks map

Mount Saint Helena is the tallest peak in Sonoma County at 4,339 feet. It is located in Robert Louis Stevenson State Park north of Calistoga, at the intersection of Sonoma, Napa, and Lake Counties. A 5.3-mile trail winds through the undeveloped park to the volcanic mountain's North Peak. The route utilizes a long and sinuous fire road on a south-facing slope, exposed to sun and wind. The popular hiking and biking route steadily climbs but is never steep. The long distance and substantial elevation gain, however, make it a strenuous hike. Throughout the hike, the views are spectacular. From the summit are 360-degree vistas that extend across Napa Valley to Mount Tamalpais, to San Francisco and the twin peaks of Mount Diablo in the south, Mount Lassen and Snow Mountain in the north, the Vaca Mountains in the east, and the coastal ranges and the ocean in the west.

To the trailhead

4625 Lake County Hwy · Calistoga   38.652694, -122.599820

Robert Louis Stevenson State Park is located in Napa Valley, northeast of Calistoga on Highway 29. Three main routes access Napa Valley from Sonoma County.

From the north, access is via Highway 128 out of Geyserville and Healdsburg. From Santa Rosa, access is via Calistoga Road off of Highway 12 (15 miles). From the south, access is via Highway 12, south of the town of Sonoma.

Calistoga. From Highway 29 and Lincoln Avenue in Calistoga, drive 8.5 miles northeast on Lincoln Avenue (Highway 29), through town and up the winding mountain road.

Park in the parking area on the left at the road's summit. Additional parking is in a larger parking area directly across the road.

The hike

Walk up the steps to a flat, grassy picnic area and posted trailhead. Head up the forested hillside on the rock-embedded path. Six switchbacks zigzag up the forested mountain. In a shady flat at 0.7 miles is the Stevenson Memorial, a stone monument by a mossy rock formation. Climb two more switchbacks to the Mount Saint Helena Trail—a T-junction with a service road at 0.85 miles. The right fork loops down the hillside back to Highway 29 (Hike 50).

Go to the left on the Mount Saint Helena Trail. The trail/fire road climbs 1,600 feet over the next 4.5 miles. As the trail climbs up the hillside, the views open to Napa Valley and the surrounding mountains. Pass above Silverado Mine on the left, which is no longer visible. At 1.6 miles, on a horseshoe right bend, is weather-chiseled Bubble Rock, a pock-marked igneous formation that is popular with rock climbers. Continue up the well-graded road cut into the chaparral-covered slope, with views across Napa County and Sonoma County. The exposed terrain is dotted with manzanita, small oaks, knobcone pines, bay laurel, and greasewood. Make a sweeping left bend at 2.25 miles, passing fractured rock columns. Cross under power lines and continue a half mile to a road junction on a saddle at 3.6 miles. The left branch leads 0.5 miles to 4,003-foot South Peak, the lower summit.

Continue north—straight ahead—between North and South Peaks, with a view of Lake Berryessa on the right. Continue to a ridge at 4.5 miles. Veer left, entering Sonoma County, and head west toward the peak. Pass through groves of sugar pines and Douglas firs, then leave the forest for the final ascent. At the summit, pass a group of communication structures to the rocky north face above Rattlesnake and Bradford canyons. After resting and savoring the views, return along the same route. ∎

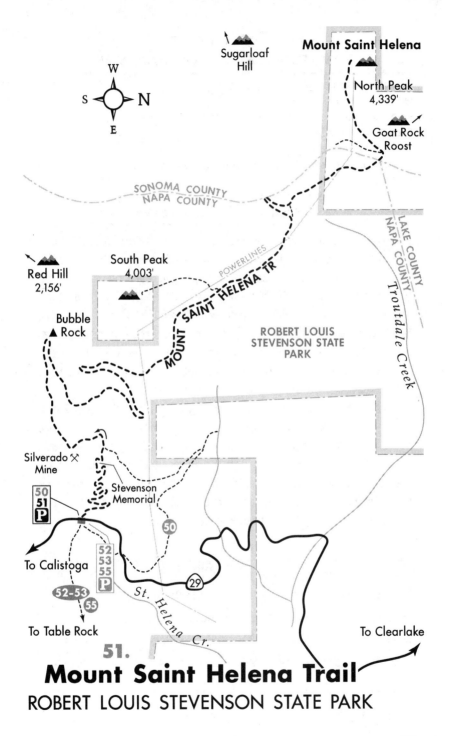

W N S E

Sugarloaf Hill

Mount Saint Helena

North Peak 4,339'

Goat Rock Roost

SONOMA COUNTY
NAPA COUNTY

LAKE COUNTY
NAPA COUNTY

Troutdale Creek

Red Hill 2,156'

South Peak 4,003'

POWERLINES

MOUNT SAINT HELENA TR

Bubble Rock

ROBERT LOUIS
STEVENSON STATE
PARK

Silverado Mine

50
51
P

Stevenson Memorial

50

To Calistoga

52
53
55
P

52-53 55

St. Helena Cr.

29

To Table Rock

To Clearlake

51.
Mount Saint Helena Trail
ROBERT LOUIS STEVENSON STATE PARK

52. Table Rock
ROBERT LOUIS STEVENSON STATE PARK

Hiking distance: 4.4 miles round trip
Hiking time: 2 hours
Configuration: out-and-back
Elevation gain: 500 feet
Difficulty: moderate
Exposure: exposed slopes with forested pockets
Dogs: not allowed
Maps: U.S.G.S. Detert Reservoir
Bothe-Napa Valley/Robert Louis Stevenson State Parks

The western parklands of Robert Louis Stevenson State Park envelop Mount Saint Helena to the west of Highway 29 (Hike 50 and 51). The next four hikes, however, explore a long rocky route on the other side of the highway, just east of the Sonoma-Napa county line. The trail along these volcanic cliffs passes through a fascinating array of boulders and rocky outcroppings. The hikes included here are three segments of the entire trail, from the Table Rock trailhead to the Historic Oat Hill Mine Road. Hike 55 is a one-way shuttle of the entire 10.6-mile trail.

This hike starts at the main parking area on Highway 29 and leads to Table Rock, following the first segment of the trail. The route utilizes an abandoned utility road and a single-tread path. The trail leads 2.2 miles through the forest to spectacular overlooks, crossing a ridge to prominent Table Rock. The massive formation sits at the head of Garnett Canyon at an elevation of 2,462 feet. It is the largest rock mass in the area.

	START	END	ONE-WAY
Hike 52	Upper Highway 29	Table Rock	2.2 mi.
Hike 53	Upper Highway 29	Holm's Place	6 mi.
Hike 54	Lower Highway 29	Holm's Place	4.5 mi.
Hike 55	Upper Highway 29	Lower Highway 29	10.6 mi. (shuttle)

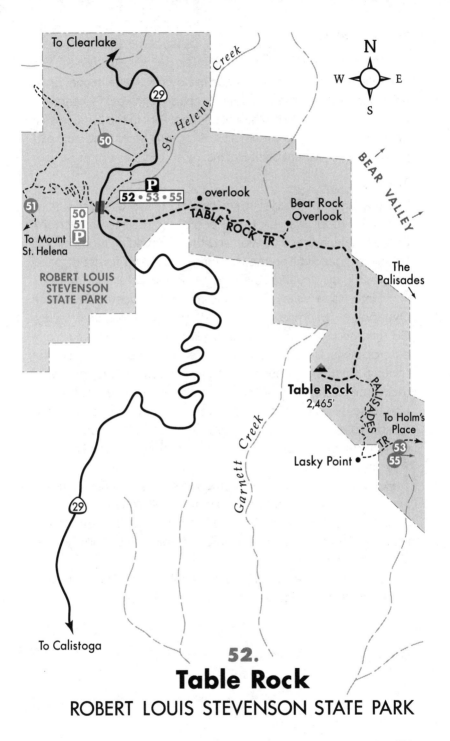

To Clearlake

N
W · E
S

St. Helena Creek

29

50

BEAR VALLEY

P
52 · 53 · 55

overlook

51

50
51
P

TABLE ROCK TR

Bear Rock
Overlook

To Mount
St. Helena

The
Palisades

ROBERT LOUIS
STEVENSON
STATE PARK

Table Rock
2,465'

PALISADES

To Holm's
Place

Garnett Creek

Lasky Point

PALISADES TR

53
55

29

To Calistoga

52.
Table Rock
ROBERT LOUIS STEVENSON STATE PARK

To the trailhead

4625 LAKE COUNTY HWY · CALISTOGA   38.652694, -122.599820

From Highway 29/Lincoln Avenue in downtown Calistoga, drive 8.5 miles northeast on Lincoln Avenue (Highway 29) through town and up the winding mountain road. Park in the parking area on the right at the road's summit. It is directly across the trailhead parking lot for Mount Saint Helena.

The hike

Pass the Table Rock Trail sign, and head up the forested hillside to an old dirt road. Bear left to the end of the road to an overlook of Saint Helena Creek Canyon and the surrounding mountains at 0.4 miles. Veer right on the trail through a mixed forest of oaks, Douglas fir, maple, and bay laurel while the vistas extend eastward into Napa Valley. Steadily climb to the posted Bear Rock Overlook at one mile, with an eastward view into Bear Valley. Go right and descend a hundred yards, passing gorgeous rock outcroppings. Descend on the loose gravel path, using careful footing. Continue through a flat in a garden of lava rock on a rock-lined path. The trail heads downhill on another steep section to seasonal Garnett Creek. Cross the creek and ascend the hillside to another natural display of volcanic rock sculptures. Climb through the rocks to a signed junction with the Palisades Trail on the left at 2.1 miles.

Head to the right, staying on the Table Rock Trail for 0.2 miles. Scramble up the loosely defined path to the edge of the volcanic cliffs atop Table Rock. After taking in the views, return to the Palisades Trail junction, the turn-around point for this hike. Return along the same trail.

Hike 53 continues southeast on the Palisades Trail to Holm's Place, four miles ahead. ■

53. Table Rock Trail—Palisades Trail

HOLM'S PLACE FROM THE NORTH

ROBERT LOUIS STEVENSON STATE PARK

Hiking distance: 12 miles round trip
Hiking time: 7 hours
Configuration: out-and-back
Elevation gain: 700 feet
Difficulty: strenuous
Exposure: exposed slopes with forested pockets
Dogs: not allowed
Maps: U.S.G.S. Detert Reservoir and Calistoga
      Bothe-Napa Valley/Robert Louis Stevenson State Parks

The rugged Palisades are precipitous volcanic cliffs that stretch southeast from Mount Saint Helena through Robert Louis Stevenson State Park. The Palisades property was acquired in 1993, raising the park's acreage to 5,272 acres.

The Palisades Trail is among the best hikes in the area. It links the Table Rock Trail (Hike 52) with the Historic Oat Hill Mine Road (Hike 54). This hike starts from the main parking area on Highway 29 and heads southward on the Table Rock trail. The route continues on the Palisades Trail after Table Rock, then leads another four miles to Karl Holm's homestead. The homestead sits among old foundations, remnants of two stone houses, and a small apple orchard. En route to Holm's Place, the trail skirts the base of the dramatic volcanic cliffs, passing awesome rocky outcroppings, overlooks, and cliffs on the sun-exposed slope. Peregrine falcons are frequently spotted from the trail. Bring an ample supply of drinking water for this long, and often hot, hike.

To the trailhead

4625 LAKE COUNTY HWY · CALISTOGA   38.652694, -122.599820

From Highway 29/Lincoln Avenue in downtown Calistoga, drive 8.5 miles northeast on Lincoln Avenue (Highway 29) through town and up the winding mountain road. Park in the parking area on the right at the road's summit. It is directly across the trailhead parking lot for Mount Saint Helena.

The hike

Pass the Table Rock Trail sign, and head up the forested hillside to an old dirt road. Bear left to the end of the road to an overlook of Saint Helena Creek Canyon and the surrounding mountains at 0.4 miles. Veer right on the trail through a mixed forest of oaks, Douglas fir, maple, and bay laurel while the vistas extend eastward into Napa Valley. Steadily climb to the posted Bear Rock Overlook at one mile, with an eastward view into Bear Valley. Go right and descend a hundred yards, passing gorgeous rock outcroppings. Descend on the loose gravel path, using careful footing. Continue through a flat in a garden of lava rock on a rock-lined path. The trail heads downhill on another steep section to seasonal Garnett Creek. Cross the creek and ascend the hillside to another natural display of volcanic rock sculptures. Climb through the rocks to a signed junction with the Palisades Trail on the left at 2.1 miles.

To the right is a short detour to Table Rock. To take the detour, scramble 0.2 miles up the loosely defined path to the edge of the volcanic cliffs atop Table Rock. After taking in the views, return back to the Palisades Trail junction.

Continue uphill (southeast) on the Palisades Trail, with views of Table Rock and Mount Saint Helena in the direction just hiked. Emerge on the west-facing slope overlooking Napa Valley, the Mayacamas Mountains, and the Sonoma County coastal range. Zigzag down the steep hillside with the aid of rock steps. Temporarily leave the state park, entering the Lasky Property on a quarter-mile trail easement. The trail leads to 2,045-foot Lasky Point at 2.7 miles, where there is a bird's-eye view of Calistoga. A plaque in the volcanic rock thanks Moses Lasky, a mountain climber and owner of the land, for sharing his land with hikers. Continue traversing the mountain, and reenter Robert Louis Stevenson State Park on the southwest face of the mountain. Follow the contours of the mountain, with awesome views of the Palisades, Garnett Canyon, and Napa Valley. Alternate between exposed grassy chaparral and stream-fed forested pockets with moss-covered boulders. At 4.6 miles, pass close to the towering lava formations and a few trickling streams. Walk under an overhanging rock grotto to a view of the Historic Oat Hill Mine Road (Hike 54), traversing the east-west cliffs. Descend on two switchbacks amid mossy boulders to the remains of the Holm's homestead in a shaded oak and bay laurel forest at 6 miles. This is the turn-around point. Return along the same path. ■

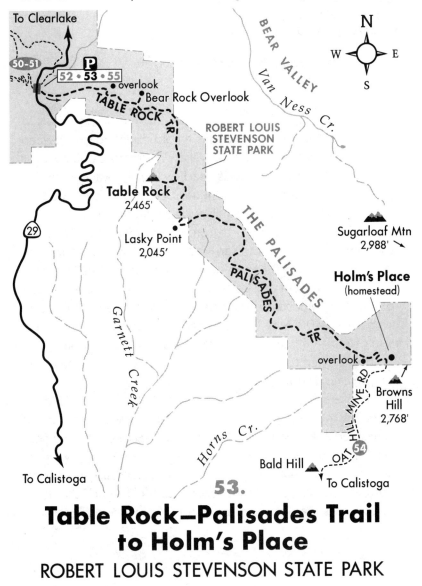

53.
Table Rock–Palisades Trail to Holm's Place
ROBERT LOUIS STEVENSON STATE PARK

54. Historic Oat Hill Mine Road

HOLM'S PLACE FROM THE SOUTH

ROBERT LOUIS STEVENSON STATE PARK

Hiking distance: 9 miles round trip
Hiking time: 5 hours
Configuration: out and back
Elevation gain: 1,900 feet
Difficulty: very strenuous
Exposure: exposed slopes with forested pockets
Dogs: not allowed
Maps: U.S.G.S. Calistoga
      Bothe-Napa Valley/Robert Louis Stevenson State Parks

The Historic Oat Hill Mine Road is an old mining road between the town of Calistoga and Pope Valley. The remote county-built road, completed in 1893, was used by freight wagons hauling quicksilver from the mines to the railroad in Calistoga. Grooves from the wagon wheels are still visible in the rockbed.

This hiking-biking trail starts from Highway 29 in Calistoga and leads northward to the old Karl Holm homestead in a shaded oak and bay laurel forest. At the 160-acre homestead are remnants of two stone houses and a small apple orchard. The rocky, rutted road to the homesteaad (closed to vehicles in 1979) rigorously climbs from 400 feet to 2,300 feet. The scenic, backcountry road offers great views of the Palisades and upper Napa Valley. The trail is open to bicyclists to Holm's Place (but not beyond). Bring an ample supply of drinking water.

This hike and the previous hike (Hike 53) both lead to Holm's Place. This hike starts from the south and heads north to the homestead. Hike 53 starts in the north and leads south. The next hike (Hike 55) is a 10.6-mile one-way shuttle hike of the entire trail. The shuttle hike begins at the north trailhead and travels south, descending along three connected trails—the Table Rock Trail, the Palisades Trail, and the Historic Oat Hill Mine Road.

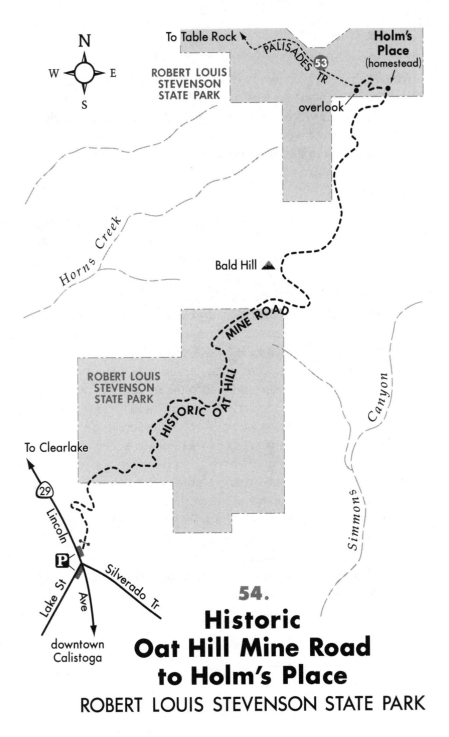

N
W E
S

To Table Rock

PALISADES TR

53

Holm's Place (homestead)

ROBERT LOUIS STEVENSON STATE PARK

overlook

Horns Creek

Bald Hill

MINE ROAD

Canyon

ROBERT LOUIS STEVENSON STATE PARK

HISTORIC OAT HILL

To Clearlake

29

Lincoln

Simmons

P

Lake St

Ave

Silverado Tr

downtown Calistoga

54.
Historic Oat Hill Mine Road to Holm's Place
ROBERT LOUIS STEVENSON STATE PARK

To the trailhead

2109 LAKE COUNTY HWY · CITY   38.589586, -122.577704

From Highway 29/Lincoln Avenue in downtown Calistoga, drive one mile northeast on Lincoln Avenue (Highway 29) through town to Silverado Trail. Drive through the intersection and park in the spaces on the right at the trailhead. If the few parking spaces are taken, park in the large dirt area on the diagonal side of the intersection by Lake Street.

The hike

Walk past the trail sign and metal gate. Gently climb the slope, walking parallel to Highway 29. Curve away from the highway under a canopy of oaks, pines, and toyon to vistas of vineyards and the town of Calistoga. Continue climbing, curving around the contours of the hill, as the vistas of Napa Valley constantly change. Steadily climb through oak groves, stands of evergreens, and manzanita that repose a thousand feet above Simmons Canyon. Loop around Bald Hill on a brush-lined slope, where old wagon wheel ruts were once carved into the rocky road. Cross a ridge and continue uphill along the towering rock wall on the right. The rock-embedded path heads through beautiful lava formations and sweeping views of the Palisades. The trail leads 4.5 miles to the old homestead of Karl Holm in a shady oak and bay laurel forest. At the 160-acre homestead are the remnants of two stone houses, a barn, and a small apple orchard.

It is worth extending the hike a short distance to an overlook of the Historic Oat Hill Mine Road. Take the Palisades Trail and climb two switchbacks amid mossy boulders to the overlook. Return along the same route.

The Palisades Trail continues 3.3 miles to Lasky Point, 3.9 miles to Table Rock, and 6 miles to the Table Rock Trailhead. ■

55. Table Rock Trail—Palisades Trail— Historic Oat Hill Mine Road

— one-way shuttle hike —

ROBERT LOUIS STEVENSON STATE PARK

Hiking distance: 10.6-mile one-way shuttle
Hiking time: 6 hours
Configuration: one-way shuttle
Elevation gain: 700 feet
Elevation loss: 1,900 feet
Difficulty: strenuous
Exposure: mostly exposed with some forested pockets
Dogs: not allowed
Maps: U.S.G.S. Detert Reservoir and Calistoga
　　　　Bothe-Napa Valley/Robert Louis Stevenson State Parks

This one-way shuttle hike combines the previous three trails into one hike—the Table Rock Trail, the Palisades Trail, and the Historic Oat Hill Mine Road. The hike follows a fantastic route along volcanic cliffs, known as the Palisades, on the east side of Robert Louis Stevenson State Park. The trail in considered to be one of the best in the area. The hike begins at the park's main parking area at the summit of Highway 29 and travels 10.6 miles southward to Calistoga, less than a half mile from downtown. Highlights of the trail include gardens of lava rock, volcanic cliffs, the Bear Rock Overlook, Garnett Creek, Table Rock, Lasky Point, a rocky grotto, and the old Holm's Place homestead. Table Rock sits at the head of Garnet Canyon at an elevation of 2,462 feet. There are great views that span from the Sonoma coastal ranges to Napa Valley. After Holm's Place, the trail follows an old mine road from 1893. Wagon wheel ruts are still visible in the rockbed.

Although the trail begins at the high end of the route and loses elevation, the hike is still quite strenuous. The trail leads though a dry, sun-exposed landscape and requires ample drinking water.

To the trailhead

4625 Lake County Hwy · Calistoga　　　38.652694, -122.599820

From Highway 29/Lincoln Avenue in downtown Calistoga, drive

8.5 miles northeast on Lincoln Avenue (Highway 29) through town and up the winding mountain road. Park in the parking area on the right at the road's summit. It is directly across from the trailhead parking lot to Mount Saint Helena.

Shuttle car

2109 LAKE COUNTY HWY · CITY   38.589586, -122.577704

Leave the shuttle car at the intersection of Lincoln Avenue (Highway 29) and Silverado Trail, located a half mile north of downtown Calistoga.

From Highway 29/Lincoln Avenue in downtown Calistoga, drive one mile northeast on Lincoln Avenue (Highway 29) through town to Silverado Trail. Drive through the intersection and park in the spaces on the right at the trailhead. If the few parking spaces are taken, park in the large dirt area on the diagonal side of the intersection by Lake Street.

The hike

Walk past the Table Rock Trail sign, and head up the forested hillside to an old dirt road. Bear left to the end of the road to an overlook of Saint Helena Creek Canyon and the surrounding mountains at 0.4 miles. Veer right on the trail through a mixed forest of oaks, Douglas fir, maple, and bay laurel while the vistas extend into Napa Valley. Steadily climb to the posted Bear Rock Overlook at one mile, with an eastward view into Bear Valley. Go right and descend a hundred yards, passing gorgeous rock outcroppings. Descend on the loose gravel path, using careful footing. Continue through a flat in a garden of lava rock on a rock-lined path. The trail heads downhill on another steep section to seasonal Garnett Creek. Cross the creek and ascend the hillside to another natural display of volcanic rock sculptures. Climb through the rocks to a signed junction with the Palisades Trail on the left at 2.1 miles.

To the right is a short detour to Table Rock. To take the detour, scramble 0.2 miles up the loosely defined path to the edge of the volcanic cliffs atop Table Rock. After enjoying the views, return back to the Palisades Trail junction.

Continue uphill (southeast) on the Palisades Trail, with views of Table Rock and Mount Saint Helena in the direction just hiked. Emerge on the west-facing slope overlooking Napa Valley, the Mayacamas Mountains, and the Sonoma County coastal range. Zigzag down the steep hillside with the aid of rock steps. Temporarily leave the state park, entering the Lasky Property on a quarter-mile trail easement. The trail leads to 2,045-foot Lasky Point at 2.7 miles, where there is a bird's-eye view of Calistoga. A plaque in the volcanic rock thanks Moses Lasky, a mountain climber and owner of the land, for sharing his land with hikers. Continue traversing the mountain, and reenter Robert Louis Stevenson State Park on the southwest face of the mountain. Follow the contours of the mountain, with awesome views of the Palisades, Garnett Canyon, and Napa Valley. Alternate between exposed grassy chaparral and stream-fed forested pockets with moss-covered boulders. At 4.6 miles, pass close to the towering lava formations and a few trickling streams. Walk under an overhanging rock grotto to a view of the Historic Oat Hill Mine Road that can be seen traversing the east-west cliffs. Descend on two switchbacks amid mossy boulders to the remains of the Holm's homestead in a shaded oak and bay laurel forest at 6 miles. The homestead sits among old foundations, remnants of two stone houses, and a small apple orchard. Enjoy a rest in the cool grove.

From the remains of the stone houses in the forest, walk gently downhill, beginning the descent to the shuttle car and Highway 29. The trail from Holm's place to the highway is shared with bicycles. Veer right on the rock-embedded path through the beautiful lava formations and sweeping views of the Palisades. Steadily descend along the towering rock wall on the left. Curve left and cross the ridge, continuing downhill on the brushy slope overlooking Napa Valley. Watch for old wagon wheel ruts ground into the slab rock. Skirt the east side of Bald Hill, overlooking forested Simmons Canyon. Loop clockwise around Bald Hill through oak groves, evergreens, and manzanita. Near the bottom are views of Calistoga, vineyards, and the sounds of civilization. Pass the gated trailhead at the junction of Highway 29 and Silverado Trail, a half mile north of downtown Calistoga. ■

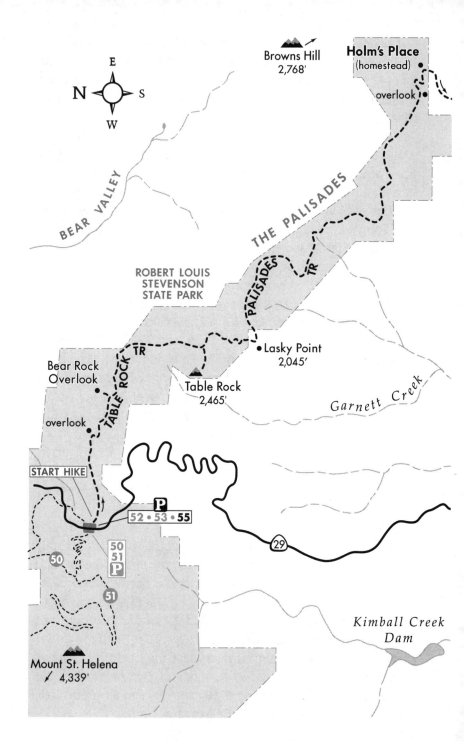

Browns Hill
2,768'

Holm's Place
(homestead)

overlook

N E S W

THE PALISADES

ROBERT LOUIS
STEVENSON
STATE PARK

PALISADES TR

Lasky Point
2,045'

Bear Rock
Overlook

TABLE ROCK TR

Table Rock
2,465'

Garnett Creek

overlook

START HIKE

P
52 • 53 • 55

50
51
P

50

51

29

Kimball Creek
Dam

Mount St. Helena
4,339'

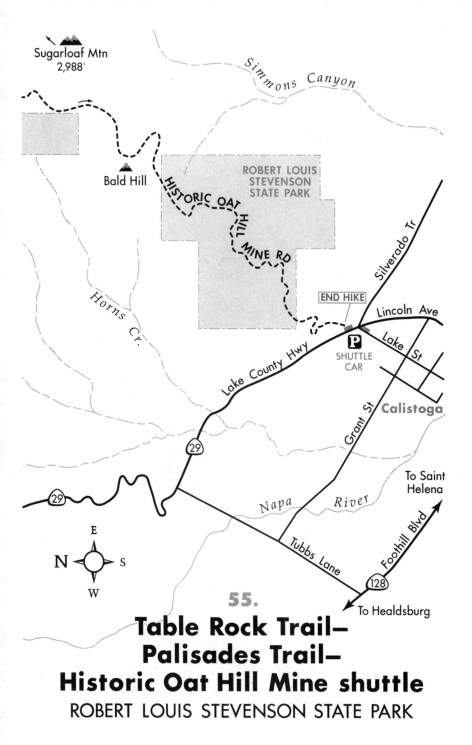

Sugarloaf Mtn
2,988'

Simmons Canyon

Bald Hill

ROBERT LOUIS
STEVENSON
STATE PARK

HISTORIC OAT HILL MINE RD

Silverado Tr

Horns Cr.

END HIKE

Lincoln Ave

P
SHUTTLE
CAR

Lake St

Lake County Hwy

Grant St

Calistoga

29

To Saint
Helena

Napa River

Foothill Blvd

29

E
N   S
W

Tubbs Lane

128

To Healdsburg

55.

Table Rock Trail–
Palisades Trail–
Historic Oat Hill Mine shuttle
ROBERT LOUIS STEVENSON STATE PARK

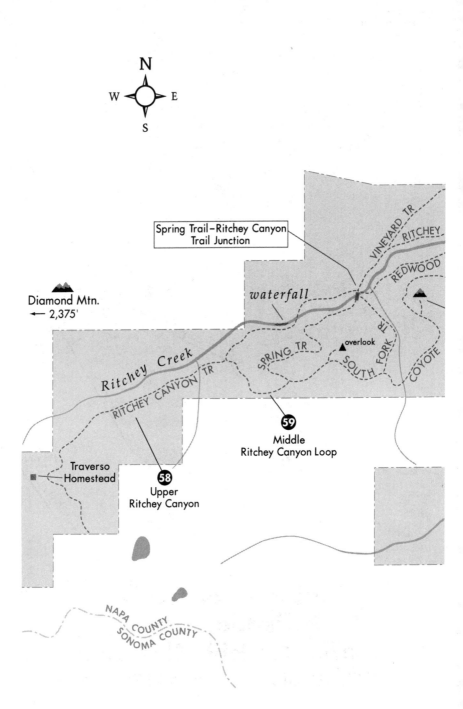

N
W E
S

Spring Trail–Ritchey Canyon
Trail Junction

VINEYARD TR

RITCHEY

REDWOOD

waterfall

Diamond Mtn.
← 2,375'

overlook

SPRING TR

SOUTH FORK TR

COYOTE

Ritchey Creek

RITCHEY CANYON TR

59

Middle
Ritchey Canyon Loop

Traverso
Homestead

58

Upper
Ritchey Canyon

NAPA COUNTY
SONOMA COUNTY

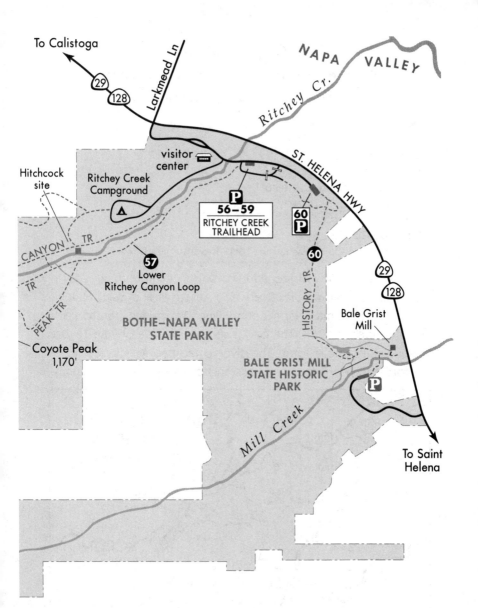

To Calistoga

NAPA VALLEY

Larkmead Ln

Ritchey Cr.

29
128

ST. HELENA HWY

visitor center

Hitchcock site

Ritchey Creek Campground

P

56–59
RITCHEY CREEK TRAILHEAD

60
P

CANYON TR

60

57

Lower Ritchey Canyon Loop

PEAK TR

TR

HISTORY TR

29
128

BOTHE–NAPA VALLEY STATE PARK

Bale Grist Mill

Coyote Peak 1,170'

BALE GRIST MILL STATE HISTORIC PARK

P

Mill Creek

To Saint Helena

HIKES 56–60
Bothe–Napa Valley State Park

56. Coyote Peak

Coyote Peak Trail—Ritchey Canyon Loop

BOTHE—NAPA VALLEY STATE PARK

Hiking distance: 4.5-mile loop
Hiking time: 2.5 hours
Configuration: loop
Elevation gain: 850 feet
Difficulty: moderate to strenuous
Exposure: mostly forested
Dogs: not allowed
Maps: U.S.G.S. Calistoga
  Bothe-Napa Valley/Robert Louis Stevenson State Parks

Bothe-Napa Valley State Park (pronounced *bo-thay*) sits in the heart of Napa Valley between Calistoga and Saint Helena along the Sonoma—Napa county line. The rugged state park was founded in 1960. The park was previously a private resort owned by Reinhold Bothe. The diverse geography includes heavily forested north-facing slopes and canyons, while the sunny

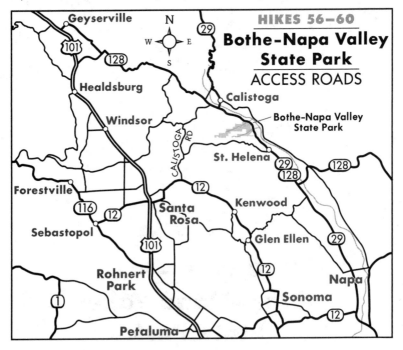

south-facing slopes are covered with brush, oaks, and manzanita. The easternmost stands of coastal redwoods grow in the lush riparian habitats near the creeks and springs.

The trail to Coyote Peak is the most popular in the park. The hike begins in lower Ritchey Canyon along Ritchey Creek under bigleaf maples, oaks, madrones, and redwoods. The Coyote Peak Trail climbs out of the canyon and moderately ascends to the 1,170-foot summit of Coyote Peak. En route to the tree-covered peak are views of Napa Valley, Mount Saint Helena, and upper Ritchey Canyon. This loop hike descends down the other side of Coyote Peak, then rejoins with trails along the creek as it returns to the trailhead.

To the trailhead

3801 St. Helena Hwy · Calistoga   38.551661, -122.520872

Bothe-Napa Valley State Park is located along Highway 29 between Calistoga and Saint Helena in Napa Valley. Three main routes access Napa Valley from Sonoma County. From the north—access is via Highway 128 out of Geyserville and Healdsburg. From Santa Rosa—access is via Calistoga Road off of Highway 12. From the south—access is via Highway 12, south of the town of Sonoma.

CALISTOGA. From Highway 29 (Lincoln Avenue) in Calistoga, drive 3.5 miles south on Highway 29 to the posted state park entrance on the right. Turn right and drive 0.4 miles to the posted Ritchey Creek Trailhead and parking area on the right.

SAINT HELENA. From Highway 29 in Saint Helena, drive 4.5 miles north on Highway 29 to the posted state park entrance on the left. Turn left and drive 0.4 miles to the posted Ritchey Creek Trailhead and parking area on the right.

The hike

Pass the trailhead sign and enter the forest. Cross a service road to the banks of Ritchey Creek. Curve left, heading upstream, and follow the south side of the creek to a trail split at 0.4 miles. The Ritchey Canyon Trail crosses the creek to the right, the return route. Begin the loop to the left on the Redwood Trail, across the creek from the campground. Traverse the moist, north-facing slope through an understory of ferns, thimbleberry, and wild rose bushes. The signed Coyote Peak Trail is on the left at 0.9 miles.

Bear left on the Coyote Peak Trail, and head up the picturesque stream-fed side canyon. Weave through the shady side canyon, and cross the drainage on a U-shaped right bend. Steadily gain elevation, contouring around the slope of the peak. Traverse the hillside path among California bays to a clearing and a trail split. Detour left on the rock-embedded path 0.1 mile to Coyote Peak, a rounded summit with a tree-obscured view. En route are views into Ritchey Canyon, with the tops of the redwoods towering over the forest canopy, and a northern view of Mount Saint Helena.

After resting, return to the trail junction and descend into Ritchey Canyon. Rock hop over a tributary stream, and stroll through a redwood grove to a posted T-junction with the South Fork Trail at 2.4 miles. The trail is an old skid road used by early loggers to haul out the redwood trees. The right fork returns for a shorter loop. For this hike, bear left and traverse the hillside. Atop a minor ridge, an unmarked side path on the right detours 60 yards to an overlook of Ritchey Canyon. Continue the descent down the South Fork Trail to a junction with the Spring Trail. The left fork leads up canyon to the Traverso Homestead (Hike 59). Bear right on the serpentine road, and gently descend through the forest. Cross a concrete spillway over the creek to the Redwood Trail on the right.

Continue straight ahead on the Vineyard Trail along the edge of Ritchey Creek. At a Y-fork, the Vineyard Trail veers left. Curve to the right on the Ritchey Canyon Trail, and continue downstream on the north side of the creek. Pass a creek crossing on the right that connects to the Redwood Trail. Continue straight, reaching the Hitchcock homesite on the right by a wood barn with a tin roof. Pass a campground access path on the left, and ford the creek to the right, completing the loop. Bear left and return 0.4 miles to the trailhead. ■

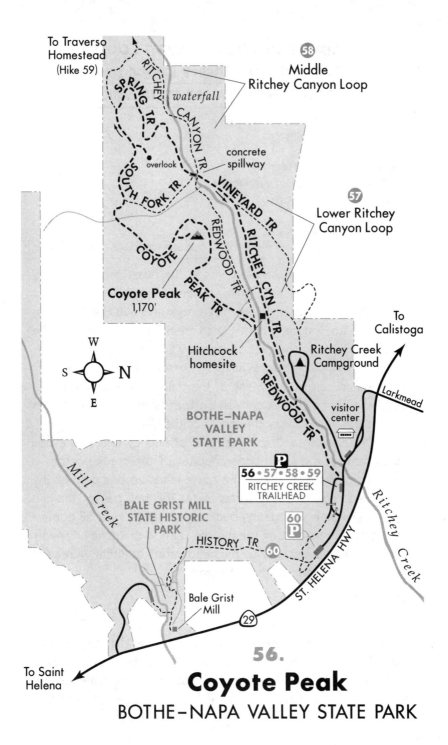

To Traverso
Homestead
(Hike 59)

SPRING TR

RITCHEY

CANYON TR

waterfall

58

Middle
Ritchey Canyon Loop

overlook

SOUTH FORK TR

concrete
spillway

VINEYARD TR

RITCHEY CYN TR

57

Lower Ritchey
Canyon Loop

COYOTE

REDWOOD TR

PEAK TR

Coyote Peak
1,170'

Hitchcock
homesite

Ritchey Creek
Campground

To
Calistoga

Larkmead

REDWOOD TR

visitor
center

W N
S E

**BOTHE-NAPA
VALLEY
STATE PARK**

P
56 • 57 • 58 • 59
RITCHEY CREEK
TRAILHEAD

60
P

HISTORY TR

60

Mill Creek

Ritchey Creek

ST. HELENA HWY

**BALE GRIST MILL
STATE HISTORIC
PARK**

Bale Grist
Mill

29

To Saint
Helena

56.

Coyote Peak
BOTHE-NAPA VALLEY STATE PARK

57. Lower Ritchey Canyon Loop
Redwood Trail—Ritchey Canyon Trail
BOTHE—NAPA VALLEY STATE PARK

Hiking distance: 3-mile loop
Hiking time: 1.5 hours
Configuration: loop
Elevation gain: 400 feet
Difficulty: easy to slightly moderate
Exposure: mostly forested
Dogs: not allowed
Maps: U.S.G.S. Calistoga
      Bothe-Napa Valley and Robert Louis Stevenson State Parks map

Bothe-Napa Valley State Park sits in the heart of Napa Valley between Calistoga and Saint Helena. The 1,900-acre park stretches along perennial Ritchey Creek and Mill Creek, reaching west into Sonoma County. Both creeks are tributaries of the Napa River, just to the east of Highway 29. The popular park offers camping, picnicking, swimming, horseback riding, and hiking along ten miles of trails. Many of the trails in the park are found along the Ritchey Creek canyon bottom. Several return options make it possible to vary the length of the hikes.

This hike explores the lower end of Ritchey Creek. The trail leads through the lush riparian habitat of the creek bottom in a redwood-lined drainage. The route leads up one side of the creek and returns on the other side. The trail passes the old Hitchcock home site, dating back to the 1870s. Hike 58 continues up the canyon along the middle section of Ritchey Canyon. Hike 59 leads all the way to the headwaters of Ritchey Creek at the upper west end of the state park.

To the trailhead

3801 ST. HELENA HWY · CALISTOGA   38.551661, -122.520872

Bothe-Napa Valley State Park is located along Highway 29 between Calistoga and Saint Helena in Napa Valley. Three main routes access Napa Valley from Sonoma County. From the north—access is via Highway 128 out of Geyserville and Healdsburg.

From Santa Rosa—access is via Calistoga Road off of Highway 12. From the south—access is via Highway 12, south of the town of Sonoma.

CALISTOGA. From Highway 29 (Lincoln Avenue) in Calistoga, drive 3.5 miles south on Highway 29 to the posted state park entrance on the right. Turn right and drive 0.4 miles to the posted Ritchey Creek Trailhead and parking area on the right.

SAINT HELENA. From Highway 29 in Saint Helena, drive 4.5 miles north on Highway 29 to the posted state park entrance on the left. Turn left and drive 0.4 miles to the posted Ritchey Creek Trailhead and parking area on the right.

The hike

Pass the trailhead sign and enter the forest. Cross a service road to the banks of Ritchey Creek. Curve left, heading upstream. Follow the south side of the creek to a trail split at 0.4 miles. The Ritchey Canyon Trail crosses the creek to the right, the return route.

Begin the loop to the left on the Redwood Trail, across the creek from the campground. Traverse the moist, north-facing slope to a second fork at 0.9 miles. The 1.5-mile Coyote Peak Trail veers left and climbs 700 feet through upland forest and chaparral to a 1,170-foot peak (Hike 56). Stay in the lush canyon on the Redwood Trail. Cross a tributary stream, and walk about 100 yards to a third junction. An access to the Ritchey Canyon Trail crosses the creek to the right. Continue straight, staying on the hiking-only section of the Redwood Trail. Weave through the forest along the creek as the canyon narrows. The Redwood Trail ends in a shaded redwood forest. Rock hop over Ritchey Creek to a dirt road and a junction at 1.5 miles. The middle creek loop—Hike 58—continues upstream on the Ritchey Canyon Trail.

For this shorter hike, bear right on the Vineyard Trail. Follow the north side of Ritchey Creek to a Y-fork. The Vineyard Trail veers left. Curve to the right on the Ritchey Canyon Trail, continuing on the north side of the creek. Pass the creek crossing on the right that leads back to the Redwood Trail. Continue straight, reaching

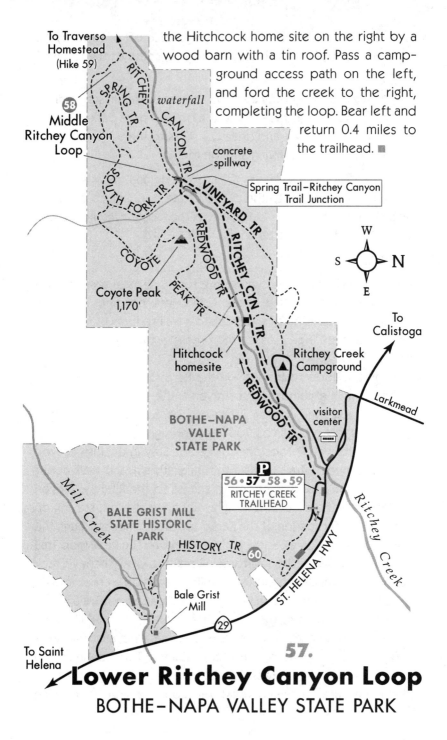

the Hitchcock home site on the right by a wood barn with a tin roof. Pass a campground access path on the left, and ford the creek to the right, completing the loop. Bear left and return 0.4 miles to the trailhead. ■

To Traverso Homestead (Hike 59)

RITCHEY CANYON TR.

SPRING TR.

waterfall

58

Middle Ritchey Canyon Loop

SOUTH FORK TR.

concrete spillway

Spring Trail–Ritchey Canyon Trail Junction

VINEYARD TR.

COYOTE

REDWOOD TR.

PEAK TR.

RITCHEY CYN. TR.

Coyote Peak 1,170'

Hitchcock homesite

Ritchey Creek Campground

REDWOOD TR.

To Calistoga

Larkmead

visitor center

W
N
S ✦ E

BOTHE–NAPA VALLEY STATE PARK

Mill Creek

BALE GRIST MILL STATE HISTORIC PARK

P
56 • **57** • 58 • 59
RITCHEY CREEK TRAILHEAD

Ritchey Creek

HISTORY TR. **60**

ST. HELENA HWY

Bale Grist Mill

29

To Saint Helena

57.
Lower Ritchey Canyon Loop
BOTHE–NAPA VALLEY STATE PARK

58. Middle Ritchey Canyon Loop
Redwood Trail—Spring Trail—Ritchey Canyon Trail
BOTHE—NAPA VALLEY STATE PARK

Hiking distance: 4.5-mile double loop
Hiking time: 2.5 hours
Configuration: double loop
Elevation gain: 850 feet
Difficulty: moderate to strenuous
Exposure: mostly forested
Dogs: not allowed
Maps: U.S.G.S. Calistoga
Bothe-Napa Valley and Robert Louis Stevenson State Parks map

Bothe-Napa Valley State Park is composed of rugged volcanic terrain that formed as far back as 3.5 million years ago. Within the park, the elevations range from 300 to 2,000 feet, producing diverse vegetation. The northern slopes and canyons are filled with an evergreen and deciduous forest, including redwoods, Douglas fir, tanbark oak, and blue oak. Bothe-Napa Valley is the farthest inland state park to contain redwood trees. The southern, exposed slopes are covered with chaparral and brush.

Ritchey Creek flows through the heart of the state park before joining the Napa River a few miles to the east. A network of trails follows the riparian corridor through stands of coastal redwoods and ferns. Three trail options are included for hiking along Ritchey Creek. This medium-length hike leads to the middle section of Ritchey Canyon, making a double loop along both sides of the creek. The trail moderately climbs into the secluded upper canyon and explores a sampling of the park's natural features.

To the trailhead

3801 St. Helena Hwy · Calistoga   38.551661, -122.520872

Bothe-Napa Valley State Park is located along Highway 29 between Calistoga and Saint Helena in Napa Valley. Three main routes access Napa Valley from Sonoma County. From the north—access is via Highway 128 out of Geyserville and Healdsburg. From Santa Rosa—access is via Calistoga Road off of Highway 12. From the south—access is via Highway 12, south of the town of Sonoma.

CALISTOGA. From Highway 29 (Lincoln Avenue) in Calistoga, drive 3.5 miles south on Highway 29 to the posted state park entrance on the right. Turn right and drive 0.4 miles to the posted Ritchey Creek Trailhead and parking area on the right.

SAINT HELENA. From Highway 29 in Saint Helena, drive 4.5 miles north on Highway 29 to the posted state park entrance on the left. Turn left and drive 0.4 miles to the posted Ritchey Creek Trailhead and parking area on the right.

The hike

Pass the trailhead sign and enter the forest. Cross a service road to the banks of Ritchey Creek. Curve left, heading upstream. Follow the south side of the creek to a trail split at 0.4 miles. The Ritchey Canyon Trail crosses the creek to the right, the return route.

Begin the loop to the left on the Redwood Trail, across the creek from the campground. Traverse the moist, north-facing slope to a second fork at 0.9 miles. The 1.5-mile Coyote Peak Trail veers left and climbs 700 feet through upland forest and chaparral to a 1,170-foot peak (Hike 56). Stay in the lush canyon on the Redwood Trail. Cross a tributary stream, and walk 100 yards to a third junction. An access to the Ritchey Canyon Trail crosses the creek to the right. Continue straight, staying on the hiking-only section of the Redwood Trail. Weave through the forest along the creek as the canyon narrows. The Redwood Trail

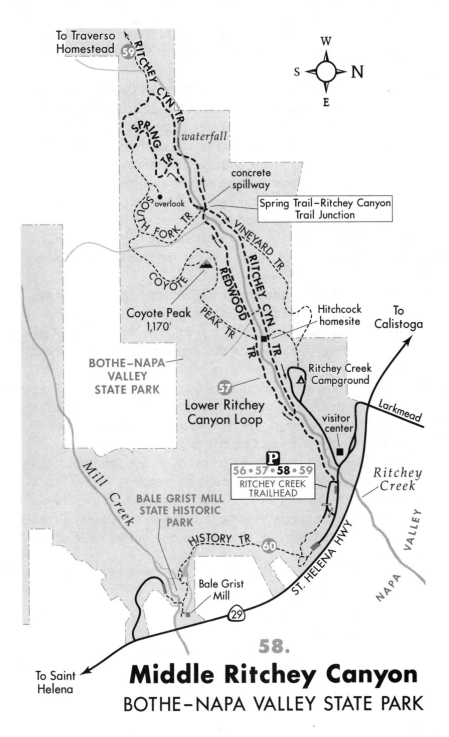

To Traverso Homestead

59 RITCHEY CYN. TR

W
S — N
E

SPRING TR

waterfall

concrete spillway

overlook

Spring Trail–Ritchey Canyon Trail Junction

SOUTH FORK TR

VINEYARD TR

COYOTE PEAK TR

REDWOOD TR

RITCHEY CYN. TR

Coyote Peak 1,170'

Hitchcock homesite

To Calistoga

BOTHE–NAPA VALLEY STATE PARK

57

Lower Ritchey Canyon Loop

Ritchey Creek Campground

Larkmead

visitor center

Mill Creek

P
56 • 57 • 58 • 59
RITCHEY CREEK TRAILHEAD

Ritchey Creek

BALE GRIST MILL STATE HISTORIC PARK

HISTORY TR

60

ST. HELENA HWY

NAPA VALLEY

Bale Grist Mill

29

To Saint Helena

58.
Middle Ritchey Canyon
BOTHE–NAPA VALLEY STATE PARK

ends in a shaded redwood forest. Rock hop over Ritchey Creek to a dirt road and a junction at 1.5 miles. The Spring Trail goes left, the return route.

Cross the road and take the posted Ritchey Canyon Trail along the north side of the creek. Climb the hillside and descend back to the creek. Rock hop over the creek, passing a cascading waterfall on the right. Climb again, back on the south side of the creek. Cross three feeder streams, and pass a moss-covered rock cave. Continue climbing steadily (with a few short, steep sections) to an open flat and a posted junction at 2.3 miles. Views of upper Ritchey Canyon and Diamond Mountain extend to the west. The right fork leads 1.2 miles into Upper Ritchey Canyon, continuing to a fruit orchard and meadow at the Traverso Homestead site from the 1880s (Hike 59).

For this hike, take the Spring Trail straight ahead. Slowly descend through a mixed forest. Curve left on a dirt road among towering redwoods, and pass a junction with the South Fork Trail on a U-bend. Follow the serpentine road on a gentle but steady downhill grade. Cross a concrete spillway over the creek, completing the upper loop back by the Redwood Trail. From the north side of the creek, continue straight ahead on the edge of the creek to a Y-fork. The Vineyard Trail veers left. Curve to the right on the Ritchey Canyon Trail, continuing on the north side of the creek. Pass a creek crossing on the right that leads to the Redwood Trail. Continue straight, reaching the Hitchcock home site on the right by the wood barn with a tin roof. Pass a campground access path on the left, and ford the creek to the right, completing the loop. Bear left and return 0.4 miles to the trailhead. ■

59. Upper Ritchey Canyon to Traverso Homestead

Redwood—Spring—Ritchey Canyon Trails

BOTHE—NAPA VALLEY STATE PARK

Hiking distance: 7 miles round trip
Hiking time: 3.5 hours
Configuration: double loop plus out-and-back to homestead
Elevation gain: 1,100 feet
Difficulty: strenuous
Exposure: mostly forested
Dogs: not allowed
Maps: U.S.G.S. Calistoga
    Bothe-Napa Valley/Robert Louis Stevenson State Parks

Ritchey Creek, a tributary of the Napa River, runs from west to east through the length of Bothe-Napa Valley State Park. Trails follow the creek canyon from the visitor center to the Traverso Homestead—the destination for this hike. The hike makes a double loop on the lower end of Ritchey Creek, then continues on the four-mile-long Ritchey Canyon Trail to the homesite near the headwaters of the creek. The old homestead sits in a pastoral meadow at the upper west end of the state park. The site dates back to the 1880s. A small fruit orchard still remains. En route, the shaded path weaves along a riparian habitat between volcanic rock cliffs, passing through groves of bigleaf maples, Douglas firs, oaks, and redwoods.

To the trailhead

3801 ST. HELENA HWY · CALISTOGA   38.551661, -122.520872

Bothe-Napa Valley State Park is located along Highway 29 between Calistoga and Saint Helena in Napa Valley. Three main routes access Napa Valley from Sonoma County. From the north—access is via Highway 128 out of Geyserville and Healdsburg. From Santa Rosa—access is via Calistoga Road off of Highway 12. From the south—access is via Highway 12, south of the town of Sonoma.

CALISTOGA. From Highway 29 (Lincoln Avenue) in Calistoga, drive 3.5 miles south on Highway 29 to the posted state park entrance on the right. Turn right and drive 0.4 miles to the posted Ritchey Creek Trailhead and parking area on the right.

SAINT HELENA. From Highway 29 in Saint Helena, drive 4.5 miles north on Highway 29 to the posted state park entrance on the left. Turn left and drive 0.4 miles to the posted Ritchey Creek Trailhead and parking area on the right.

The hike

This route makes a figure-8 double loop along the lower and middle sections of Ritchey Creek, then continues on the Ritchey Canyon Trail to the Traverso Homestead. To begin, pass the trailhead sign and enter the forest. Cross a service road to the banks of Ritchey Creek. Curve left, heading upstream. Follow the south side of the creek to a trail split at 0.4 miles. The Ritchey Canyon Trail crosses the creek to the right, the return route.

Begin the first loop to the left on the Redwood Trail, across the creek from the campground. Traverse the moist, north-facing slope to a second fork at 0.9 miles. The 1.5-mile Coyote Peak Trail veers left and climbs 700 feet through upland forest and chaparral to a 1,170-foot peak (Hike 56). Stay in the lush canyon on the Redwood Trail. Cross a tributary stream, and walk about 100 yards to a third junction. An access to the Ritchey Canyon Trail crosses the creek to the right. Continue straight, staying on the hiking-only section of the Redwood Trail. Weave through the forest along the creek as the canyon narrows. The Redwood Trail ends in a shaded redwood forest. Rock hop over Ritchey Creek to a dirt road and a junction at 1.5 miles. This is the junction between the first and second loops. The Spring Trail goes left, the return route.

Cross the road and take the posted Ritchey Canyon Trail along the north side of the creek. Climb the hillside and descend back to the creek. Rock hop over the creek back to the south side, passing a cascading waterfall on the right. Climb again, crossing three feeder streams and a moss-covered rock cave. Steadily gain elevation (with a few short, steep sections) to an open

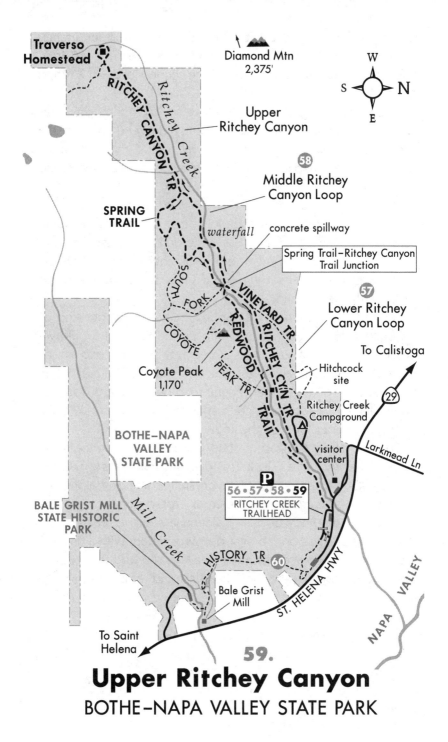

Traverso Homestead

Diamond Mtn 2,375'

W N E S

RITCHEY CANYON TR

Ritchey Creek

Upper Ritchey Canyon

58

Middle Ritchey Canyon Loop

SPRING TRAIL

waterfall

concrete spillway

Spring Trail–Ritchey Canyon Trail Junction

SOUTH FORK

COYOTE

VINEYARD TR

RITCHEY CYN TR

57

Lower Ritchey Canyon Loop

To Calistoga

Coyote Peak 1,170'

REDWOOD PEAK TR

Hitchcock site

29

BOTHE–NAPA VALLEY STATE PARK

RITCHEY CANYON TRAIL

Ritchey Creek Campground

visitor center

Larkmead Ln

BALE GRIST MILL STATE HISTORIC PARK

Mill Creek

P

56 • 57 • 58 • 59
RITCHEY CREEK TRAILHEAD

HISTORY TR

60

Bale Grist Mill

ST. HELENA HWY

NAPA VALLEY

To Saint Helena

59.

Upper Ritchey Canyon
BOTHE–NAPA VALLEY STATE PARK

flat and a posted junction at 2.3 miles. Views of upper Ritchey Canyon and Diamond Mountain extend to the west. The left fork, the Spring Trail, is the upper end of the second loop—the return route.

To continue to the Traverso Homestead, go to the right, staying on the Ritchey Canyon Trail. Gently descend through the forest on the north-facing canyon wall. Cross a stair-stepping tributary stream, and pass redwood fairy rings, maple trees, and ferns. Follow the undulating path, emerging from the dense forest to chaparral, grasslands, and an unsigned junction at 3.5 miles. The left fork makes a horseshoe left bend and climbs the south canyon wall. The right fork crosses the drainage at the Traverso Homestead in a clearing with old rusted debris and a fruit orchard. It is a pastoral setting, but it takes some imagination to visualize the homestead.

Return to the junction with Spring Trail at the upper end of the second loop. Stay to the right on the Spring Trail. Slowly descend through a mixed forest. Curve left on a dirt road among towering redwoods, and pass a junction with the South Fork Trail on a U-bend. Follow the serpentine road on a gentle but steady downhill grade. Cross a concrete spillway over the creek, completing the upper loop by the Redwood Trail.

Continue straight ahead on the Vineyard Trail along the north edge of the creek to a Y-fork. The Vineyard Trail veers left. Curve to the right on the Ritchey Canyon Trail, continuing along the north side of the creek. Pass the creek crossing on the right that connects to the Redwood Trail. Continue straight, reaching the Hitchcock homesite on the right by a wood barn with a tin roof. Pass a campground access path on the left, and ford the creek to the right, completing the loop. Bear left and return 0.4 miles to the trailhead. ■

60. Bale Grist Mill State Historic Park

History Trail

BOTHE—NAPA VALLEY STATE PARK

Hiking distance: 2.4 miles round trip
Hiking time: 1.5 hours
Configuration: out-and-back
Elevation gain: 200 feet
Difficulty: easy
Exposure: mostly forested
Dogs: not allowed
Maps: U.S.G.S. Calistoga
Bothe-Napa Valley and Robert Louis Stevenson State Parks map

Dr. Edward Bale built a grist mill at this site in 1846. The mill was used for grinding grain (grist) into wheat flour. Water from Mill Creek was diverted into Mill Pond and delivered by redwood flumes to the top of the waterwheel. The weight of the water turned the 20-foot wheel, which turned the millstones, which ground the grist. The water-powered mill was used until 1905. The mill has since been restored with a larger 36-foot diameter wheel. It is one of only two surviving water-driven mills west of the Mississippi River.

Bale Grist Mill State Historic Park is adjacent to Bothe-Napa Valley State Park. The parks are connected by Highway 29 and the 1.2-mile History Trail. This hike begins from the east end of Bothe-Napa Valley State Park and leads to Bale Grist Mill State Historic Park. The trail passes an old pioneer cemetery with marked graves dating back to the mid-1800s. The hike climbs a ridge under a forest canopy, then descends into the Mill Creek drainage and the mill.

To the trailhead

3315 ST. HELENA HWY · ST. HELENA   38.539905, –122.511323

Bothe-Napa Valley State Park is located along Highway 29 between Calistoga and Saint Helena.

CALISTOGA. From Highway 29 (Lincoln Avenue) in Calistoga, drive 3.5 miles south on Highway 29 to the posted state park entrance on the right. Turn right and drive 0.7 miles to the last parking lot.

SAINT HELENA. From Highway 29 in Saint Helena, drive 4.5 miles north on Highway 29 to the posted state park entrance on the left. Turn left and drive 0.7 miles to the last parking lot.

To hike the trail in reverse, park at the Bale Grist Mill State Historic Park. The entrance is located on Highway 29—1.6 miles south of Bothe-Napa Valley State Park and 2.9 miles north of Saint Helena.

The hike

From the picnic area, take the posted path south, parallel to Highway 29. Curve right, away from the highway, to an open meadow and the historic White Church Cemetery. A side path on the left leads to the rock headstones.

Back on the main trail, enter the forest of madrone, Douglas fir, and oaks. Climb the shaded hillside to the ridge. Follow the ridge, topping out in a half mile. The serpentine path slowly descends into the Mill Creek drainage to a tributary stream. Cross the stream and follow its west bank downstream to a posted junction at 0.9 miles. The left fork detours along the creek to the site of the old Mill Pond and the dam built in 1859. The History Trail crosses a wooden bridge over a seasonal stream to a trail split at Mill Creek. The left fork leads to the historic Grist Mill buildings. The right fork crosses a long wooden bridge over Mill Creek to the Bale Grist Mill parking lot. After exploring the mill and granary, return by retracing your steps. ■

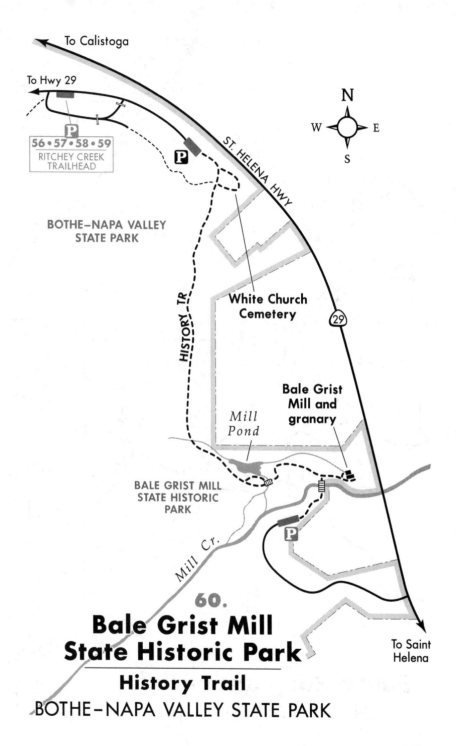

To Calistoga

To Hwy 29

P

56 • 57 • 58 • 59
RITCHEY CREEK
TRAILHEAD

P

ST. HELENA HWY

N
W   E
S

BOTHE–NAPA VALLEY
STATE PARK

HISTORY TR

White Church
Cemetery

29

Bale Grist
Mill and
granary

*Mill
Pond*

BALE GRIST MILL
STATE HISTORIC
PARK

P

Mill Cr.

60.
Bale Grist Mill
State Historic Park

History Trail

BOTHE–NAPA VALLEY STATE PARK

To Saint
Helena

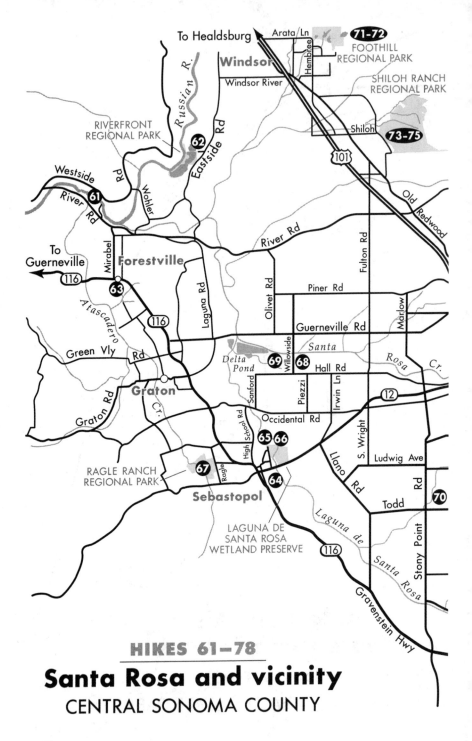

HIKES 61–78

Santa Rosa and vicinity
CENTRAL SONOMA COUNTY

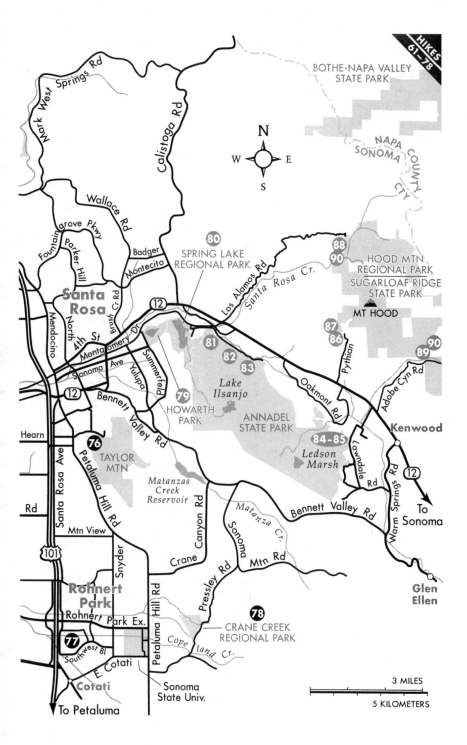

BOTHE-NAPA VALLEY
STATE PARK

NAPA COUNTY
CTY

SONOMA

Mark West Springs Rd

Calistoga Rd

N
W E
S

Wallace Rd

Fountaingrove Pkwy

Parker Hill

Badger

Montecito

Brush Cr Rd

Santa Rosa

Mendocino

North

4th St

Montgomery Dr

Sonoma Ave

Yulupa

Summerfield

Los Alamos Rd

Santa Rosa Cr.

⑫

⑳

SPRING LAKE
REGIONAL PARK

⑧⑧
⑨⑩

HOOD MTN
REGIONAL PARK
SUGARLOAF RIDGE
STATE PARK

MT HOOD

⑧⑦
⑧⑥

⑨⓪
⑧⑨

Adobe Cyn Rd

Pythian

⑧①

⑧②
⑧③

Lake
Ilsanjo

⑲

Howarth
Park

Bennett Valley Rd

⑫

Hearn

⑫

⑦⑥

TAYLOR
MTN

Matanzas
Creek
Reservoir

Oakmont Rd

ANNADEL
STATE PARK

Ledson
Marsh

⑧④-⑧⑤

Lawndale Rd

Kenwood

Warm Springs Rd

⑫

To
Sonoma

Santa Rosa Ave

Petaluma Hill Rd

Mtn View

Rd

101

Snyder

Crane Canyon Rd

Sonoma

Matanza Cr.

Bennett Valley Rd

Mtn Rd

Pressley Rd

Crane

**Rohnert
Park**

Rohnert Park Ex.

⑦⑦

Southwest Bl

E. Cotati

Cotati

To Petaluma

Petaluma Hill Rd

Cope land Cr.

⑦⑧

CRANE CREEK
REGIONAL PARK

Sonoma
State Univ.

Glen
Ellen

3 MILES

5 KILOMETERS

217

61. Steelhead Beach Regional Park

Hiking distance: 1.5-mile loop
Hiking time: 45 minutes
Configuration: loop
Elevation gain: level
Difficulty: easy
Exposure: forested riverfront and open beaches
Dogs: allowed
Maps: U.S.G.S. Camp Meeker and Guerneville
Steelhead Beach Regional Park map

The Russian River originates in the Mayacamas Mountains above Lake Mendocino. The twisting river winds through vineyards, plains, redwood forests and canyons, draining a million acres across 120 miles before emptying into the sea at Jenner. Steelhead Beach Regional Park is a 26-acre oasis on the banks of the Russian River at the north end of Forestville and east of Guerneville. The park is a popular river access site for fishing, kayaking, rafting, and canoeing. This natural stretch of the Russian River has endangered coho salmon and threatened steelhead (rainbow) trout. A loop trail follows the south side of the river between Steelhead Beach and Children's Beach. The hike weaves through three plant communities—an alluvial stand of large redwoods; riparian scrub with thickets of willows; and a riparian forest with cottonwoods, walnuts, Oregon ash, bigleaf maple, California bay, bamboo, and box elder.

To the trailhead

9000 RIVER ROAD · FORESTVILLE   38.495735, -122.899282

From Highway 116 in Forestville, drive 1.4 miles north on Mirabel Road to River Road. Turn left and continue a quarter mile to the posted park entrance on the right. Turn right and park in the lot 0.1 mile ahead. A parking fee is required.

From Guerneville, drive 7 miles east on River Road to the park entrance on the left.

The hike

Take the paved path west to the group picnic area, where the pavement ends. Continue on the dirt path, crossing the boat ramp road near the boat launch, to the posted Willow Trail. Weave through the mixed riparian forest on the low bluffs above the Russian River. Pass a junction with the Seasonal Trail on the right, and follow the river downstream to a junction with the Osprey Trail. The right fork leads to sandy Children's Beach. Return on the Osprey Trail, meandering through the forest between River Road and the Willow Trail. Cross the boat ramp road, returning to the parking lot. ∎

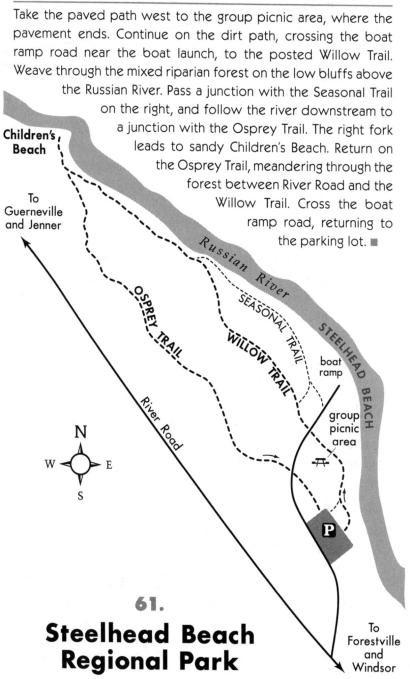

Children's Beach

To Guerneville and Jenner

Russian River

OSPREY TRAIL

SEASONAL TRAIL

WILLOW TRAIL

STEELHEAD BEACH

boat ramp

group picnic area

River Road

N
W E
S

P

To Forestville and Windsor

61.

Steelhead Beach Regional Park

62. Riverfront Regional Park

Hiking distance: 2-mile loop
Hiking time: 1 hour
Configuration: loop
Elevation gain: level
Difficulty: easy
Exposure: forested pockets and open lakeshore
Dogs: allowed
Maps: U.S.G.S. Healdsburg · Riverfront Regional Park map

Riverfront Regional Park is adjacent to the Russian River in the town of Windsor. The 300-acre park, once a gravel quarry, was opened to the public in 2005. It includes a picnic area in a large redwood grove and two recreational lakes used for fishing and non-motorized boating. The park has more than two miles of lakeshore trails that circle the lakes. From January through July, the area is a nesting site for the great blue heron, North America's largest wading water bird. Their nests can be spotted high in the trees. This hike follows the perimeter of Lake Benoist and skirts the banks of the Russian River and the east shore of Lake Wilson.

To the trailhead

7821 EASTSIDE ROAD · WINDSOR   38.521472, -122.849633

From Highway 101 in Windsor, exit on Central Windsor. Drive 2.1 miles west on Windsor River Road to Eastside Road. Turn left and continue 1.8 miles to the signed park entrance on the right. Turn right and drive 0.5 miles to the trailhead parking lot. A parking fee is required.

The hike

Walk past the trailhead kiosk, and follow the Lake Trail southwest (a dirt road). Skirt a dense redwood forest and picnic area on the left and Lake Wilson on the right. Continue to a junction at the north end of Lake Benoist at 0.3 miles. The right fork (the return route) crosses a berm separating the two lakes. Begin the loop on the left fork, and follow the southwest side of the lake on the forested path through redwoods, willow, bamboo, and bay laurel. Cross over an inlet stream at a concrete spillway and a few other rock-lined inlet streams. At the far west end of the lake is a great view across the length of the lake. Cross a stream and begin the return. A lower footpath skirts the edge of the lake. If the water level is high, cross the rocky dam and follow the top of the berm along the Russian River. The two paths merge atop the ridge and continue east, overlooking the lake. Descend and cross a stream, completing the loop. ∎

Russian River

Lake Benoist

To
Forestville and
Guerneville

LAKE

Lake McLaughlin

TRAIL

Lake Wilson

W
S ✧ N
E

redwood
grove

P

Eastside Road

To Windsor and
Healdsburg

62.
Riverfront
Regional Park

63. West County Regional Trail

FORESTVILLE to GRATON

Hiking distance: 4 miles round trip
Hiking time: 1.5 hours
Configuration: out-and-back
Elevation gain: level
Difficulty: easy
Exposure: mostly exposed with forested pockets
Dogs: allowed
Maps: U.S.G.S. Camp Meeker and Sebastopol
West County and Rodota Trails map

A rails-to-trails system has been developed on the old Petaluma and Santa Rosa Railroad line, which connects Petaluma and Santa Rosa with Sebastopol and Forestville. The West County Regional Trail, a segment of the trail system, is a 5.5-mile trail that runs from Forestville to Sebastopol. This hike follows the first section of the trail in a tree-lined corridor from Forestville to the small town of Graton. The trail parallels a water channel, meanders alongside pastures and vineyards, and passes through the Fish and Game's Atascadero Marsh Ecological Reserve. The mostly paved path is a popular hiking, biking, and dog-walking route.

From Graton, the walk can be extended another 1.75 miles south to Occidental Road and another 3.5 miles to Sebastopol. From Sebastopol, the trail continues west to Santa Rosa along the Joe Rodota Trail (Hike 64). The entire rails-to-trails system is 14 miles, from Forestville to Sebastopol to Santa Rosa.

To the trailhead

HWY 116/2ND ST · FORESTVILLE   38.473518, -122.893444

From downtown Forestville on Highway 116, park along the south side of the street between Second Street and Mirabel Road, or pull into the open area off the road.

The hike

Walk down the gravel road alongside houses and buildings on the left. As the road curves left, leave the road to the right. Walk toward the tree grove to the posted trailhead. Take the paved

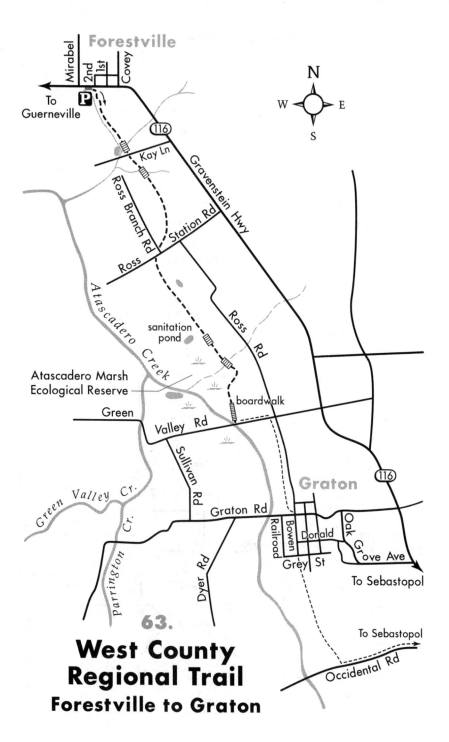

63.
West County Regional Trail
Forestville to Graton

path through a tunnel of trees alongside a stream and a vineyard on the right. Follow the tree-lined corridor, cross a bridge over the creek, and cross Kay Lane, a private road. Cross a second bridge over a stream. Continue south to Ross Branch Road at 0.8 miles. Bear left 30 yards to Ross Station Road. Walk 40 yards to the right, and pick up the posted trail on the left. Stroll between vineyards and a few farm houses, gradually descending past horse stables and corrals. Pass the Graton Sanitation Pond on the right, then cross a bridge over the creek and another bridge over a wetland pond. Curve right, where the pavement ends, and follow the dirt path between a pond and a vineyard. Curve left through the Atascadero Marsh Ecological Reserve. Cross the wetland on a 160-yard boardwalk to Green Valley Road. This is the turn-around spot.

To extend the hike, walk a quarter mile to the left on Green Valley Road, picking up the trail again on the right. The path continues south 1.5 miles through the town of Graton to Occidental Road in Sebastopol. ■

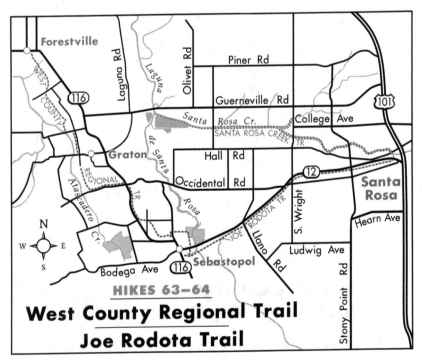

HIKES 63–64

West County Regional Trail
Joe Rodota Trail

64. Joe Rodota Trail
FROM SEBASTOPOL

Hiking distance: 1.5 miles round trip
Hiking time: 45 minutes
Configuration: out-and-back
Elevation gain: level
Difficulty: very easy
Exposure: mostly exposed with forested pockets
Dogs: allowed
Maps: U.S.G.S. Sebastopol · West County & Rodota Trails map

A 14-mile rails-to-trails system runs from the cities of Forestville to Sebastopol to Santa Rosa along an abandoned railroad right-of-way. The Joe Rodota Trail is the section of the trail that links Sebastopol to Santa Rosa. The paved multi-use trail is named for the first director of the Sonoma County Regional Parks. The entire trail is 8.5 miles long.

This walk begins at the west end of the trail in Sebastopol and heads east along the first 0.75-mile length of the trail. The route leads through grasslands and a thick riparian forest in the Laguna de Santa Rosa wetlands under valley oak, willow, Oregon ash, and black walnut trees. Throughout the hike are sweeping views of dairy pastures, vineyards, creeks, and the Santa Rosa Plain. This is a popular trail for hiking, biking, jogging, dog walking, and bird watching.

To the trailhead

MAIN ST/BURNETT ST · SEBASTOPOL   38.401024, -122.823300

From Sebastopol Road (Highway 12) and Main Street in downtown Sebastopol, drive 0.1 mile south on Main Street to a parking lot on the left, south of Burnett Street.

The hike

From the east end of the parking lot, cross Petaluma Avenue to the posted trailhead. Pass the map kiosk and head east on the paved path alongside oak and walnut trees. At 150 yards, pass a trail on the left that crosses two bridges over Calder Creek and leads to Highway 12, continuing to the Laguna de Santa Rosa

Wetlands Preserve (Hikes 65 and 66). Stay straight on the main trail. Cross a bridge over Laguna de Santa Rosa in a riparian habitat with willow trees and poison oak. Cross a second, 120-foot bridge over the Laguna Waterway. Follow the tree-lined path as it runs parallel to Highway 12, with views of the open, grassy wetlands. The trees soon give way to open meadows and a another bridge over a waterway. This is the turn-around point for a 1.5-mile round-trip walk.

To extend the hike, the trail continues 8 miles east, parallel to Highway 12, to downtown Santa Rosa by Railroad Square. ■

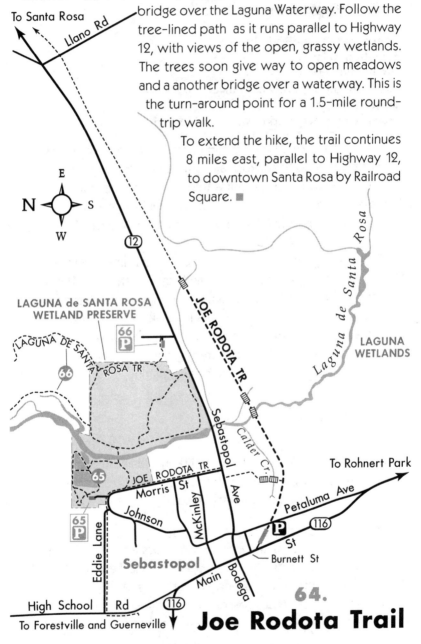

64.
Joe Rodota Trail

65. Laguna de Santa Rosa
Wetland Preserve

Hiking distance: 0.8 miles round trip
Hiking time: 30 minutes
Configuration: loop with out-and-back
Elevation gain: level
Difficulty: every easy
Exposure: open grasslands
Dogs: allowed
Maps: U.S.G.S. Sebastopol · Laguna de Santa Rosa Trail Map

The Laguna de Santa Rosa waterway is the main artery in a 250-square-mile watershed between Sonoma Mountain and Sebastopol. It is the largest freshwater wetland on the northern California coast. The river is also the largest and southernmost tributary of the Russian River, extending 22 miles from Cotati to its confluence with the Russian River north of Forestville. The sinuous Laguna de Santa Rosa meanders through a 30,000-acre complex of creeks, pools, and oak woodlands. This area is prime bird habitat and an important stop for migrating waterfowl on the Pacific Flyway.

The Laguna de Santa Rosa Wetland Preserve in Sebastopol is among the best places to observe the laguna from the waterway itself. The short and easy trail follows a raised gravel road that passes ponds, marshes, stands of valley oak, black walnuts, Oregon ash, and blackberries, offering sweeping views of the expansive watershed.

To the trailhead

595 MORRIS ST · SEBASTOPOL   38.408936, -122.820539

From Sebastopol Road (Highway 12) and Main Street in downtown Sebastopol, drive a quarter mile east on Sebastopol Road to Morris Street. Turn left and continue 0.4 miles, passing the community center and youth annex on the right. Turn right into the trailhead parking lot, just beyond the youth annex.

The hike

At the trailhead arbor are three paths. Begin the loop on the left fork. Walk 100 yards to a bench at an overlook of the wetlands. Loop to the right and descend to a junction with the middle trail at a pond. The right fork leads back to the arbor. Bear left and skirt the edge of the pond on the right and open grasslands to the left. At the end of the first pond is a trail junction. The right fork cuts across between the two ponds. Continue straight on the left fork, skirting the north edge of the second pond. Curve right and head southwest between two ponds to another trail split by the left field of a baseball diamond. The right fork leads back to the trailhead by the youth annex, the return route.

First, detour on the left fork, and head south between the baseball field and lagoon. During the summer, a floating bridge is in place over the Laguna de Santa Rosa, offering a connection to the trails on the opposite side of the waterway (Hike 66). This trail on the west side of the creek ends at Morris Street by the community center. Return to the junction and complete the loop to the left. ▪

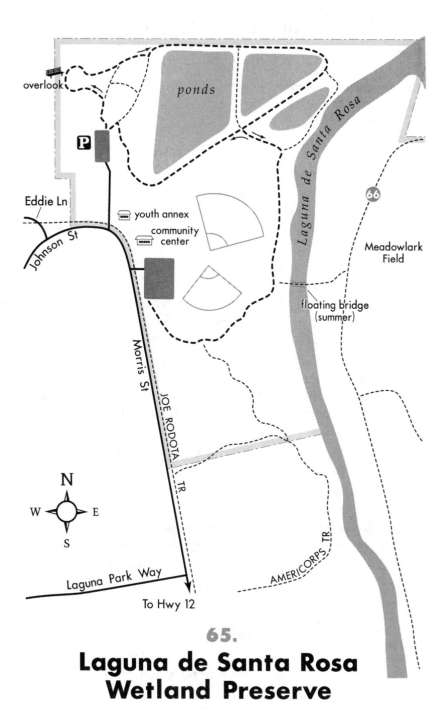

overlook

ponds

P

Laguna de Santa Rosa

Eddie Ln

Johnson St

youth annex

community center

66

Meadowlark Field

floating bridge (summer)

Morris St

JOE RODOTA TR

AMERICORPS TR

N
W E
S

Laguna Park Way

To Hwy 12

65.
Laguna de Santa Rosa Wetland Preserve

66. Laguna de Santa Rosa Trail

Hiking distance: 2.4-mile double loop
Hiking time: 1.5 hours
Configuration: double loop
Elevation gain: 50 feet
Difficulty: easy
Exposure: mostly open meadows
Dogs: allowed
Maps: U.S.G.S. Sebastopol
Laguna de Santa Rosa Trail Map

The Laguna de Santa Rosa is Sonoma's largest freshwater wetland, comprised of a 30,000-acre complex of open waters, verdant wetlands, expansive grasslands, perennial marshes, oak and ash savanna, riparian forest, vernal pools, and ponds. The wetland, extending from Forestville to Cotati, serves as a huge storage pond during heavy rains and is a critical flood basin for the Russian River. The laguna provides a stopover for thousands of native and migrating birds along the Pacific Flyway, with more than 200 species of birds.

The Laguna de Santa Rosa Trail is a multi-use hiking, biking, and equestrian trail that winds along the east side of the waterway's main channel. A 1.8-mile trail connects Highway 12 in Sebastopol with Occidental Road just to the north, with trailheads along each road. The trails opened to the public in 2012.

This hike winds through the Laguna de Santa Rosa Wetland Preserve and the adjacent Kelly Farm along a 2.4-mile double loop. The route travels through mostly open grasslands dotted with oaks, eucalyptus, and blackberry vines. The trail circles Kelly Pond, frequently teeming with birds. There is a bench that offers an overlook of the pond and a distant view of Mount Saint Helena. A pedestrian-only path drops into the floodplain and parallels the Laguna waterway in lush riparian forest.

To the trailhead

HWY 12 · SEBASTOPOL   38.405262, -122.811029

The Highway 12 (southern trailhead) is located along the eastern edge of Sebastopol.

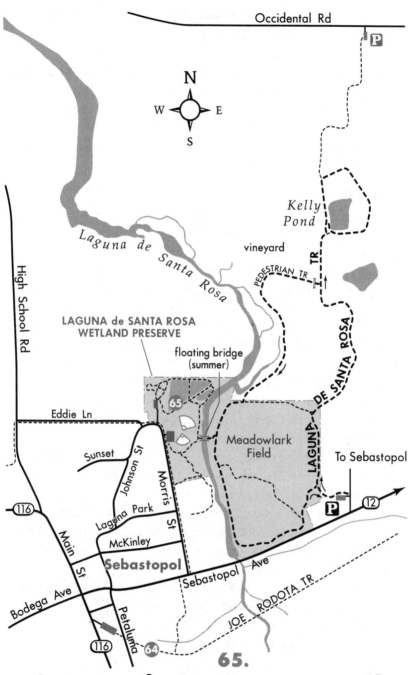

Laguna de Santa Rosa Trail

Occidental Rd

N
W E
S

Laguna de Santa Rosa

Kelly Pond

vineyard

PEDESTRIAN TR

TR

LAGUNA de SANTA ROSA WETLAND PRESERVE

floating bridge (summer)

LAGUNA DE SANTA ROSA

High School Rd

Eddie Ln

Sunset

Johnson St

Morris St

Laguna Park

McKinley

116

Main St

Bodega Ave

Petaluma

116

64

Sebastopol

Sebastopol Ave

Meadowlark Field

To Sebastopol

12

JOE RODOTA TR

65.

65

P

P

From Sebastopol Road (Highway 12) and Main Street in downtown Sebastopol, drive 0.7 miles east on Sebastopol Road to the signed Laguna de Santa Rosa Trail turnoff on the left. It is located just east of the Chevron gas station. Turn left, then another quick left into the parking lot. A parking fee is not required.

From Santa Rosa, drive 5.5 miles west on Highway 12 to the posted trailhead turnoff on the right.

The northern trailhead is located at 5420 Occidental Road, Santa Rosa.

The hike

From the trailhead kiosk, take the well-defined trail north to a posted junction at 100 yards. The left fork (the return route) leads to the Laguna Wetland Preserve. Begin the loop straight ahead, staying on the Laguna de Santa Rosa Trail. Skirt the east edge of Meadowlark Field to a signed Y-fork at 0.3 miles. Stay to the right and follow the raised path, overlooking the open meadows and a view of Mount Saint Helena. Continue to a gated pedestrian trail on the left at 0.8 miles. To the left is the return route. For now, continue straight along the east side of a vineyard to an overlook with benches at Kelly Pond. A half-mile trail circles the pond, a popular habitat for the birds. Views of the pond extend along the west and south sides. From here, it is 0.6 miles north to the Occidental Road trailhead.

After circling the pond, return 0.2 miles to the pedestrian gate, now on the right. Pass through the gate and head west through the meadow. Curve left and walk south to a T-junction. Bear right and stroll through a mixed riparian forest (predominantly oaks) to a signed junction with the Laguna Wetland Preserve on the right (Hike 65). Walk 35 yards to the right to the banks of the wide creek channel and a summer floating bridge.

Return to the forested main trail and proceed south, parallel to the creek channel. Follow the east banks of the waterway towards Highway 12. Curve left, skirting the south end of the preserve to complete the second loop. ■

67. Ragle Ranch Regional Park

Hiking distance: 1.7-mile loop
Hiking time: 1 hour
Configuration: loop
Elevation gain: 50 feet
Difficulty: easy
Exposure: a mix of open grasslands and shaded forest
Dogs: allowed
Maps: U.S.G.S. Sebastopol · Ragle Ranch Regional Park

Ragle Ranch Regional Park covers 157 acres on the west side of Sebastopol. The eastern portion of the park has athletic fields, a playground, picnic areas, and a paved jogging path. The western portion of the park is the wild, natural side. It includes oak woodlands, a memorial redwood grove, open grasslands, and riparian wetlands overgrown with blackberry bushes. Atascadero Creek cuts through the scenic park. A multi-use hiking, biking, and equestrian trail loops around the undeveloped parkland. This hike circles the perimeter of the park on a trail through the wetlands, crossing bridges over small streams and Atascadero Creek.

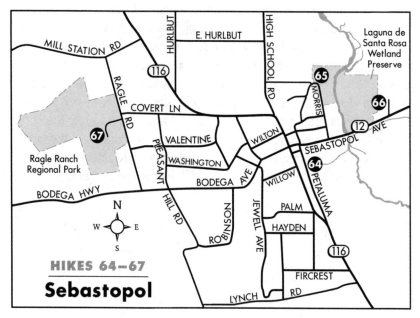

To the trailhead

From Highway 101 in Santa Rosa, drive 7 miles west on Highway 12 to Ragle Road in Sebastopol. (En route, Highway 12 becomes Sebastopol Road, then Bodega Avenue.) Turn right on Ragle Road, and continue 0.5 miles to Ragle Ranch Road on the left—the park entrance. Turn left and enter the park. A parking fee is required. Free parking is available along the east side of Ragle Road.

The hike

Follow the paved path along the west side of the park road to the gazebo picnic area and the posted junction for the Veteran's Memorial Grove. Head west and veer left, leaving the paved path. Continue on the dirt path 100 yards to the gated Blackberry Trail. Head down the hillside through an old pear orchard to bridge 4 and the Hilltop Trail on the right. Cross the bridge over the tributary stream, and quickly cross bridge 3 over Atascadero Creek. Enter the wetlands and pass the Thistle Trail, a cut-across route paralleling Atascadero Creek. Stroll through the riparian wetlands, passing large pockets of blackberry bushes while gradually gaining elevation from the basin. Loop around the perimeter of the wetland along the park's west boundary, passing black oak, willow, and ash groves. Skirt the north edge of the park to bridge 2 by the north end of the Thistle Trail. Bear left, crossing the bridge over Atascadero Creek. Parallel the north side of the creek through grasslands, a vineyard on the left, and an oak grove. Cross bridge 1 and head south. The dirt trail ends at a paved fork. The Hilltop Trail on the right leads to the Veteran's Memorial Grove, a planted redwood grove. The Blackberry Trail continues south back to the parking area. ■

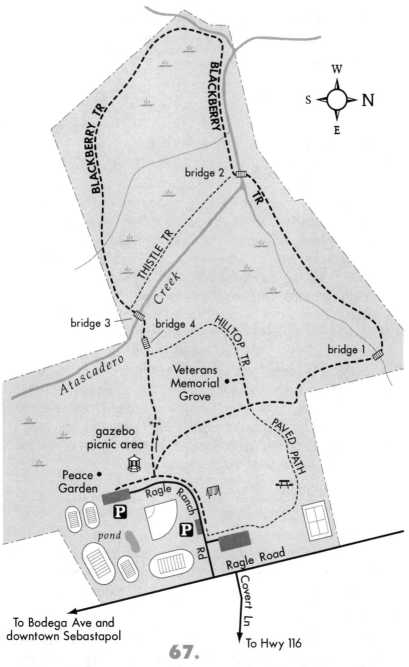

W N
S E

BLACKBERRY TR

BLACKBERRY TR

bridge 2

THISTLE TR

Creek

bridge 3

bridge 4

HILLTOP TR

bridge 1

Atascadero

Veterans
Memorial
Grove

gazebo
picnic area

PAVED PATH

Peace
Garden

Ragle Ranch

P

P

pond

Rd

Ragle Road

To Bodega Ave and
downtown Sebastapol

Covert Ln

To Hwy 116

67.

Ragle Ranch Regional Park

68. Santa Rosa Creek Trail—East
Willowside Road east to Fulton Road

Hiking distance: 4 miles round trip
Hiking time: 2 hours
Configuration: out-and-back
Elevation gain: level
Difficulty: easy
Exposure: mostly exposed with partial shade
Dogs: allowed
Maps: U.S.G.S. Sebastopol

Santa Rosa Creek forms in the upper slopes of Red Hill between Sugarloaf Ridge State Park and Hood Mountain Regional Park. The creek flows through the heart of Santa Rosa and joins the Laguna de Santa Rosa north of Sebastopol. The Santa Rosa Creek Trail follows along the creek for 6.5 miles, from downtown Santa Rosa to Laguna de Santa Rosa by Delta Pond.

Hikes 68 and 69 follow a section of the trail from Willowside Road between Santa Rosa and Sebastopol. This hike heads east along a raised gravel road on the south side of the Santa Rosa Creek Flood Channel. The trail runs under the shade of oak, black walnut, Oregon ash, and willow trees. It is a popular route for walkers, joggers, dog walkers, and bikers. A trail also follows the north side of the creek and may be used as an optional return route. The trail on the north side of the creek is paved, and the trail on the south side of the creek is gravel.

To the trailhead

WILLOWSIDE ROAD · SANTA ROSA   38.444843, -122.806771

From Highway 101 in Santa Rosa, exit on Guerneville Road. Drive 4.5 miles west to Willowside Road and turn left. Continue 0.5 miles south to the trailhead on the south side of Santa Rosa Creek. Park on the narrow shoulder along the road.

The hike

From the east side of Willowside Road, pass the trailhead posts, heading east. Follow the south side of Santa Rosa Creek upstream. The gravel path leads through the riparian corridor among oak,

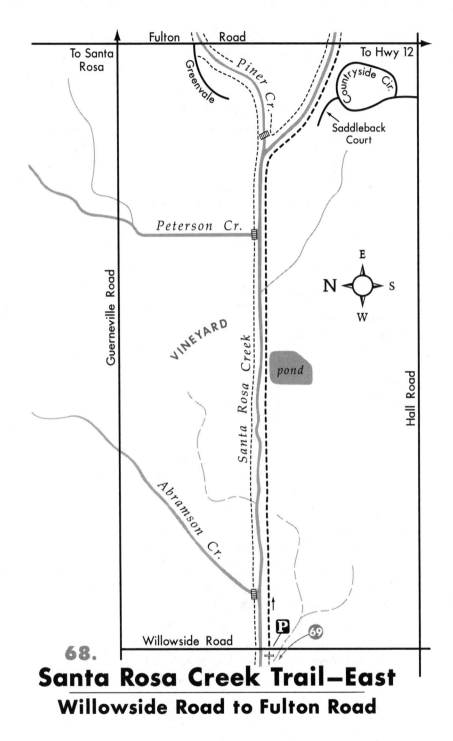

Fulton Road

To Santa Rosa

To Hwy 12

Greenvale

Piner Cr.

Countryside Cir.

Saddleback Court

Peterson Cr.

Guerneville Road

VINEYARD

Santa Rosa Creek

pond

E
N
S
W

Hall Road

Abramson Cr.

P
69

Willowside Road

68.

Santa Rosa Creek Trail–East
Willowside Road to Fulton Road

walnut, and willow trees. Pass Abramson Creek, a feeder stream joining Santa Rosa Creek from the north. Meander along a vineyard, then pass pastureland to the south. Continue atop the levee to a large pond on the right at 1.5 miles. Pass another vineyard that straddles both sides of the trail. Curve right at the confluence with Piner Creek. Stroll between the creek and the backside of homes fronting Saddleback Court and Countryside Circle to Fulton Road at 2 miles.

To extend the hike, the trail continues 2.8 miles east to downtown Santa Rosa, where it becomes Prince Memorial Greenway. ∎

69. Santa Rosa Creek Trail—West
Willowside Road west to Delta Pond

Hiking distance: 3 miles round trip
Hiking time: 1.5 hours
Configuration: out-and-back
Elevation gain: level
Difficulty: easy
Exposure: mostly exposed with partial shade
Dogs: allowed
Maps: U.S.G.S. Sebastopol

Delta Pond is a mile-long manmade pond along the Santa Rosa Creek Trail. It is an important stop for migrating waterfowl on the Pacific Flyway. It is also a thriving rookery for great blue herons, great egrets, and double-crested cormorants. The rookery is home to more than 150 nests. The Santa Rosa Creek Trail runs along the creek for 6.5 miles, from Santa Rosa to the trail's west end at Delta Pond, where the creek joins the Laguna de Santa Rosa. At the east end, the Santa Rosa Creek Trail connects to the Joe Rodota Trail west of Olive Park.

Hikes 68 and 69 follow a popular segment of the trail, traveling in opposite directions from Willowside Road. This hike heads west from Willowside Road (directly across from Hike 68.) The trail begins on a gated gravel road maintained by the Sonoma

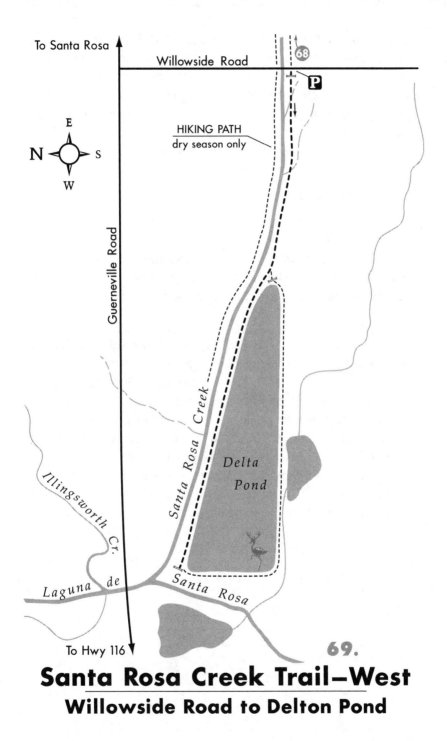

To Santa Rosa

Willowside Road

68

P

HIKING PATH
dry season only

N E S W

Guerneville Road

Santa Rosa Creek

Delta Pond

Illingsworth Cr.

Laguna de

Santa Rosa

To Hwy 116

69.

Santa Rosa Creek Trail–West
Willowside Road to Delton Pond

County Water Agency. The trail follows the downstream course of Santa Rosa Creek under towering oaks, Oregon ash, black walnuts, and willows trees. The path skirts the north side of Delta Pond along the creek to the Laguna de Santa Rosa waterway. The pond is contained by a tall berm and is fenced. Public access up to the rim overlooking the pond is restricted.

During the wet winter months, this path may be muddy or covered with pools of water.

To the trailhead

WILLOWSIDE ROAD · SANTA ROSA   38.444843, -122.806771

From Highway 101 in Santa Rosa, exit on Guerneville Road. Drive 4.5 miles west to Willowside Road and turn left. Continue 0.5 miles south to the trailhead on the south side of Santa Rosa Creek. Park on the narrow shoulder along the road.

The hike

Pass the vehicle gate and head west on the gravel road. Follow the south edge of Santa Rosa Creek downstream through a lush, riparian corridor with walnut and willow trees. Walk through pastureland on the dirt path to the gated east end of Delta Pond at 0.7 miles. At the fence, leave the road and veer right on the grassy path. Skirt the north side of the pond between the berm and Santa Rosa Creek. The berm supporting Delta Pond prevents a view of the pond. At 1.5 miles, the trail ends by a gate at the far west end of Delta Pond, where the creek meets the Laguna Channel. Return along the same route. ■

70. Colgan Creek Trail

Hiking distance: 2.2 miles round trip to Bellevue Avenue
4.6 miles round trip to Victoria Drive
Hiking time: 1 hour
Configuration: out-and-back
Elevation gain: level
Difficulty: easy
Exposure: mostly open grasslands
Dogs: allowed
Maps: U.S.G.S. Santa Rosa

Colgan Creek originates in the oak woodlands of Taylor Mountain. The creek flows westward across the Santa Rosa Plain, draining nearly 5,000 acres. Colgan Creek, part of the Laguna de Santa Rosa watershed, is a flood control channel. It joins the south side of the Laguna between Sebastopol and Rohnert Park. This mile-long trail follows a portion of the creek from Todd Road by Stony Point Road to Elsie Allen High School. The trail is not a wilderness hike but a scenic stroll on a paved streamside path. There are sweeping views of the Laguna watershed across the Santa Rosa Plain to Sonoma Mountain.

To the trailhead

3600 STONY POINT RD · SANTA ROSA   38.388803, -122.741459

ROHNERT PARK. From Highway 101, just north of Rohnert Park, exit on Todd Road. Drive 1.3 miles west to Stony Point Road and turn right. Continue 0.1 miles to the posted trailhead on the right. Park along the shoulder of the road.

SANTA ROSA. From Highway 12 in Santa Rosa, exit on Stony Point Road, located 1.3 miles west of Highway 101. Drive 3 miles south to Todd Road. The trailhead is 0.1 miles north of Todd Road. Turn around and park along the shoulder of the road.

The hike

Take the paved path along the south edge of Colgan Creek. Weave between a sheep ranch to the northwest and a cattle ranch to the southeast. Meander through the flat pasturelands passing barns and taking in the views of Sonoma Mountain in the distance. At

0.8 miles, bend slightly right, following the creek through oaks and blackberries. The path reaches Bellevue Avenue, across the road from the track and baseball fields of Elsie Allen High School. This is the turn-around point for a 2.2-mile round-trip hike.

To extend the walk, cross Bellevue Avenue and parallel the north side of Colgan Creek, heading east. At just under a half mile, the path curves left and continues north for 0.7 miles to Victoria Drive, where the trail ends. Return by retracing your steps. ▪

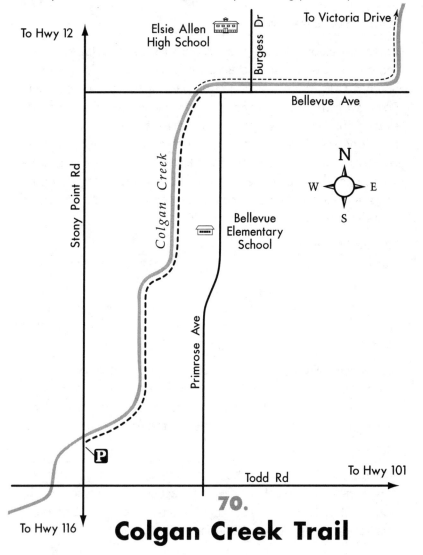

70.
Colgan Creek Trail

71. Perimeter Loop
FOOTHILL REGIONAL PARK

Hiking distance: 2.6-mile loop
Hiking time: 1.5 hours
Configuration: loop
Elevation gain: 460 feet
Difficulty: easy
Exposure: open oak groves and rolling grasslands
Dogs: allowed
Maps: U.S.G.S. Healdsburg · Foothill Regional Park map

Foothill Regional Park sits in the rolling hills at the northeast corner of Windsor between Highway 101 and Chalk Hill Valley. The 211-acre parkland was a cattle ranch until the mid-1980s. The land is covered in oak savanna that is scattered with several species of oaks, bay, madrone, and buckeye trees. Many of the trails that weave through the rolling hills are old ranch roads. This hike loops around the perimeter of the park on several connecting trails. The hike passes three ponds and climbs oak-dotted hills to scenic overlooks of the Santa Rosa Plain, the Russian River Valley, and the town of Windsor.

To the trailhead

1351 ARATA LANE · WINDSOR   38.560989, -122.797775

From Highway 101 in Windsor, take the Central Windsor exit. Drive 0.7 miles southeast on Old Redwood Highway to Hembree Lane and turn left. Continue 1.3 miles to the posted park entrance on the right. A fee for parking in the lot is required. Free parking is available along both sides of the road.

From the north end of Windsor, drive 1.4 miles east of Highway 101 on Arata Lane to the park entrance on the left.

The hike

Walk up the gravel road past the restrooms and vehicle gate to a trail junction. Stay to the right on the Three Lakes Trail, beginning the loop counter-clockwise. Walk for about 100 yards to a junction with the Pond A Trail on the left. Stay straight along the south side of the pond through an open oak grove. Climb to the crest of the hill to a junction on the left with the Westside Trail. Stay on the Three Lakes Trail, and descend to the edge of Pond B. Cross the earthen dam. Pass the second Pond B trail junction and the Oakwood Trail, reaching Pond C. Cross a bridge over the outlet stream. Skirt the southern edge of Pond C to a trail split at the end of the Three Lakes Trail at 0.8 miles. Take the right fork on the posted Alta Vista Trail, and climb the oak-dotted hillside. Steadily climb the spine to the upper reaches of Foothill Park. At 1.1 miles, the trail reaches an overlook at 660 feet, the highest point in the park.

Curve to the left and descend across the rolling grasslands to a junction with the Oakwood Trail at a post-and-rail fence. Take the Oakwood Trail to the right, continuing along the east perimeter of the park. Pass the Ravine Trail on the left, and cross a wooden bridge over a seasonal stream. Weave through the forest, overlooking the ponds, the town of Windsor, and the Russian River Valley. Continue to a Y-fork with the Westside Trail at 2.4 miles. Veer to the right, passing the Bobcat Trail on the left, and steadily descend through oak-dotted grasslands. Pass the Pond A Trail and walk 150 yards, completing the loop at the trailhead. ■

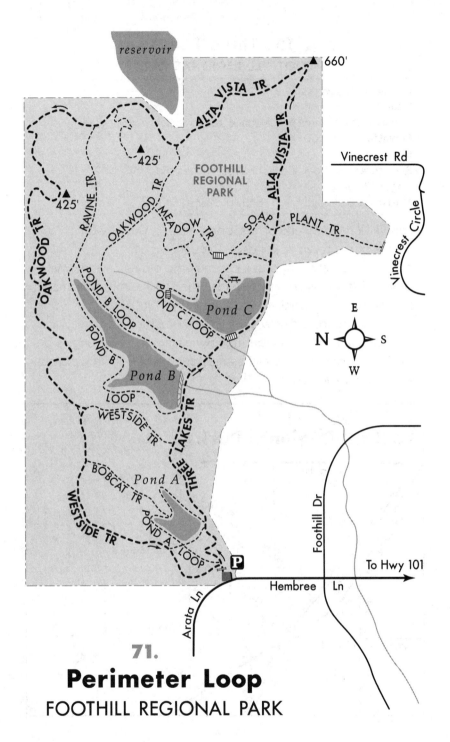

reservoir

660'

ALTA VISTA TR

ALTA VISTA TR

Vinecrest Rd

Vinecrest Circle

425'

425'

FOOTHILL
REGIONAL
PARK

RAVINE TR

OAKWOOD TR

OAKWOOD TR

MEADOW TR

SOAP   PLANT TR

POND B LOOP

POND B

POND C LOOP

Pond C

Pond B

LOOP

N

E

S

W

WESTSIDE TR

THREE LAKES TR

BOBCAT TR

Pond A

WESTSIDE TR

POND A LOOP

P

Foothill Dr

To Hwy 101

Hembree Ln

Arata Ln

71.
Perimeter Loop
FOOTHILL REGIONAL PARK

72. The Three Ponds
FOOTHILL REGIONAL PARK

Hiking distance: 1.4-mile multi-loop
Hiking time: 1 hour
Configuration: three loops connected to an out-and-back trail
Elevation gain: 100 feet
Difficulty: easy
Exposure: open oak groves and rolling grasslands
Dogs: allowed
Maps: U.S.G.S. Healdsburg · Foothill Regional Park map

Foothill Regional Park offers open, scenic views within easy access of the town of Windsor. The park has almost seven miles of multi-use trails that crisscross over the old ranchland. (Many of the trails follow old ranch roads.) The park has three manmade ponds that were originally created in the 1960s when it was a ranch. The ponds are now a drinking source for wild animals and may be used for fishing but not swimming. This hike begins on the Three Lakes Trail and circles the perimeter of all three ponds, forming three loops.

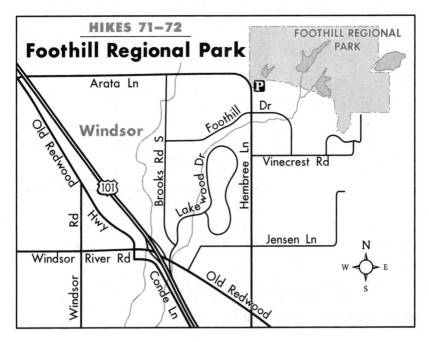

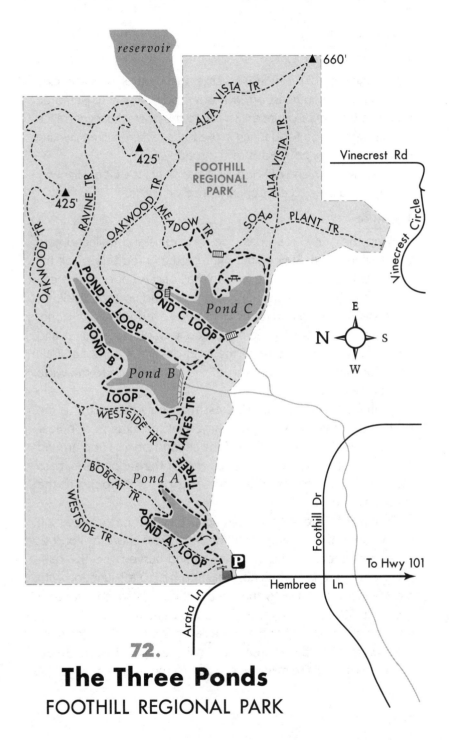

72.
The Three Ponds
FOOTHILL REGIONAL PARK

To the trailhead

From Highway 101 in Windsor, take the Central Windsor exit. Drive 0.7 miles southeast on Old Redwood Highway to Hembree Lane and turn left. Continue 1.3 miles to the posted park entrance on the right. A fee for parking in the lot is required. Free parking is available along both sides of the road.

From the north end of Windsor, drive 1.4 miles east of Highway 101 on Arata Lane to the park entrance on the left.

The hike

Walk up the gravel road past the restrooms and trailhead gate to a trail junction. Stay to the right on the Three Lakes Trail for about 100 yards to a junction with the Pond A Loop on the left. Bear left on the west side of the pond. Head up the hillside on the footpath, rising above the dam to an overlook of the pond. Stay to the right, skirting the pond's edge through manzanita and oak. Follow the curvature of the lake, passing the Bobcat Trail. After looping around two arms of the pond, return to the wide Three Lakes Trail.

Continue to the left (east). Crest the hill and descend to the southeast corner of Pond B, the largest of the three ponds. Bear left and follow the west side of the second pond. Loop around both arms of the pond. At the far end of the second arm, pass the Ravine Trail and return on the east side of the pond to the Three Lakes Trail.

Continue to the left to the Pond C Trail, just before crossing the wooden bridge. Bear left along the west shore of Pond C. Cross a bridge over the inlet stream and curve right. The path soon leaves the lake at its northeast corner to a T-junction with the Meadow Trail. Go to the right and cross a footbridge to a trail split. Stay to the right, as the Soap Plant Trail curves to the left. Twenty yards shy of the Three Lakes Trail, a path on the right leads 0.1 mile to a picnic area overlooking the pond. At the Three Lakes Trail, return 0.6 miles west, back to the trailhead. ■

73. Ridge Trail—Canyon Trail Loop
SHILOH RANCH REGIONAL PARK

Hiking distance: 4.1-mile loop
Hiking time: 2 hours
Configuration: out-and-back with large loop
Elevation gain: 550 feet
Difficulty: moderate
Exposure: mostly forested
Dogs: not allowed
Maps: U.S.G.S. Healdsburg and Mark West Springs
Shiloh Ranch Regional Park map

Shiloh Ranch Regional Park is a forested enclave north of Santa Rosa. Located in the foothills of the Mayacamas Mountains, the rugged landscape contains forests of mixed evergreens, a variety of oaks (including the arching limbs of coastal live oaks), Douglas fir, bigleaf maples, and madrones. The parkland has eight miles of looping trails ranging in elevation from 200 to 850 feet. The trails are a mix of old ranch roads and single track paths leading through canyons, stream-fed valleys, rolling hills, and across ridges. There are magnificent vistas across the Santa Rosa Plain to a scenic year-round pond.

This hike forms a loop on the south side of the park. The hike follows the ridge up to overlooks, drops down to the pond in a stream-fed valley, then returns down a scenic canyon.

To the trailhead

5750 FAUGHT ROAD · SANTA ROSA   38.518380, -122.757864

From Highway 101 in Windsor, exit on Shiloh Road. Drive 1.4 miles east to Faught Road at the base of the hills. Turn right (south) and continue 0.6 miles (passing the main parking lot) to the sharp right bend in the road. The posted trailhead is on the left along the bend. Park along the edge of the turnout on the left by the trailhead gate.

The hike

Walk past the trailhead gate and map kiosk. Head up the foothill slope on the South Ridge Trail. Steadily climb through an open forest, passing overlooks of the Santa Rosa Plain and the town of Windsor. At 0.6 miles is a junction with the Big Leaf Trail, located by an overlook with a bench and hitching post in a savannah of mostly blue oak. Minutes ahead is a junction with the Canyon Trail, the return loop.

Begin the loop to the left, staying on the South Ridge Trail, and ascend through a forest of majestic oaks, bigleaf maple, Douglas fir, and madrones. Weave a half mile up the mountain to the Vista Trail, where a short 30-yard spur trail leads to an overlook with three benches and sweeping panoramic vistas. Return to the main trail and continue through the forest to a signed junction with the Ridge Trail at 1.6 miles. The trail to the right is posted as the Pond Trail, but it is the Ridge Trail, which then leads to the Pond Trail. Bear right and slowly descend, perched on the north-facing canyon wall among mossy tree trunks and a ground cover of ferns. Emerge into the rolling meadows to a junction with the Creekside Trail, just shy of the valley floor. Bear left on the Creekside Trail, and walk 0.3 miles to a junction at the pond. Go to the right on the Pond Trail and loop around the pond and picnic site. Walk south, surrounded by open, rolling hills, to a junction. Bear left, staying on the Pond Trail. At 2.5 miles is a signed junction where the Pond Trail ends. The dead-end Mark West Creek Trail continues east, straight ahead.

Take the Canyon Trail to the right. Weave through the canyon along the south canyon wall. Cross a wooden bridge over the drainage in the bucolic forest and wind up the canyon slope. Continue down canyon on the south-facing slope, looping in and out of a couple side canyons. Ascend the canyon wall to the ridge and the South Ridge Trail, completing the loop. Return to the trailhead 0.7 miles to the left. ■

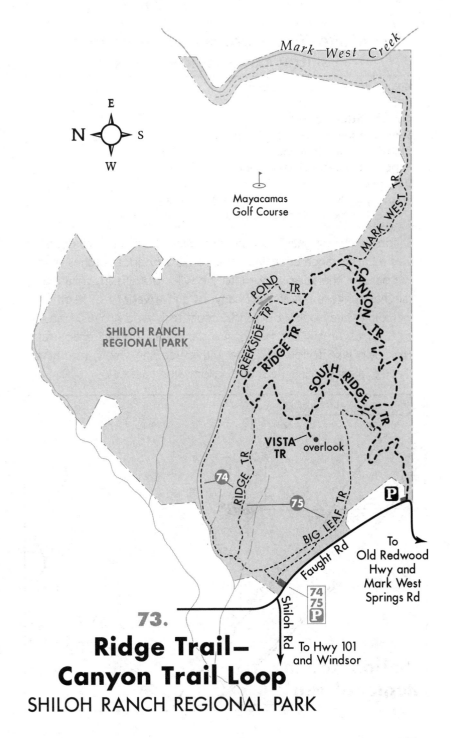

Mark West Creek

N E S W

Mayacamas
Golf Course

SHILOH RANCH
REGIONAL PARK

MARK WEST TR

POND TR

CREEKSIDE TR

RIDGE TR

CANYON TR

SOUTH RIDGE TR

VISTA
TR ● overlook

RIDGE TR

74

75

BIG LEAF TR

P

To
Old Redwood
Hwy and
Mark West
Springs Rd

Faught Rd

Shiloh Rd

74
75
P

To Hwy 101
and Windsor

73.

Ridge Trail–
Canyon Trail Loop
SHILOH RANCH REGIONAL PARK

74. Ridge Trail—Creekside Trail Loop
SHILOH RANCH REGIONAL PARK

Hiking distance: 2.8-mile loop
Hiking time: 2 hours
Configuration: loop
Elevation gain: 550 feet
Difficulty: easy to moderate
Exposure: forested hills and open ridge
Dogs: not allowed
Maps: U.S.G.S. Healdsburg and Mark West Springs
Shiloh Ranch Regional Park map

Shiloh Ranch Regional Park is north of Santa Rosa near Windsor. It was a cattle ranch until 1988. The 860-acre park stretches from the base of the valley floor into the wild foothills. The hilly terrain has rugged, stream-fed canyons and a variety of habitats, including valley oak woodlands, coast redwood groves, stands of Douglas fir, bigleaf maple, grasslands, and mixed chaparral. This loop hike follows a ridge with sweeping vistas, returning through a canyon in a riparian corridor along a creek.

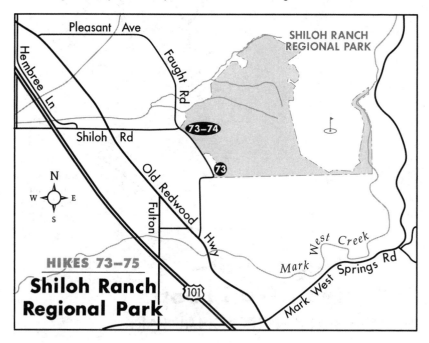

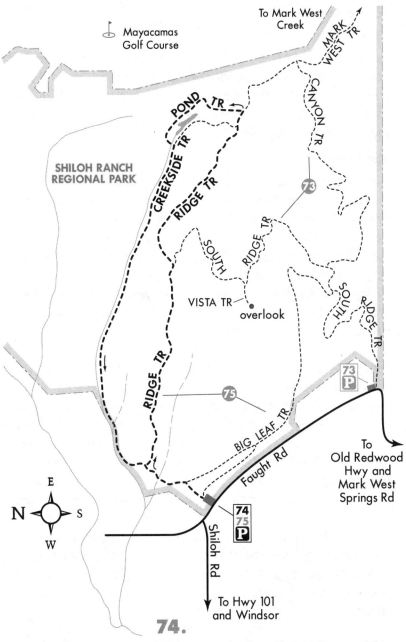

Mayacamas
Golf Course

To Mark West
Creek

MARK WEST TR

POND TR

CANYON TR

CREEKSIDE TR

RIDGE TR

SHILOH RANCH
REGIONAL PARK

73

SOUTH RIDGE TR

SOUTH RIDGE TR

VISTA TR
overlook

RIDGE TR

73
P

75

BIG LEAF TR.

Faught Rd

To
Old Redwood
Hwy and
Mark West
Springs Rd

74
75
P

Shiloh Rd

E
N ← → S
W

To Hwy 101
and Windsor

74.

Ridge Trail–Creekside Trail
SHILOH RANCH REGIONAL PARK

To the trailhead

From Highway 101 in Windsor, exit on Shiloh Road. Drive 1.4 miles east to Faught Road at the base of the hills. Turn right (south) and continue 0.1 mile to the posted park entrance on the left. A fee for parking in the lot is required. Free parking is available along the shoulder of Faught Road.

The hike

Walk past the trailhead map panel and restrooms on the wide gravel path. Stroll through an oak-shaded picnic area to a junction at 50 yards. The Big Leaf Trail (Hike 75) goes to the right. Continue straight on the Ridge Trail. Cross a seasonal stream on the west edge of the park. Curve right and climb 150 yards to a posted junction with the Creekside Trail.

Begin the loop on the right fork, staying on the Ridge Trail. Weave up the hillside through oaks and madrones to overlooks of the town of Windsor, the expansive Santa Rosa Plain, and the Mayacamas Mountains. Follow the ridge between two steep canyons, steadily gaining elevation. The trail tops out by power lines and descends 50 yards to a posted Y-fork. The South Ridge Trail veers off to the right. Curve left and slowly descend along the north-facing canyon wall. Just shy of the grassy valley floor is the Creekside Trail. Continue straight for 100 yards and veer left on the Pond Trail. Follow the north side of the creek, surrounded by open, rolling hills. Loop around the pond and picnic site on the left. Join the Creekside Trail on the west end of the pond by the outlet stream. Go to the right and head down canyon along the south edge of the creek under pines and mossy oaks in a shaded, fern-filled glen. Traverse the narrow south canyon slope, and cross a bridge over a stream. Complete the loop 100 yards ahead at the Ridge Trail. Retrace your route straight ahead. ■

75. Big Leaf Trail—Ridge Trail Loop
SHILOH RANCH REGIONAL PARK

Hiking distance: 3-mile loop
Hiking time: 2 hours
Configuration: loop
Elevation gain: 550 feet
Difficulty: easy to moderate
Exposure: forested hills and open ridge
Dogs: not allowed
Maps: U.S.G.S. Healdsburg and Mark West Springs
Shiloh Ranch Regional Park map

This hike forms a loop in the central section of Shiloh Ranch Regional Park. The hike offers a sampling of the park's natural features—from the shady valley floor to the ridge with panoramic views. The trail begins along the lower hillside slopes through oak groves, then climbs the South Ridge Trail to a vista point with broad vistas of the Mayacamas Mountains, the expansive basin, and the north end of Sonoma County. The hike returns along a ridge with gorgeous views across the Santa Rosa Plain.

To the trailhead

5750 FAUGHT ROAD · SANTA ROSA   38.525095, –122.762905

From Highway 101 in Windsor, exit on Shiloh Road. Drive 1.4 miles east to Faught Road at the base of the hills. Turn right (south) and continue 0.1 mile to the posted park entrance on the left. A fee for parking in the lot is required. Free parking is available along the shoulder of Faught Road.

The hike

Walk past the trailhead map panel and restrooms on the wide gravel path. Stroll through an oak-shaded picnic area to a junction at 50 yards. Bear right on the Big Leaf Trail and begin the loop. Head southeast, traversing the hill parallel to Faught Road. Continue through oaks and manzanita with views of the vineyards on the valley floor. Pass a trail on the right that ascends from the parking lot. Curve left, skirting a small vineyard on private land. Climb a short, forested slope, and continue at a level grade through majestic oaks, madrones, bigleaf maple, and towering Douglas fir. Climb at a gentle grade. Make a U-shaped bend to an oak-studded grassland and a junction with the South Ridge Trail at an overlook with a bench of the Santa Rosa Plain. The right fork leads to a trailhead on Faught Road at the southwest corner of the park. Bear left and pass the Canyon Trail on the right. Cross a saddle with views of the Mayacamas Mountains and the town of Windsor. Weave a half mile up the mountain to the Vista Trail on the left by a power pole. Detour 100 yards left to an overlook with three benches and sweeping panoramic vistas.

Return to the main trail, and continue to a signed junction with the Ridge Trail at two miles (Hike 74). Go to the left and follow the ridge downhill, overlooking the basin. Pass the Creekside Trail on the right. Cross a seasonal drainage and complete the loop, 50 yards shy of the trailhead. ■

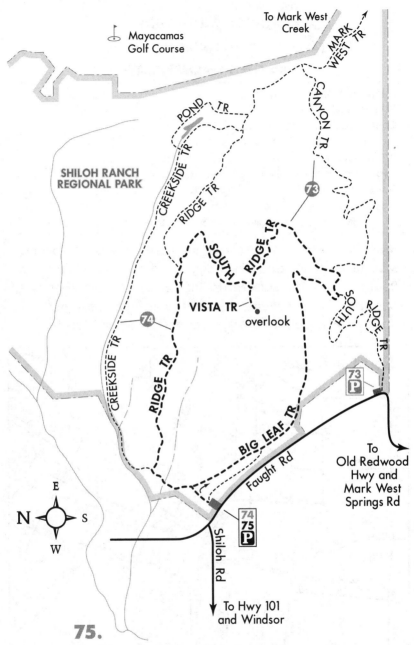

Mayacamas
Golf Course

To Mark West
Creek

MARK WEST TR

To Mark West Creek

POND TR

CANYON TR

SHILOH RANCH
REGIONAL PARK

CREEKSIDE TR

RIDGE TR

73

SOUTH RIDGE TR

VISTA TR
overlook

SOUTH RIDGE TR

74

CREEKSIDE TR

RIDGE TR

73 P

BIG LEAF TR

Faught Rd

To
Old Redwood
Hwy and
Mark West
Springs Rd

74 75 P

Shiloh Rd

E
N — S
W

To Hwy 101
and Windsor

75.
Big Leaf Trail–Ridge Trail Loop
SHILOH RANCH REGIONAL PARK

76. Taylor Mountain

TAYLOR MOUNTAIN REGIONAL PARK
and OPEN SPACE PRESERVE

Hiking distance: 4.5 miles round trip
Hiking time: 2.5 hours
Configuration: loop with out-and-back
Elevation gain: 1,100 feet
Difficulty: moderate to strenuous
Exposure: exposed hillside and forested pockets
Dogs: allowed
Maps: U.S.G.S. Santa Rosa
   Taylor Mountain Regional Park & Open Space Preserve map

Taylor Mountain is a summit at the northern end of Sonoma Mountain with a descending ridge that drops down into Santa Rosa. The city lies adjacent to the preserve's northwest end, but the open space remains undeveloped. The headwaters for Colgan Creek, Cooper Creek, Matanzas Creek, and Todd Creek

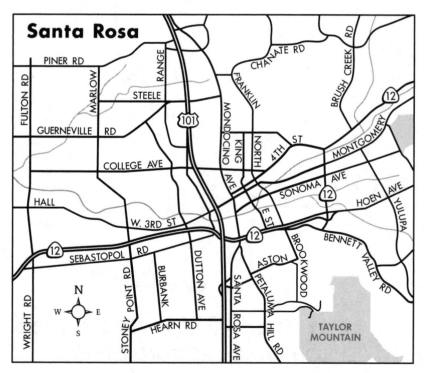

originate from the mountain. Taylor Mountain is named for Gold Rush pioneer John Taylor, who settled on the scenic slopes in the 1850s to raise dairy cows and plant a vineyard. Keeping with its agricultural history, cattle grazing continues within the park to this day. Prior to agricultural development, the Southern Pomo Indians inhabited the site until the 19th century.

Taylor Mountain Open Space Preserve encompasses more than 1,100 acres. It was opened to the public in 2013. There are four miles of hiking, biking, and equestrian trails along two routes. Future plans include the development of a 17-mile trail system with six loops and another trailhead from Petaluma Hill Road.

This loop hikes begin from the main trailhead at the north end of the preserve. The trail passes through shaded oak woodlands, open grassland meadows, and wetlands en route to the 1,400-foot summit of Taylor Mountain. The route utilizes old ranch roads and paths that cross the rolling terrain to the high mountain pastures. From the summit are panoramic views of Bennett Valley, Annadel State Park, Hood Mountain, and Bald Mountain to the north; the entire Santa Rosa Plain and the coastal range, including Mount Tamalpais, to the west; the Mayacamas Mountains, including Mount Saint Helena, to the east; and Mount Diablo to the south.

To the trailhead

2080 KAWANA TERRACE · SANTA ROSA   38.415369, −122.692924

SOUTHBOUND ON HIGHWAY 101 IN SANTA ROSA. Take the Hearn Avenue exit. Immediately turn right on Corby Avenue and go one block to Hearn Avenue. Turn right, crossing over the freeway to Santa Rosa Avenue at the first intersection. Turn left and go one block to Kawana Springs Road. Turn right and continue 0.6 miles to Franz Kafka Avenue. Turn right and quickly turn left onto Kawana Terrace. Drive 0.6 miles and turn right into Taylor Mountain Regional Park. Turn right again into the parking lot. A parking fee is required.

NORTHBOUND ON HIGHWAY 101 IN SANTA ROSA. Take the Yolanda Avenue/Hearn Avenue exit. Turn left on Santa Rosa Avenue at the first intersection. Drive 0.2 miles to Kawana Springs Road.

Turn right and continue 0.6 miles to Franz Kafka Avenue. Turn right and quickly turn left onto Kawana Terrace. Drive 0.6 miles and turn right into Taylor Mountain Regional Park. Turn right again into the parking lot.

The hike

Walk through the trailhead gate onto the Western Trail, passing two huge water tanks on the left. The Western Trail follows the more gradual side of the ridge ascent. Follow the gravel road, parallel to Todd Creek, into an oak grove. Stroll through the intermittent shade from the majestic oaks. Leave the forest, passing through open, rolling meadows while steadily climbing at a moderate grade. At one mile, the path temporarily levels out on an open flat with vistas across the entire Santa Rosa Plain. Cross the gently rolling flat while taking in the views, continuing to a four-way junction with the Eastern Trail.

The steep, direct route goes right on the Eastern Trail. A preferable alternative is to wind up Taylor Mountain on the path straight ahead. The path switchbacks across the Eastern Trail four times on an easier grade. After the fourth intersection, continue on the Eastern Trail. Walk through a forested pocket with mossy tree trunks and rocks. Near the summit, make a sweeping S-curve and pass a historic rock wall to the preserve's northern boundary. The 360-degree vistas extend as far as the air quality will allow. Veer right to the trail's end by a vineyard and additional panoramas.

After resting at the summit, return to the four-way junction of the Western Trail and Eastern Trail. Continue straight head on the Eastern Trail, descending to the trailhead parking lot on the steeper east side of the loop. ■

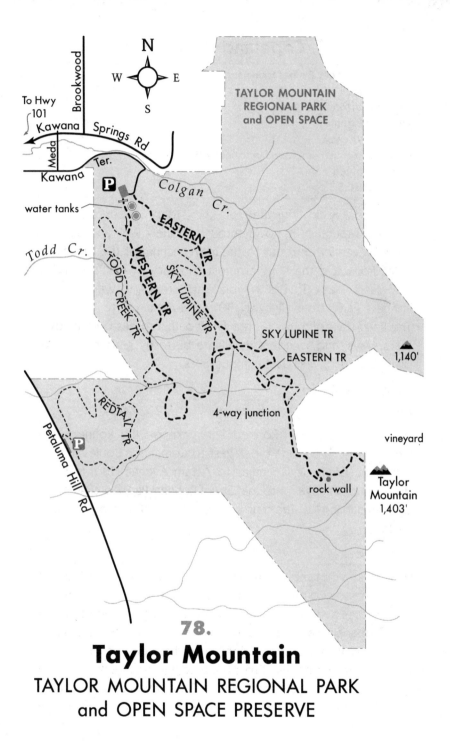

78.
Taylor Mountain
TAYLOR MOUNTAIN REGIONAL PARK
and OPEN SPACE PRESERVE

77. Copeland Creek Trail

Hiking distance: 5 miles round trip
Hiking time: 2.5 hours
Configuration: out-and-back
Elevation gain: level
Difficulty: easy
Exposure: mostly exposed with shady tree groves
Dogs: allowed
Maps: U.S.G.S. Cotati

Copeland Creek originates on the steep, upper slopes of Sonoma Mountain. It flows through Rohnert Park and Sonoma State University en route to the main channel of the Laguna de Santa Rosa. It is the southernmost tributary of the laguna. The Copeland Creek Trail is a wonderful creekside walk through Rohnert Park, from Highway 101 to Sonoma State University. The level trail follows the tree-lined path, crosses bridges over waterways, and wanders through a butterfly garden, a native plant sanctuary, and past campus lakes.

To the trailhead

6750 COMMERCE BLVD · ROHNERT PARK   38.342904, -122.711301

From Highway 101 in Rohnert Park, exit on the Rohnert Park Expressway. Drive one block east to Commerce Boulevard and turn right. Continue 0.5 miles to Avram Avenue. Turn left and quickly turn left again into the City of Rohnert Park Administrative Offices parking lot. The trailhead is at the north end of the parking lot.

The hike

Head east along the south side of Copeland Creek. Follow the paved, tree-lined path upstream, passing a wooden footbridge that crosses over the creek at 0.15 miles. The level path passes a mix of riparian plants, including willows, bay, fir, oaks, and a few redwoods. Pass a second bridge over the creek, and walk 200 yards to Seedfarm Drive. Cross the road, railroad tracks, a bridge over a water channel, and Country Club Drive in rapid succession. Continue east along the waterway, passing a third bridge

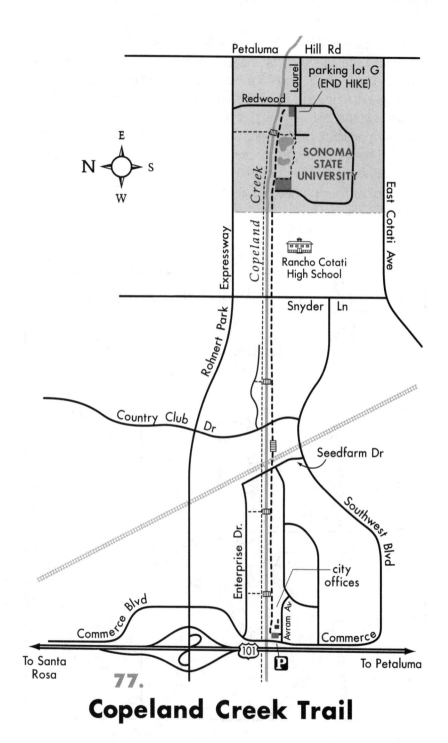

Copeland Creek Trail

over Copeland Creek. Continue to Snyder Lane at 1.3 miles. Cross Snyder Lane and skirt the edge of the athletic fields of Rancho Cotati High School. Enter Sonoma State University, passing a few school buildings and more redwood trees. The paved path soon ends and the dirt path begins. Walk past two large ponds and a grassy parkland on the right to a fourth bridge over the creek. Pass a native plant shadehouse, an interpretive demonstration garden, and a bird and butterfly garden. A small nature trail loops around the main path. The trail ends at parking lot G in the university at 2.5 miles. ■

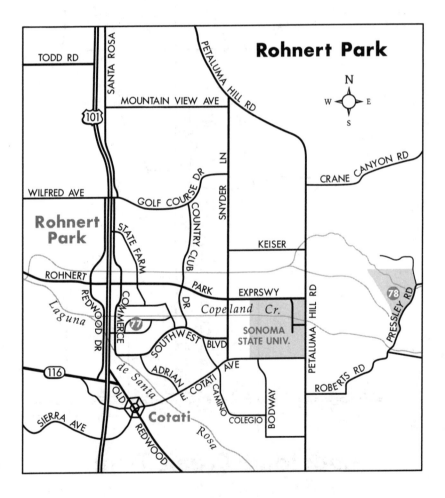

78. Crane Creek Regional Park

Hiking distance: 2-mile loop
Hiking time: 1 hour
Configuration: loop
Elevation gain: 100 feet
Difficulty: easy
Exposure: mostly open, rolling hills with forested pockets
Dogs: allowed
Maps: U.S.G.S. Cotati · Crane Creek Regional Park map

Crane Creek Regional Park encompasses 128 acres of rolling, grassy meadows on the east side of Rohnert Park. This diverse park contains oak savanna, riparian woodland, vernal pools, and bunchgrass meadows. Crane Creek and a seasonal stream flow through the wildflower-covered meadows. The park is bordered with black oak, white alder, California buckeye, and maple. Hiking, biking, and horse trails loop around the perimeter of the park. Several additional hiking-only trails explore the interior of the park. This hike leads to ridgetop overlooks of the park, then down to the bucolic setting along Crane Creek.

To the trailhead

6107 Pressley Rd · Rohnert Park   38.344030, -122.644431

From Highway 101 in Rohnert Park, exit on the Rohnert Park Expressway. Drive 2.7 miles east to a T-junction at Petaluma Hill Road. Turn right and head 1.2 miles south to Roberts Road. Turn left and continue 1.9 miles to the posted park entrance on the left. (En route, Roberts Road becomes Pressley Road.) Turn left and park in the lot. A parking fee is required.

The hike

Two paths leave from the parking lot. Begin the loop on the Fiddleneck Trail to the west (left). Pass the map kiosk and head up the open, grassy slope to a junction. The Overlook Loop Trail veers left and rejoins the Fiddleneck Trail a short distance ahead. The Hawk Ridge Trail goes to the right. Stay on the main Fiddleneck Trail, and climb to a knoll with a bench. From the overlook are views of the entire park and the cattle-grazed hillsides. Follow the ridge to a second knoll and a junction with the Hawk Ridge Trail on the right at 0.3 miles. Detour right on the Hawk Ridge Trail to the Bowden Bluff Overlook. Return to the junction and descend from the knoll. Pass stately, twisted oaks to the fenced west boundary at the valley floor. Cross a stream to a junction with the Poppy Trail and another 50 yards farther to the Lupine Trail. Stay on the Fiddleneck Trail to a junction with the Northern Loop Trail. Veer left on the Northern Loop, following the stream to the northwest corner of the park. Curve right along the north boundary to a four-way junction at a gate.

Cross the Fiddleneck Trail and pass through the gate on the Creek Trail. Stroll through the open meadow along the south edge of Crane Creek, lined with willows, alders, and bays. Pass mature bay laurels, buckeyes, and gnarled valley oaks to the east end of the Lupine Trail. Continue along Crane Creek, then curve away from the creek to a junction. The Sunset Trail crosses Crane Creek, links to the Buckeye Trail, and climbs 0.4 miles to a 466-foot overlook. The Creek Trail continues to the right, crossing a bridge over a steam to the east end of the Poppy Trail. Bear left, staying on the Creek Trail, and return to the trailhead parking lot. ∎

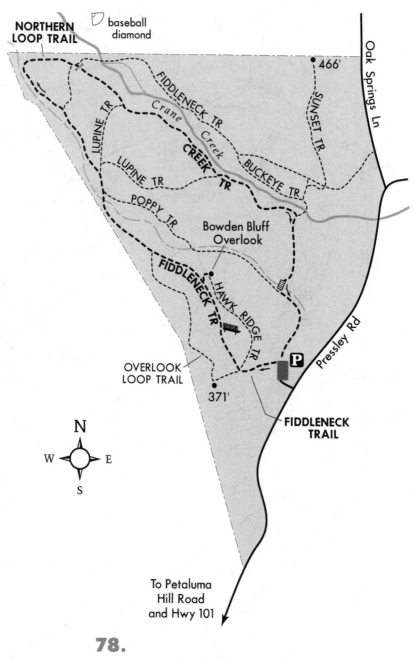

NORTHERN LOOP TRAIL

baseball diamond

FIDDLENECK TR

Crane Creek

CREEK TR

LUPINE TR

LUPINE TR

POPPY TR

BUCKEYE TR

SUNSET TR

466'

Oak Springs Ln

Bowden Bluff Overlook

FIDDLENECK TR

HAWK RIDGE TR

OVERLOOK LOOP TRAIL

371'

P

Pressley Rd

FIDDLENECK TRAIL

N
W E
S

To Petaluma Hill Road and Hwy 101

78.
Crane Creek Regional Park

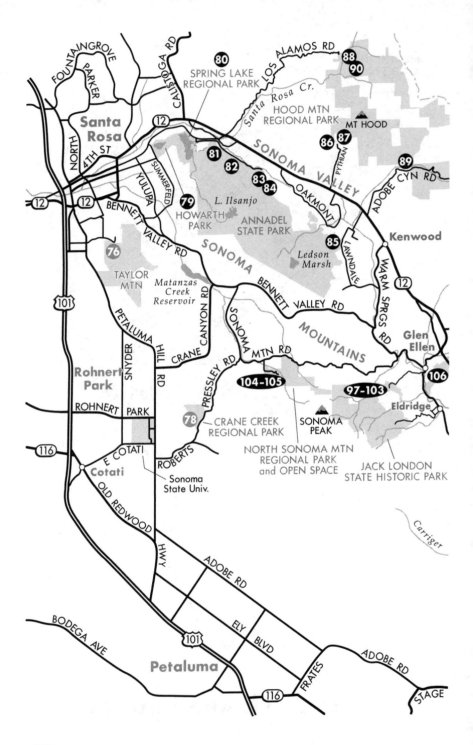

FOUNTAINGROVE PARKER

CALISTOGA RD

LOS ALAMOS RD

88
90

NORTH

Santa Rosa

4TH ST

12

80

SPRING LAKE REGIONAL PARK

Santa Rosa Cr.

HOOD MTN REGIONAL PARK

MT HOOD

SONOMA VALLEY

86 87

89

ADOBE CYN RD

12

12

SUMMERFIELD

YULUPA

BENNETT VALLEY RD

79

HOWARTH PARK

L. Ilsanjo

81

82

83
84

OAKMONT

ANNADEL STATE PARK

85

Ledson Marsh

PYTHIAN

LAWNDALE

Kenwood

76

TAYLOR MTN

Matanzas Creek Reservoir

CRANE CANYON RD

SONOMA

BENNETT VALLEY RD

MOUNTAINS

WARM SPRGS RD

12

Glen Ellen

101

PETALUMA HILL RD

PRESSLEY RD

SONOMA MTN RD

104-105

97-103

106

Rohnert Park

SNYDER

ROHNERT PARK

78

CRANE CREEK REGIONAL PARK

SONOMA PEAK

NORTH SONOMA MTN REGIONAL PARK and OPEN SPACE

Eldridge

JACK LONDON STATE HISTORIC PARK

116

E COTATI

ROBERTS

Cotati

Sonoma State Univ.

OLD REDWOOD HWY

ADOBE RD

Carriger

BODEGA AVE

101

ELY BLVD

FRATES

ADOBE RD

Petaluma

116

STAGE

Santa Rosa to Sonoma
Sonoma Valley
SOUTH CENTRAL SONOMA COUNTY

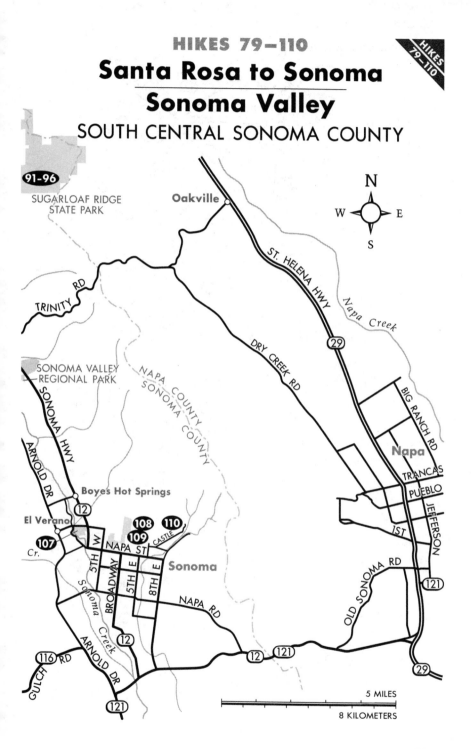

91-96

SUGARLOAF RIDGE
STATE PARK

Oakville

N
W · E
S

ST. HELENA HWY

Napa Creek

TRINITY RD

DRY CREEK RD

29

SONOMA VALLEY
REGIONAL PARK

NAPA COUNTY
SONOMA COUNTY

BIG RANCH RD

Napa

SONOMA HWY

ARNOLD DR

Boyes Hot Springs

12

TRANCAS

PUEBLO

JEFFERSON

El Verano

108
110
109
CASTLE

1ST

107
Cr.

5TH W

NAPA ST

Sonoma

OLD SONOMA RD

121

5TH E

8TH E

BROADWAY

Sonoma Creek

NAPA RD

NAPA RD

12

121

116 RD

ARNOLD DR

GULCH

12

121

29

5 MILES

8 KILOMETERS

121

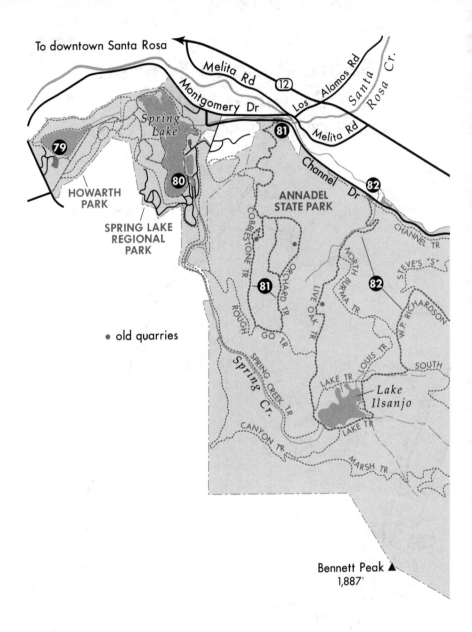

To downtown Santa Rosa

Melita Rd **12**

Los Alamos Rd

Santa Rosa Cr.

Montgomery Dr

Melita Rd

81

Channel Dr

82

Spring Lake

79

80

HOWARTH
PARK

SPRING LAKE
REGIONAL
PARK

ANNADEL
STATE PARK

CHANNEL TR

COBBLESTONE TR

ORCHARD TR

81

NORTH BURMA TR

LIVE OAK TR

82

STEVE'S "S"

W.P. RICHARDSON

● old quarries

ROUGH

GO TR

SPRING CREEK TR

Spring Cr.

LAKE TR

LOUIS TR

SOUTH

Lake Ilsanjo

CANYON TR

LAKE TR

MARSH TR

Bennett Peak ▲
1,887'

Annadel State Park
with HOWARTH PARK and
SPRING LAKE REGIONAL PARK

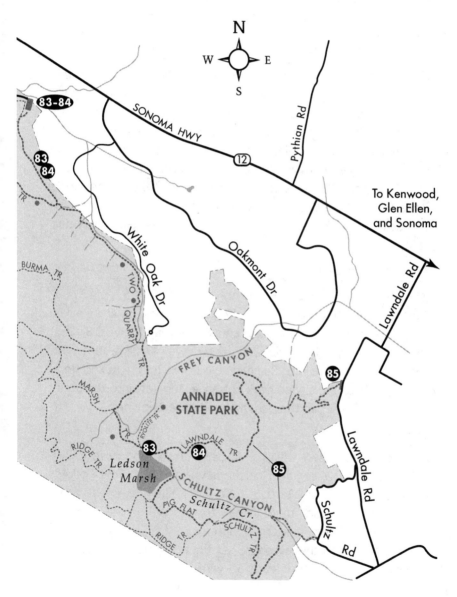

79. Howarth Park

Hiking distance: 0.9-mile loop
Hiking time: 30 minutes
Configuration: loop
Elevation gain: level
Difficulty: easy
Exposure: a mix of open grasslands and shaded forest
Dogs: allowed
Maps: U.S.G.S. Santa Rosa · Howarth Park Map and Trail Guide

Howarth Park lies adjacent to Spring Lake Regional Park on the east side of Santa Rosa. The diverse 152-acre community park is one of the city's oldest and largest parks. It includes tennis courts; a softball field; a climbing wall; an amusement area with a train, carousel, and animal barn; and a 25-acre lake with boat rentals. Hiking and biking trails surround Lake Ralphine in the center of the park. The trails connect with Spring Lake Regional Park (Hike 80) and continue into Annadel State Park (Hikes 81—85). This easy hike makes a pleasant loop around Lake Ralphine under stands of oaks.

To the trailhead

630 SUMMERFIELD ROAD · SANTA ROSA   38.453347, –122.668170

From Highway 101 and Highway 12 in Santa Rosa, drive 1.5 miles west on Highway 12 to Farmers Lane. Turn left and drive 0.8 miles to Montgomery Drive, following the Highway 12 signs. Turn right and continue one mile to Summerfield Road. Turn right and go a quarter mile to the signed park entrance. Turn left into the park, and drive 0.2 miles to the parking lot at Lake Ralphine.

The hike

From the south end of Lake Ralphine, take the paved Old Fisherman's Trail, a segment of the Bay Area Ridge Trail. Follow the east side of the lake to a fork at 0.1 mile. Curve left onto a dirt path. Meander through oak trees and a mixed riparian forest with willows, manzanita, and madrones. Pass short side paths that lead to the lakeshore. At the north tip of the lake is a junction. The right fork leads 50 yards to the paved path and continues into Spring Lake Regional Park. Descend on the left fork—the Eagle Scout Trail—and cross a wooden bridge over the lake's inlet stream. Continue on the north side of the lake, staying close to the shoreline. Traverse the forested hillside above the lake toward the dam. Bear left and cross a bridge over the outlet stream channel. Walk across Lake Ralphine Dam, completing the loop. ■

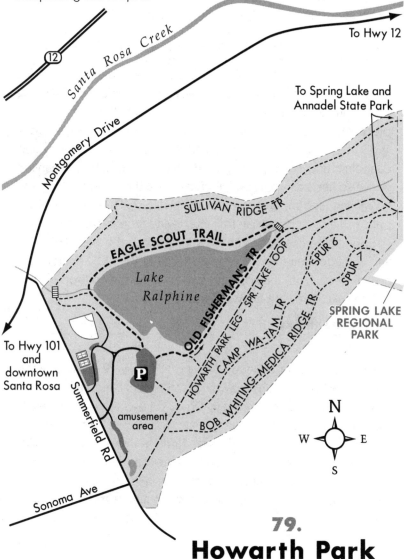

To Hwy 12

Santa Rosa Creek

12

Montgomery Drive

To Spring Lake and Annadel State Park

SULLIVAN RIDGE TR.

EAGLE SCOUT TRAIL

Lake Ralphine

OLD FISHERMAN'S TR.

HOWARTH PARK LEG - SPR. LAKE LOOP

CAMP WA-TAM TR.

BOB WHITING-MEDICA RIDGE TR.

SPUR 6

SPUR 7

SPRING LAKE REGIONAL PARK

To Hwy 101 and downtown Santa Rosa

Summerfield Rd

P

amusement area

Sonoma Ave

N
W ✦ E
S

79.
Howarth Park

80. Spring Lake Regional Park
Spring Lake Loop

Hiking distance: 2.6-mile loop
Hiking time: 1.5 hours
Configuration: loop
Elevation gain: 50 feet
Difficulty: easy
Exposure: a mix of open grasslands and shaded forest
Dogs: allowed
Maps: U.S.G.S. Santa Rosa · Spring Lake Regional Park map

Spring Lake Regional Park sits in the foothills of eastern Santa Rosa between Howarth Park and Annadel State Park. The 320-acre park is among the most popular parks in Santa Rosa. The center-piece of the park is Spring Lake, a 72-acre lake constructed in 1962 as a flood control reservoir. The lake is used for sailing, canoeing, and fishing (bass, bluegill, and trout). The expansive park also has a campground, picnic area, a three-acre spring-fed swimming lagoon, and miles of multi-use trails. A paved biking path and a dirt equestrian trail intertwine around the lake.

Spring Lake lies between Howarth Park to the west (Hike 79) and Annadel State Park to the east (Hikes 81—85). Several con-nector paths from the adjacent park join this paved loop around Spring Lake. Bikes are allowed on the loop.

To the trailhead

393 VIOLETTI ROAD · SANTA ROSA   38.454579, -122.647726

SANTA ROSA. From Highway 101 and Highway 12 in Santa Rosa, drive 1.5 miles west on Highway 12 to Farmers Lane. Turn left and drive 0.8 miles to Montgomery Drive, following the Highway 12 signs. Turn right and continue 2.7 miles to Channel Drive. Turn right and go 0.2 miles to Violetti Road. Turn right and drive 0.2 miles to the posted park entrance on Violetti Road. Turn right, passing the entrance station, and drive straight ahead 0.2 miles to the parking lot at Spring Lake and the swimming lagoon. A parking fee is required.

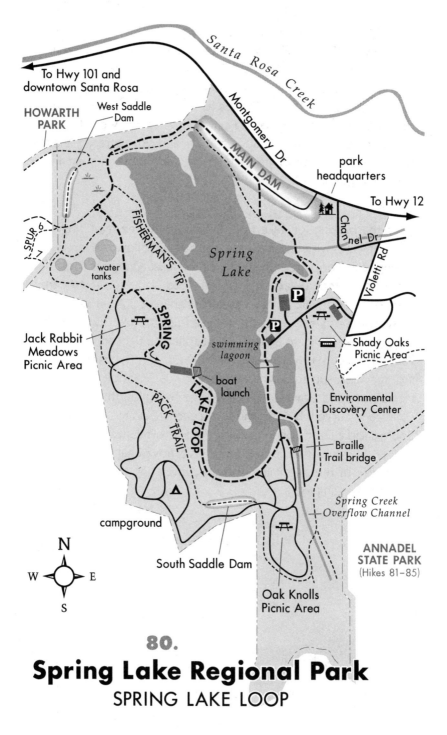

To Hwy 101 and downtown Santa Rosa

Santa Rosa Creek

HOWARTH PARK

West Saddle Dam

Montgomery Dr

MAIN DAM

park headquarters

To Hwy 12

Channel Dr

Violetti Rd

SPUR 6
7

water tanks

FISHERMAN'S TR

Spring Lake

P

P

SPRING

LAKE LOOP

PACK TRAIL

Jack Rabbit Meadows Picnic Area

swimming lagoon

boat launch

Shady Oaks Picnic Area

Environmental Discovery Center

Braille Trail bridge

Spring Creek Overflow Channel

campground

N
W   E
S

South Saddle Dam

ANNADEL STATE PARK
(Hikes 81–85)

Oak Knolls Picnic Area

80.
Spring Lake Regional Park
SPRING LAKE LOOP

KENWOOD. From the town of Kenwood, drive 5.5 miles north on Highway 12 (Sonoma Highway) to Los Alamos Road. Turn left and drive 0.2 miles to Melita Road. Turn right and immediately veer left onto Montgomery Drive. Continue a half mile to Channel Drive and turn left. Drive 0.2 miles to Violetti Road. Turn right and drive 0.2 miles to the posted park entrance on Violetti Road. Turn right, passing the entrance station, and drive straight ahead 0.2 miles to the parking lot at Spring Lake and the swimming lagoon. A parking fee is required.

The hike

From the parking lot, take the paved path to the right, walking counter-clockwise around the lake. The trail follows the edge of Spring Lake. Loop around a finger of the lake, and cross over the Santa Rosa Creek Diversion Channel. Head up to the top of the main dam, and walk northwest across the dam. After crossing, slowly descend, following the north end of the lake. Curve south through oak groves to a posted trail split. The right fork leads to Lake Ralphine in Howarth Park (Hike 79). Curve left, passing water storage tanks on the right. Weave into Jack Rabbit Meadows Picnic Area and down to the boat launch. Follow the shoreline south, and curve left along the south end of Spring Lake beneath South Saddle Dam. Continue along the shoreline. Cross the Braille Trail Bridge over the Spring Creek Overflow Channel. Skirt the west side of the swimming lagoon, completing the loop at the trailhead parking lot. ■

Annadel State Park

HIKES 81–85

6201 Channel Drive • Santa Rosa
open sunrise to sunset

Annadel State Park lies on the eastern edge of Santa Rosa at the north end of the Sonoma Mountains. The largely undeveloped park covers more than 5,500 pristine acres of oak woodlands, Douglas fir and redwood forests, and exposed chaparral slopes. The state park includes broad meadows, rolling hills, narrow ridges, stream-fed canyons, creeks, old cobblestone quarries, a 26-acre lake, and a wetland marsh. More than 40 miles of inter-connecting hiking, jogging, mountain biking, and horseback riding trails weave through the park's diverse habitats. The next five hikes explore the wide range of terrain and landscape found at Annadel State Park.

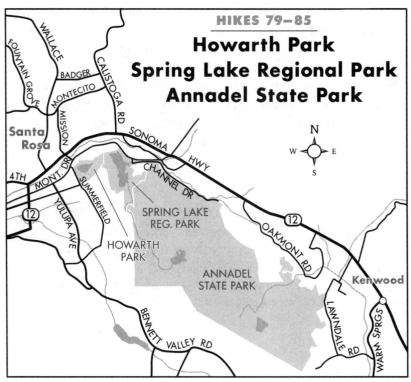

81. Cobblestone Trail— Orchard Trail Loop

ANNADEL STATE PARK

Hiking distance: 4.7-mile loop
Hiking time: 2.5 hours
Configuration: loop
Elevation gain: 400 feet
Difficulty: easy to moderate
Exposure: a mix of shaded forest and open meadows
Dogs: not allowed
Maps: U.S.G.S. Santa Rosa · Annadel State Park map

This hike forms a loop on the Cobblestone and Orchard Trails in the northwestern end of Annadel State Park. The Cobblestone Trail is named for the basalt cobblestones that were mined out of the area's quarries. The stones were once used for paving roads. The old cobblestones can still be seen on the streets of San Francisco and Sacramento. The trail passes the Wymore Quarry, where a gravity-powered tram transported cobblestones to a railroad line at Channel Drive. The return route on the Orchard Trail runs through the remains of an old orchard. The loop travels through several diverse habitats and landscapes, including oak and manzanita savanna, open meadows, and a stream-fed draw. En route, the trail crosses a narrow ridge and leads to vistas of upper Sonoma Valley and the Santa Rosa Plain.

To the trailhead

6201 CHANNEL DR · SANTA ROSA   38.456695, -122.639052

SANTA ROSA. From Highway 101 and Highway 12 in Santa Rosa, drive 1.5 miles west on Highway 12 to Farmers Lane. Turn left and drive 0.8 miles to Montgomery Drive, following the Highway 12 signs. Turn right and continue 2.7 miles to Channel Drive. Turn right and go 0.6 miles to the posted Cobblestone Trail on the right. Park in the pullout on the left.

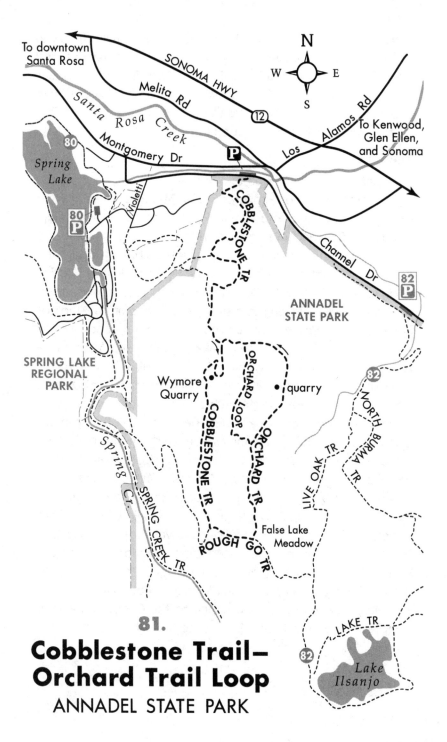

81.
Cobblestone Trail–
Orchard Trail Loop
ANNADEL STATE PARK

KENWOOD. From the town of Kenwood, drive 5.5 miles north on Highway 12 (Sonoma Highway) to Los Alamos Road. Turn left and drive 0.2 miles to Melita Road. Turn right and immediately veer left onto Montgomery Drive. Drive a half mile to Channel Drive and turn left. Continue 0.6 miles to the posted Cobblestone Trail on the right. Park in the pullout on the left.

The hike

Walk past the map kiosk on the Cobblestone Trail, entering the shady forest with moss-covered rocks. Pass through an oak and manzanita grassland, and weave up the north-facing hillside. Head up a draw and level out in a wide, open meadow. Skirt the west edge of the meadow, then curve left and cross through the grassland to a junction at 0.7 miles. The right fork leads to Spring Lake Regional Park (Hike 80). Stay left and reenter the mixed forest. Continue climbing to a sitting bench and an overlook of upper Sonoma Valley. Cross a minor ridge to a second junction with a path that leads to Spring Lake Regional Park. A short distance ahead is a junction with the Orchard Trail at 1.2 miles.

Begin the loop to the right, staying on the Cobblestone Trail. Cross the narrow ridge with two steep drop-offs. Make a sweeping right bend, then a left bend, passing the Wymore Quarry on the left. Traverse the hillside, enjoying the views west across the Santa Rosa Plain. Continue to a posted T-junction at 2.2 miles. Bear left on the Rough Go Trail. Walk 0.2 miles, passing an open meadow rimmed with oaks, to a junction with the Orchard Trail. The right fork leads to Lake Ilsanjo (Hike 82). Bear left on the Orchard Trail, and follow the west edge of False Lake Meadow to a junction. The two paths form a loop around the knoll just ahead, rejoining in a half mile. The left fork is slightly shorter. The right fork passes an old quarry. Both paths rejoin at 3.4 miles, then lead a short distance to the Cobblestone Trail, completing the loop. Return 1.2 miles to the right. ■

82. Lake Ilsanjo Loop
ANNADEL STATE PARK

Hiking distance: 6.2-mile loop
Hiking time: 3.5 hours
Configuration: loop
Elevation gain: 600 feet
Difficulty: moderate to slightly strenuous
Exposure: a mix of shaded forest and open meadows
Dogs: not allowed
Maps: U.S.G.S. Santa Rosa and Kenwood · Annadel State Park map

In the 1930s, Joe Coney bought the land that is now Annadel State Park. In the 1950s, he built Lake Ilsanjo on Spring Creek and named it after himself and his wife, Ilse. Joe used the 26-acre lake as a hunting and fishing retreat for his friends. Lake Ilsanjo is now the highlight of the park, popular with picnickers, mountain bikers, joggers, equestrians, hikers, and anglers hoping to catch bluegill and bass. The lake is surrounded by meadows filled with wildflowers.

This hike leads to Lake Ilsanjo from midway along Channel Drive. The trail circles the lakeshore and returns via the Richardson Trail, making a large loop through the center of the park. The Richardson Trail is an old ranch road shaded by redwoods and mixed oak woodlands.

To the trailhead

6201 CHANNEL DR · SANTA ROSA   38.451912, -122.633382

SANTA ROSA. From Highway 101 and Highway 12 in Santa Rosa, drive 1.5 miles west on Highway 12 to Farmers Lane. Turn left and drive 0.8 miles to Montgomery Drive, following the Highway 12 signs. Turn right and continue 2.7 miles to Channel Drive. Turn right and go 1.5 miles to the posted North Burma Trail and Channel Trail. Park along the right side of the road. A parking fee is required.

KENWOOD. From the town of Kenwood, drive 5.5 miles north on Highway 12 (Sonoma Highway) to Los Alamos Road. Turn left and drive 0.2 miles to Melita Road. Turn right and immediately veer left onto Montgomery Drive. Drive a half mile to Channel Drive and turn left. Continue 1.5 miles to the posted North Burma Trail and Channel Trail. Park along the right side of the road. A parking fee is required.

The hike

Head up the forested slope on the North Burma Trail. Follow the west side of a stream, originating from False Lake Meadow. Rock-hop over the creek and climb two switchbacks. Pass a 15-foot cataract, reaching a posted trail split on a flat at 0.7 miles. The North Burma Trail goes left. Stay straight on the Live Oak Trail and traverse the hillside, skirting the east side of grassy False Lake Meadow. At the summit, pass the site of an old quarry on the left. Gradually descend and cross a small bridge, emerging from the shady oak forest into False Lake Meadow. Cross the tree-rimmed grasslands to a junction with the Rough Go Trail at 1.6 miles. Follow the Rough Go Trail straight ahead through the rocky grassland. At just over 2 miles, the Rough Go Trail ends at a junction with the Lake Trail on the west side of Lake Ilsanjo. Both directions circle the lake.

For this hike, curve right, crossing the dam and spillway. Loop around the south and east sides of the picturesque lake. Cross two of the lake's feeder streams and a picnic area with a side loop on the left. At the north end of the lake is a four-way junction at 3 miles. The left fork loops back to the Rough Go Trail. The Louis Trail continues straight ahead for a shorter 5.1-mile hike.

For this hike, bear right on the W.P. Richardson Trail, an old ranch road. Head up the dirt road, staying left past a junction with the South Burma Trail. Traverse the hill, passing the North Burma Trail. Begin an easy descent through a forest of redwoods, Douglas fir, and coast live oak, passing Steve's "S" Trail at 3.9 miles. (The "S" Trail is a steep, hiking-only trail.) Pass a picnic area, water tank, and wood steps to a quarry site, all on the right. At 4.6 miles, pass the Two Quarry Trail on a horseshoe left bend (Hike 83). Continue down to the parking lot at the east end of Channel Drive at 5.5 miles. Head left and walk 0.7 miles on forested Channel Drive, or take the Channel Trail (parallel to the road) back to the trailhead. ■

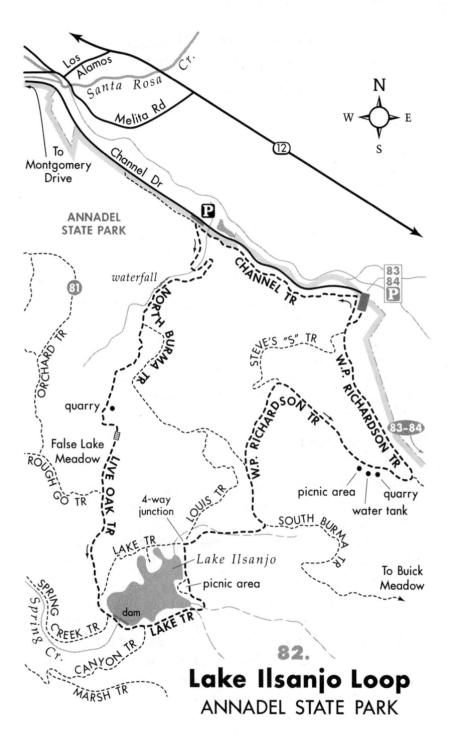

Los Alamos Cr.

Santa Rosa

Melita Rd

12

N
W E
S

To Montgomery Drive

Channel Dr

P

ANNADEL STATE PARK

waterfall

CHANNEL TR

83 84 P

81

ORCHARD TR

NORTH BURMA TR

STEVE'S "S" TR

W.P. RICHARDSON TR

W.P. RICHARDSON TR

83-84

quarry

LIVE OAK TR

False Lake Meadow

ROUGH GO TR

4-way junction

LOUIS TR

picnic area

water tank

quarry

LAKE TR

SOUTH BURMA TR

Lake Ilsanjo

picnic area

To Buick Meadow

SPRING CREEK TR

CANYON TR

dam

LAKE TR

Spring Cr.

MARSH TR

82.
Lake Ilsanjo Loop
ANNADEL STATE PARK

83. Two Quarry Trail to Ledson Marsh
ANNADEL STATE PARK

Hiking distance: 7 miles round trip
Hiking time: 4 hours
Configuration: out-and-back
Elevation gain: 800 feet
Difficulty: moderate to strenuous
Exposure: a mix of shaded forest and open meadows
Dogs: not allowed
Maps: U.S.G.S. Kenwood · Annadel State Park map

Ledson Marsh sits in a large 1,100-foot-high circular depression on the quieter, southeast end of the park. The 30-acre marsh was built in the 1930s as a reservoir to water eucalyptus trees. It is now a mosaic of waterways, overgrown with cattails, tules, and native grasses. It is a popular bird observation site with more than 100 species of birds that are known to inhabit the area. The Two Quarry Trail, named for two basalt quarry sites along the trail, leads into the eastern portion of the park to Ledson Marsh. The hike begins on the Warren Richardson Trail at the east end of Channel Drive and joins with the Two Quarry Trail. For a one-way shuttle hike to Ledson Marsh, see Hike 84.

To the trailhead

6201 CHANNEL DR · SANTA ROSA   38.444569, -122.615691

SANTA ROSA. From Highway 101 and Highway 12 in Santa Rosa, drive 1.5 miles west on Highway 12 to Farmers Lane. Turn left and drive 0.8 miles to Montgomery Drive, following the Highway 12 signs. Turn right and continue 2.7 miles to Channel Drive. Turn right and go 2.2 miles to the large parking lot at the end of the road. A parking fee is required.

KENWOOD. From the town of Kenwood, drive 5.5 miles north on Highway 12 (Sonoma Highway) to Los Alamos Road. Turn left and drive 0.2 miles to Melita Road. Turn right and immediately veer left onto Montgomery Drive. Drive a half mile to Channel Drive and turn left. Continue 2.2 miles to the large parking lot at the end of the road. A parking fee is required.

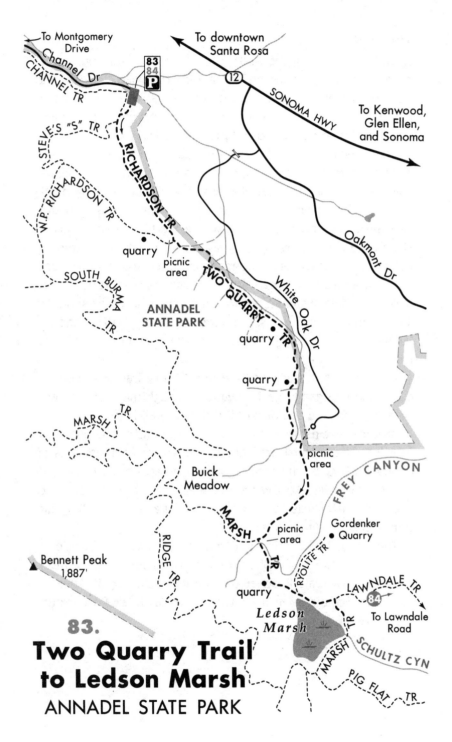

To Montgomery Drive

Channel Dr

CHANNEL TR

83 84 P

To downtown Santa Rosa

12

SONOMA HWY

To Kenwood, Glen Ellen, and Sonoma

STEVE'S "S" TR

W.P. RICHARDSON TR

RICHARDSON TR

quarry

picnic area

TWO QUARRY TR

Oakmont Dr

White Oak Dr

SOUTH BURMA TR

ANNADEL STATE PARK

quarry

quarry

MARSH TR

picnic area

Buick Meadow

FREY CANYON

RIDGE TR

MARSH TR

picnic area

Gordenker Quarry

Bennett Peak 1,887'

quarry

RYOLITE TR

LAWNDALE TR

84

To Lawndale Road

Ledson Marsh

MARSH TR

SCHULTZ CYN

PIG FLAT TR

83.
Two Quarry Trail
to Ledson Marsh
ANNADEL STATE PARK

The hike

From the far end of the parking lot, take the hikers-only foot-path to the W.P. Richardson Trail, a wide dirt road. Bear left and head up the old boulder-studded ranch road to an oak-rimmed meadow with a view of Sugarloaf Ridge to the east. At 0.9 miles, on a horseshoe right bend, is a picnic area and junction.

Leave the road and take the Two Quarry Trail to the left. Cross a stream and head east on the footpath through bay laurel and towering Douglas fir trees. Traverse the hillside, walking parallel to the creek on the left. Cross three small feeder streams. Pass a rock quarry on the right, where the trail begins to climb. Head up the lush canyon, rising above the creek, then returning back to the creek. Pass a second distinct quarry on the right, and curve away from the creek. Stroll through the quiet forest, cross another tributary stream, and return to the creek by a series of small waterfalls and pools. Hop over the creek to a T-junction at 2.4 miles. The left fork is an access to White Oak Drive, a private road.

Go to the right, staying on the Two Quarry Trail (which is now a dirt road). Steadily gain elevation through the dense forest, weaving along the contours of the canyon wall. Leave the canyon to an expansive meadow with a picnic area and posted junction. Bear left on the Marsh Trail, crossing a stream. Pass remnants of another quarry on the right to the northwest corner of Ledson Marsh at 3.3 miles. Follow the north edge of the reed-covered marsh a quarter mile to a junction with the Lawndale Trail, the turn-around point for this hike.

The Marsh Trail continues to the right along the east side of Ledson Marsh. Straight ahead—Hike 84—leads nearly 3 miles down to Lawndale Road at the northeast corner of Annadel State Park. For the 6.4-mile shuttle hike to Lawndale Road, reference Hike 84. ■

84. Ledson Marsh Shuttle

Two Quarry Trail from Channel Drive to Lawndale Trail at Lawndale Road

ANNADEL STATE PARK

Hiking distance: 6.4-mile one-way shuttle
Hiking time: 3.5 hours
Configuration: one-way shuttle
Elevation gain: 800 feet
Difficulty: moderate to strenuous
Exposure: a mix of shaded forest and open meadows
Dogs: not allowed
Maps: U.S.G.S. Kenwood · Annadel State Park map

Between 1870 and 1920, Italian stonecutters worked in the basalt quarries of present-day Annadel State Park. The cobblestones were used for paving streets throughout northern California. After the 1920s, when roads were then primarily used by automobiles, the cobblestones were no longer used for paving.

This hike utilizes a shuttle car. The route begins at Channel Drive, leads to Ledson Marsh, then continues to the shuttle car trailhead on Lawndale Road. The hike travels through the quieter eastern end of the park on the Two Quarry Trail, passing old quarries en route to Ledson Marsh. (The quarries have since been reclaimed by moss.) Ledson Marsh is a popular site for observing birds. The marsh lies within a circular depression at 1,100 feet. The hike then descends from Ledson Marsh to Lawndale Road, weaving through redwood and Douglas fir forests to vistas of Sonoma Valley and the surrounding mountains.

To the trailhead

6201 CHANNEL DR · SANTA ROSA   38.444569, -122.615691

SANTA ROSA. From Highway 101 and Highway 12 in Santa Rosa, drive 1.5 miles west on Highway 12 to Farmers Lane. Turn left and drive 0.8 miles to Montgomery Drive, following the Highway 12 signs. Turn right and continue 2.7 miles to Channel Drive. Turn right and go 2.2 miles to the large parking lot at the end of the road. A parking fee is required.

KENWOOD. From the town of Kenwood, drive 5.5 miles north on Highway 12 (Sonoma Highway) to Los Alamos Road. Turn left and drive 0.2 miles to Melita Road. Turn right and immediately veer left onto Montgomery Drive. Drive a half mile to Channel Drive and turn left. Continue 2.2 miles to the large parking lot at the end of the road. A parking fee is required.

Shuttle Car

1606 LAWNDALE RD · KENWOOD	38.417671, -122.575008

SANTA ROSA. From Highway 101 and Highway 12 in Santa Rosa, drive 1.5 miles west on Highway 12 to Farmers Lane. Turn left and drive one mile to 4th Street, following the Highway 12 signs. Turn right and continue 8.4 miles to Lawndale Road. Turn right and go 1.1 mile to the trailhead parking lot on the right at the base of the mountains.

KENWOOD. From the town of Kenwood, drive 2 miles north on Highway 12 (Sonoma Highway) to Lawndale Road. Turn left and continue 1.1 mile to the trailhead parking lot on the right at the base of the mountains.

The hike

From the far end of the parking lot, take the hikers-only footpath to the W.P. Richardson Trail, a wide dirt road. Bear left and head up the old boulder-studded ranch road to an oak-rimmed meadow with a view of Sugarloaf Ridge to the east. At 0.9 miles, on a horseshoe right bend, is a picnic area and junction.

Leave the road and take the Two Quarry Trail to the left. Cross a stream and head east on the footpath through bay laurel and towering Douglas fir trees. Traverse the hillside, walking parallel to the creek on the left. Cross three small feeder streams. Pass a rock quarry on the right, where the trail begins to climb. Head up the lush canyon, rising above the creek, then returning back to the creek. Pass a second distinct quarry on the right, and curve away from the creek. Stroll through the quiet forest, cross another tributary stream, and return to the creek by a series of

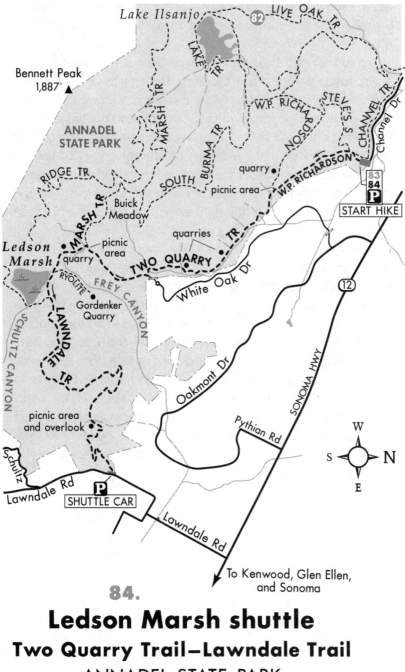

Lake Ilsanjo

82 LIVE OAK TR

Bennett Peak
1,887'

ANNADEL
STATE PARK

LAKE TR

MARSH TR

W.P. RICHARDSON

STEVE'S S

CHANNEL TR

Channel Dr

RIDGE TR

SOUTH BURMA TR

quarry

picnic area

W.P. RICHARDSON

83
84
P

START HIKE

MARSH TR

Buick
Meadow

quarries

TWO QUARRY TR

Ledson
Marsh

picnic
area

quarry

RYOLITE

FREY CANYON

White Oak Dr

Gordenker
Quarry

12

LAWNDALE TR

SCHULTZ CANYON

Oakmont Dr

Sonoma Hwy

picnic area
and overlook

Pythian Rd

W

S   N

E

Schultz

Lawndale Rd

P

SHUTTLE CAR

Lawndale Rd

To Kenwood, Glen Ellen,
and Sonoma

84.

Ledson Marsh shuttle
Two Quarry Trail–Lawndale Trail
ANNADEL STATE PARK

small waterfalls and pools. Hop over the creek to a T-junction at 2.4 miles. The left fork is an access to White Oak Drive, a private road.

Go to the right, staying on the Two Quarry Trail (which is now a dirt road). Steadily gain elevation through the dense forest, weaving along the contours of the canyon wall. Leave the canyon to an expansive meadow with a picnic area and posted junction. Bear left on the Marsh Trail, crossing a stream. Pass remnants of another quarry on the right to the northwest corner of Ledson Marsh at 3.3 miles. Follow the north edge of the reed-covered marsh a quarter mile to a junction with the Lawndale Trail. The Marsh Trail continues to the right along the east side of Ledson Marsh.

From the Lawndale Trail–Marsh Trail junction, continue straight ahead (east) on the Lawndale Trail at a level grade. Descend through oak trees into the canyon. Traverse the canyon walls under a forest canopy of firs and redwoods. Head downhill to a right bend under powerlines. The vistas extend across Sonoma Valley to Sugarloaf Ridge, Bald Mountain, and Red Mountain. Continue traversing the steep hillside and make a sharp left bend, crossing over a seasonal drainage. Emerge from the forest to a grassy knoll and picnic area overlooking Sonoma Valley. Loop around the knoll and curve left over another drainage. Zigzag down two switchbacks, crossing a drainage on the second bend. Wind down to the base of the mountain and the trailhead/shuttle car on Lawndale Road. ∎

85. Lawndale Trail—Ledson Marsh
Schultz Canyon Loop
ANNADEL STATE PARK

Hiking distance: 7-mile loop
Hiking time: 4 hours
Configuration: loop
Elevation gain: 700 feet
Difficulty: moderate to strenuous
Exposure: a mix of shaded forest and open meadows
Dogs: not allowed
Maps: U.S.G.S. Kenwood · Annadel State Park map

This hike makes a large loop through the quieter east end of Annadel State Park in Sonoma Valley. The route begins on the Lawndale Trail, an old road once used by stonecutters working in the area's basalt quarries. The road follows a stream drainage, climbs to knolls with overlooks, weaves under a canopy of redwoods and Douglas firs, and emerges at Ledson Marsh at 1,100 feet. The marsh is prime bird habitat. The water collected in Ledson Marsh overflows into Schultz Canyon, where the hike returns. The trail descends through the remote canyon, following the forested watercourse. The loop returns to the trailhead along quiet, narrow roads that border the state park. Along the route are views of Sugarloaf Ridge, Hood Mountain, and Sonoma Valley.

To the trailhead

1606 LAWNDALE RD · KENWOOD   38.417671, -122.575008

SANTA ROSA. From Highway 101 and Highway 12 in Santa Rosa, drive 1.5 miles west on Highway 12 to Farmers Lane. Turn left and drive one mile to 4th Street, following the Highway 12 signs. Turn right and continue 8.4 miles to Lawndale Road. Turn right and go 1.1 mile to the trailhead parking lot on the right at the base of the mountains.

KENWOOD. From the town of Kenwood, drive 2 miles north on Highway 12 (Sonoma Highway) to Lawndale Road. Turn left and continue 1.1 mile to the trailhead parking lot on the right at the base of the mountains.

The hike

Walk past the trailhead gate, and head up the grassy slope dotted with oak, madrone, and buckeye trees. Loop around a lush, stream-fed canyon and continue up the hillside through moss-covered valley oaks and manzanita. Curve right, crossing the drainage, and emerge to a grassy knoll with a picnic area and open vistas. The views extend across Sonoma Valley to Sugarloaf Ridge, Hood Mountain, Bald Mountain, and Red Mountain. Loop left around the knoll, and reenter a cool Douglas fir and redwood forest with several species of ferns covering the forest floor. Cross two more seasonal drainages, steadily climbing on a gentle grade. After gaining 500 feet in elevation, the trail switchbacks to the left beneath power lines. Top a minor ridge and slowly curve right around a hill. Cross under the power lines, where the trail levels out.

Continue to a junction with the Marsh Trail at 2.9 miles. Bear left on the Marsh Trail, and cross a bridge over Schultz Creek, the outlet steam of Ledson Marsh. Skirt the east edge of the reed-filled marsh to a signed junction with a picnic area overlooking the wetland at 3.3 miles. Bear left on the Pig Flat Trail, and cross the flat through oaks and manzanita to a staggered junction at 3.8 miles. To the right is the Ridge Trail.

Twenty yards ahead, bear left and head east on the Schultz Trail. Cross a tributary of Schultz Creek, and meander through the forest down the south wall of Schultz Canyon. Curve out of the canyon and switchback left to vistas down Sonoma Valley. Pass a picnic area and overlook on the left, and return into Schultz Canyon. At the canyon floor, follow the creek downstream 150 yards and hop over the creek. Traverse the hill to the east edge of Annadel State Park, reaching the gate at Schultz Road.

Bear left on Schultz Road, and climb 0.8 miles up the narrow, winding road to Lawndale Road. Go to the left and continue a half mile downhill to the trailhead at the base of the mountain. ∎

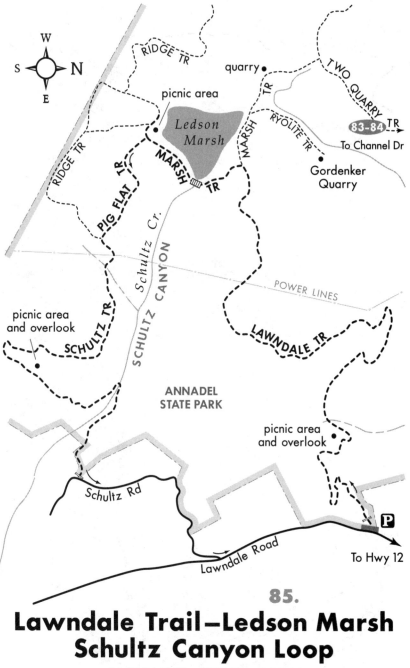

Lawndale Trail–Ledson Marsh
Schultz Canyon Loop
ANNADEL STATE PARK

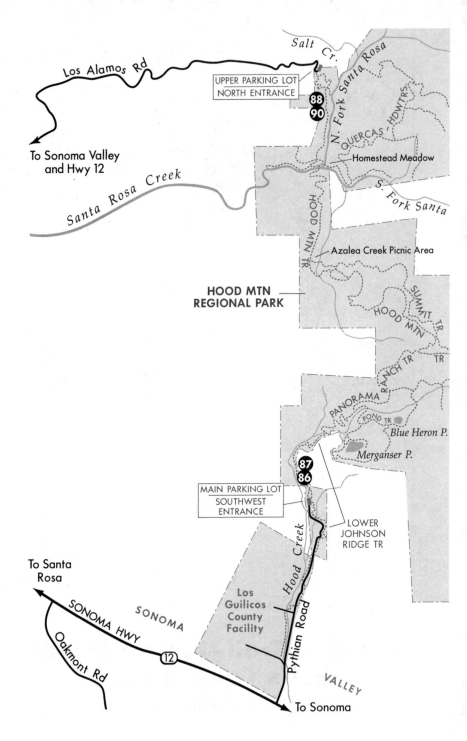

Salt Cr.

Los Alamos Rd

N. Fork Santa Rosa

UPPER PARKING LOT
NORTH ENTRANCE

88
90

QUERCAS HDWTRS

Homestead Meadow

To Sonoma Valley
and Hwy 12

Santa Rosa Creek

S. Fork Santa

HOOD MTN TR

Azalea Creek Picnic Area

**HOOD MTN
REGIONAL PARK**

SUMMIT TR

HOOD MTN

RANCH TR

TR

PANORAMA

POND TR

Blue Heron P.

Merganser P.

87
86

MAIN PARKING LOT
SOUTHWEST
ENTRANCE

LOWER
JOHNSON
RIDGE TR

To Santa
Rosa

SONOMA HWY

SONOMA

Hood Creek

Oakmont Rd

12

Los
Guilicos
County
Facility

Pythian Road

VALLEY

To Sonoma

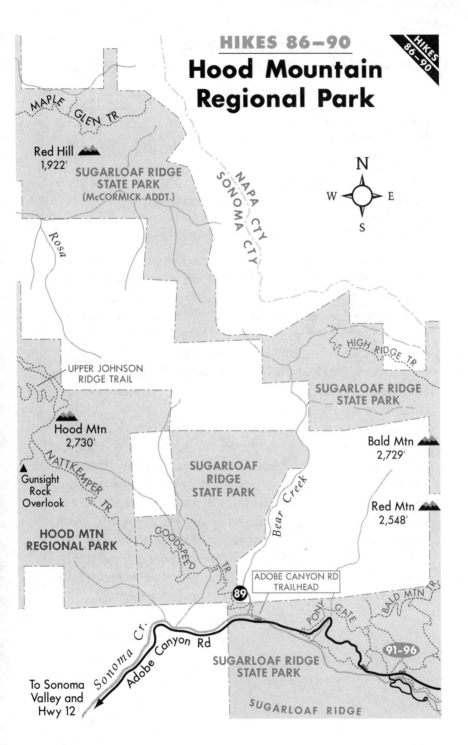

Hood Mountain Regional Park

MAPLE GLEN TR

Red Hill
1,922'

SUGARLOAF RIDGE
STATE PARK
(McCORMICK ADDT.)

NAPA CTY
SONOMA CTY

Rosa

N
W   E
S

UPPER JOHNSON
RIDGE TRAIL

HIGH RIDGE TR

SUGARLOAF RIDGE
STATE PARK

Hood Mtn
2,730'

Bald Mtn
2,729'

NATTKEMPER TR

Gunsight
Rock
Overlook

SUGARLOAF
RIDGE
STATE PARK

Bear Creek

Red Mtn
2,548'

HOOD MTN
REGIONAL PARK

GOODSPEED TR

ADOBE CANYON RD
TRAILHEAD

89

PONY GATE

BALD MTN TR

91-96

Sonoma Cr.

Adobe Canyon Rd

SUGARLOAF RIDGE
STATE PARK

To Sonoma
Valley and
Hwy 12

SUGARLOAF RIDGE

86. Lower Johnson Ridge Trail
to Merganser Pond and Blue Heron Pond
HOOD MOUNTAIN REGIONAL PARK

Hiking distance: 4-mile loop
Hiking time: 2 hours
Configuration: loop
Elevation gain: 1,000 feet
Difficulty: moderate to strenuous
Exposure: mostly shaded forest with open meadows
Dogs: allowed
Maps: U.S.G.S. Kenwood · Hood Mountain Regional Park

Hood Mountain Regional Park sits in the Mayacamas Mountains five miles east of Santa Rosa. The park lies adjacent to Sugarloaf Ridge State Park. Interconnecting trails link the two parks. The 5,800-acre wilderness park has elevations ranging from 650 feet to 2,730 feet atop the crest of Hood Mountain. The park contains the headwaters of Santa Rosa Creek and tributaries that feed Sonoma Creek. The diverse parkland includes rolling meadows, deep canyons, sheer wooded slopes, and dramatic rock outcroppings.

This hike begins from the main trailhead parking lot at Pythian Road. The trail climbs through the 247-acre Lawson Property, which provides public access from the Sonoma Valley floor. The hike follows the Lower Johnson Ridge Trail to Merganser Pond and Blue Heron Pond, climbing through mixed woodland forests and grassland habitats while overlooking Hood Creek Canyon. Despite the thousand-foot elevation gain, the trail winds only halfway up to the summit of Hood Mountain. From the ponds, however, are views overlooking Sonoma Valley, Annadel State Park and Glen Ellen. (Hike 87 continues up to the summit.)

To the trailhead

1450 PYTHIAN ROAD · SANTA ROSA   38.451714, -122.574100

NORTH SONOMA VALLEY. From Highway 12 and Calistoga Road on the north end of Sonoma Valley, drive 4.6 miles southeast on Highway 12 (Sonoma Highway) to Pythian Road. Turn left and continue 1.3 miles to the trailhead parking lot on the right at the end of the public road. A parking fee is required.

KENWOOD. From the town of Kenwood in Sonoma Valley, drive 2 miles north on Highway 12 (Sonoma Highway) to Pythian Road on the right. Turn right and continue 1.3 miles to the trailhead parking lot on the right at the end of the public road. A parking fee is required.

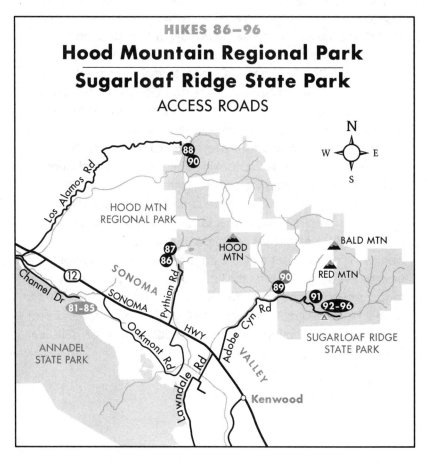

The hike

Walk north up the hill, passing a mileage sign, into the mixed forest on the Lower Johnson Ridge Trail. Stroll among the oak, Douglas fir, madrone, and bigleaf maple trees. Pass a couple of homes on the right. Merge with an asphalt road, and head 0.3 miles up the steep road high above Hood Creek. Curve right as the pavement ends. Walk 40 yards and switchback left, returning to the Lower Johnson Ridge Trail. Zigzag up the hill on the footpath, passing three water tanks. Steadily climb to a posted junction with the Panorama Ranch Trail on the left at 1.5 miles. The Ranch Trail continues to the Hood Mountain summit and the Gunsight Rock Overlook (Hike 87).

Curve right, staying on the Lower Johnson Ridge Trail. Cross a bridge over Hood Creek to a Y-fork with the Pond Trail. The right fork descends to Merganser Pond. Begin the loop on the left fork to a junction with the Valley View Trail—the return route. First, detour straight ahead 100 yards to the south shore of Blue Heron Pond. At the north end of the pond is a picnic table under a mature walnut tree. The Pond Trail continues north and joins the Upper Johnson Ridge Trail up to Hood Mountain.

After enjoying the pastoral site, return to the Valley View Trail. Bear left and descend, overlooking Sonoma Valley and Annadel State Park. Loop around the canyon, high above Merganser Pond, to an overlook of the valley above Kenwood and Glen Ellen. Drop down on a couple of switchbacks to a junction near Merganser Pond. The right fork leads 50 yards to the southwest shore. The side path follows a berm on the edge of the pond and rejoins the main trail at a junction with the Pond Trail. A side path on the right loops around to the east side of the pond and ends by picnic tables. From the junction, head uphill on the Pond Trail and veer left, completing the loop at the Lower Johnson Ridge Trail. Bear left and retrace your steps. ■

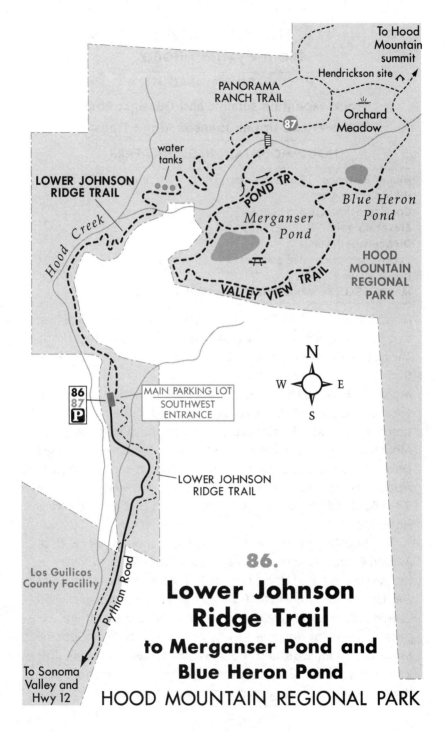

To Hood
Mountain
summit

Hendrickson site

PANORAMA
RANCH TRAIL

87

Orchard
Meadow

water
tanks

LOWER JOHNSON
RIDGE TRAIL

Blue Heron
Pond

POND TR

*Merganser
Pond*

Hood Creek

HOOD
MOUNTAIN
REGIONAL
PARK

VALLEY VIEW TRAIL

N
W   E
S

86
87
P

MAIN PARKING LOT
SOUTHWEST
ENTRANCE

LOWER JOHNSON
RIDGE TRAIL

Los Guilicos
County Facility

Pythian Road

86.

Lower Johnson
Ridge Trail
to Merganser Pond and
Blue Heron Pond
HOOD MOUNTAIN REGIONAL PARK

To Sonoma
Valley and
Hwy 12

87. Hood Mountain from Pythian Road

HOOD MOUNTAIN: ROUTE 1

Hood Mountain summit and Gunsight Rock

Lower and Upper Johnson Ridge Trails

HOOD MOUNTAIN REGIONAL PARK

Hiking distance: 7.2 miles round trip
Hiking time: 4 hours
Configuration: out and back
Elevation gain: 1,900 feet
Difficulty: strenuous
Exposure: a mix of shaded forest and open meadows
Dogs: allowed
Maps: U.S.G.S. Kenwood · Hood Mountain Regional Park

Hood Mountain is a 2,730-foot mountain with a craggy rock face that overlooks Sonoma Valley just east of the city of Santa Rosa. The headwaters of Santa Rosa Creek and Sonoma Creek form on the slopes of the mountain, which is the centerpiece of Hood Mountain Regional Park. Gunsight Rock Overlook lies just southwest of the summit. The overlook is an extensive rock formation with a notch. Three routes climb to the summit of Hood Mountain and the Gunsight Rock Overlook. The next three hikes (Hikes 87—89) include the three routes, which access the peak from three different trailheads. A fourth hike—Hike 90—is a 9.4-mile shuttle hike that travels the length of the park across Hood Mountain.

This hike begins at the southwest entrance at the end of Pythian Road. The trailhead is accessed from Sonoma Valley at the western base of Hood Mountain. The route takes the Lower and Upper Johnson Ridge Trails to the 2,730-foot summit and Gunsight Rock Overlook. From the vertical rock perch are expansive views of Sonoma Valley, Annadel State Park, Sonoma Mountain, Santa Rosa, and the coastal mountains. The hike follows along Hood Creek Canyon, the headwaters of Hood Creek, through a dense coniferous woodland, then continues to a freshwater wetland and the Hendrickson Homestead site. The trail ascends the crest of Hood Mountain to its summit and to the Gunsight Rock Overlook.

To the trailhead

1450 PYTHIAN ROAD · SANTA ROSA   38.451714, –122.574100

NORTH SONOMA VALLEY. From Highway 12 and Calistoga Road on the north end of Sonoma Valley, drive 4.6 miles southeast on Highway 12 (Sonoma Highway) to Pythian Road. Turn left and continue 1.3 miles to the trailhead parking lot on the right at the end of the public road. A parking fee is required.

KENWOOD. From the town of Kenwood in Sonoma Valley, drive 2 miles north on Highway 12 (Sonoma Highway) to Pythian Road on the right. Turn right and continue 1.3 miles to the trailhead parking lot on the right at the end of the public road. A parking fee is required.

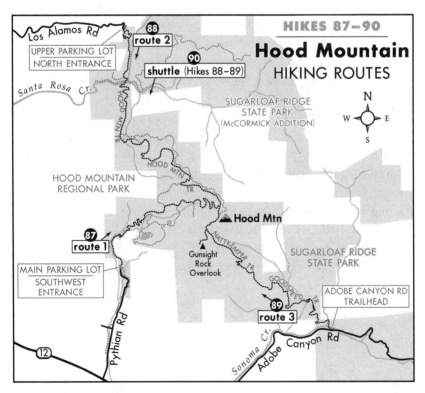

The hike

Walk north up the hill, passing a mileage sign, into the mixed forest on the Lower Johnson Ridge Trail. Stroll among the oak, Douglas fir, madrone, and bigleaf maple trees. Pass a couple of homes on the right. Merge with an asphalt road, and head 0.3 miles up the steep road high above Hood Creek. Curve right as the pavement ends. Walk 40 yards and switchback left, returning to the Lower Johnson Ridge Trail. Zigzag up the hill on the footpath, passing three water tanks on the right. Steadily climb to a posted junction with the Panorama Ranch Trail on the left at 1.5 miles. The right fork leads to Blue Heron Pond and Merganser Pond (Hike 86).

For this hike, go left on the Panorama Ranch Trail and steadily climb. Skirt Orchard Meadow on the right to a junction. Bear right on the Orchard Meadow Trail, and walk 0.15 miles to a junction with Upper Johnson Ridge Trail. Bear left past the Hendrickson Historical Homesite on the left, which includes two old wood houses, a stone root cellar, and a brick chimney. Head north, zigzagging up the mountain and passing Knight's Retreat Trail. Continue climbing to the Hood Mountain Trail atop the ridge. Go to the right and climb another 0.2 miles through the shaded forest to the Hood Mountain summit at just over 3 miles.

From the summit, descend 0.2 miles on the Nattkemper Trail through manzanita and multi-colored lava rock outcroppings to the signed Gunsight Rock Trail. The left fork—the Nattkemper Trail—continues into Sugarloaf Ridge State Park to Adobe Canyon Road. Veer right on the Gunsight Rock Trail, and walk 0.2 miles to a massive jumble of rocks overlooking Sonoma Valley. The vistas extend to San Pablo Bay and the Santa Rosa Valley, Sonoma Mountain to Mount Tamalpais in Marin County, and Mount Diablo in Contra Costa County. Return by retracing your route. ■

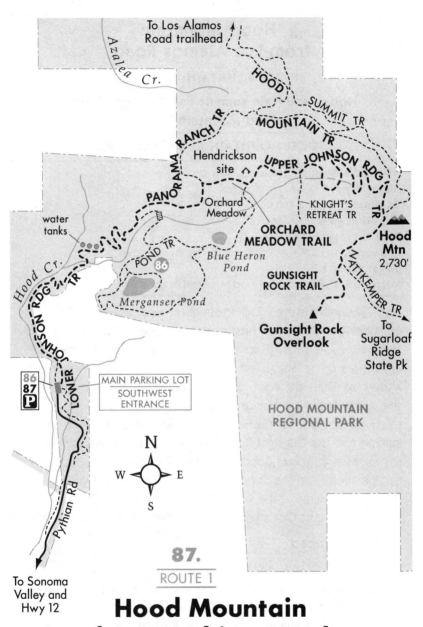

To Los Alamos Road trailhead

Azalea Cr.

HOOD MOUNTAIN TR

SUMMIT TR

PANORAMA RANCH TR

Hendrickson site

UPPER JOHNSON RDG

PANORAMA

water tanks

Orchard Meadow

KNIGHT'S RETREAT TR

ORCHARD MEADOW TRAIL

Hood Cr.

JOHNSON RDG TR

POND TR

86

Blue Heron Pond

Merganser Pond

GUNSIGHT ROCK TRAIL

ZATTKEMPER TR

Hood Mtn 2,730'

▲ **Gunsight Rock Overlook**

To Sugarloaf Ridge State Pk

86 87 P

LOWER

MAIN PARKING LOT SOUTHWEST ENTRANCE

HOOD MOUNTAIN REGIONAL PARK

N
W · E
S

Pythian Rd

To Sonoma Valley and Hwy 12

87.
ROUTE 1

Hood Mountain from Pythian Road
Lower and Upper Johnson Ridge Trails
HOOD MOUNTAIN REGIONAL PARK

88. Hood Mountain from Los Alamos Road

HOOD MOUNTAIN: ROUTE 2

Hood Mountain summit and Gunsight Rock
Hood Mountain Trail

HOOD MOUNTAIN REGIONAL PARK

Hiking distance: 11.8 miles round trip
Hiking time: 6 hours
Configuration: out and back
Elevation gain: 2,100 feet
Difficulty: very strenuous
Exposure: a mix of shaded forest and open meadows
Dogs: allowed
Maps: U.S.G.S. Kenwood · Hood Mountain Regional Park

Hood Mountain is the 2,730-foot centerpiece of Hood Mountain Regional Park. It is the highest peak between Sonoma Valley and Napa Valley. The 5,800-acre wilderness park includes three hiking routes up to the summit and the nearby craggy overlook known as Gunsight Rock. This hike accesses the summit from the upper (north) entrance at the end of Los Alamos Road. The strenuous route takes the Hood Mountain Trail (a fire road) to the summit and the Gunsight Rock Overlook. The massive jumble of rocks sits high above Sonoma Valley. (The prominent rock face can be seen from the Sonoma Highway.) From the overlook are spectacular vistas of the valley. On a clear day, the Golden Gate Bridge, the Pacific Ocean, and the Sierra Nevada Range are visible.

To the trailhead

3000 LOS ALAMOS RD · SANTA ROSA   38.488809, -122.572103

NORTH SONOMA VALLEY. From Highway 12 and Calistoga Road on the north end of Sonoma Valley, drive 1.1 miles southeast on Highway 12 (Sonoma Highway) to Los Alamos Road. Turn left and drive 4.7 miles up the narrow, winding mountain road to the park entrance gate. Continue another 0.6 miles downhill to the trailhead parking area on the right. A parking fee is required.

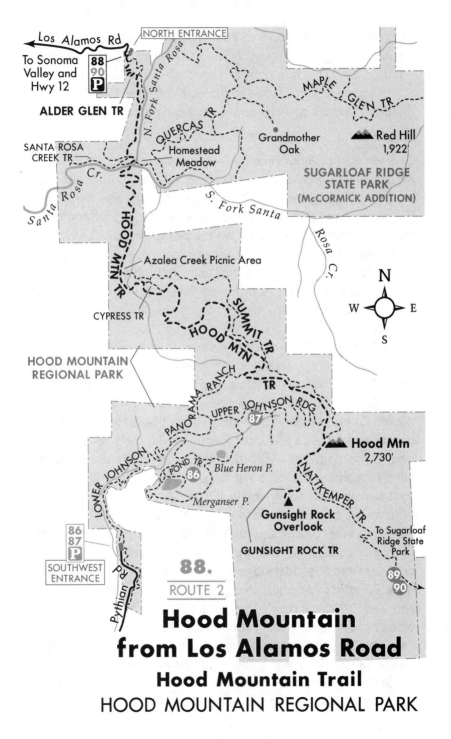

Los Alamos Rd →

NORTH ENTRANCE

To Sonoma
Valley and
Hwy 12

88
90
P

ALDER GLEN TR

N. Fork Santa Rosa

QUERCAS TR

MAPLE GLEN TR

Grandmother
Oak

Red Hill
1,922'

SANTA ROSA
CREEK TR

Santa Rosa Cr.

Homestead
Meadow

S. Fork Santa

**SUGARLOAF RIDGE
STATE PARK**
(McCORMICK ADDITION)

Rosa Cr.

HOOD MTN TR

Azalea Creek Picnic Area

N
W · E
S

CYPRESS TR

SUMMIT TR

HOOD MTN

**HOOD MOUNTAIN
REGIONAL PARK**

PANORAMA RANCH TR

UPPER JOHNSON RDG

87

Hood Mtn
2,730'

LOWER JOHNSON

POND TR

86

Blue Heron P.

NATTKEMPER TR

Merganser P.

▲ Gunsight Rock
Overlook

To Sugarloaf
Ridge State
Park

86
87
P

SOUTHWEST
ENTRANCE

Pythian Rd

GUNSIGHT ROCK TR

89
90

88.
ROUTE 2

Hood Mountain
from Los Alamos Road
Hood Mountain Trail
HOOD MOUNTAIN REGIONAL PARK

KENWOOD. From the town of Kenwood in Sonoma Valley, drive 5.5 miles north on Highway 12 (Sonoma Highway) to Los Alamos Road on the right. Turn right and continue 4.7 miles up the narrow, winding mountain road to the park entrance gate. Continue another 0.6 miles downhill to the trailhead parking area.

The hike

Take the posted Alder Glen Trail, which soon joins with the Hood Mountain Trail. Weave down the wide, forested path under the shade of evergreens, maples, oaks, bays, figs, and madrone. Follow the west canyon wall into Homestead Meadow, engulfed by the surrounding mountains, to the picnic area and T-junction at 1.1 miles. The right fork is a service road. Bear left and drop down 100 yards to a signed trail split. The left fork enters the 1,200-acre McCormick Addition of Sugarloaf Ridge State Park. Stay to the right for 30 yards to Santa Rosa Creek amid alders and bays.

Rock hop over the creek, and head up the slope among horsetail ferns. The long, steady climb leads to the posted Azalea Creek Picnic Area on the left and restrooms on the right at 2.5 miles. Climb a short distance, passing the Summit Trail. Cross over Azalea Creek, and climb to vistas of Mount Saint Helena and the coastal range. Pass a few more junctions with the Summit Trail, a parallel footpath that winds through a pygmy forest. Both routes head east and merge on a flat circular clearing atop the 2,730-foot summit of Hood Mountain at 5.5 miles.

From the summit, descend on the Nattkemper Trail through manzanita and colorful lava outcrops for 0.2 miles to the signed Gunsight Rock Trail. The left fork—the Nattkemper Trail—continues into Sugarloaf Ridge State Park to Adobe Canyon Road (Hike 90—the shuttle hike). Veer right on the Gunsight Rock Trail and walk 0.2 miles, passing volcanic outcroppings to a massive block of rocks overlooking Sonoma Valley. The vistas extend to San Pablo Bay and the Santa Rosa Valley, Sonoma Mountain to Mount Tamalpais in Marin County, and Mount Diablo in Contra Costa County. Return by retracing your route, or take the alternate Summit Trail back to the Azalea Creek Picnic Area. ■

89. Hood Mountain from Adobe Canyon Road

Hood Mountain Summit and Gunsight Rock
Goodspeed—Nattkemper Trails

SUGARLOAF RIDGE STATE PARK and
HOOD MOUNTAIN REGIONAL PARK

Hiking distance: 7 miles round trip
Hiking time: 4 hours
Configuration: out and back
Elevation gain: 2,100 feet
Difficulty: very strenuous
Exposure: a mix of shaded forest and open meadows
Dogs: allowed in Hood Mountain; not allowed in Sugarloaf Ridge
Maps: U.S.G.S. Kenwood · Sugarloaf Ridge State Park
Hood Mountain Regional Park

Hood Mountain Regional Park and Sugarloaf Ridge State Park lie adjacent to each other in the Mayacamas Mountains, a 52-mile range that stretches between Sonoma Valley and Napa Valley. Three routes access the 2,730-foot summit of Hood Mountain. This trail begins from Adobe Canyon Road on the west side of the mountain in Sugarloaf Ridge State Park. The hike utilizes the Goodspeed and Nattkemper Trails, overlooking Sonoma Valley while crossing the southwest-facing, sun-exposed slope of Hood Mountain. About midway through the hike, the trail enters Hood Mountain Regional Park. The trail continues to the 2,730-foot summit and the Gunsight Rock Overlook, a distinctive formation of massive rocks perched on the cliffs just beneath the summit. The trail is strenuous, but the views from the overlook are fantastic. On a clear day, the vistas extend to the Golden Gate Bridge, the Pacific Ocean, and the Sierra Nevada Range.

To the trailhead

2605 ADOBE CANYON RD · KENWOOD   38.442542, -122.530889

NORTH SONOMA VALLEY. From Highway 12 and Calistoga Road on the north end of Sonoma Valley, drive 6 miles southeast on Highway 12 (Sonoma Highway) to Adobe Canyon Road. Turn left and continue 2.3 miles up the winding mountain road to the dirt parking area on the left.

KENWOOD. From the town of Kenwood in Sonoma Valley, drive 0.9 miles north on Highway 12 (Sonoma Highway) to Adobe Canyon Road on the right. Turn right and continue 2.3 miles up the winding mountain road to the dirt parking area on the left.

The hike

Take the posted Goodspeed Trail from the lower west end of the parking area. Immediately enter a lush redwood grove, and cross a wooden bridge over Sonoma Creek. Loop clockwise around a hill among moss-covered rocks, ferns, and bigleaf maples. Cross a bridge over Bear Creek, a tributary of Sonoma Creek. Follow the creek a short distance, and curve left up the hillside through a predominant Douglas fir forest. Climb at a moderate grade on the rock-embedded path. The views extend from forested Adobe Canyon to volcanic Sugarloaf Ridge. Zigzag up the mountain through chaparral and manzanita, with views of Bald Mountain, Red Mountain, Brushy Peaks, and Sonoma Mountain across the valley. Cross a gravel road at 0.9 miles. Descend via four switchbacks, and cross a boulder-filled tributary of Sonoma Creek. Ascend the mountainside, leaving the chaparral, and enter the shade of a Douglas fir forest with manzanita. Make a horseshoe right bend, and steadily climb up the exposed, rock-strewn ridge. Cross a seasonal stream in a pocket of trees to the open, southwest-facing slope. Traverse the grassland while enjoying the amazing vistas. Continue to the posted Hood Mountain Regional Park boundary and a map kiosk at two miles. The Goodspeed Trail becomes the Nattkemper Trail at the boundary.

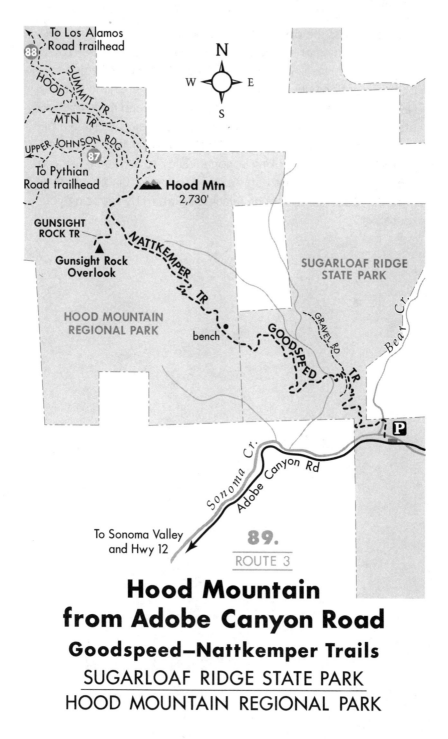

To Los Alamos
Road trailhead

88

HOOD SUMMIT TR

MTN TR

UPPER JOHNSON RDG

87

To Pythian
Road trailhead

▲▲ **Hood Mtn**
2,730'

GUNSIGHT
ROCK TR

NATTKEMPER TR

▲ Gunsight Rock
Overlook

HOOD MOUNTAIN
REGIONAL PARK

bench

GOODSPEED

SUGARLOAF RIDGE
STATE PARK

GRAVEL RD

TR

Bear Cr.

N
W E
S

P

Sonoma Cr.

Adobe Canyon Rd

To Sonoma Valley
and Hwy 12

89.
ROUTE 3

Hood Mountain
from Adobe Canyon Road
Goodspeed–Nattkemper Trails
SUGARLOAF RIDGE STATE PARK
HOOD MOUNTAIN REGIONAL PARK

Head across the open grasslands on the Nattkemper Trail. Pass a bench and memorial plaque to Clark Nattkemper (1914—2001), with views stretching to San Pablo Bay. Continue climbing to a posted junction with the Gunsight Overlook Trail on the left. The Nattkemper Trail continues 0.2 miles straight ahead through thickets of live oak to the 2,730-foot Hood Mountain summit in a circular clearing. The Gunsight Rock Trail heads 0.2 miles to a massive jumble of rocks overlooking Sonoma Valley to San Pablo Bay and the Santa Rosa Plain. The vistas extend to Mount Diablo and over Sonoma Mountain to Mount Tamalpais. Return by retracing your route. ■

90. Hood Mountain Shuttle Hike

Los Alamos Road to Adobe Canyon Road

Hood Mountain Trail—
Goodspeed Trail—Nattkemper Trail

HOOD MOUNTAIN REGIONAL PARK and
SUGARLOAF RIDGE STATE PARK

Hiking distance: 9.4-mile one-way shuttle
Hiking time: 5 hours
Configuration: one-way shuttle
Elevation gain: 2,100 feet
Difficulty: very strenuous
Exposure: a mix of shaded forest and open meadows
Dogs: allowed in Hood Mountain / not allowed in Sugarloaf Ridge
Maps: U.S.G.S. Kenwood · Hood Mountain Regional Park
Sugarloaf Ridge State Park

This hike leads from the upper Hood Mountain trailhead on Los Alamos Road to Adobe Canyon Road, combining Hike 88 and Hike 89 into a 9.4-mile, one-way shuttle. The strenuous hike leads from the upper reaches of Sonoma Valley, up to the Hood Mountain summit, and down into Adobe Canyon, following the length of Hood Mountain Regional Park. The 2,730-foot Hood Mountain lies on the southern end of the Mayacamas Range between Sonoma Valley and Napa Valley. It is the highest peak along the Sonoma-Napa county line. A short side path near the summit leads to the Gunsight Rock Overlook, a massive array of rocks that sits high above Sonoma Valley. Along the trail are expansive views of the valley and the coastal mountains. On clear days, the views extend from San Francisco to the Sierra Nevada Range. The diverse route winds through canyons; climbs over ridgetops; and passes through open grasslands, mixed woodlands, Sargent cypress, and a pygmy forest of Mendocino cypress.

The shuttle car is left at the trailhead along Adobe Canyon Road in Sugarloaf Ridge State Park. The hike begins from the upper, north Hood Mountain trailhead at the end of Los Alamos Road.

To the trailhead

3000 LOS ALAMOS RD · SANTA ROSA   38.488809, -122.572103

NORTH SONOMA VALLEY. From Highway 12 and Calistoga Road on the north end of Sonoma Valley, drive 1.1 miles southeast on Highway 12 (Sonoma Highway) to Los Alamos Road. Turn left and drive 4.7 miles up the narrow, winding mountain road to the road gate and trailhead parking area on the right. A parking fee is required.

KENWOOD. From the town of Kenwood in Sonoma Valley, drive 5.5 miles north on Highway 12 (Sonoma Highway) to Los Alamos Road on the right. Turn right and drive 4.7 miles up the narrow, winding mountain road to the road gate and trailhead parking area on the right. A parking fee is required.

Shuttle car

2605 ADOBE CANYON RD · KENWOOD   38.442542, -122.530889

NORTH SONOMA VALLEY. From Highway 12 and Calistoga Road on the north end of Sonoma Valley, drive 1.1 miles southeast on Highway 12 (Sonoma Highway) to Los Alamos Road. Turn left and drive 4.7 miles up the narrow, winding mountain road to the park entrance gate. Continue another 0.6 miles downhill to the trailhead parking area on the right. A parking fee is required.

KENWOOD. From the town of Kenwood in Sonoma Valley, drive 5.5 miles north on Highway 12 (Sonoma Highway) to Los Alamos Road on the right. Turn right and continue 4.7 miles up the narrow, winding mountain road to the park entrance gate. Continue another 0.6 miles downhill to the trailhead parking area on the right. A parking fee is required.

The hike

Take the posted Alder Glen Trail, which soon joins with the Hood Mountain Trail. Weave down the wide, forested path under the shade of evergreens, maples, oaks, bays, figs, and madrone. Follow the west canyon wall into Homestead Meadow, engulfed by the surrounding mountains, to the picnic area and T-junction at 1.1 miles. The right fork is a service road. Bear left and drop down 100 yards to a signed trail split. The left fork enters the 1,200-acre McCormick Addition of Sugarloaf Ridge State Park. Stay to the right for 30 yards to Santa Rosa Creek amid alders and bays.

Rock hop over the creek, and head up the slope among horsetail ferns. The long, steady climb leads to the posted Azalea Creek Picnic Area on the left and restrooms on the right at 2.5 miles. Climb a short distance, passing the Summit Trail. Cross over Azalea Creek, and climb to vistas of Mount Saint Helena and the coastal range. Pass a few more junctions with the Summit Trail, a parallel footpath that winds through a pygmy forest. Both routes head east and merge on a flat circular clearing atop the 2,730-foot summit of Hood Mountain at 5.5 miles.

From the summit, descend on the Nattkemper Trail through manzanita and colorful lava outcrops for 0.2 miles to the signed Gunsight Rock Trail. This hike continues on the Nattkemper Trail to the left, but for now, veer right on the Gunsight Rock Trail. Walk 0.2 miles, passing volcanic outcroppings to a massive block of rocks overlooking Sonoma Valley. The vistas extend to San Pablo Bay and the Santa Rosa Valley, Sonoma Mountain to Mount Tamalpais in Marin County, and Mount Diablo in Contra Costa County.

After enjoying the views from the overlook, head back up the Gunsight Rock Trail and continue southeast on the Nattkemper Trail. Cross the open grasslands with world-class views. Pass a bench and memorial plaque to Clark Nattkemper (1914-2001). At 7 miles, the trail reaches Sugarloaf Ridge State Park by a map kiosk. The Nattkemper Trail becomes the Goodspeed Trail at the boundary.

Continue on the Goodspeed Trail and pass through a pocket of fir trees. Cross a seasonal stream and steadily descend on the rock-strewn, southwest-facing slope. Enter the shade of a Douglas fir forest, and cross a boulder-filled tributary of Sonoma Creek. Climb via four switchbacks to a gravel road. Cross the road and zigzag down the mountain through chaparral and manzanita, with views of Bald Mountain, Red Mountain, Brushy Peaks, and Sugarloaf Ridge in the heart of Sugarloaf Ridge State Park. Curve

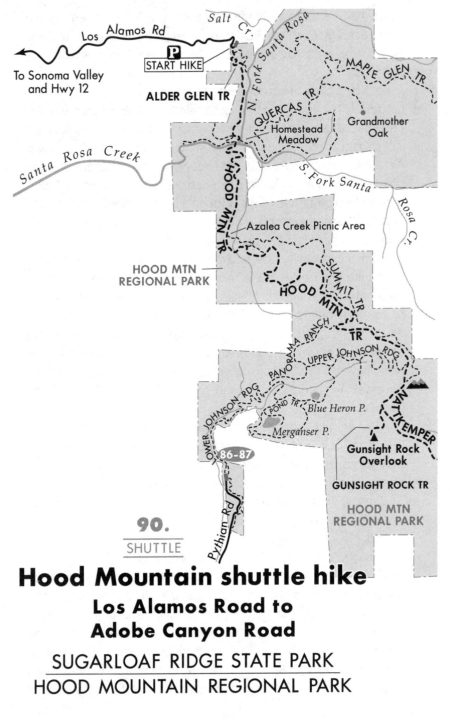

Hood Mountain shuttle hike

Los Alamos Road to Adobe Canyon Road

SUGARLOAF RIDGE STATE PARK
HOOD MOUNTAIN REGIONAL PARK

90.

SHUTTLE

right through a predominant Douglas fir forest to Bear Creek. Cross a wooden footbridge over the creek. Loop around a hill among moss-covered rocks and through a lush redwood grove to Sonoma Creek. Cross a bridge over the creek, and ascend the slope to the shuttle car parking area at Adobe Canyon Road. ■

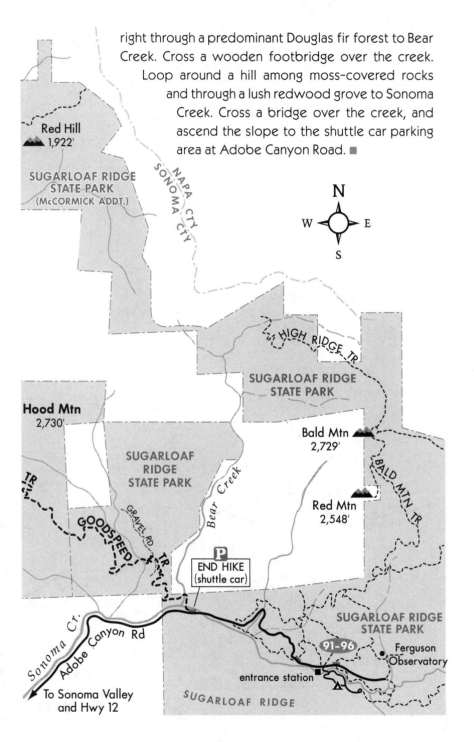

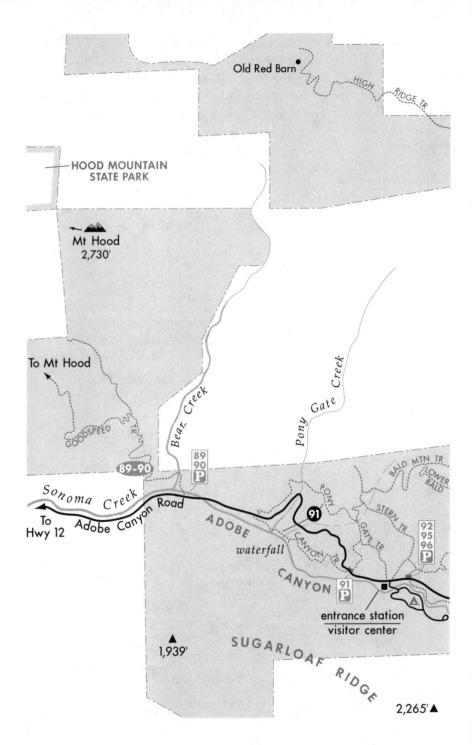

Old Red Barn

HIGH RIDGE TR

HOOD MOUNTAIN
STATE PARK

Mt Hood
2,730'

To Mt Hood

GOODSPEED TR

Bear Creek

Pony Gate Creek

89-90

89
90
P

Sonoma Creek

Adobe Canyon Road

To
Hwy 12

ADOBE

CANYON

waterfall

91

PONY

CANYON TR

GATE TR

STERN TR

BALD MTN TR

LOWER
BALD

92
95
96
P

91
P

entrance station
visitor center

1,939'

SUGARLOAF RIDGE

2,265' ▲

Sugarloaf Ridge State Park

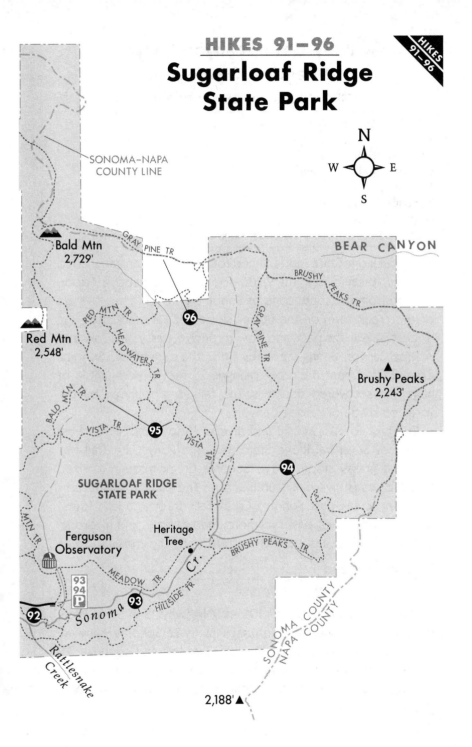

SONOMA-NAPA
COUNTY LINE

N
W E
S

GRAY PINE TR

BEAR CANYON

Bald Mtn
2,729'

BRUSHY PEAKS TR

RED MTN TR

HEADWATERS TR

GRAY PINE TR

96

Red Mtn
2,548'

Brushy Peaks
2,243'

BALD MTN TR

VISTA TR

95

VISTA TR

94

SUGARLOAF RIDGE
STATE PARK

Ferguson
Observatory

Heritage
Tree

BRUSHY PEAKS TR

MTN TR

Cr.

MEADOW TR

HILLSIDE TR

93
94
P

93

Sonoma

92

SONOMA COUNTY
NAPA COUNTY

Rattlesnake
Creek

2,188' ▲

91. Pony Gate—Canyon Loop to Sonoma Creek Falls

SUGARLOAF RIDGE STATE PARK

Hiking distance: 1.7-mile loop
Hiking time: 1 hour
Configuration: loop
Elevation gain: 450 feet
Difficulty: easy
Exposure: shaded forest
Dogs: not allowed
Maps: U.S.G.S. Kenwood · Sugarloaf Ridge State Park map

Sugarloaf Ridge State Park is named for its distinct conical-shaped ridge of volcanic rock. The 2,200-foot ridge rises above Adobe Canyon from the south edge of Sonoma Creek. The headwaters of the creek form on the upper slopes of Bald Mountain, the highest peak in the park, and flow through a grassy meadow into Adobe Canyon. Along the valley floor, the path passes Sonoma Creek Falls, where the creek plunges 25 feet over a jumble of huge, moss-covered boulders. The falls is surrounded by the forested shade of Adobe Canyon.

This hike forms a scenic and diverse loop in the lower west corner of Sugarloaf Ridge State Park. The Pony Gate Trail traverses a grassy slope above Sonoma Creek through a mixed forest of coast live oak, laurel, and fir. The Canyon Trail returns along the creak past Sonoma Creek Falls through a lush forest of redwoods, oaks, bay, sycamore, maple, alder, and madrone. Sonoma Creek is seasonal and is often dry by the end of summer.

To the trailhead

2605 ADOBE CANYON RD · KENWOOD   38.438267, -122.518804

SANTA ROSA. From Highway 101 and Highway 12 in Santa Rosa, drive 11.4 miles west and south on Highway 12 (Sonoma Highway) to Adobe Canyon Road on the left. Turn left and continue 3.2 miles up the winding mountain road to the posted trailhead parking area on the left. It is located 0.2 miles before the park entrance station.

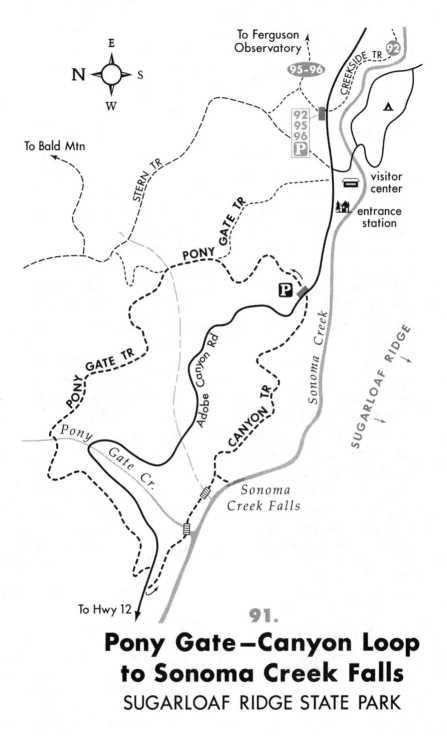

91.

Pony Gate—Canyon Loop
to Sonoma Creek Falls
SUGARLOAF RIDGE STATE PARK

KENWOOD. From the town of Kenwood, drive 0.9 miles north on Highway 12 (Sonoma Highway) to Adobe Canyon Road on the right. Turn right and continue 3.2 miles up the winding mountain road to the posted trailhead parking area on the left. It is located 0.2 miles before the park entrance station.

The hike

Take the posted trail from the upper east end of the parking area, and head up the forested hillside. The vistas extend across Adobe Canyon to the forested wall of Sugarloaf Ridge and across Sonoma Valley to Sonoma Mountain. Traverse the hillside to a junction with the Pony Gate Trail at 0.2 miles. Bear left and cross a tributary of Sonoma Creek to a Y-fork. Stay to the left and descend under a canopy of oaks, pines, and madrones to Pony Gate Creek. Follow the cascading creek 20 yards downstream, and rock-hop across the gulch. Climb up the hill and weave through the shady forest. Steadily descend to Adobe Canyon Road at 1.1 mile at the far end of the loop.

Cautiously walk 50 yards down the road to the posted Canyon Trail on the left. Descend steps into a redwood, oak, and fern-filled forest. Head southeast in lush Adobe Canyon above Sonoma Creek. Follow the creek upstream, and cross a wooden footbridge over Pony Gate Creek. Cross a second bridge over the tributary stream to a junction at 1.3 miles. Detour 50 yards to the right to Sonoma Creek Falls, tumbling through a rocky ravine amid redwoods, Douglas firs, and moss-covered boulders. After enjoying the falls, return to the main trail. Climb steps, steadily gaining elevation through the dense forest. Emerge from the forest at Adobe Canyon Road across from the trailhead, completing the loop. ■

92. Creekside Nature Trail
SUGARLOAF RIDGE STATE PARK

Hiking distance: 0.75-mile loop
Hiking time: 30 minutes
Configuration: loop
Elevation gain: 100 feet
Difficulty: very easy
Exposure: mostly shaded forest
Dogs: not allowed
Maps: U.S.G.S. Kenwood · Sugarloaf Ridge State Park
Creekside Nature Trail interpretive guide

The Creekside Nature Trail is an easy 0.75-mile loop on the valley floor of Sugarloaf Ridge State Park. The trail meanders along the banks of Sonoma Creek and Rattlesnake Creek through a forest of coast live oak, white oak, black oak, Douglas fir, California bay laurel, coyote brush, and Oregon ash. En route are overlooks of Hood Mountain, Red Mountain, Bald Mountain, and Sugarloaf Ridge. The nature trail has 17 numbered posts that correspond with a free pamphlet available from the ranger station by the park entrance.

To the trailhead

2605 ADOBE CANYON RD · KENWOOD   38.437811, -122.514194

SANTA ROSA. From Highway 101 and Highway 12 in Santa Rosa, drive 11.4 miles west and south on Highway 12 (Sonoma Highway) to Adobe Canyon Road on the left. Turn left and continue 3.5 miles up the winding mountain road to the large trailhead parking area on the left. It is located 0.1 mile past the park entrance station. A parking fee is required.

KENWOOD. From the town of Kenwood in Sonoma Valley, drive 0.9 miles north on Highway 12 (Sonoma Highway) to Adobe Canyon Road on the right. Turn right and continue 3.5 miles up the winding mountain road to the large trailhead parking area on the left. It is located 0.1 mile past the park entrance station. A parking fee is required.

The hike

Cross the road to the picnic area and signed Creekside Nature Trail. Follow the log-rail fence above Sonoma Creek, and pass the picnic area on the right. Stroll through the lush forest with coast live oak, white oak, Douglas fir, white alder, and coyote brush. Traverse the hillside past scattered serpentine rock. Cross a wood footbridge and skirt the Campfire Center amphitheater on the left. Veer left on the gravel path, passing interpretive stations. At signpost 11, take a 45-yard detour to the left. Climb the knoll to a bench and huge black oak tree with views of Hood Mountain, Bald Mountain, and Red Mountain. Return to the main trail and continue east. At signpost 12, cross a wood bridge over Sonoma Creek, and climb to a junction with the Hillside Trail at the far end of the loop.

Bear right and follow the Hillside Trail 80 yards. Bear right again, continuing back on the Creekside Nature Trail. A view of volcanic Sugarloaf Ridge stretches to the south. Descend past a water tank on the right, and rock-hop over Rattlesnake Creek. Traverse the northern base of Sugarloaf Ridge, and enter the campground at site 25. Follow the campground road in a tree-rimmed meadow. Cross the bridge over Sonoma Creek by camp-site 12, completing the loop back at the Campfire Center. Curve left, cross the footbridge, and return to the left. ■

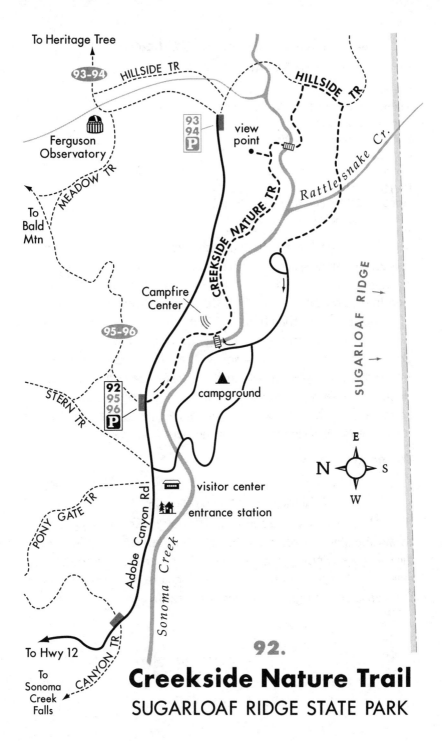

To Heritage Tree

HILLSIDE TR

93-94

HILLSIDE TR

Ferguson Observatory

93 94 P

view point

Rattlesnake Cr.

MEADOW TR

CREEKSIDE NATURE TR

To Bald Mtn

SUGARLOAF RIDGE

Campfire Center

95-96

STERN TR

92 95 96 P

campground

N E S W

PONY GATE TR

Adobe Canyon Rd

visitor center

entrance station

Sonoma Creek

CANYON TR

To Hwy 12

To Sonoma Creek Falls

92.
Creekside Nature Trail
SUGARLOAF RIDGE STATE PARK

93. Meadow—Hillside Loop
SUGARLOAF RIDGE STATE PARK

Hiking distance: 2.2-mile loop
Hiking time: 1 hour
Configuration: loop
Elevation gain: 250 feet
Difficulty: easy
Exposure: a mix of shaded forest and open meadows
Dogs: not allowed
Maps: U.S.G.S. Kenwood and Rutherford
Sugarloaf Ridge State Park map

Sugarloaf Ridge State Park encompasses 4,020 acres of steep, rugged hills ranging in elevation from 600 to 2,729 feet. The park includes a campground, primitive campsites, picnic areas, rolling meadows, an observatory with three telescopes, and 25 miles of hiking and equestrian trails.

The Meadow Trail strolls along the north side of Sonoma Creek in a scenic, grassy meadow. The path leads to Heritage Tree, a massive bigleaf maple tree in a creekside picnic area. The Hillside Trail traverses the forested hills on the opposite side of Sonoma Creek at the foot of Sugarloaf Ridge. These two trails form an easy loop in the heart of the park.

To the trailhead

2605 ADOBE CANYON RD · KENWOOD   38.436576, -122.508801

SANTA ROSA. From Highway 101 and Highway 12 in Santa Rosa, drive 11.4 miles west and south on Highway 12 (Sonoma Highway) to Adobe Canyon Road on the left. Turn left and continue 3.8 miles up the winding mountain road to the end of the road, 0.4 miles past the park entrance station. The posted trailhead parking area is on the right. A parking fee is required.

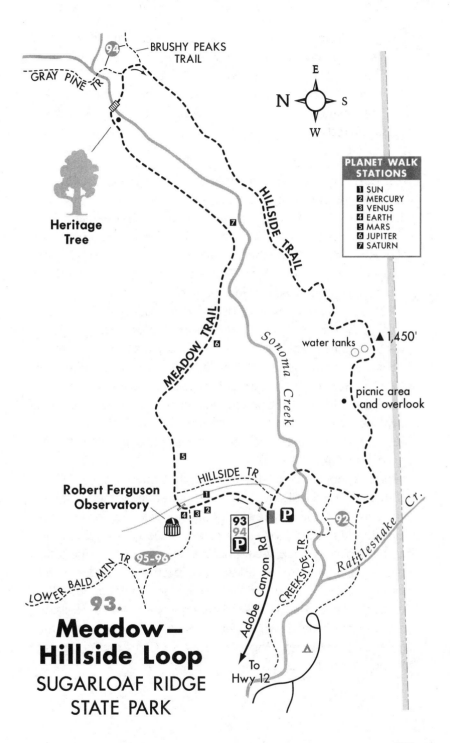

BRUSHY PEAKS TRAIL

GRAY PINE TR

94

Heritage Tree

HILLSIDE TRAIL

MEADOW TRAIL

N
E
W
S

PLANET WALK STATIONS
1 SUN
2 MERCURY
3 VENUS
4 EARTH
5 MARS
6 JUPITER
7 SATURN

7

6

Sonoma Creek

water tanks ○○

▲ 1,450'

● picnic area and overlook

5

HILLSIDE TR

Robert Ferguson Observatory

1

4 3 2

93
94
P

P

92

CREEKSIDE TR

Rattlesnake Cr.

LOWER BALD MTN TR 95-96

Adobe Canyon Rd

To Hwy 12

93.
Meadow–Hillside Loop
SUGARLOAF RIDGE STATE PARK

KENWOOD. From the town of Kenwood, drive 0.9 miles north on Highway 12 (Sonoma Highway) to Adobe Canyon Road on the right. Turn right and continue 3.8 miles up the winding mountain road to the end of the road, 0.4 miles past the park entrance station. The posted trailhead parking area is on the right. A parking fee is required.

The hike

Walk past the vehicle gate and observatory sign, following the wide gravel road along a stream. Pass the Robert Ferguson Observatory on its right, and walk through the trail gate. The Planet Walk begins near the observatory. The interpretive trail follows the first half of this hike along the Meadow Trail, then continues on the Brushy Peaks Trail—Hike 94. Along the Meadow Trail are signs about the sun and the first six planets.

Just after the gate by the observatory, cross over the stream and pass the Hillside Trail. Skirt the north edge of the large meadow to Sonoma Creek at a half mile. Follow the creek upstream through towering oaks and bay laurel. At 0.9 miles, pass the sprawling Heritage Tree in a picnic area on the banks of Sonoma Creek. Cross the wood bridge over the creek to a junction with Gray Pine Trail on the left, then the Brushy Peaks Trail on the left. These trails both make larger loops through the higher elevations of the park (Hikes 94—96).

For this shorter loop, stay to the right both times, then head southwest on the Hillside Trail along the edge of the meadow. Gradually climb the hillside toward Sugarloaf Ridge. Traverse the slope through grasslands and a forest of Douglas fir, California bay, and coast live oak. Weave up the hill to 1,450 feet, the highest point along the trail. Head downhill past two wooden water tanks and a picnic area overlook to a posted junction with the Creekside Nature Trail (Hike 92). Bear right, staying on the Hillside Trail, and continue downhill. Pass a second junction with the Creekside Nature Trail. Hop over Sonoma Creek and complete the loop at the trailhead. ∎

94. Brushy Peaks—Gray Pine Loop and The Planet Walk

SUGARLOAF RIDGE STATE PARK

Hiking distance: 6.5-mile loop
Hiking time: 3.5 hours
Configuration: loop
Elevation gain: 1,000 feet
Difficulty: moderate to strenuous
Exposure: a mix of shaded forest and open meadows
Dogs: not allowed
Maps: U.S.G.S. Kenwood and Rutherford
      Sugarloaf Ridge State Park

Sugarloaf Ridge State Park contains three distinct ecological systems. In Sonoma Creek Canyon are riparian redwood forests that also include Douglas fir, gray pines, bigleaf maple, California bay laurel, and California buckeye. Along the open meadows are oak and fir woodlands. Atop the dry exposed ridges are chaparral varieties, including manzanita, toyon, coyote brush, and chamise.

This loop hike explores all three habitats. The first half of the hike follows the Planet Walk along the canyon. The interpretive trail illustrates the magnitude of the solar system by proportionately reducing its size over two billion times to fit within the park boundaries. Informative panels represent the sun and each of the nine planets. The Planet Walk begins at the gated road by the Robert Ferguson Observatory and ends on the ridge straddling Napa and Sonoma counties. The hike continues up to the dry ridge, following the rolling ridge over six peaks. The expansive views span across the Mayacamas Mountains and down Napa Valley. The return loop steadily descends from the ridge back to the Sonoma Creek floor.

To the trailhead

2605 ADOBE CANYON RD · KENWOOD   38.436576, -122.508801

SANTA ROSA. From Highway 101 and Highway 12 in Santa Rosa, drive 11.4 miles west and south on Highway 12 (Sonoma Highway) to Adobe Canyon Road on the left. Turn left and continue 3.8

miles up the winding mountain road to the end of the road, 0.4 miles past the park entrance station. The posted trailhead parking area is on the right. A parking fee is required.

KENWOOD. From the town of Kenwood, drive 0.9 miles north on Highway 12 (Sonoma Highway) to Adobe Canyon Road on the right. Turn right and continue 3.8 miles up the winding mountain road to the end of the road, 0.4 miles past the park entrance station. The posted trailhead parking area is on the right. A parking fee is required.

The hike

Walk past the vehicle gate and observatory sign, following the wide gravel road along a stream. The Planet Walk signs begin with the sun at the observatory parking lot. Throughout the first half of the hike, the route will pass by all the Planet Walk signs, ending with Pluto near Brushy Peaks.

Pass the Robert Ferguson Observatory on its right side, and walk through the trail gate. Cross over the stream and pass the Hillside Trail. Skirt the north edge of the large meadow to Sonoma Creek at a half mile. Follow the creek upstream through

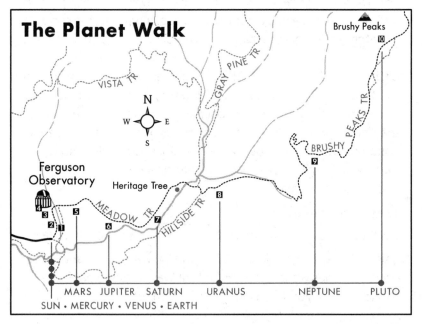

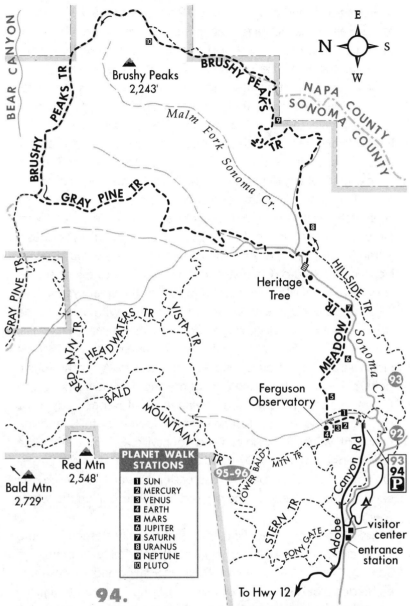

PLANET WALK STATIONS

1 SUN
2 MERCURY
3 VENUS
4 EARTH
5 MARS
6 JUPITER
7 SATURN
8 URANUS
9 NEPTUNE
10 PLUTO

94.
Brushy Peaks—Gray Pine Loop and The Planet Walk
SUGARLOAF RIDGE STATE PARK

towering oaks and bay laurel. At 0.9 miles is a sprawling bigleaf maple called the Heritage Tree in a picnic area on the banks of Sonoma Creek. Cross the wood bridge over the creek to a junction with the Gray Pine Trail on the left—the return route.

Begin the loop straight ahead, and walk sixty yards to a posted junction. The Hillside Trail—straight ahead—makes a short return loop back to the trailhead (Hike 93). Instead, bear left on the Brushy Peaks Trail. Traverse the forested hillside under a canopy of oak, manzanita, and toyon. Parallel the Malm Fork of Sonoma Creek, gradually gaining elevation. Cross a small branch of the Malm Fork, and climb the east wall of the canyon on a series of switchbacks. The climb levels out and curves left to a clearing overlooking Sugarloaf Ridge, Sonoma Valley, and the coastal range. En route are more interpretive panels about Uranus, Neptune, and Pluto. The distance from the signs to the observatory help to visualize the scale and size of the solar system.

Continue uphill to a grassy meadow dotted with oaks and the ridge. Follow the rolling ridge for a half mile over four peaks, with views of Red Mountain, Bald Mountain, and sweeping vistas across Napa County and Sonoma County. After the fourth peak, curve left, straddling the county line. The views extend to the Mayacamas Mountains, the vineyards of Napa Valley, Lake Hennessey and Rector Reservoir in the lower foothills, and the towns of Mount Saint Helena and Yountville. Continue along the rolling ridge on a rocky fire road over a series of dips and peaks. On top of the sixth peak, cross under power lines. After the seventh rise, descend to the posted Gray Pine Trail on the left at four miles.

Bear left on the Gray Pine Trail, and steadily descend on the wide dirt trail. At 4.8 miles, curve left and follow a branch of Sonoma Creek in an oak grove. Make an S-bend and cross another feeder creek. Parallel and hop over Sonoma Creek to a junction with the Vista Trail at 5.3 miles. Ford the creek again, reaching a T-junction with the Meadow Trail, which completes the loop. Bear right and cross a wood bridge over Sonoma Creek to the Heritage Tree. Retrace your steps on the Meadow Trail back to the Ferguson Observatory and the trailhead. ■

95. Lower Loop
Red Mountain—Bald Mountain

Bald Mountain Trail—Headwaters Trail—Vista Trail

SUGARLOAF RIDGE STATE PARK

Hiking distance: 5.2-mile loop
Hiking time: 2.5 hours
Configuration: loop
Elevation gain: 1,000 feet
Difficulty: moderate to strenuous
Exposure: a mix of shaded forest and open meadows
Dogs: not allowed
Maps: U.S.G.S. Kenwood and Rutherford
      Sugarloaf Ridge State Park

Upper Sonoma Creek, in Sugar Loaf Ridge State Park, is framed by Sugarloaf Ridge to the south and the slopes of Red Mountain and Bald Mountain to the north. Sonoma Creek forms from three ephemeral forks that drain from the peaks. This hike makes a loop along the lower half of the mountain slope, while Hike 96 makes a longer and more strenuous loop up to the ridgeline.

The hike begins on the Bald Mountain Trail and steadily ascends a thousand feet to the headwaters of Sonoma Creek. The Headwaters Trail is a scenic half-mile trail that skirts the western fork of Sonoma Creek in a fern-filled oasis at the upper end of the loop. The hike then heads down the Vista Trail through a lush forested corridor, crossing a couple of ravines and a grassy hillside. The trail returns through a meadow along the banks of Sonoma Creek.

To the trailhead

2605 ADOBE CANYON RD · KENWOOD   38.437811, -122.514194

SANTA ROSA. From Highway 101 and Highway 12 in Santa Rosa, drive 11.4 miles west and south on Highway 12 (Sonoma Highway) to Adobe Canyon Road on the left. Turn left and continue 3.5 miles up the winding mountain road to the large trailhead parking area on the left. It is located 0.1 mile past the park entrance station. A parking fee is required.

KENWOOD. From the town of Kenwood in Sonoma Valley, drive 0.9 miles north on Highway 12 (Sonoma Highway) to Adobe Canyon Road on the right. Turn right and continue 3.5 miles up the winding mountain road to the large trailhead parking area on the left. It is located 0.1 mile past the park entrance station. A parking fee is required.

The hike

Walk past the trailhead map and head up the grassy slope. Weave through an oak grove to a meadow and a triangle junction. The right fork leads to the observatory on the Meadow Trail—the return route. Go to the left on the Lower Bald Mountain Trail, beginning the loop. Climb to the upper end of the meadow, and enter an oak grove with manzanita and madrone. At one mile the trail reaches the Bald Mountain Trail, a paved fire road. Bear right and head up the narrow road to sweeping views of Sonoma Valley and the surrounding mountains. Pass the Vista Trail at 1.2 miles on a U-shaped bend. (For a shorter 4.5-mile loop, take the Vista Trail to the right.) Continue straight, weaving up the contours of the forested mountain. Pass a couple of stream-fed gullies and overlooks to the Red Mountain Trail at two miles. The Bald Mountain Trail continues straight ahead to the summit (Hike 96).

For this hike, leave the road and bear right on the Red Mountain Trail along the southeast flank of Red Mountain. Weave through the forest on the footpath, and descend 0.2 miles to a signed junction with the Headwaters Trail. The Red Mountain Trail crosses the upper reaches of Sonoma Creek in a moss-filled rocky grotto and climbs to the ridge straddling the county line. For this hike, take the Headwaters Trail to the right, and follow a seasonal fork of Sonoma Creek. Descend through the shaded forest along the west side of the creek, passing lush rock walls, ferns, moss-covered trees, and pools of water. The half-mile trail ends in an oak grove at a T-junction with the Vista Trail. Bear left on the Vista Trail, and traverse the hillside while overlooking the park valley, Brushy Peaks, and Sugarloaf Ridge. The serpentine path

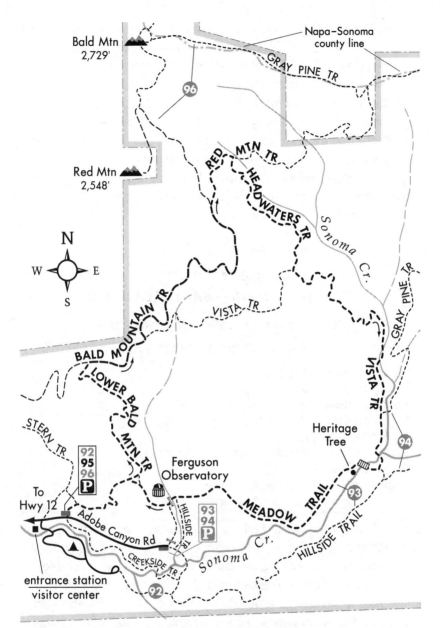

Bald Mtn
2,729'

Napa–Sonoma
county line

GRAY PINE TR

96

Red Mtn
2,548'

RED MTN TR

HEADWATERS TR

Sonoma Cr.

N
W E
S

VISTA TR

BALD MOUNTAIN TR

VISTA TR

GRAY PINE TR

STERN TR

LOWER BALD MTN TR

92
95
96
P

Heritage
Tree

94

To
Hwy 12

Ferguson
Observatory

MEADOW TRAIL

93

Adobe Canyon Rd

HILLSIDE TR

93
94
P

HILLSIDE TRAIL

CREEKSIDE TR

Sonoma Cr.

entrance station
visitor center

92

95. Lower Loop
Red Mountain–Bald Mountain
SUGARLOAF RIDGE STATE PARK

steadily loses elevation through a mixed forest with bigleaf maples, oaks, and ferns. Continue along the watercourse of Sonoma Creek to the valley floor at the Gray Pine Trail at 3.6 miles.

Veer to the right on the old dirt road. Cross Sonoma Creek to the Meadow Trail. Bear right and cross a wood bridge over Sonoma Creek to Heritage Tree, a massive bigleaf maple on the banks of the creek. Stroll through the open meadow along Sonoma Creek to the Ferguson Observatory at 4.5 miles. Leave the road and continue on the Meadow Trail to the right. Walk up the slope and veer left at the triangle junction, completing the loop. Retrace your steps 0.4 miles to the left. ∎

96. Upper Loop
Red Mountain—Bald Mountain

Bald Mountain Trail—Gray Pine Trail
SUGARLOAF RIDGE STATE PARK

Hiking distance: 7-mile loop
Hiking time: 4 hours
Configuration: loop
Elevation gain: 1,600 feet
Difficulty: strenuous
Exposure: a mix of shaded forest and open meadows
Dogs: not allowed
Maps: U.S.G.S. Kenwood and Rutherford
　　　　　Sugarloaf Ridge State Park map

Sugarloaf Ridge State Park is located in the heart of the Mayacamas Mountains high above the town of Kenwood. Towering Bald Mountain, the park's highest peak at 2,729 feet, straddles the county line between Sonoma and Napa Counties. This hike forms a large loop from the lower sloping meadow to the Bald Mountain summit. At the summit are 360-degree vistas that span from the Sierra Nevada Range to the San Francisco skyline and the Golden Gate Bridge. The views extend down both Sonoma Valley and Napa Valley. Two illustrated panels point out more than 30 of the surrounding peaks, towns, and valleys. The Gray Pine Trail (the return route) follows the isolated Sugarloaf Ridge for over a mile along the county border, then descends along the headwaters of Sonoma Creek.

To the trailhead

2605 ADOBE CANYON RD · KENWOOD   38.437811, -122.514194

SANTA ROSA. From Highway 101 and Highway 12 in Santa Rosa, drive 11.4 miles west and south on Highway 12 (Sonoma Highway) to Adobe Canyon Road on the left. Turn left and continue 3.5 miles up the winding mountain road to the large trailhead parking area on the left. It is located 0.1 mile past the park entrance station. A parking fee is required.

KENWOOD. From the town of Kenwood, drive 0.9 miles north on Highway 12 (Sonoma Highway) to Adobe Canyon Road on the right. Turn right and continue 3.5 miles up the winding mountain road to the large trailhead parking area on the left. It is located 0.1 mile past the park entrance station. A parking fee is required.

The hike

Walk past the trailhead map and head up the grassy slope. Weave through an oak grove to a meadow and a triangle junction. The right fork leads to the observatory on the Meadow Trail. Go to the left on the Lower Bald Mountain Trail, beginning the loop. Climb to the upper end of the meadow, and enter an oak grove with manzanita and madrone. At one mile the trail reaches the Bald Mountain Trail, a paved fire road.

Bear right and head up the narrow road to sweeping views of Sonoma Valley and the surrounding mountains. Pass the Vista Trail at 1.2 miles on a U-shaped bend. (For a shorter 4.5-mile loop, take the Vista Trail to the right.) Continue straight, weaving up the contours of the forested mountain. Pass a couple of stream-fed gullies and overlooks. At two miles, the Red Mountain Trail cut-across breaks off to the right.

For this hike, continue 0.4 miles to a road on the left that leads up to the top of Red Mountain. The short quarter-mile paved road leads up to the microwave tower at the 2,548-foot summit of Red Mountain. The road ends at a gate before reaching the tower. Back on the main trail, weave up the dirt road on the upper mountain slope to amazing vistas. The final ascent curves clockwise to a junction with the High Ridge Trail. Bear right and walk 80 yards to the Gray Pine Trail on the left, just short of the summit. Detour right to the 2,729-foot bald summit with a bench, 360-degree vistas, and two interpretive maps.

After resting and savoring the views, return 20 yards to the Gray Pine Trail. Descend along the rolling grassy ridge, which follows the Napa-Sonoma county line. The views extend down both valleys from the ridge. Enter a mixed forest and continue east, staying on the ridge to the junction with the east end of Red Mountain Trail and a picnic bench at 3.6 miles. At just under four miles, curve right, leaving the ridge, and head south to a signed junction with the Brushy Peaks Trail.

Bend right, staying on the Gray Pine Trail, and steadily descend on the wide dirt trail. At 4.8 miles, curve left and follow a branch of Sonoma Creek in an oak grove. Make an S-bend and cross another feeder creek. Parallel and hop over Sonoma Creek to a junction with the east end of the Vista Trail at 5.3 miles. Ford the creek again, reaching a T-junction with the Meadow Trail.

Bear right and cross a wood bridge over Sonoma Creek to Heritage Tree, a massive bigleaf maple tree on the banks of Sonoma Creek. Stroll through the open meadow along Sonoma Creek to the Ferguson Observatory at 6.4 miles. Leave the road and take the Meadow Trail to the right. Walk up the slope and veer left at the triangle junction, completing the loop at 6.6 miles. Retrace your steps 0.4 miles to the left, back to the parking lot. ■

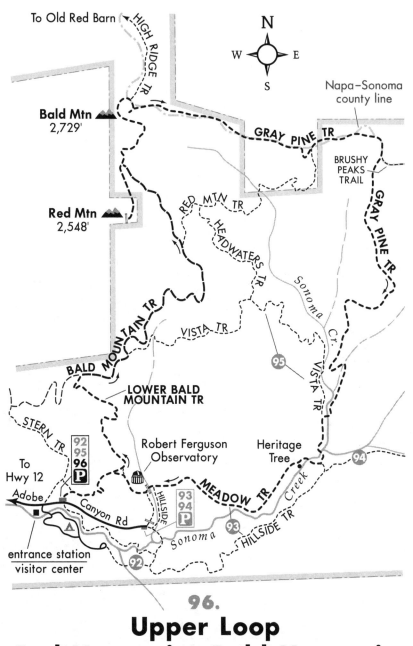

To Old Red Barn

HIGH RIDGE TR

N
W E
S

Napa–Sonoma
county line

GRAY PINE TR

Bald Mtn
2,729'

BRUSHY
PEAKS
TRAIL

GRAY PINE TR

Red Mtn
2,548'

RED MTN TR

HEADWATERS TR

Sonoma Cr.

VISTA TR

BALD MOUNTAIN TR

VISTA TR

95

VISTA TR

**LOWER BALD
MOUNTAIN TR**

STERN TR

92
95
96
P

Robert Ferguson
Observatory

Heritage
Tree

94

To
Hwy 12

HILLSIDE TR

93
94
P

MEADOW TR

Creek

Adobe

Canyon Rd

Sonoma

93

HILLSIDE TR

△

entrance station
visitor center

92

96.
Upper Loop
Red Mountain–Bald Mountain
SUGARLOAF RIDGE STATE PARK

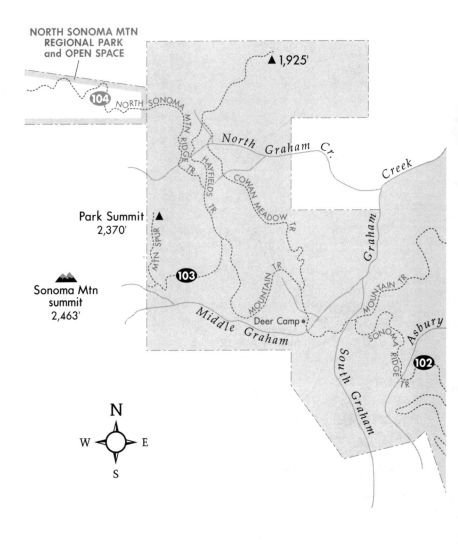

NORTH SONOMA MTN
REGIONAL PARK
and OPEN SPACE

▲ 1,925'

104 NORTH SONOMA

North Graham Cr.

MTN RIDGE TR.

HAYFIELDS TR.

COWAN MEADOW TR.

Creek

Graham

Park Summit ▲
2,370'

MTN SPUR

103

MOUNTAIN TR.

MOUNTAIN TR.

Sonoma Mtn
summit
2,463'

Middle Graham

Deer Camp •

SONOMA RIDGE TR.

Asbury

102

South Graham

N
W ⬥ E
S

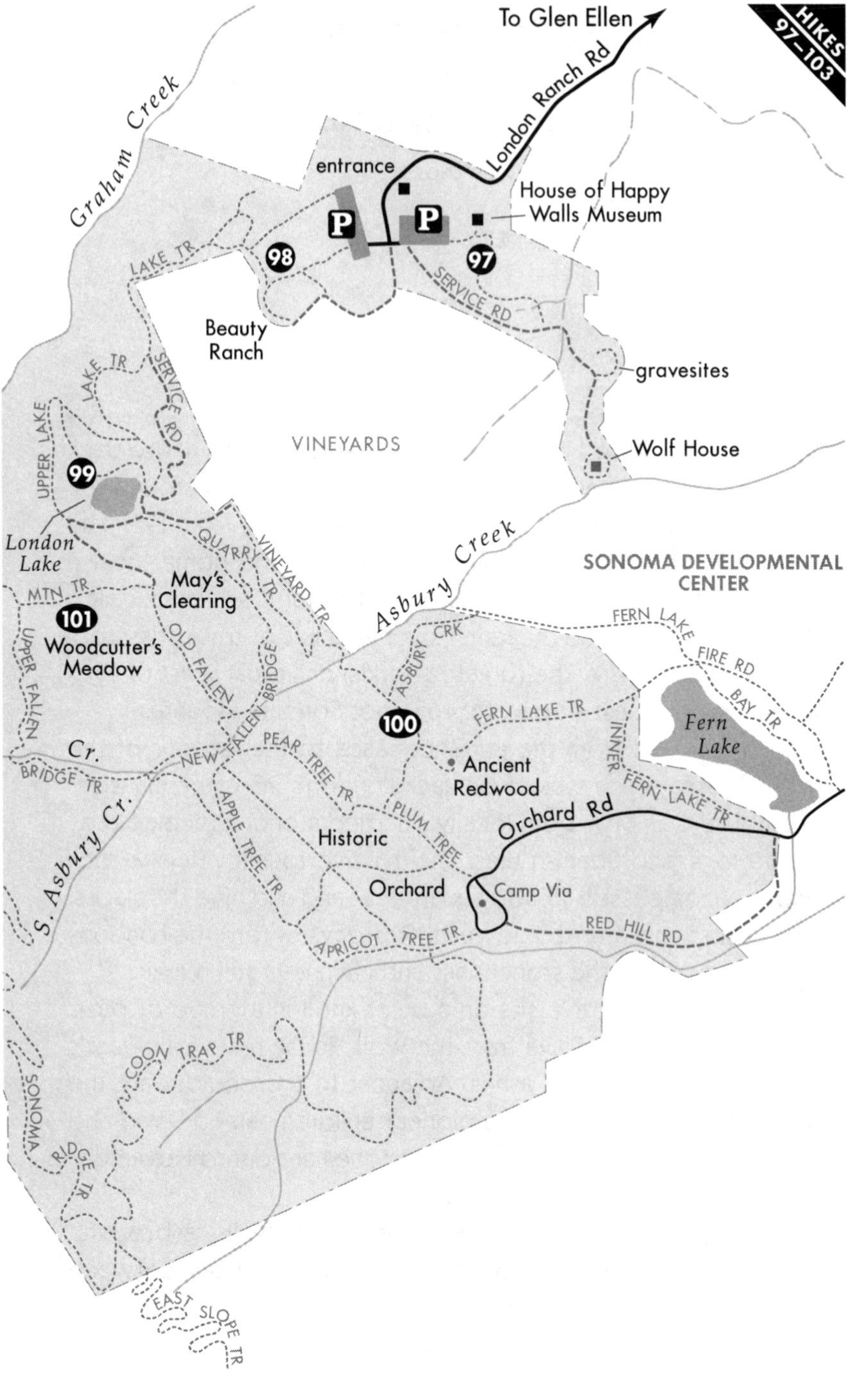
HIKES 97–103
To Glen Ellen
London Ranch Rd
Graham Creek
entrance
House of Happy Walls Museum
P
P
98
97
LAKE TR
SERVICE RD
Beauty Ranch
gravesites
LAKE TR
LAKE TR
SERVICE RD
UPPER LAKE
VINEYARDS
Wolf House
99
London Lake
QUARRY TR
VINEYARD TR
Asbury Creek
SONOMA DEVELOPMENTAL CENTER
MTN TR
May's Clearing
101
Woodcutter's Meadow
OLD FALLEN
BRIDGE
ASBURY CRK
FERN LAKE
FIRE RD
BAY TR
UPPER FALLEN
100
FERN LAKE TR
INNER
Fern Lake
Cr.
NEW FALLEN BRIDGE
PEAR TREE TR
Ancient Redwood
BRIDGE TR
FERN LAKE TR
S. Asbury Cr.
APPLE TREE TR
PLUM TREE
Orchard Rd
Historic
Orchard
Camp Via
RED HILL RD
APRICOT TREE TR
COON TRAP TR
SONOMA RIDGE TR
EAST SLOPE TR

97. Wolf House Ruins and Jack London's Grave

JACK LONDON STATE HISTORIC PARK

Hiking distance: 1.5 miles round trip
Hiking time: 1 hour
Configuration: out-and-back
Elevation gain: 150 feet
Difficulty: easy
Exposure: shaded forest
Dogs: not allowed
Maps: U.S.G.S. Glen Ellen · Jack London State Historic Park map

Jack London State Historic Park serves as a memorial to Jack London, a prolific author of adventure stories from around the turn-of-the-20th Century. London lived at the site from 1911 until his death in 1916. Near the park entrance are his home (now a museum), several historic buildings, and his farm, which he called Beauty Ranch. Beyond the ranch, over 26 miles of trails crisscross the 1,400-acre park. The forested parklands lie just west of Glen Ellen along the east slope of 2,463-foot Sonoma Mountain.

A short walk from the entrance leads to the remains of the Wolf House, which was to be Jack London's 26-room mansion. The house was built from locally quarried stone, unpeeled redwood logs, and Spanish tiles. The massive four-level, lava-rock house encompassed 15,000 square feet and had nine fireplaces. His dream house burned down in 1913, days before the Londons were to move in. The stone walls and chimneys still remain.

Jack London's grave sits on a quiet knoll in a grove of oaks. A large block of red lava from the Wolf House rests atop Jack's and his wife Charmian's ashes. Adjacent to the boulder are the marked older graves of two pioneer children named David and Lillie Greenlaw. Their wooden headstones are dated November 1876, the year Jack London was born.

This walk begins at the House of Happy Walls, a beautiful stone building built by London's widow, Charmian, between 1919 and 1922. The two-story structure was modeled after the Wolf House. It now functions as a museum and visitor center.

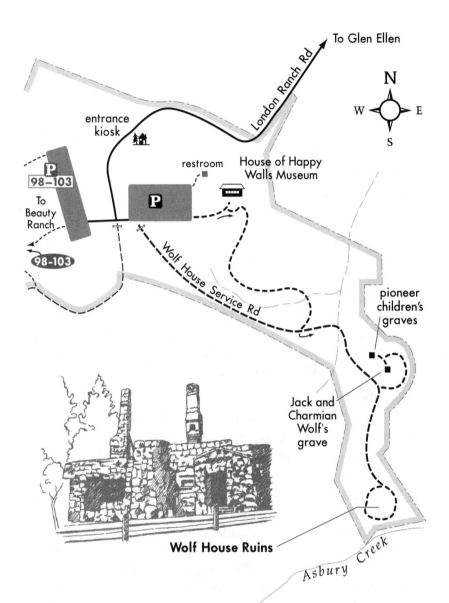

To Glen Ellen

London Ranch Rd

N
W · E
S

entrance
kiosk

restroom

House of Happy
Walls Museum

P
98-103

To
Beauty
Ranch

98-103

Wolf House Service Rd

pioneer
children's
graves

Jack and
Charmian
Wolf's
grave

Wolf House Ruins

Asbury Creek

97.

Wolf House Ruins
Jack London's grave
JACK LONDON STATE HISTORIC PARK

The building is dedicated to Jack London and his work. It houses mementos and collections from London's worldwide travels and personal possessions, including his writings, letters, photographs, art, home furnishings, and clothes. The trail then leads through a mixed forest en route to his gravesite and the Wolf House ruins in the redwoods above Asbury Creek. A path loops around the house and climbs to a platform overlooking the second floor.

To the trailhead

2400 LONDON RANCH RD · GLEN ELLEN   38.356397, -122.543732

Jack London State Historic Park is located in Sonoma Valley off of Highway 12 in the town of Glen Ellen. The turnoff to Glen Ellen—Arnold Drive—is 6 miles north of Sonoma and 3.6 miles south of Kenwood. Take Arnold Drive to downtown Glen Ellen and the intersection with London Ranch Road on the west.

Take London Ranch Road 1.3 miles west. Wind up the hill to the park entrance station. After the kiosk, turn left into the museum parking lot. A parking fee is required.

The hike

From the far end of the parking lot, walk up the paved path to the House of Happy Walls Museum, a fieldstone structure with Spanish roof tiles. After visiting the museum and the exhibits, take the signed trail from the southeast corner of the building. Gently descend on the forested dirt path through bay laurel, madrone, and oaks. Cross a stream, reaching the Wolf House Service Road at 0.3 miles. Bear left on the narrow road, parallel to the creek on the left. Cross over the creek and head uphill to a road fork. Detour left and wind around about 110 yards to Jack London's gravesite on a knoll. On the left are the graves of Jack and his wife Charmian, dated 11-26-16. A lava boulder from the house ruins sits atop their ashes. To the right are the graves of the two pioneer children. Return to the main trail and continue 0.15 miles to the Wolf House in a redwood grove. A path circles the ruins, with views of the gorgeous lava rock arches and fireplaces. A raised platform overlooks the pool and the house. Return on the same trail. ■

98. Beauty Ranch
JACK LONDON STATE HISTORIC PARK

Hiking distance: 0.75 miles round trip
Hiking time: 1 hour
Configuration: inter-connecting trails
Elevation gain: 50 feet
Difficulty: very easy
Exposure: open, rolling foothills
Dogs: not allowed
Maps: U.S.G.S. Glen Ellen · Jack London State Historic Park map

Jack London's Beauty Ranch is tucked into the foothills of Sonoma Mountain above the town of Glen Ellen. When London moved to this property, he fully embraced farming and living off the land. His experimental ranch is now part of the state historic park, which still contains the original structures. The wood-framed cottage is where London lived and wrote many of his books from 1905 until his death in 1916. Over the course of 16 prolific years, Jack London wrote 51 books and nearly 200 short stories, including *Call of the Wild* and *The Sea Wolf.* Sonoma Valley became known as Valley of the Moon from London's 1913 novel by the same name.

There are several unusual structures amongst the ranch buildings. The innovative Pig Palace is a circular piggery with a central feeding and round storage tower designed by London. Two 40-foot silos were built in 1914, the first cement silos in California. A rock sherry barn, part of the old Kohler-Frohling winery, was built by Chinese laborers in 1884, then converted into a stable for London's English shire horses. London hired Italian masons to build an additional stallion barn and a rock manure pit. A distillery building from the old winery still exists, as well as other ruins from the 1880s winery damaged by the 1906 earthquake. This interpretive hike loops through the grounds of the historic former ranch.

To the trailhead

2400 LONDON RANCH RD · GLEN ELLEN   38.356397, -122.543732

Jack London State Historic Park is located in Sonoma Valley off of Highway 12 in the town of Glen Ellen. The turnoff to Glen Ellen—Arnold Drive—is 6 miles north of Sonoma and 3.6 miles south of Kenwood. Take Arnold Drive to downtown Glen Ellen and the intersection with London Ranch Road on the west.

Take London Ranch Road 1.3 miles west. Wind up the hill to the park entrance station. After the kiosk, turn right and drive 0.1 mile to the trailhead parking lot. A parking fee is required.

The hike

From the trailhead kiosk, take the posted Beauty Ranch-Mountain Trails path. Walk through a eucalyptus grove and picnic area to a T-junction by the sherry barn on the left. Bear left past the barn to the rock-walled manure pit and stallion barn. Curve right on the paved service road. Continue along the edge of a vineyard on the left to the Jack London Cottage on the right and a view of the terraced hillside. Curve right, passing the cottage to the rock-wall ruins of the historic winery. Stroll past the rock walls or enter the open structure.

Curve left, staying on the edge of the vineyard toward the two 40-foot silos erected between 1912 and 1915. As the gravel road curves left (before reaching the silos) veer to the right on the grassy path. Climb to the circular rock-walled Pig Palace in an oak grove. Loop around the central feed tower and the ring of 17 pig pens. Continue to the cement-block silos and a junction. A side path goes right to a rock smokehouse behind the Pig Palace. Return to the main road. The right fork on the Lake Trail leads to the lake, bathhouse, and the backcountry of the state park (Hikes 99—103). For this hike, bear left and return to the trail split by the winery ruins. Curve left, passing the distillery building constructed in 1888. Complete the trail at the sherry barn. Return to the left. ■

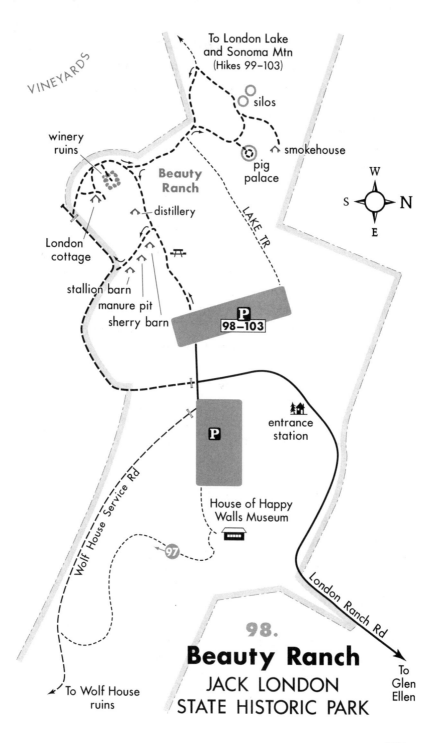

VINEYARDS

To London Lake
and Sonoma Mtn
(Hikes 99–103)

silos

smokehouse

winery
ruins

Beauty
Ranch

pig
palace

distillery

LAKE TR

London
cottage

W

N

S

E

stallion barn

manure pit

sherry barn

P
98–103

P

entrance
station

Wolf House Service Rd

House of Happy
Walls Museum

97

London Ranch Rd

98.
Beauty Ranch
JACK LONDON
STATE HISTORIC PARK

To Wolf House
ruins

To
Glen
Ellen

99. Lake Trail Loop
Beauty Ranch to London Lake
JACK LONDON STATE HISTORIC PARK

Hiking distance: 2.5 miles round trip
Hiking time: 1.5 hours
Configuration: out-and-back with two loops
Elevation gain: 400 feet
Difficulty: easy
Exposure: mix of open meadows and shaded forest
Dogs: not allowed
Maps: U.S.G.S. Glen Ellen · Jack London State Historic Park map

Jack London acquired this property just west of Glen Ellen as a quiet, natural retreat. He soon became preoccupied with restoring the old ranchland back to a working farm, which he named Beauty Ranch. London built a lake in 1915 as a five-acre irrigation reservoir for the ranch. It quickly became a swimming hole and entertainment area for the Londons and their guests. The lake, now known as London Lake, sits at the foot of Sonoma Mountain surrounded by redwood groves. A redwood bathhouse on the northeast shore and a curved stone dam to the south were also built by London. Encroaching vegetation and sediment have since reduced the lake's size in half. Cattails rim the shore and redwoods cover the mountain slope. This picturesque trail strolls through Beauty Ranch past London's living quarters and the old ranch buildings, then loops around the lake to vista points and overlooks.

To the trailhead

2400 LONDON RANCH RD · GLEN ELLEN   38.356397, -122.543732

Jack London State Historic Park is located in Sonoma Valley off of Highway 12 in the town of Glen Ellen. The turnoff to Glen Ellen—Arnold Drive—is 6 miles north of Sonoma and 3.6 miles south of Kenwood. Take Arnold Drive to downtown Glen Ellen and the intersection with London Ranch Road on the west.

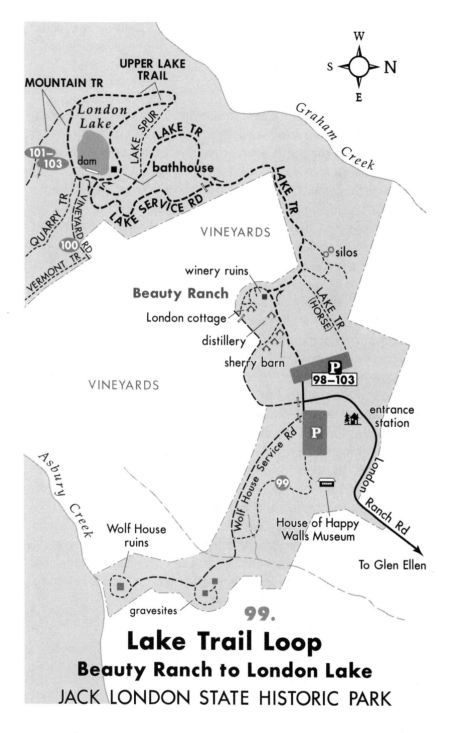

Lake Trail Loop
Beauty Ranch to London Lake
JACK LONDON STATE HISTORIC PARK

Take London Ranch Road 1.3 miles west. Wind up the hill to the park entrance station. After the kiosk, turn right and drive 0.1 mile to the trailhead parking lot. A parking fee is required.

The hike

From the trailhead kiosk, take the posted Beauty Ranch–Mountain Trails path. Walk through a eucalyptus grove and picnic area to a T-junction by the sherry barn on the left. Go to the right, passing the distillery and winery ruins to a trail split. Veer to the right, skirting the Jack London Vineyard, and curve left, passing the 40-foot silos on the right. Leave Beauty Ranch on the Lake Trail, with close-up views of Sonoma Mountain. Follow the dirt road through oak groves, pines, and madrones to a posted junction.

Leave the road and begin the first loop on the Lake Trail to the right, a hiking-only trail. Walk through the dense forest with redwoods and bay laurel, then rejoin the Lake Service Road at one mile. Continue 20 yards to the right, and veer right on the footpath, located to the east side of London Lake by the redwood bathhouse and the stone dam. Take the Upper Lake Trail, beginning the second loop. Pass the old log bathhouse, and follow the north side of the lake. Pass the Lake Spur Trail on the right. Make a U-shaped left bend, and traverse the hillside to an overlook of the lake. Descend to the Mountain Trail (an unpaved multi-use road) on a horseshoe bend. The right fork heads up to Woodcutter's Meadow, Sonoma Ridge, and the summit of Sonoma Mountain (Hikes 100–103). For this hike, go to the left and cross the lake's inlet stream. Follow the south side of London Lake to the Quarry Trail, then walk another 15 yards to the Vineyard Trail. Bear left along the rock dam, completing the second loop. Follow the winding dirt service road downhill and back to the vineyards, completing the first loop. Return to Beauty Ranch and the trailhead. ■

100. Ancient Redwood
Fern Lake • Historic Orchard
JACK LONDON STATE HISTORIC PARK

Hiking distance: 8.2 miles round trip (for all three destinations)
- 4 miles round trip to Ancient Redwood
- add 3 miles round trip for loop around Fern Lake
- add 1.2 miles round trip for loop around Historic Orchard

Hiking time: 4 hours total (for all three destinations)
- 2 hours to Ancient Redwood
- 3.5 hours to Ancient Redwood and Fern Lake
- 2.5 hours to Ancient Redwood and Historic Orchard

Configuration: out-and-back with two loop options
Elevation gain: 300—400 feet
Difficulty: moderate to slightly strenuous
Exposure: mostly shaded forest with exposed pockets
Dogs: not allowed
Maps: U.S.G.S. Glen Ellen
Jack London State Historic Park map

In 2006, land was annexed from the Sonoma Developmental Center to Jack London State Historic Park. The Sonoma Developmental Center, just south of Glen Ellen, is a state-owned facility for the mentally and physically impaired. The 1,600-acre facility is part of the small town of Eldridge, with its own post office and fire department. The annexed land is accessible from the main entrance to the state park, and includes trails to an enormous redwood tree (known as Ancient Redwood), a historic orchard, and Fern Lake.

The Ancient Redwood, also known as Grandmother Redwood or Grandmother Tree, is a massive first growth redwood in a quiet grove. The giant tree has a huge girth with a 14-foot diameter and is estimated to be nearly 2,000 years old. The top of the stately tree is gone, either snapped off by the 1906 earthquake or destroyed by fire. The gnarled limbs and bark are visually striking. Owls are frequently spotted in the tree.

The Historic Orchard was originally planted in the early 1900s as a working farm for the residents to grow and sell fruit. The orchard encompasses 80 acres of fruit bearing trees, including apple, peach, plum, pear, prune, apricot, and cherry. Most of the original orchard remains today.

Fern Lake is a gorgeous lake surrounded by rolling hills and evergreen forest. The lake was used for irrigating the orchard.

This hike begins from Beauty Ranch at the entrance to Jack London State Historic Park. The route winds through redwood groves and passes London Lake en route to the Ancient Redwood. It is two miles from the trailhead to the redwood. From the redwood tree, the hike includes two options. A loop to the west circles the Historic Orchard. A trail to the east loops around Fern Lake.

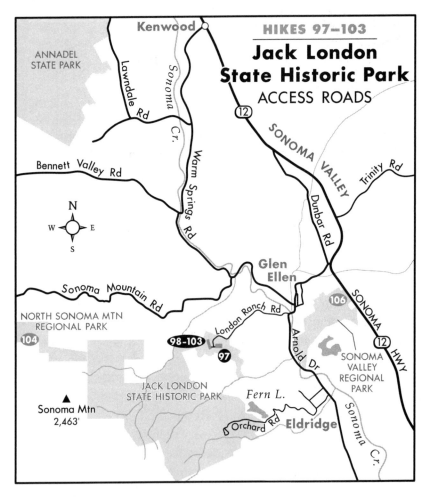

To the trailhead

Jack London State Historic Park is located in Sonoma Valley off of Highway 12 in the town of Glen Ellen. The turnoff to Glen Ellen—Arnold Drive—is 6 miles north of Sonoma and 3.6 miles south of Kenwood. Take Arnold Drive to downtown Glen Ellen and the intersection with London Ranch Road on the west.

Take London Ranch Road 1.3 miles west. Wind up the hill to the park entrance station. After the kiosk, turn right and drive 0.1 mile to the trailhead parking lot. A parking fee is required.

The hike

From the trailhead kiosk, take the posted Beauty Ranch–Mountain Trails path. Walk through a eucalyptus grove and picnic area to a T-junction by the sherry barn on the left. Go to the right, passing the distillery and winery ruins to a trail split. Veer to the right, skirting the Jack London Vineyard, and curve left, passing the 40-foot silos on the right.

Leave Beauty Ranch on the Lake Trail. Follow the dirt trail through oak groves, pines, and madrones to a posted junction. Go right, staying on the Lake Trail, now a hiking-only trail. Traverse the lower mountain slope. Stroll through the dense forest amidst several redwood rings. (Redwood rings are a circle of redwood trees sprouted from the trunk of a damaged or fallen central tree.) Pass the Lake Spur Trail on the right, then veer right as the footpath merges with the service road. Weave up the road to the southeast corner of London Lake at one mile. Walk along the base of the rock-walled dam to a signed junction. The Mountain Trail goes to the right (Hikes 101–103).

Take the Vineyard Trail to the left and gently descend. Parallel the vineyard on the left and the natural forest on the right. Pass a junction with the Quarry Trail at 1.4 miles, and continue through the redwood forest. Cross Asbury Creek to a signed junction with the Asbury Creek Trail on the left. Continue on the Vineyard Trail for 0.1 mile to a three-way junction with picnic benches and hitching posts. The left fork leads to Fern Lake and the right fork leads to the Historic Orchard—the two hiking options. For

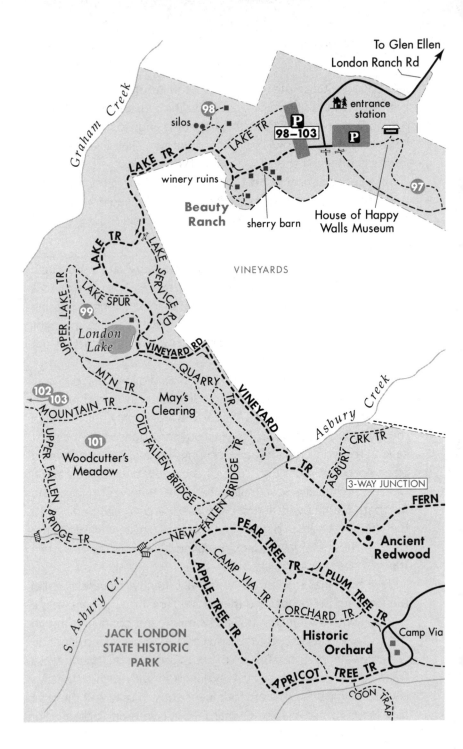

To Glen Ellen
London Ranch Rd

98

silos

LAKE TR

LAKE TR

P
98-103

entrance
station

P

97

winery ruins

VINEYARDS

Beauty
Ranch

sherry barn

House of Happy
Walls Museum

LAKE TR

LAKE SERVICE RD

UPPER LAKE TR

LAKE SPUR

99

London
Lake

VINEYARD RD

QUARRY TR

VINEYARD TR

Asbury Creek

MTN TR

102
103

MOUNTAIN TR

May's
Clearing

OLD FALLEN BRIDGE

101

Woodcutter's
Meadow

UPPER FALLEN BRIDGE TR

NEW FALLEN BRIDGE TR

FALLEN BRIDGE TR

ASBURY CRK TR

3-WAY JUNCTION

FERN

Ancient
Redwood

PEAR TREE TR

CAMP VIA TR

PLUM TREE TR

ORCHARD TR

Camp Via

S. Asbury Cr.

JACK LONDON
STATE HISTORIC
PARK

APPLE TREE TR

Historic
Orchard

APRICOT TREE TR

COON TRAP

100.
Ancient Redwood
Fern Lake • Historic Orchard
JACK LONDON STATE HISTORIC PARK

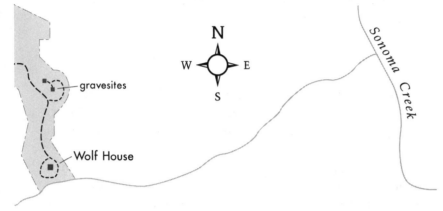

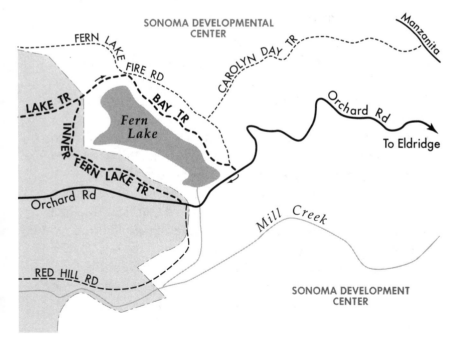

now, take the middle fork. Walk about 100 yards to the massive Ancient Redwood on the left, where the trail ends. A bench offers a respite in the shade of the forest.

ANCIENT REDWOOD TO FERN LAKE: From the three-way junction by the Ancient Redwood, head east on the posted Fern Lake Trail. Steadily descend, dropping a couple hundred feet to the park boundary. Fern Lake lies below to the right. Leave the state park and cross the north end of the lake on the Sonoma Developmental Center land. Veer right on the Bay Trail, skirting the length of the lake on a hillside perch. The trail ends at a four-way junction with the Fern Lake Fire Road and Carolyn Day Trail. Bear right on the fire road to the paved Orchard Road. Walk to the right and cross the earthen dam of Fern Lake. Just after the dam, leave the paved road and veer right on the unsigned Inner Fern Lake Trail, back inside Jack London State Park. Stroll through the forest, with hills blocking the view of the lake. Complete the loop back at the park boundary at the north end of Fern Lake. Return 0.4 miles to the junction by the Ancient Redwood. Return back to the parking lot by retracing your steps, or continue to the Historic Orchard.

ANCIENT REDWOOD TO HISTORIC ORCHARD: From the three-way junction by the Ancient Redwood, head south on the posted Vineyard Trail, climbing 0.1 mile to a T-junction with the Pear Tree Trail. Begin the loop of the Historic Orchard to the right. Follow the edge of the large orchard at the base of upper Sonoma Mountain. Pass the Camp Via Trail on the left, which cuts through the center of the orchard. Seventy yards ahead, the New Fallen Bridge Trail veers into the forest on the right (Hike 101).

Now on the Apple Tree Trail, continue looping southeast along the foot of the mountain. The trail becomes the Apricot Tree Trail and leads to an overlook of Camp Via. Traverse the hillside above the orchard. At the paved Orchard Road, go to the left 0.1 mile, and pick up the Plum Tree Trail on the left. Complete the loop back at the Vineyard Trail on the right. Walk 0.1 mile back to the junction by the Ancient Redwood. Return back to the parking lot by retracing your steps. ∎

101. Woodcutters Meadow— Asbury Creek Loop

JACK LONDON STATE HISTORIC PARK

Hiking distance: 4 miles round trip
Hiking time: 2 hours
Configuration: out-and-back with loop
Elevation gain: 700 feet
Difficulty: moderate
Exposure: mostly shaded forest
Dogs: not allowed
Maps: U.S.G.S. Glen Ellen
　　　　　Jack London State Historic Park map

Woodcutter's Meadow is a large grassy meadow above London Lake in Jack London State Historic Park. From the meadow are views down Sonoma Valley to San Pablo Bay and across the valley to the Mayacamas Mountains. Asbury Creek cascades along the southern side of the meadow. The creek tumbles downstream through a dense forest of redwoods.

This hike begins at Beauty Ranch, a group of historic buildings that once comprised London's mountainside ranch. The trail leads to London Lake, a reservoir and former swimming hole used by the Londons, then begins a two-mile loop. The loop route leads to May's Clearing, an open grassy slope above the lake, and Woodcutter's Meadow. The trail traverses the forested slopes of Sonoma Mountain and parallels Asbury Creek, crossing two bridges over the creek.

To the trailhead

2400 LONDON RANCH RD · GLEN ELLEN   38.356397, -122.543732

Jack London State Historic Park is located in Sonoma Valley off of Highway 12 in the town of Glen Ellen. The turnoff to Glen Ellen— Arnold Drive—is 6 miles north of Sonoma and 3.6 miles south of Kenwood. Take Arnold Drive to downtown Glen Ellen and the intersection with London Ranch Road on the west.

Take London Ranch Road 1.3 miles west. Wind up the hill to the park entrance station. After the kiosk, turn right and drive 0.1 mile to the trailhead parking lot. A parking fee is required.

The hike

From the trailhead kiosk, take the posted Beauty Ranch–Mountain Trails path. Walk through a eucalyptus grove and picnic area to a T-junction by the sherry barn on the left. Go to the right, passing the distillery and winery ruins to a trail split. Veer to the right, skirting the Jack London Vineyard, and curve left, passing the 40-foot silos on the right.

Leave Beauty Ranch on the Lake Trail. Follow the dirt trail through oak groves, pines, and madrones to a posted junction. Go right, staying on the Lake Trail, now a hiking-only trail. Traverse the lower mountain slope. Stroll through the dense forest amidst several redwood rings. (A redwood ring is a circle of redwood trees sprouted from the trunk of a damaged or fallen central tree.) Pass the Lake Spur Trail on the right, then veer right as the footpath merges with the service road. Weave up the road to the southeast corner of London Lake at one mile. Walk along the base of the rock-walled dam to a signed junction. The Vineyard Trail to the Ancient Redwood goes to the left (Hike 100). Take the Mountain Trail to the right 15 yards to the posted Quarry Trail on the left.

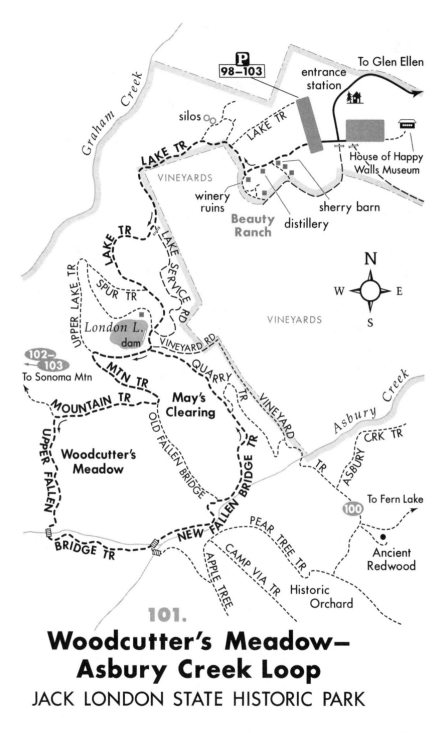

To Glen Ellen

P 98–103

entrance station

silos

LAKE TR

LAKE TR

VINEYARDS

House of Happy Walls Museum

winery ruins

Beauty Ranch

distillery

sherry barn

Graham Creek

LAKE TR

LAKE SERVICE RD

SPUR TR

UPPER LAKE TR

London L.
dam

N
W · E
S

VINEYARDS

VINEYARD RD

102–103
To Sonoma Mtn

MTN TR

MOUNTAIN TR

May's Clearing

QUARRY TR

VINEYARD TR

Asbury Creek

ASBURY CRK TR

UPPER FALLEN

Woodcutter's Meadow

OLD FALLEN BRIDGE

NEW FALLEN BRIDGE TR

ASBURY TR

100
To Fern Lake

Ancient Redwood

BRIDGE TR

PEAR TREE TR

CAMP VIA TR

APPLE TREE

Historic Orchard

101.
Woodcutter's Meadow–
Asbury Creek Loop
JACK LONDON STATE HISTORIC PARK

Begin the loop to the right, staying on the Mountain Trail. Climb 0.2 miles along a switchback to an overlook of May's Clearing, the large grassy meadow. At the overlook is a bench and a junction with the Old Fallen Bridge Trail, which crosses through May's Clearing. The views span for 60 miles from the overlook. Continue uphill on the main trail in a lush forest with redwoods, madrones, bay laurel, and ferns to the signed Upper Fallen Bridge Trail on the left. Bear left and walk through Woodcutter's Meadow and a forest to North Asbury Creek.

Cross a bridge over the perennial creek and curve left. Descend along the stair-stepping creek under the shade of the towering redwoods to the lower bridge and junction. The trail straight ahead leads to the historic orchard (Hike 100). Bear left and cross the bridge over North Asbury Creek. Follow the creek on the New Fallen Bridge Trail, a cliffside path, to a posted trail split with the Quarry Trail. Stay to the left on the Quarry Trail, and complete the two-mile loop back at the Mountain Trail by London Lake. From here, retrace your steps back to Beauty Ranch and the parking lot. ■

102. Sonoma Ridge Trail
JACK LONDON STATE HISTORIC PARK

Hiking distance: 9.5 miles round trip
Hiking time: 6 hours
Configuration: out-and-back
Elevation gain: 1,300 feet
Difficulty: strenuous
Exposure: mostly shaded forest with pockets of open meadows
Dogs: not allowed
Maps: U.S.G.S. Glen Ellen · Jack London State Historic Park map

Sonoma Mountain encompasses a long forested ridge running north and south that forms the backbone of Jack London State Historic Park. This hike along the Sonoma Ridge Trail, a segment of the Bay Area Ridge Trail, follows the east side of the ridge through the 1,400-acre state park, steadily climbing south. The hike begins at Beauty Ranch and ascends the forested slope beyond London Lake. The trail passes through deep woods, redwood groves, and open meadows, offering sweeping vistas down Sonoma Valley to San Pablo Bay and across to the Mayacamas Mountains.

To the trailhead

2400 LONDON RANCH RD · GLEN ELLEN   38.356397, -122.543732

Jack London State Historic Park is located in Sonoma Valley off of Highway 12 in the town of Glen Ellen. The turnoff to Glen Ellen—Arnold Drive—is 6 miles north of Sonoma and 3.6 miles south of Kenwood. Take Arnold Drive to downtown Glen Ellen and the intersection with London Ranch Road on the west.

Take London Ranch Road 1.3 miles west. Wind up the hill to the park entrance station. After the kiosk, turn right and drive 0.1 mile to the trailhead parking lot. A parking fee is required.

The hike

From the trailhead kiosk, take the posted Beauty Ranch-Mountain Trails path. Walk through a eucalyptus grove and picnic area to a T-junction by the sherry barn on the left. Go to the right, passing the distillery and winery ruins to a trail split. Veer to the right, skirting the Jack London Vineyard, and curve left, passing the 40-foot silos on the right.

Leave Beauty Ranch on the Lake Trail. Follow the dirt trail through oak groves, pines, and madrones to a posted junction. Go right, staying on the Lake Trail, now a hiking-only trail. Traverse the lower mountain slope. Stroll through the dense forest amidst several redwood rings. (A redwood ring is a circle of redwood trees sprouted from the trunk of a damaged or fallen central tree.) Pass the Lake Spur Trail on the right, then veer right as the footpath merges with the service road. Weave up the road to the southeast corner of London Lake at one mile. Walk along the base of the rock-walled dam to a signed junction. The Vineyard Trail goes to the left (Hike 100).

Take the Mountain Trail to the right. Continue past the posted Quarry Trail on the left, and climb 0.2 miles along a switchback to an overlook of May's Clearing, the large grassy meadow. At the overlook is a bench and a junction with the Old Fallen Bridge Trail, which crosses through May's Clearing. The views span for 60 miles from the overlook. Continue uphill on the main trail in a lush forest with redwoods, madrones, bay laurel, and ferns to the signed Upper Fallen Bridge Trail on the left. The loop around Woodcutter's Meadow goes to the left (Hike 101). Go to the right, staying straight on the Mountain Trail. Pass Pine Tree Meadows, a small glade on the right. Continue to the Sonoma Ridge Trail by a map kiosk on the left at 2.2 miles.

Bear left on the Sonoma Ridge Trail, and angle up the side of the mountain. Stroll through a forest of Douglas fir, madrone, and bay to rocky North Asbury Creek in a redwood grove. Cross over to the south side of the creek, and zigzag up switchbacks at an easy grade. The far-reaching vistas extend to a grassy slope below the ridgeline at 2,100 feet. At 5.3 miles is a road split, forming a 0.3-mile loop at the park boundary. From the east side of the loop, the East Slope Trail (Bay Area Ridge Trail) continues along the ridge, while the Coon Trap Trail links to the Historic Orchard. Circle the loop, then retrace your steps back to the trailhead parking lot. ■

N
W   E
S

To Glen Ellen

P 98–103

entrance

silos

98

LAKE TR

museum

97

winery ruins

sherry barn

Beauty Ranch

distillery

LAKE TR

LAKE SERVICE

99

LAKE SPUR

UPPER LAKE TR

London Lake

VINEYARDS

Graham Creek

Pine Tree Meadows

VINEYARD

QUARRY TR

May's Clearing

MOUNTAIN TR

Asbury Creek

VINEYARD TR

OLD FALLEN BRDG

101 Woodcutter's Meadow

UPPER FALLEN

BRDG TR

NEW FALLEN BRDG

FERN LAKE TR

100 Ancient Redwood

MTN TR

103 To Sonoma Mtn

SONOMA

RIDGE

S. Asbury

Historic Orchard

Orchard Rd

Camp Via

S. Graham

TR

JACK LONDON STATE HISTORIC PARK

COON TRAP TR

EAST SLOPE TR

102.
Sonoma Ridge Trail
JACK LONDON STATE HISTORIC PARK

103. Sonoma Mountain Trail to summit
JACK LONDON STATE HISTORIC PARK

Hiking distance: 8 miles round trip
Hiking time: 5 hours
Configuration: out-and-back
Elevation gain: 1,800 feet
Difficulty: strenuous
Exposure: mostly shaded forest with pockets of open meadows
Dogs: not allowed
Maps: U.S.G.S. Glen Ellen · Jack London State Historic Park map

Sonoma Mountain stretches from Santa Rosa to Sonoma. The volcanic range forms the western side of the 17-mile-long Sonoma Valley. Sonoma Valley is also known as the Valley of the Moon, named after the Jack London book of the same name.

This hike climbs to the summit of the range through the back-country of Jack London State Historic Park. The hike, which mainly follows a fire road, leads through unspoiled forests with redwoods, bigleaf maple, black oak, buckeye, bay, and madrone to the Park Summit. Park Summit is a short distance east of the 2,463-foot summit of Sonoma Mountain. (The actual summit sits just outside the park boundary on private land.)

To the trailhead

2400 LONDON RANCH RD · GLEN ELLEN   38.356397, -122.543732

Jack London State Historic Park is located in Sonoma Valley off of Highway 12 in the town of Glen Ellen. The turnoff to Glen Ellen—Arnold Drive—is 6 miles north of Sonoma and 3.6 miles south of Kenwood. Take Arnold Drive to downtown Glen Ellen and the intersection with London Ranch Road on the west.

Take London Ranch Road 1.3 miles west. Wind up the hill to the park entrance station. After the kiosk, turn right and drive 0.1 mile to the trailhead parking lot. A parking fee is required.

The hike

From the trailhead kiosk, take the posted Beauty Ranch–Mountain Trails path. Walk through a eucalyptus grove and picnic area to a T-junction by the sherry barn on the left. Go to the right, passing the distillery and winery ruins to a trail split. Veer to the right, skirting the Jack London Vineyard, and curve left, passing the 40-foot silos on the right.

Leave Beauty Ranch on the Lake Trail. Follow the dirt trail through oak groves, pines, and madrones to a posted junction. Go right, staying on the Lake Trail, now a hiking-only trail. Traverse the lower mountain slope. Stroll through the dense forest amidst several redwood rings. (A redwood ring is a circle of redwood trees sprouted from the trunk of a damaged or fallen central tree.) Pass the Lake Spur Trail on the right, then veer right as the footpath merges with the service road. Weave up the road to the southeast corner of London Lake at one mile. Walk along the base of the rock-walled dam to a signed junction. The Vineyard Trail goes to the left (Hike 100).

Take the Mountain Trail to the right. Continue past the posted Quarry Trail on the left, and climb 0.2 miles along a switchback to an overlook of May's Clearing, the large grassy meadow. At the overlook is a bench and a junction with the Old Fallen Bridge Trail, which crosses through May's Clearing. The views span for 60 miles from the overlook. Continue uphill on the main trail in a lush forest with redwoods, madrones, bay laurel, and ferns to the signed Upper Fallen Bridge Trail on the left. The loop around Woodcutter's Meadow goes to the left (Hike 101). Go to the right, staying straight on the Mountain Trail. Pass Pine Tree Meadows, a small glade on the right. Continue to the Sonoma Ridge Trail by a map kiosk on the left at 2.2 miles. The Sonoma Ridge Trail heads left/south (Hike 102).

To continue to the summit, walk straight ahead through the forest. Cross South Graham Creek and continue on the Mountain Trail. In a short distance, cross Middle Graham Creek to the Deer Camp rest area in a redwood grove on the north side of the creek, once a camping site for Jack London and his guests. Climb through a meadow while enjoying the views of Sonoma Valley and the Mayacamas Mountains. At the Cowan Meadow Trail, stay left, continually climbing to the north canyon wall above Middle Graham Creek. Climb through meadows and oak forests to the Hayfields Trail, veering off to the right en route to the park's north boundary. (A junction on the Hayfields Trail connects with the North Sonoma Mountain Ridge Trail, Hike 104). Stay to the left on the Mountain Trail, contouring through a large meadow to the north branch of the Middle Graham Creek headwaters. Climb along the creek to the west boundary of the park. Curve right and climb a quarter mile to the 2,370-foot park summit, a short distance from (and 90 feet lower than) the privately owned Sonoma Mountain summit. Return along the same route. ■

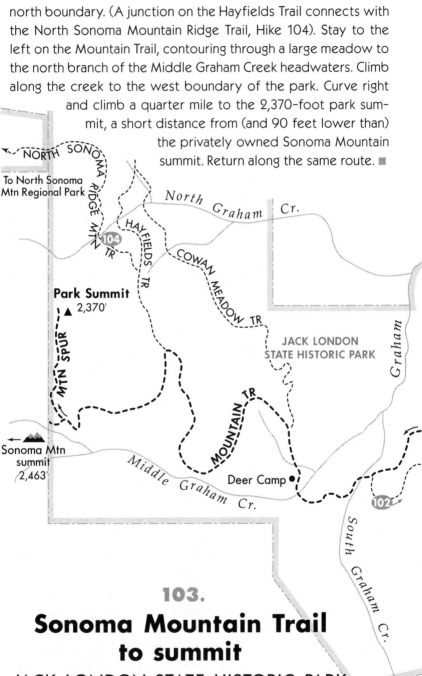

103.

Sonoma Mountain Trail
to summit

JACK LONDON STATE HISTORIC PARK

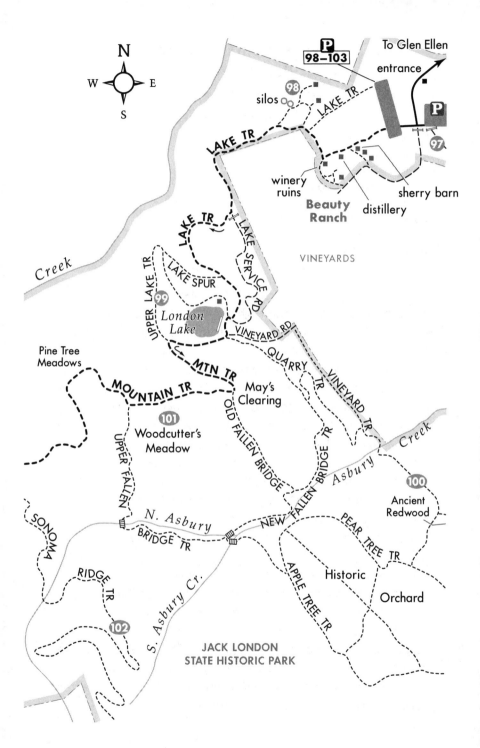

N
W   E
S

To Glen Ellen
entrance

P 98-103

P

97

98

silos

LAKE TR

LAKE TR

LAKE TR

winery ruins

Beauty Ranch

distillery

sherry barn

Creek

LAKE TR

LAKE TR

LAKE SERVICE RD

LAKE SPUR

UPPER LAKE TR

99

London Lake

VINEYARDS

VINEYARD RD

Pine Tree Meadows

MTN TR

MOUNTAIN TR

MTN TR

May's Clearing

QUARRY TR

VINEYARD TR

101

Woodcutter's Meadow

OLD FALLEN BRIDGE

NEW FALLEN BRIDGE TR

Asbury Creek

100

Ancient Redwood

UPPER FALLEN

N. Asbury BRIDGE TR

NEW FALLEN BRIDGE TR

PEAR TREE TR

SONOMA

RIDGE TR

102

S. Asbury Cr.

APPLE TREE TR

Historic

Orchard

JACK LONDON STATE HISTORIC PARK

104. North Sonoma Mountain Ridge Trail

NORTH SONOMA MOUNTAIN REGIONAL PARK and OPEN SPACE PRESERVE

Hiking distance: 8 miles round trip
Hiking time: 4.5 hours
Configuration: out and back
Elevation gain: 1,000 feet
Difficulty: moderate to strenuous
Exposure: mostly shaded forest
Dogs: not allowed
Maps: U.S.G.S. Glen Ellen
North Sonoma Mountain Regional Park and Open Space Preserve

Sonoma Mountain is the prominent 14-mile-long range that separates Petaluma and the Highway 101 corridor from scenic Sonoma Valley. The prominent landform tops out at 2,463 feet and is among the highest points in Sonoma County.

North Sonoma Mountain Regional Park and Open Space Preserve, opened to the public in 2014, is a stunning 820-acre parkland on the north slope of the mountain. The open space is located southeast of Santa Rosa between Rohnert Park and Sonoma Valley. The land lies adjacent to Jack London State Historic Park on its west side. Within the regional park are numerous creeks surrounded by dense forests of coast live oak, black oak, bigleaf maple, Pacific madrone, Douglas fir, bay laurel, and coast redwoods, with an understory of blackberry, toyon, and western poison oak. The open slopes are covered with chaparral and grasslands.

A 4.25-mile trail climbs to the mountain summit. Atop the ridge, the trail seamlessly connects to Jack London State Historic Park via the Hayfields Trail near the summit. The trail gently winds through diverse landscapes, including dark shaded forests, broad meadows, and upland valleys. From the trail are sweeping views of Sonoma Valley, the Santa Rosa Plain, the coastal range to the Pacific Ocean, and the Mayacamas Mountains. The multi-use trail is open to hiking, biking, and equestrians.

The North Sonoma Mountain Trail is part of the Bay Area Ridge Trail around the San Francisco Bay area. To date, about 340 miles of the Bay Area Ridge Trail are complete. This trail has added another vital link in the projected 550-mile loop.

To the trailhead

5297 SONOMA MOUNTAIN RD · SANTA ROSA   38.363259, -122.604776

SANTA ROSA. Take Bennett Valley Road 6 miles to Sonoma Mountain Road and turn right. Continue 2.2 miles to a road fork with Pressley Road. Veer left, staying on Sonoma Mountain Road, and drive 0.7 miles to the North Sonoma Mountain Park turnoff on the right. Turn right and go 0.5 miles, crossing a bridge over Matanzas Creek, to the trailhead parking lot on the left. A parking fee is required.

PETALUMA. Take Petaluma Hill Road 2.5 miles north to Roberts Road and turn right. Continue 4.2 miles to Sonoma Mountain Road. (En route, Roberts Road becomes Pressley Road at 1.3 miles.) Turn right on Sonoma Mountain Road, and drive 0.7 miles to the North Sonoma Mountain Park turnoff on the right. Turn right and go 0.5 miles, crossing a bridge over Matanzas Creek, to the trailhead parking lot on the left.

GLEN ELLEN. Take Warm Springs Road 2.4 miles west to Bennett Valley Road and turn left. Continue 6.6 miles to Sonoma Mountain Road and turn left. Go 2.2 miles to a road fork with Pressley Road. Veer left, staying on Sonoma Mountain Road, and drive 0.7 miles to the North Sonoma Mountain Park turnoff on the right. Turn right and go 0.5 miles, crossing a bridge over Matanzas Creek, to the trailhead parking lot on the left.

SCENIC MOUNTAIN ROUTE FROM GLEN ELLEN. Take Warm Springs Road 1.2 miles west to Sonoma Mountain Road and turn left. Continue 4.6 miles to the North Sonoma Mountain Park turnoff on the left. Turn left and go 0.5 miles, crossing a bridge over Matanzas Creek, to the trailhead parking lot on the left.

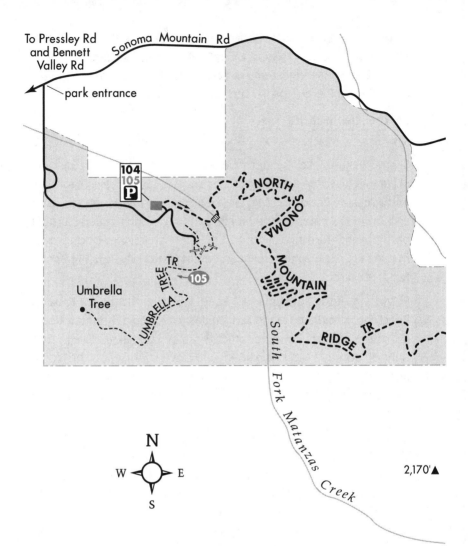

To Pressley Rd
and Bennett
Valley Rd

Sonoma Mountain Rd

park entrance

104
105
P

NORTH SONOMA MOUNTAIN

UMBRELLA TREE TR

105

Umbrella
Tree

RIDGE TR

South Fork Matanzas Creek

N
W E
S

2,170'▲

104.
North Sonoma Mountain
Ridge Trail
NORTH SONOMA MOUNTAIN REGIONAL PARK
and OPEN SPACE PRESERVE

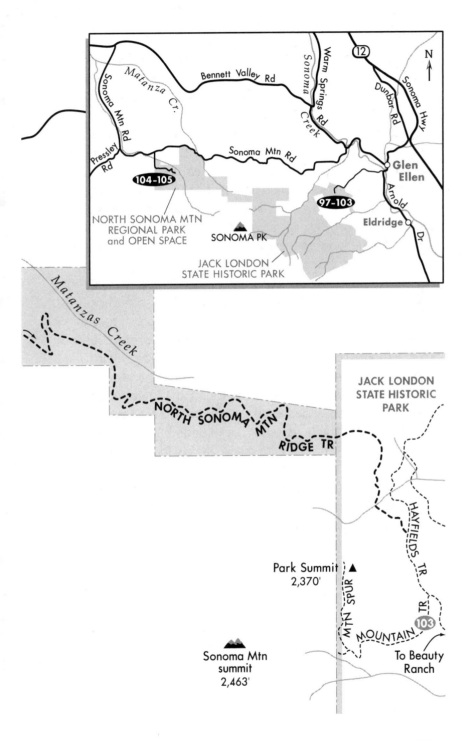

N

12

Bennett Valley Rd

Matanza Cr.

Sonoma Mtn Rd

Pressley Rd

Warm Springs Rd

Sonoma Creek

Dunbar Rd

Sonoma Hwy

104-105

Sonoma Mtn Rd

97-103

Glen Ellen

NORTH SONOMA MTN
REGIONAL PARK
and OPEN SPACE

SONOMA PK

Eldridge

Arnold Dr

JACK LONDON
STATE HISTORIC PARK

Matanzas Creek

NORTH SONOMA MTN
RIDGE TR

JACK LONDON
STATE HISTORIC
PARK

HAYFIELDS TR

Park Summit
2,370'

MTN SPUR

103

MOUNTAIN TR

To Beauty
Ranch

Sonoma Mtn
summit
2,463'

The hike

Take the trail past the restrooms to the signed trailhead. Enter the shade of the mixed forest under redwoods, black oaks, and bay laurel. At 200 yards is a trail split by creekside picnic tables on the left. The Umbrella Tree Trail curves right (Hike 105). Stay on the North Sonoma Mountain Ridge Trail, walking through a damp forest with redwood groves and oaks. Cross the bridge over perennial South Fork Matanzas Creek. Temporarily leave the forest and cross the open rolling hills, skirting the edge of a vineyard. Wend up the meadows, passing a log rail fence by a paved easement road. Veer away from the road and traverse the hillside, entering the shade of the forest again. Long, easy switchbacks zigzag up the mountain at a gradual grade, making the pastoral climb easy. In clearings are sweeping vistas across the Santa Rosa Plain to the west and the Mayacamas Mountains to the northeast.

Continue through the damp, atmospheric forest to a minor ridge. Make a horseshoe right bend and follow the ridge. Continue to a Y-fork by a ranch gate on the left. The wider right fork, a dirt road, leads to the open rolling grasslands and radio towers atop the mountain. For this hike, take the lower left branch. The footpath gently descends through the forest to a trail gate. Pass through the gate, entering Jack London State Historic Park. Continue to a T-junction with the Hayfields Trail. This is the turnaround point

To extend the hike, the right fork leads 0.8 miles to the 2,370-foot Park Summit (just east of the actual 2,463-foot summit). Return by retracing your route. ■

105. Umbrella Tree Trail

NORTH SONOMA MOUNTAIN REGIONAL PARK
and OPEN SPACE PRESERVE

Hiking distance: 1.8 miles round trip
Hiking time: 1 hour
Configuration: out and back
Elevation gain: 450 feet
Difficulty: slightly moderate
Exposure: shaded redwood forest & exposed grassy hilltop
Dogs: not allowed
Maps: U.S.G.S. Glen Ellen
        North Sonoma Mountain Regional Park and Open Space Preserve

Umbrella Tree is a massive multi-trunk bay laurel tree in a compact grouping of six old-growth trees. The tree sits on a 2,160-foot knoll along the Sonoma Mountain range. From the knoll are sweeping vistas across Santa Rosa and Bennett Valley to the coastal range.

This short but rewarding hike is in North Sonoma Mountain Regional Park and Open Space Preserve, a 736-acre parkland on the north slope of Sonoma Mountain. (The 14-mile Sonoma Mountain range forms the southwest side of Sonoma Valley.) En route to the Umbrella Tree, the hike travels through a redwood grove on the banks of South Fork Matanzas Creek, ascends the mountainside slope through a dense forest, then crosses the open hilltop meadows to an overlook with a picnic bench beside the tree.

To the trailhead

5297 SONOMA MOUNTAIN RD · SANTA ROSA   38.363259, –122.604776

SANTA ROSA. Take Bennett Valley Road 6 miles to Sonoma Mountain Road and turn right. Continue 2.2 miles to a road fork with Pressley Road. Veer left, staying on Sonoma Mountain Road, and drive 0.7 miles to the North Sonoma Mountain Park turnoff on the right. Turn right and go 0.5 miles, crossing a bridge over Matanzas Creek, to the trailhead parking lot on the left. A parking fee is required.

PETALUMA. Take Petaluma Hill Road 2.5 miles north to Roberts Road and turn right. Continue 4.2 miles to Sonoma Mountain Road. (En route, Roberts Road becomes Pressley Road at 1.3 miles.) Turn right on Sonoma Mountain Road, and drive 0.7 miles to the North Sonoma Mountain Park turnoff on the right. Turn right and go 0.5 miles, crossing a bridge over Matanzas Creek, to the trailhead parking lot on the left.

GLEN ELLEN. Take Warm Springs Road 2.4 miles west to Bennett Valley Road and turn left. Continue 6.6 miles to Sonoma Mountain Road and turn left. Go 2.2 miles to a road fork with Pressley Road. Veer left, staying on Sonoma Mountain Road, and drive 0.7 miles to the North Sonoma Mountain Park turnoff on the right. Turn right and go 0.5 miles, crossing a bridge over Matanzas Creek, to the trailhead parking lot on the left.

SCENIC MOUNTAIN ROUTE FROM GLEN ELLEN. Take Warm Springs Road 1.2 miles west to Sonoma Mountain Road and turn left. Continue 4.6 miles to the North Sonoma Mountain Park turnoff on the left. Turn left and go 0.5 miles, crossing a bridge over Matanzas Creek, to the trailhead parking lot on the left.

The hike

The hike begins on the North Sonoma Mountain Ridge Trail. Take the trail past the restrooms to the signed trailhead. Enter the shade of the mixed forest with redwoods, black oaks, and bay laurel. At 200 yards is a trail split and creekside picnic tables on the left. The North Sonoma Mountain Ridge Trail continues straight to a bridge crossing perennial South Fork Matanzas Creek (Hike 104).

For this hike, curve right on the Umbrella Tree Trail. Head up the path in a dense forest of redwoods. Pass through a ranch gate. Curve right and go through a second gate. Emerge from the forest to a junction in an open meadow with views across Santa Rosa. The right fork leads back to the trailhead. Bear left and follow the fenceline to a third and final gate. Go through the gate, and re-enter the shade of the forest among bigleaf maples, twisted black oaks, and bay laurel. Continue uphill on the old ranch road through the mixed forest. At 0.6 miles, leave the forest to the open, rolling grassland. Follow the grassy path and curve to the right. Climb up to the bald summit alongside Umbrella Tree. At the knoll is an overlook and a picnic bench. After enjoying the vistas, return along the same route. ■

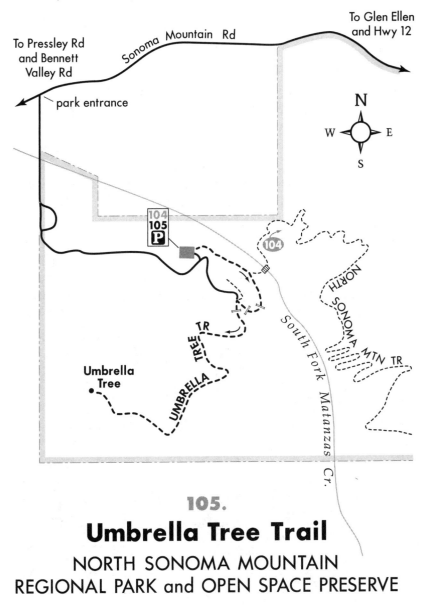

105.
Umbrella Tree Trail
NORTH SONOMA MOUNTAIN
REGIONAL PARK and OPEN SPACE PRESERVE

106. Sonoma Valley Regional Park

Hiking distance: 2.5-mile loop
Hiking time: 1.5 hours
Configuration: loop
Elevation gain: 225 feet
Difficulty: easy
Exposure: a mix of open meadows and shaded forest
Dogs: allowed (plus off-leash allowed in Liz Perrone dog park)
Maps: U.S.G.S. Glen Ellen • Sonoma Valley Regional Park map

Sonoma Valley Regional Park is tucked into the base of the Sonoma Mountains along the verdant valley floor. The park sits on the west edge of the wide valley, just south of the creekside town of Glen Ellen and six miles north of Sonoma. The 202-acre park is filled with rolling oak woodlands and grassy meadows and is known for its beautiful displays of California poppies, wild irises, and lupines. The park has picnic areas and the Liz Perrone Dog Park, a one-acre fenced grassland for off-leash canines. Dirt and paved trails used for hiking, biking, and horseback riding weave through the streamside corridor. This hike stays on the wide main route, climbing the rolling hillside to the picturesque ridge and returning through the stream-fed meadow with gorgeous blue oaks.

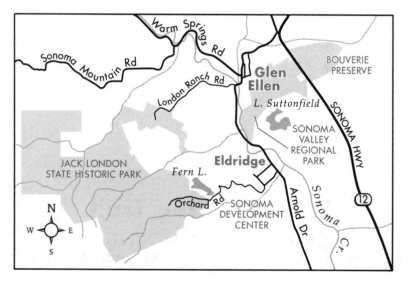

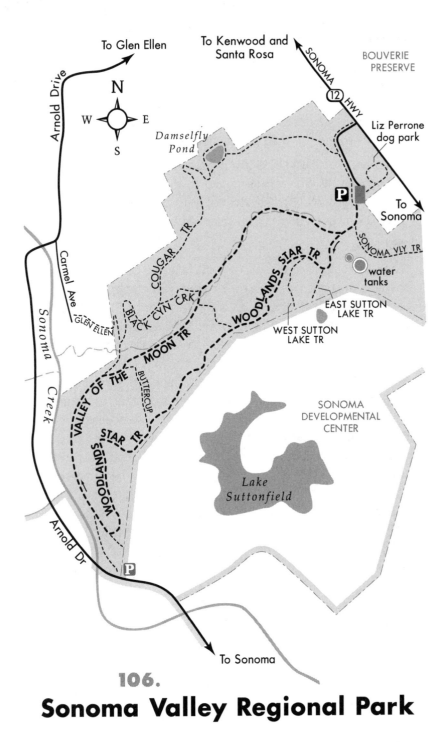

To Glen Ellen

To Kenwood and
Santa Rosa

BOUVERIE
PRESERVE

Arnold Drive

SONOMA HWY

12

Liz Perrone
dog park

N

W · E

S

*Damselfly
Pond*

P

To
Sonoma

Carmel Ave

COUGAR TR.

SONOMA VLY TR

water
tanks

Sonoma Creek

BLACK CYN CRK

WOODLANDS STAR TR

EAST SUTTON
LAKE TR

GLEN ELLEN

VALLEY OF THE MOON TR

WEST SUTTON
LAKE TR

BUTTERCUP

WOODLANDS STAR TR.

SONOMA
DEVELOPMENTAL
CENTER

*Lake
Suttonfield*

Arnold Dr

P

To Sonoma

106.
Sonoma Valley Regional Park

To the trailhead

13630 SONOMA HWY 12 · GLEN ELLEN   38.364486, -122.512241

KENWOOD. From the town of Kenwood, drive 4 miles south on Highway 12 (Sonoma Highway) to the posted park entrance. (It is located 0.4 miles south of Arnold Drive.) Turn right and drive 0.2 miles to the trailhead parking lot. A parking fee is required.

SONOMA. From East Napa Street in Sonoma, drive 5.5 miles north on Highway 12 (Sonoma Highway) to the park entrance on the left. (It is located 1.8 miles north of Madrone Road.) Turn left and drive 0.2 miles to the trailhead parking lot.

The hike

From the far end of the parking lot, take the paved path. Curve towards the right, passing a road to the water tanks, to a trail fork at 100 yards. Begin the loop to the left on the Ridge Trail, and climb up to the ridge. Curve to the right and follow the grassy ridge dotted with oaks to an overlook with sitting benches. The views include the Sonoma Mountains, the Mayacamas Mountains, Sonoma Valley, and Lake Suttonfield. Continue through the oak savanna, passing a series of side paths that veer off from the main route. Stay on the wider, main route to a fenceline. The trail beyond the fence enters the Sonoma Developmental Center.

Bear right, keeping the fence to your left, and descend 40 yards to a junction. Go to the left and traverse the hillside along the park boundary through a forest of oak, madrone, and manzanita. Curve right and weave down the hillside to the open rolling grasslands on the valley floor near Arnold Drive. Take the Canyon Trail to the right, and parallel a seasonal tributary of Sonoma Creek. Meander through the stream-fed meadow. Blue oaks draped with strands of lace lichen dot the meadow. Cross over the seasonal creek seven times, completing the loop. Stay to the left, returning to the trailhead. ■

107. Maxwell Farms Regional Park

Hiking distance: 1-mile loop
Hiking time: 35 minutes
Configuration: loop
Elevation gain: level
Difficulty: easy
Exposure: a mix of shaded forest and open meadows
Dogs: allowed
Maps: U.S.G.S. Sonoma · Maxwell Farms Regional Park map

Maxwell Farms Regional Park is located at the northwest end of Sonoma just south of Boyes Hot Springs. The 85-acre park borders Sonoma Creek in a lush riparian corridor. The park has two distinct personalities. The developed northeast portion of the park includes picnic areas, athletic fields, a playground, and a Boys and Girls Club. The southwest half of the park is a natural 40-acre oasis with woodlands that are dominated by immense California bays and lush grassland meadows. The Maxwell family lived on this land from 1859 to 1968. They planted plum and apricot orchards in the late 1800s, which are still productive. This hike loops around the natural area and follows the watercourse of Sonoma Creek.

To the trailhead

100 VERANO AVE · SONOMA   38.302469, -122.478389

SONOMA. From Sonoma Plaza in downtown Sonoma, drive one mile west on West Napa Street to Highway 12 (Sonoma Highway). Turn right and continue 0.6 miles to Verano Avenue. Turn left and go 0.1 mile to the posted park entrance on the left. Turn left and park in the lot. A parking fee is required.

KENWOOD. From the town of Kenwood, drive 8 miles south on Highway 12 (Sonoma Highway) to Verano Avenue and turn right. Continue 0.1 mile to the posted park entrance on the left. Turn left and park in the lot. A parking fee is required.

The hike

From the far, southeast end of the parking lot, walk down the service road past the Valley of the Moon Boys and Girls Club. Curve right to the group picnic area on the left and a posted junction. Continue straight ahead on the Three Meadow Trail—a dirt footpath—to a four-way junction.

Begin the loop to the left on the Bay Tree Trail through oaks, bay laurels, and blackberry bushes to the south park boundary and another junction. The left fork loops back to the ranger residence and returns to the group picnic area. Curve to the right on the Back Meadow Trail, skirting the south end of the park. The trail merges with the Three Meadow Trail and continues along the park boundary 20 feet above Sonoma Creek. Follow the creek upstream, heading north to the west end of the Bay Tree Trail. Bear right on the Bay Tree Trail, and stroll through an amazing tunnel of massive bay laurels. Complete the loop at the junction with the Three Meadows Trail. Return left to the parking lot. ■

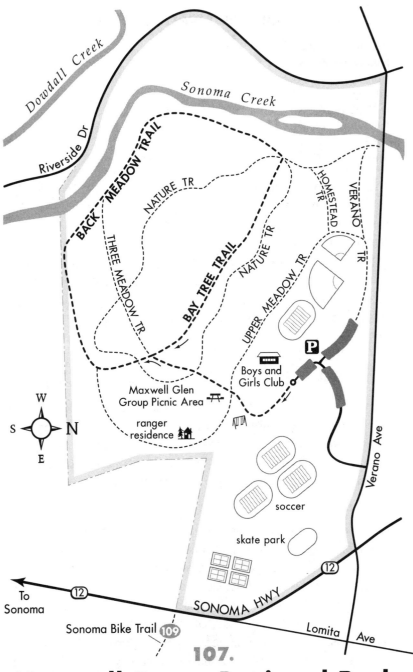

Dowdall Creek

Sonoma Creek

Riverside Dr

BACK MEADOW TRAIL

NATURE TR

THREE MEADOW TR

BAY TREE TRAIL

NATURE TR

NATURE TR

UPPER MEADOW TR

HOMESTEAD TR

VERANO TR

P

Boys and Girls Club

Maxwell Glen Group Picnic Area

ranger residence

W
S ✦ N
E

soccer

skate park

Verano Ave

To Sonoma

(12)

(12)

SONOMA HWY

Sonoma Bike Trail (109)

Lomita Ave

107.

Maxwell Farms Regional Park

108. Sonoma Overlook Trail

Hiking distance: 3 miles round trip
Hiking time: 1.5 hours
Configuration: out-and-back
Elevation gain: 400 feet
Difficulty: easy
Exposure: a mix of open meadows and forested pockets
Dogs: not allowed
Maps: U.S.G.S. Sonoma · Sonoma Overlook Trail map

The Sonoma Overlook Trail is a gorgeous hike that is a short half mile from the Sonoma Plaza in downtown Sonoma. The trail traverses the hillside above the north end of town to a grassy plateau below the summit of Schocken Hill. The hike begins at Mountain Cemetery and leads to the plateau through a mixed woodland forest. A short trail loops around the plateau to a memorial bench with a bird's-eye view of Sonoma, the sloping ridge of Sonoma Mountain, and vistas across Sonoma Valley to San Pablo Bay.

To the trailhead

1ST STREET WEST · SONOMA   38.299574, -122.457297

From West Napa Street by the Sonoma Plaza in downtown Sonoma, drive 0.5 miles north on First Street West (along the west edge of the plaza) to the posted Mountain Cemetery on the right. It is across the street from Depot Park and just before the hill. Turn right and park by the signed trailhead.

The hike

Pass the trailhead panel and walk up the grassy slope, skirting the west edge of the cemetery. Cross a seasonal stream in a small canyon, and zigzag up the hillside in a grove of oaks and California bays. Pass a moss-covered lava rock and an old rock wall. Emerge from the forest to a clearing in a sloping meadow and a Y-fork with a vista of Sonoma and the surrounding mountains. The Toyon Trail veers right and descends to Toyon Road at the upper end of Mountain Cemetery. This trail can be used on the return route by winding down the cemetery roads to the entrance and trailhead. For now, continue straight on the left fork. Steadily gain elevation through manzanita and majestic, twisted valley oaks. Switchback to the left, and gently climb to a junction at the Upper Meadow at 1.25 miles.

Begin the loop around the meadow to the right. Pass basalt outcroppings en route to sweeping vistas, including the sloping ridge of Sonoma Mountain. At the south end of the loop is a memorial stone bench. Just beyond the bench is a trail split. The right fork curves to the upper end of the meadow and ends at the fenced boundary. The main trail stays on the plateau to the left and completes the loop. Return on the same trail, or use the alternative Toyon Trail. ■

Schocken Hill ▲▲
658'

memorial bench

seasonal stream

Norrbom Road

TOYON TR

Toyon
Cedar
Laurel
Circle
Circle
Willow
Cypress

P

MOUNTAIN CEMETERY

N
W ⊕ E
S

1st St West

Arnold Field

1st St East

2nd St East

DEPOT PARK

Depot Hotel ■

To downtown Sonoma

108.
Sonoma Overlook Trail

109. Sonoma Bike Path

Hiking distance: 3 miles round trip
Hiking time: 1.5 hours
Configuration: out-and-back
Elevation gain: level
Difficulty: easy
Exposure: mostly exposed
Dogs: allowed
Maps: U.S.G.S. Sonoma · Sonoma State Historic Park map

The Sonoma Bike Path is a hiking, biking, and jogging trail that crosses through the heart of Sonoma just north of Sonoma Plaza. The path stretches from Fourth Street East, by Sebastiani Vineyards and Winery, to the Sonoma Highway across from Maxwell Farms Regional Park. The dog-friendly path travels past vineyards, Depot Park, the Sonoma Depot Museum (built as a replica of the Sonoma's first train depot of 1880), Sonoma State Historic Park, and the open grasslands around General Vallejo's Gothic Revival home on 20 acres. The historic park contains Mission San Francisco Solano, built in 1823. Known as Sonoma Mission, it is the northernmost of California's 21 Franciscan missions. The path is popular with locals as well as visitors.

To the trailhead

4TH STREET EAST · SONOMA   38.294644, -122.449347

From East Napa Street by the Sonoma Plaza in downtown Sonoma, drive 0.5 miles east on East Napa Street to 4th Street East. Turn left and continue a quarter mile to the posted trail across from Lovall Valley Road by the Sebastiani Vineyards. Park along either side of the street.

The hike

From Fourth Street East at the west end of Lovall Valley Road, head west on the paved path through the Sebastiani Vineyards. Cross Second Street East, and continue through a landscaped greenbelt to First Street East at 0.35 miles. Cross the street and enter Depot Park, with a eucalyptus grove, historical museum, and train cars on the left. Athletic fields are on the right.

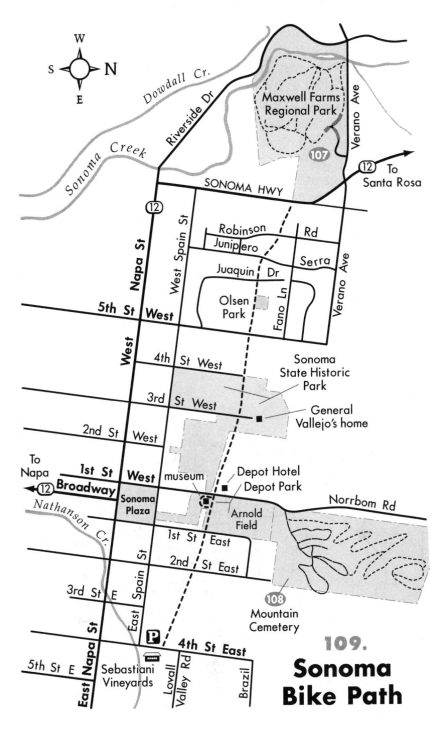

W N
S E

Dowdall Cr.

Riverside Dr

Sonoma Creek

Maxwell Farms
Regional Park

(107)

Verano Ave

SONOMA HWY

(12) To
Santa Rosa

(12)

Napa St

West Spain St

Robinson Rd

Junipero

Serra

Juaquin Dr

Fano Ln

Olsen Park

Verano Ave

5th St West

West

4th St West

Sonoma
State Historic
Park

3rd St West

2nd St West

General
Vallejo's home

To
Napa

1st St West

museum

Depot Hotel
Depot Park

(12) Broadway

Sonoma
Plaza

Norrbom Rd

Nathanson Cr.

Arnold
Field

1st St East

East Spain St

2nd St East

3rd St E

(108)

Mountain
Cemetery

P

East Napa St

4th St East

5th St E

Sebastiani
Vineyards

Lovall Valley Rd

Brazil

109.
Sonoma
Bike Path

383

A side path circles the museum and train cars. At a half mile is First Street West and the historic Depot Hotel, built in 1870 and closed in 1923. Cross through the vast grasslands of Sonoma State Historic Park to Third Street West. To the right, the forested road leads to General Mariano Vallejo's home, dating back to the 1850s. Continue straight ahead through the open meadow to Fourth Street West. Cross the street, leaving the state park, and pass through a greenbelt corridor between homes. Cross Fifth Street West at just over one mile, and continue through the corridor. Pass Olsen Park, Juaquin Drive, Junipero Serra Drive, and Robinson Road to the end of the trail at the Sonoma Highway (Highway 12). Across the highway is Maxwell Farms Regional Park (Hike 107). Return by retracing your steps. ■

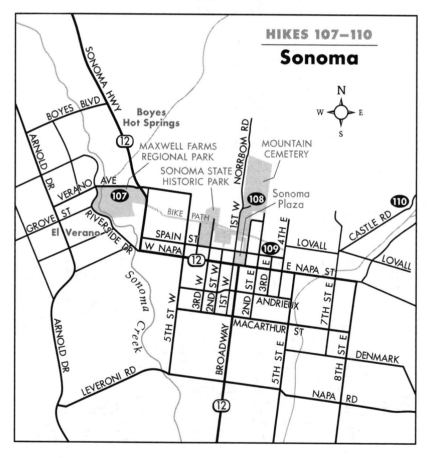

110. Bartholomew Memorial Park

(Closed from January 1 to April 1)

Hiking distance: 2.4-mile loop
Hiking time: 1.5 hours
Configuration: loop
Elevation gain: 450 feet
Difficulty: easy to moderate
Exposure: a mix of open meadows and shaded forest
Dogs: allowed
Maps: U.S.G.S. Sonoma · Bartholomew Foundation Trail Map

Bartholomew Memorial Park is a little known gem tucked into the hills less than two miles northeast of Sonoma. The 375-acre park leases part of its diverse land to Bartholomew Winery. This hike is not a meandering stroll through a winery, it only begins and ends there. The trail is a backcountry hike winding through oak-covered mountain slopes and redwood groves. The hike follows portions of Arroyo Seco and the South Fork of Arroyo Seco to a pond, lake, cave, and two impressive overlooks.

To the trailhead

1695 CASTLE ROAD · SONOMA   38.300560, -122.426523

From East Napa Street by the Sonoma Plaza in downtown Sonoma, drive one mile east on East Napa Street to 7th Street East. Turn left and continue 0.3 miles to Castle Road. Turn right and drive a 0.4 miles to the Bartholomew Park Winery entrance. Enter the winery grounds and go a quarter mile to a road fork. The right fork leads to the tasting room. Veer left 0.1 mile to the trailhead parking lot.

A second trailhead is located off of Old Winery Road. From East Napa Street, just east of 8th Street East, turn north on Old Winery Road. Drive 0.75 miles to the posted trailhead parking area on the left.

The hike

From the north end of the parking lot, follow the posted trail 40 yards to Duck Pond. Curve right along the east side of the pond to a trail gate. Pass through the gate and cross a stream in an oak, manzanita, and madrone forest. Climb the hill on the Grape Stomp Trail and traverse the slope, parallel to the stream. Head up the shaded draw and recross the stream. Climb steps and zigzag up the hill to Grape Stomp Bench and an overlook of Sonoma and San Pablo Bay. Weave along the contours of the hills with small dips and rises. Descend to a fork of Arroyo Seco Creek by a private road.

Rock-hop over the creek and cross the road. Climb eight steps and head up the forested hillside. Follow the north side of Arroyo Seco Creek, passing above Benicia's Lake. Descend steps and hop over the creek upstream of the lake. Enter a redwood grove with Douglas fir and continue climbing. A side path on the right leads to the east shore of the lake. The main trail continues to a posted junction at one mile. Angel's Flight Trail descends to the right for a slightly shorter and easier loop.

Bear left on the You-Walk Miwok Trail, climbing to the 640-foot summit that is just past a bench. On clear days, the vistas extend as far as the Golden Gate Bridge. Descend from the upper slope, with the aid of dirt and log steps, to the Shortcut Trail on the right. Stay straight 20 yards to a side path on the right to Szeptaj Point bench, with beautiful views of Sonoma from under a canopy of oaks. Continue downhill on the main trail to a posted junction. Detour to the left 80 yards. Follow the South Fork of Arroyo Seco upstream, passing small waterfalls. Continue over mossy boulders to Solano's Hideaway, a massive rock formation with caves. Solano was an Indian chief of the Suisun Tribe and a friend of General Vallejo.

Return to the junction and continue west, passing a junction with the lower south end of Angel's Flight Trail. Pass through a trail gate and skirt the backside of the Buena Vista Winery. Pass through a second gate to a narrow paved road by a gazebo on the left. Cross a rock bridge over Arroyo Seco Stream and follow the path on the right side of the road. Cross Castle Road and complete the loop at the trailhead parking lot. ■

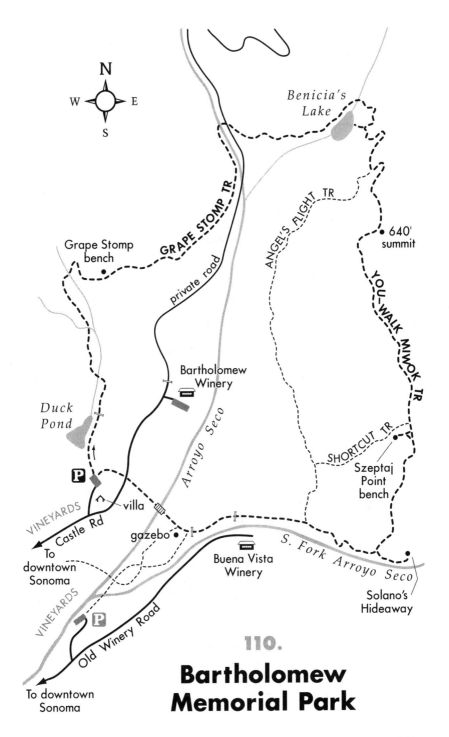

N
W ◆ E
S

Benicia's Lake

GRAPE STOMP TR.

ANGEL'S FLIGHT TR.

• 640' summit

Grape Stomp bench •

private road

YOU-WALK MIWOK TR.

Bartholomew Winery

Arroyo Seco

Duck Pond

SHORTCUT TR.

Szeptaj Point bench •

P

villa

VINEYARDS

To Castle Rd

gazebo •

Buena Vista Winery

S. Fork Arroyo Seco

• Solano's Hideaway

To downtown Sonoma

VINEYARDS

P

Old Winery Road

110.

Bartholomew Memorial Park

To downtown Sonoma

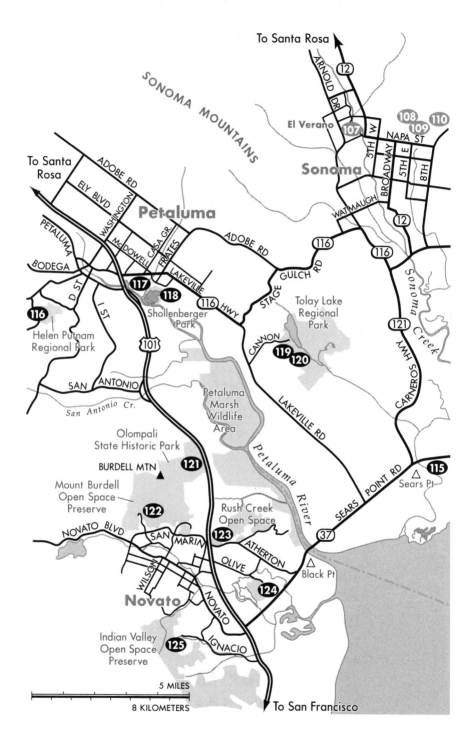

To Santa Rosa

SONOMA MOUNTAINS

12

Arnold Dr

El Verano

107

5TH W

Sonoma

108 110
109

NAPA ST

BROADWAY

5TH E

8TH

To Santa Rosa

ADOBE RD

ELY BLVD

WASHINGTON

Petaluma

WATMAUGH

PETALUMA

BODEGA

McDOWELL

CASA GR.

FRATES

LAKEVILLE

ADOBE RD

GULCH RD

STAGE

12

116

116

116

D ST

1 ST

117

118

116 HWY

Shollenberger Park

Helen Putnam Regional Park

101

Tolay Lake Regional Park

CANNON

119 120

Sonoma Creek

121

CARNEROS HWY

SAN ANTONIO

San Antonio Cr.

Petaluma Marsh Wildlife Area

LAKEVILLE RD

Olompali State Historic Park

BURDELL MTN ▲

121

Petaluma River

115

Sears Pt

SEARS POINT RD

Mount Burdell Open Space Preserve

122

Rush Creek Open Space

123

37

NOVATO BLVD

SAN MARIN

ATHERTON

OLIVE

Black Pt

WILSON

124

Novato

NOVATO

Indian Valley Open Space Preserve

125

IGNACIO

5 MILES

8 KILOMETERS

To San Francisco

388

Southern Sonoma County

SAN PABLO BAY • NAPA–SONOMA MARSHES

NOVATO to PETALUMA

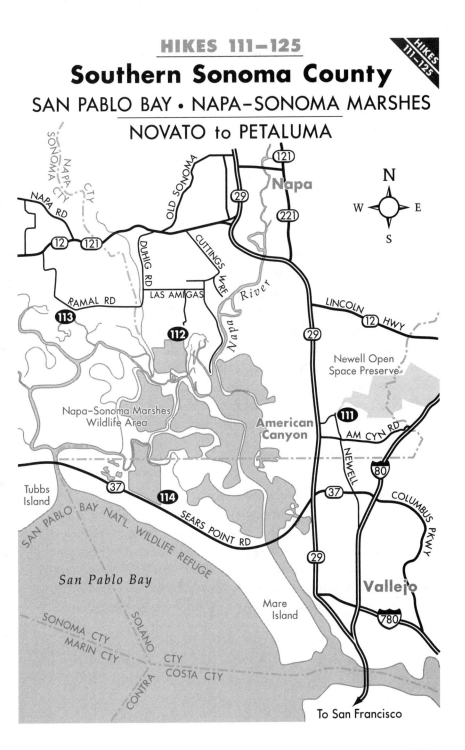

111. Newell Open Space Preserve

Hiking distance: 6-mile loop
Hiking time: 3 hours
Configuration: loop
Elevation gain: 700 feet
Difficulty: moderate
Exposure: mostly open rolling grassland
Dogs: not allowed
Maps: U.S.G.S. Cordelia

Newell Open Space Preserve encompasses 642 acres in the eastern hills above the city of American Canyon. The preserve's land stretches from American Canyon to the Solano County line, connecting with Lynch Canyon Open Space in Solano County. In 1999, Jack and Bernice Newell donated the ranchland to the city to preserve the hillsides, protect wildlife, and offer outdoor recreation to the public. The land is a raptor migration resting area and forms a protected wildlife corridor of 10,000 acres, extending eastward to Suisun Marsh. The preserve contains rolling grasslands, coast live oak, and bay laurel woodlands. Cattle still graze on the property. Remote dirt roads and footpaths, open to hikers and bikers, weave through the hills.

To the trailhead

DONALDSON WAY/NEWELL DR · AM. CANYON   38.175872, -122.242982

From Napa Street by the Sonoma Plaza in downtown Sonoma, drive 1.1 mile south on Broadway (Highway 12) to Napa Road. Turn left and continue 4.3 miles to the Carneros Highway (Highway 121) and turn left (east). Go 5.1 miles east to Highway 29 and turn right, towards Fairfield/Vallejo. Drive 3.7 miles south to Donaldson Way and turn left (east). Continue 0.7 miles to a T-junction at Newell Drive. Park in the unpaved parking area across the road.

The hike

Walk past the trailhead map-kiosk and follow the wide grassy path between the wire fence on the left and the tree-lined stream on the right. Stroll through the lush, green farmland to a signed Y-fork at 1.1 mile.

Begin the loop to the right, and cross over the seasonal drainage. Climb a slope and pass through a gate. Continue ascending, completely surrounded by the rolling hills. Pass a small pond on the left side of the trail to a Y-fork at 1.3 miles. For a shorter 4.1-mile hike, bear left, staying on the Newell Loop.

For this hike, stay to the right. Climb to the 830-foot ridge and the signed Prairie Ridge Trail. The ridge is on the boundary of Lynch Canyon Open Space and Solano County. The 360-degree vistas include San Pablo Bay, the Benicia Bridge, San Francisco Bay, the Golden Gate Bridge, Mount Tamalpais, Sonoma Mountain, the Mayacamas Range, and the Vaca Mountains. Go to the left on the Prairie Ridge Trail and follow the ridge, passing bay trees, oak trees, and beautiful sandstone boulders. Traverse the east-facing slope within Lynch Canyon Open Space to a signed junction with the Kestrel Trail. Curve left, returning to the ridge and westward views. Follow the ridge on the county line, savoring the landscape and vistas. The faint path cuts through an opening in the trees and outcroppings to a posted junction. Bear right, staying on the Prairie Ridge Trail, and follow the oak-dotted ridge. Descend along the spine of the hill to the Saddle Trail at 3 miles.

Go to the left and walk 0.3 miles to a junction with the Newell Loop Trail, the lower cut-across trail. Pass through the gate and head down canyon on the wide, grassy path for one mile, completing the loop. Bear right and retrace your steps back to the trailhead. ■

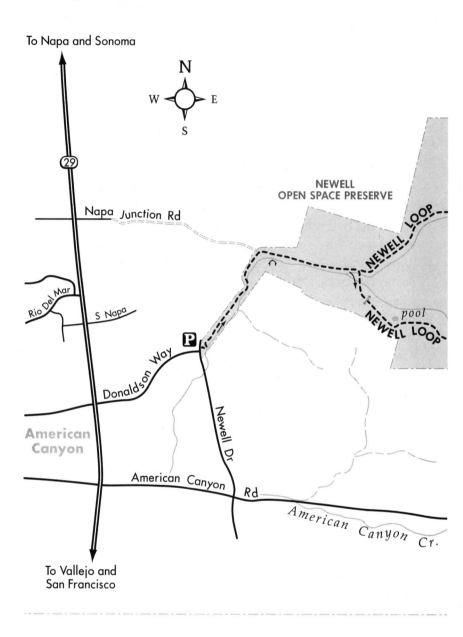

To Napa and Sonoma

N
W E
S

29

Napa Junction Rd

NEWELL
OPEN SPACE PRESERVE

NEWELL LOOP

Rio Del Mar

S Napa

pool

NEWELL LOOP

P

Donaldson Way

Newell Dr

American
Canyon

American Canyon Rd

American Canyon Cr.

To Vallejo and
San Francisco

111.
Newell Open Space Preserve

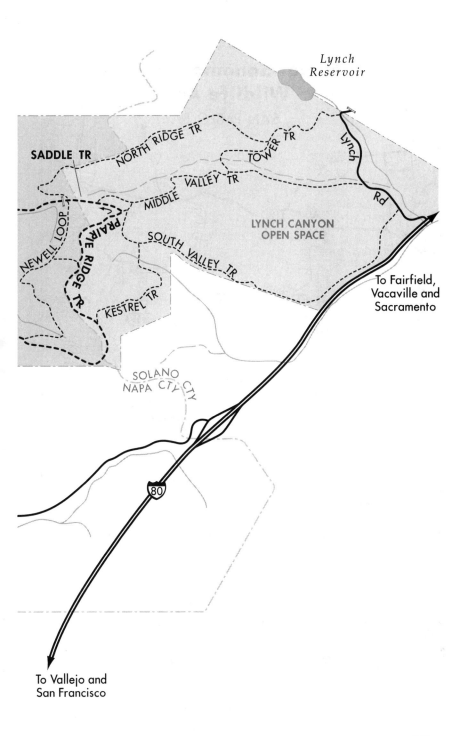

Lynch Reservoir

NORTH RIDGE TR

SADDLE TR

TOWER TR

Lynch Rd

VALLEY TR

MIDDLE

LYNCH CANYON OPEN SPACE

NEWELL LOOP

PRAIRIE RIDGE TR

SOUTH VALLEY TR

KESTREL TR

To Fairfield, Vacaville and Sacramento

SOLANO CTY
NAPA CTY

80

To Vallejo and San Francisco

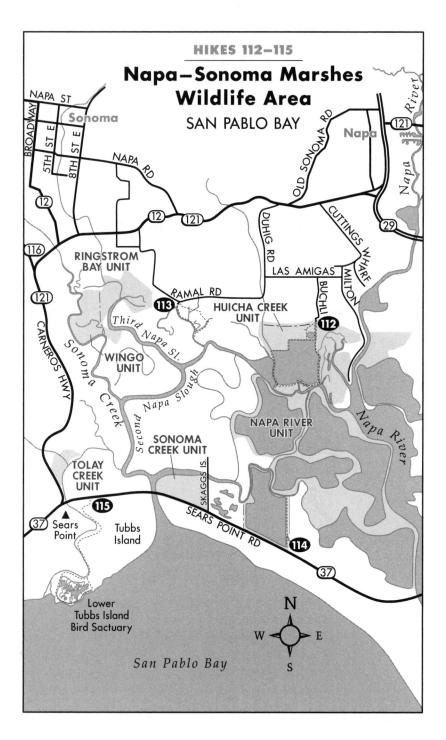

Napa–Sonoma Marshes
Wildlife Area

SAN PABLO BAY

NAPA ST

Sonoma

BROADWAY

5TH ST E

8TH ST E

NAPA RD

Napa River

121

Napa

OLD SONOMA RD

12

121

12

DUHIG RD

CUTTINGS WHARF

29

116

RINGSTROM BAY UNIT

LAS AMIGAS

MILTON

121

RAMAL RD

113

HUICHA CREEK UNIT

BUCHLI

112

CARNEROS HWY

Third Napa Sl.

Sonoma Creek

WINGO UNIT

Second Napa Slough

NAPA RIVER UNIT

Napa River

SONOMA CREEK UNIT

TOLAY CREEK UNIT

SKAGGS IS.

115

37

Sears Point

Tubbs Island

SEARS POINT RD

114

37

Lower Tubbs Island Bird Sactuary

San Pablo Bay

N
W   E
S

112. Huichica Creek Unit
NAPA—SONOMA MARSHES WILDLIFE AREA

Hiking distance: Hike 1: 1.5 miles out-and-back or 3.5-mile loop
Hike 2: 1.3-mile loop
Hiking time: 1—2 hours
Configuration: out-and-back or two loops
Elevation gain: level
Difficulty: easy
Exposure: exposed marshland
Dogs: allowed
Maps: U.S.G.S. Cuttings Wharf
Napa-Sonoma Marshes Wildlife Area map

The Napa-Sonoma Marshes Wildlife Area covers 48,000 acres on the north edge of San Pablo Bay. The marshlands lie between Highway 12 on the north and Highway 37 on the south, straddling Napa, Sonoma, and Solano counties. Within the marsh are saltwater ponds, tidal marshes, seasonally flooded wetlands, agricultural fields, sloughs, and rivers. The rich wetland is fed by the Napa River (which drains Napa Valley) and Sonoma Creek (which drains Sonoma Valley). It is a premier place to observe wildlife and an important habitat for fish, shorebirds, and waterfowl. The tidal marsh was diked for agricultural uses in the late 1800s and early 1900s. In the early 1950s the Leslie Salt Company purchased much of the land and developed it for salt production.

Hikes 112—115 access the Napa-Sonoma Marshes from northern and southern points. This hike leads through the north end of the wetlands in the 1,091-acre Huichica Creek Unit. Two paths follow the levees above mudflats, a 300-acre salt pond, water channels, and grasslands.

To the trailhead

BUCHLI STATION RD · NAPA 38.214957, -122.331962

From Sonoma Plaza in downtown Sonoma, drive 1.1 mile south on Broadway to Napa Road. Turn left (east) and continue 4.3 miles to a T-junction with Highway 121/Highway 12. Turn left (east) and go 2.8 miles to Duhig Road. Turn right (south) and drive 2.2 miles to Las Amigas Road. Turn left and continue 1.3 miles to Buchli Station Road. Turn right and proceed 1.3 miles to the trailhead parking lot at the end of the road, just south of the railroad tracks.

The hike

HIKE 1. Walk south past the yellow gate on the wide gravel levee. Stroll through the wetlands, passing water channels, mudflats, and ponds. At a half mile, follow the east edge of a 300-acre pond with a row of dead eucalyptus trees along the eastern edge of the pond. Once used as salt evaporation ponds, the grove of bare tree trunks are the result of the high saltwater content. This area forms the upper ponds of the Napa River Unit at the southern end of the Napa-Sonoma Marsh. The levee passes Fly Bay on the east and leads to Napa Slough at 1.5 miles. The views extend across the flatlands to Mount Tamalpais in the west. Choose your own turn-around point.

HIKE 2. From the trailhead, head west along the north edge of the wetland to a junction at a quarter mile. Detour straight ahead to the old bunker, an old army communication center from World War II. After checking out the structure, return to the junction. Head south and loop around the reed-filled pond. Curve left and follow the west edge of the water channel, returning to the trailhead. ■

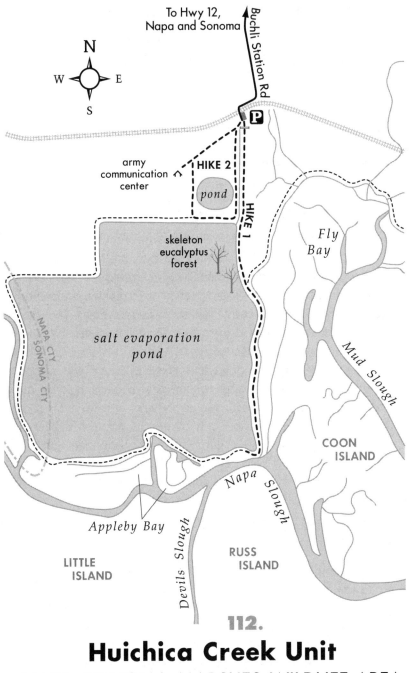

To Hwy 12, Napa and Sonoma

Buchli Station Rd

N
W E
S

P

army communication center

HIKE 2

pond

HIKE 1

Fly Bay

skeleton eucalyptus forest

salt evaporation pond

NAPA CTY
SONOMA CTY

Mud Slough

COON ISLAND

Napa Slough

Appleby Bay

Devils Slough

RUSS ISLAND

LITTLE ISLAND

112.

Huichica Creek Unit
NAPA-SONOMA MARSHES WILDLIFE AREA

113. Hudeman Slough Nature Trail
RINGSTROM BAY UNIT of the
NAPA—SONOMA MARSHES WILDLIFE AREA

Hiking distance: 2.5-mile loop
Hiking time: 1.5 hours
Configuration: loop
Elevation gain: level
Difficulty: easy
Exposure: exposed marshland
Dogs: allowed
Maps: U.S.G.S. Sears Point
       Napa-Sonoma Marshes Wildlife Area map

The Napa-Sonoma Marshes Wildlife Area encompasses over 13,000 acres of mainly abandoned salt evaporation ponds. The high salt content in the ponds killed the trees, leaving visible skeleton forests. The ponds are part of an extensive restoration program that is in the early stages of development. The goal of the restoration effort is to reclaim former tidal marshes that were diked many years ago.

The sizeable expanse of marshland is a productive estuarine ecosystem, providing habitat for millions of birds. It is an important wintering habitat for Pacific Flyway waterfowl. Most of the wildlife area is accessible only by boat or footpaths. Levees offer foot access and are regularly used by fisherman, hunters, photographers, bird watchers, bikers, boaters, and hikers. This hike loops through Hudeman Slough on the north end of the wildlife area.

To the trailhead

RAMAL ROAD · SONOMA   38.221035, -122.395232

From Sonoma Plaza in downtown Sonoma, drive 1.1 mile south on Broadway to Napa Road. Turn left (east) and continue 4.3 miles to a T-junction with Highway 121/Highway 12. Turn left (east) and go 2.8 miles to Duhig Road. Turn right and drive 5 miles to the large metal barn on the left. (En route, Duhig Road becomes Ramal Road.) Turn left and park in the lot on the right.

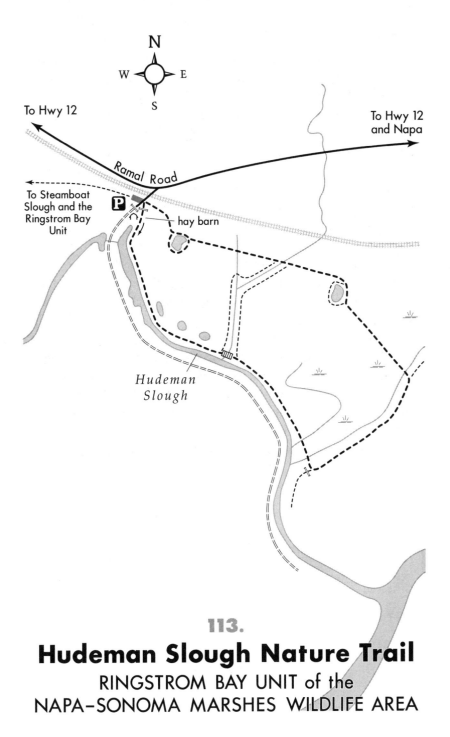

N
W   E
S

To Hwy 12

To Hwy 12
and Napa

Ramal Road

To Steamboat
Slough and the
Ringstrom Bay
Unit

P

hay barn

*Hudeman
Slough*

113.
Hudeman Slough Nature Trail
RINGSTROM BAY UNIT of the
NAPA-SONOMA MARSHES WILDLIFE AREA

The hike

From the access gate at the east end of the parking lot, follow the grassy berm on the edge of Hudeman Slough. Gradually curve left following the curvature of the slough. Pass a series of ponds on the left to a footbridge at a half mile. Cross the bridge and curve right on the levee, savoring the expansive vistas. At a 90-degree bend, bear left and leave the banks of Hudeman Slough. Parallel a wide water channel on the left and agricultural fields on the right to a junction. Bear left and follow the levee between the wetlands. Walk up the grassy slope to a pond in a berm-lined basin. Go to the right and circle the pond counter clockwise to its north end. Descend to the dirt road and continue west. Climb a small rise to another pond and a Y-fork that circles the pond. Take either route, circling the pond to the northwest corner. Descend and parallel the railroad tracks 200 yards to the trailhead.

To extend the hike, from the west end of the parking lot, a trail leads 3 miles to Sonoma Creek and the 408-acre Ringstrom Bay Unit of the Napa-Sonoma Marshes Wildlife Area. The path leads 0.8 miles to a levee on the edge of the Steamboat Slough wetlands, passing an information kiosk and following a grassy path west past ponds and a major water channel from Steamboat Slough. The levees continue to Railroad Slough and Sonoma Creek. ■

114. Napa River Unit
NAPA—SONOMA MARSHES WILDLIFE AREA

Hiking distance: 2.4 miles round trip
Hiking time: 1 hour
Configuration: out and back
Elevation gain: level
Difficulty: easy
Exposure: exposed coastal marshland
Dogs: not allowed March 2—June 30
Maps: U.S.G.S. Cuttings Wharf
Napa-Sonoma Marshes Wildlife Area map

This hike begins at the north edge of San Pablo Bay—the northern arm of San Francisco Bay—in the expansive Napa-Sonoma Marshes. The wetland habitat is located primarily between the Napa River and Sonoma Creek where they drain into San Pablo Bay. The trail follows a levee from the south end of the wildlife area through seasonal freshwater marshes and tidal salt marshes. This land was originally diked for hay and grain production. The area is now part of the former salt pond system. The Leslie Salt Company flooded the diked islands in the early 1950s for salt production.

The hike offers easy waterfowl and shorebird observation, a wide diversity of flora and fauna, and unobstructed vistas of the surrounding mountains.

To the trailhead

1158 SEARS POINT RD · VALLEJO   38.135153, -122.344540

From Sonoma Plaza in downtown Sonoma, drive 1.1 mile south on Broadway (Highway 12) to Napa Road. Turn left (east) and continue 4.3 miles to the Carneros Highway (Highway 121) and turn left (east). Go 5.1 miles east to Highway 29 and turn right, towards Fairfield/Vallejo. Drive 10 miles south to Highway 37 (Sears Point Road). Curve right onto Highway 37 and drive 6 miles west to the large pullout on the right by an eight-foot chain link fence. The pullout is located 3.6 miles west of the bridge over the Napa River.

The hike

Walk through the trailhead gate, and head north on the gravel levee. Follow a water channel on the right and a massive pond on the left. The 360-degree vistas include the Mayacamas Range in Napa County, the Sonoma Mountain Range in Sonoma County, Mount Tamalpais in Marin County, and Mount Diablo in Contra Costa County. At 1.2 miles, the trail crosses under power lines, just before reaching South Slough. The trail north of the towers is closed to hunting, fishing, and hiking. ■

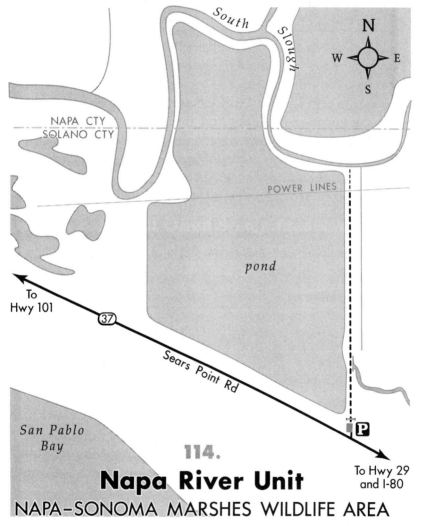

114.
Napa River Unit
NAPA-SONOMA MARSHES WILDLIFE AREA

115. San Pablo Bay National Wildlife Refuge

LOWER TUBBS ISLAND • TOLAY CREEK

Hiking distance: 5.5—8 miles round trip
Hiking time: 3—5 hours
Configuration: lollipop
Elevation gain: level
Difficulty: moderate
Exposure: exposed coastal marshland
Dogs: not allowed past picnic area
Maps: U.S.G.S. Sears Point and Petaluma Point

San Pablo Bay National Wildlife Refuge lies along San Pablo Bay at the northern reaches of San Francisco Bay. The wildlife refuge encompasses 13,000 acres between the mouth of the Petaluma River and Mare Island by Vallejo, including tidal wetlands, mud flats, salt marshes, and open water. Numerous waterways drain through the surrounding terrain, including the Napa River, Petaluma River, Sonoma Creek, Tolay Creek, and many sloughs. The waterways are interspersed with grasslands, oak woodlands, and agricultural fields. Lower Tubbs Island, near Tolay Creek, is the most accessible portion of the national wildlife refuge, luring bird watchers, wildlife photographers, and hikers. Lower Tubbs Island Bird Sanctuary is a 332-acre preserve within the refuge. It is a sanctuary for migrating birds, waterfowl, and shorebirds.

This trail follows a dirt levee 2.75 miles to the bird sanctuary on Lower Tubbs Island, then continues another 1.5 miles to Midshipman Point at the tip of the open waters. The terrain is flat, exposed, and windswept with wide open vistas.

To the trailhead

5202 SEARS POINT RD · SONOMA   38.153294, -122.436086

From downtown Sonoma, drive 8 miles south on Highway 121 (the Carneros Highway) to a T-junction with Highway 37 (Sears Point Road). Turn left and head east on Highway 37. Drive 0.7 miles, crossing over Tolay Creek and skirting the lagoon, to the first right turn. Turn right and park on the right at the posted trailhead.

The hike

Pass the trailhead gate and map panel on the dirt road. Follow the levee of Tolay Creek south along the edge of the wetlands and agricultural fields. At 0.4 miles curve left, passing a picnic area with an information map on the left. (Dogs are not allowed past the picnic area.) Continue southeast and bend right, with views of Mount Tamalpais and Mount Diablo in the distance. A parallel path follows the top of the levee on the right, overlooking the Tolay Creek Lagoon. At 1.6 miles, veer left and pass a metal pumping station on the left. Continue southeast to a trail split at 2.3 miles, located by an information kiosk, the viewing area, and the entrance into the Lower Tubbs Island Bird Sanctuary.

Begin the loop to the right between Lower Tolay Lagoon and Lower Tubbs Island, surrounded by tidal sloughs and salt marshes. Pass a group of red barns on the right, and curve left to the mouth of Tolay Creek. Follow the edge of San Pablo Bay on the levee road, where there is a view of Midshipman Point (the obvious promontory) and the mouth of the Petaluma River. At the east end of Lower Tubbs Island is a road split. Stay to the left along the Tubbs Island setback and complete the loop. Return to the right. ▪

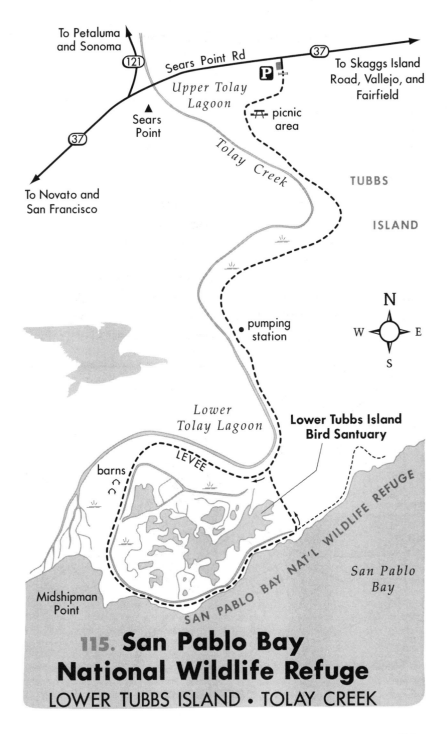

To Petaluma
and Sonoma

121

Sears Point Rd

37

To Skaggs Island
Road, Vallejo, and
Fairfield

P

*Upper Tolay
Lagoon*

▲
Sears
Point

picnic
area

37

To Novato and
San Francisco

Tolay Creek

TUBBS

ISLAND

N
W ✦ E
S

• pumping
station

*Lower
Tolay Lagoon*

**Lower Tubbs Island
Bird Santuary**

LEVEE

barns

SAN PABLO BAY NAT'L WILDLIFE REFUGE

*San Pablo
Bay*

Midshipman
Point

SAN PABLO BAY NAT'L WILDLIFE REFUGE

**115. San Pablo Bay
National Wildlife Refuge**
LOWER TUBBS ISLAND • TOLAY CREEK

116. Helen Putnam Regional Park

Hiking distance: 2.2-mile loop
Hiking time: 1.5 hours
Configuration: loop
Elevation gain: 300 feet
Difficulty: easy
Exposure: a mix of open meadows and shaded woodlands
Dogs: allowed
Maps: U.S.G.S. Petaluma · Helen Putnam Regional Park map

Helen Putnam Regional Park is located in the Petaluma country-side two miles southwest of downtown. The 216-acre park lies across rolling open meadows punctuated by mature oak savan-nah. The park also includes a shaded picnic area, playground, and a fishing pond. Hiking, biking, and equestrian trails wind through the hills, with panoramic vistas of southern Sonoma County and northern Marin County. Eight well-marked trails wind through the park. This route follows the park's perimeter and visits Fish Pond.

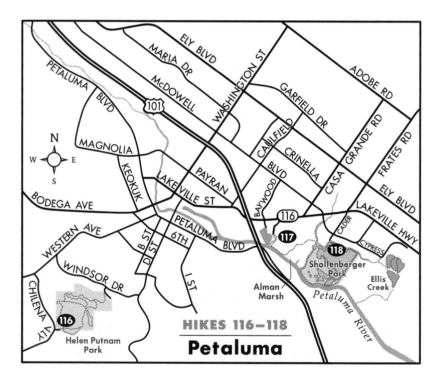

HIKES 116–118
Petaluma

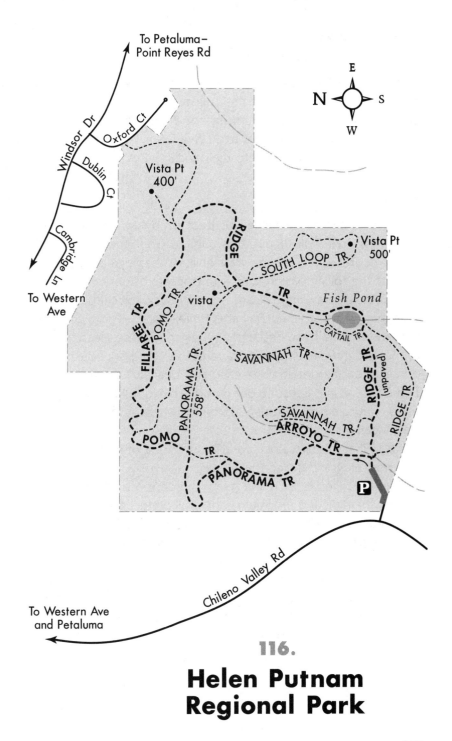

To Petaluma–
Point Reyes Rd

E
N S
W

Windsor Dr

Oxford Ct

Dublin Ct

Vista Pt
400'

Cambridge Ln

To Western
Ave

FILLAREE TR

POMO TR

vista

RIDGE

SOUTH LOOP TR

TR

Vista Pt
500'

Fish Pond

CATTAIL TR

SAVANNAH TR

PANORAMA TR 558'

SAVANNAH TR

POMO

TR

ARROYO TR

RIDGE TR
(unpaved)

RIDGE TR

P

PANORAMA TR

Chileno Valley Rd

To Western Ave
and Petaluma

116.

Helen Putnam
Regional Park

To the trailhead

411 CHILENO VALLEY RD · PETALUMA   38.212608, -122.664466

From Highway 101 in Petaluma, exit on Washington Street. Drive one mile southwest to Petaluma Boulevard. Turn left and go one block to Western Avenue. Turn right and continue 1.8 miles to Chileno Valley Road. Turn left and drive 0.8 miles to the posted park entrance. Turn left into the parking lot. A parking fee is required.

The hike

From the far end of the parking lot, bear left by the map kiosk on the Arroyo Trail. Walk 0.1 mile to a junction. Go to the left on the Panorama Trail and climb the grassy hill. At the ridge is an overlook of the rolling pastureland with pockets of oaks. A bench sits next to a sprawling, majestic coast live oak. Top the slope to a junction with the Pomo Trail at 0.4 miles. Bear left, staying on the Panorama Trail, and descend on the gentle slope. Head uphill to the oak grove and horse pasture at the west park boundary. Continue on the upper ridge east, and bear left on the Pomo Trail. Descend into a shaded oak woodland and follow the ridge. Loop right to a posted fork at 0.9 miles. Bear left on the Fillaree Trail. Meander through the oaks to a T-junction with the paved Ridge Trail at 1.3 miles, located at an overlook of Petaluma, the Chileno Valley, and the coastal hills.

Take the right fork up the gentle grade, passing the Pomo Trail on the right and the South Loop Trail on the left. (The loop trail leads to a 500-foot vista point.) Sheltered by hills on three sides, begin descending. Walk parallel to a small seasonal creek to Fish Pond at 1.9 miles. Curve around the east shore of the oval pond to a junction. Leave the paved Ridge Trail, and veer right along the south end of the pond to the water tank. Go to the left on the Ridge Trail and traverse the hillside. Pass the Savannah Trail on the right, returning to the parking lot. ■

117. Alman Marsh
PETALUMA MARINA to SHOLLENBERGER PARK

Hiking distance: 2 miles round trip
Hiking time: 1 hour
Configuration: out-and-back
Elevation gain: level
Difficulty: easy
Exposure: exposed marshland
Dogs: allowed
Maps: U.S.G.S. Petaluma River
Shollenberger Park Self-Guided Tour map

Alman Marsh is comprised of 80 acres of former pastures and wetlands along the Petaluma River in the city of Petaluma. The undeveloped wetlands are part of Petaluma's public marshlands, which also include Shollenberger Park and the Ellis Creek water recycling facility ponds, both to the east. The Alman marshlands were allowed to reflood in the 1980s, returning to a mix of salt-water and freshwater. Many bird species inhabit the area.

The Alman Marsh Trail is a one-mile trail linking the Petaluma Marina (along the Petaluma River) with Shollenberger Park. The trail follows a short section of the river, where bass and sturgeon fishing is a popular pastime, then veers away from the river en route to the dredge ponds at Shollenberger Park. The path meanders through scenic and fertile tidal marsh, wetlands, open fields with freshwater channels, and around a seasonal pond.

The trail skirts Rocky Memorial Dog Park, a nine-acre grassland bordering Alman Marsh. The park sits on the site of the old city landfill and is accessed from Casa Grande Road.

To the trailhead

781 BAYWOOD DR · PETALUMA   38.230220, -122.612082

From Highway 101 in Petaluma, exit on Lakeville Highway (Highway 116). Drive 0.1 mile east to Baywood Drive and turn right. Continue 0.2 miles to the far southeast end of the parking lot (passing the Sheraton Hotel) to the posted trailhead. Park in the spaces near the footbridge.

The hike

Cross the footbridge over the freshwater channel into the wetland. Head south to the Petaluma River and curve left, following the river downstream. Cross a 120-foot boardwalk over the wetland and curve inland, away from the river. Cross a bridge over another water channel and skirt the east side of Rocky Memorial Dog Park, an off-leash grassland. Zigzag northeast, passing a seasonal pond on the right to a metal bridge. Cross the pedestrian bridge over Adobe Creek to a T-junction with the Shollenberger Park Trail at the dredge spoils ponds, just north of viewing station 5 (Hike 118). Return by retracing your route, or continue around the ponds for an additional two miles. ■

118. Shollenberger Park

Hiking distance: 2-mile loop
Hiking time: 1 hour
Configuration: loop
Elevation gain: level
Difficulty: easy
Exposure: exposed marshland
Dogs: allowed
Maps: U.S.G.S. Petaluma River
Shollenberger Park Self-Guided Tour map

Shollenberger Park is part of the Petaluma wetlands complex, 500 acres of tidal and freshwater marshes along the banks of the Petaluma River in southern Petaluma. The river is actually a 14-mile tidal slough that stretches from Petaluma to San Pablo Bay. The 240-acre city park, created in 1995, was the site for materials dredged from the bottom of the shallow Petaluma River, allowing river navigation.

A circular two-mile path loops around the dredge ponds, overlooking the preserved wildlife sanctuary, the wetlands, tidal marshes, and open fields. It is prime bird habitat for shorebirds and migrating waterfowl. The trail is popular for dog walking,

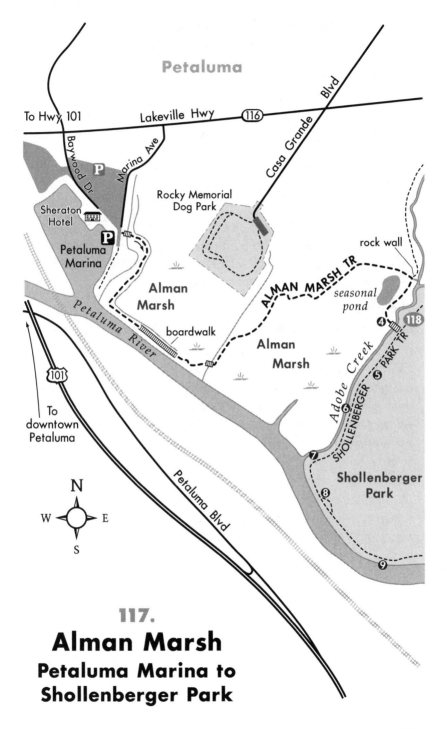

Petaluma

To Hwy 101   Lakeville Hwy   116

Baywood Dr

Marina Ave

Casa Grande Blvd

P

Sheraton
Hotel

P

Petaluma
Marina

Rocky Memorial
Dog Park

rock wall

ALMAN MARSH TR

seasonal
pond

Alman
Marsh

4   118

boardwalk

Alman
Marsh

Petaluma River

Adobe Creek

SHOLLENBERGER PARK TR

5

6

101

To
downtown
Petaluma

7

8

Shollenberger
Park

N
W — E
S

Petaluma Blvd

9

117.
Alman Marsh
Petaluma Marina to
Shollenberger Park

jogging, bird watching, wildlife photography, and nature study, with sweeping vistas of southern Sonoma County and northern Marin County. Along the trail loop are several informative panels that describe the wetland's ecology and history. Trail brochures are available at the trailhead.

From the loop, a trail connects to the west to Alman Marsh (Hike 117) and to the northeast to the ponds at the water recycling facility along Ellis Creek.

To the trailhead

1400 CADER LANE · PETALUMA   38.229555, –122.598144

From Highway 101 in Petaluma, exit on Lakeville Highway (Highway 116). Drive one mile east to South McDowell Boulevard and turn right. Continue 0.3 miles to Cader Lane on the left. Turn right into the posted park entrance and parking lot.

The hike

Follow the paved path south past the restrooms and map kiosk to a junction. Pick up the interpretive trail guide, which corresponds with 15 numbered learning stations. Begin the loop on the right fork, and head southwest along Adobe Creek on the right. Just before reaching viewing station five is a junction. The Alman Marsh Trail crosses a bridge over the creek and follows the wetlands one mile to the Petaluma River and marina. Continue straight on the west side of the dredge spoils ponds. The south end of the far pond parallels the serpentine Petaluma River, while the east side overlooks the wetlands. As you continue around the ponds, use the guide to learn about the history, geology, restoration, ponds, animals, birds, and wetland ecology of the immediate area. ■

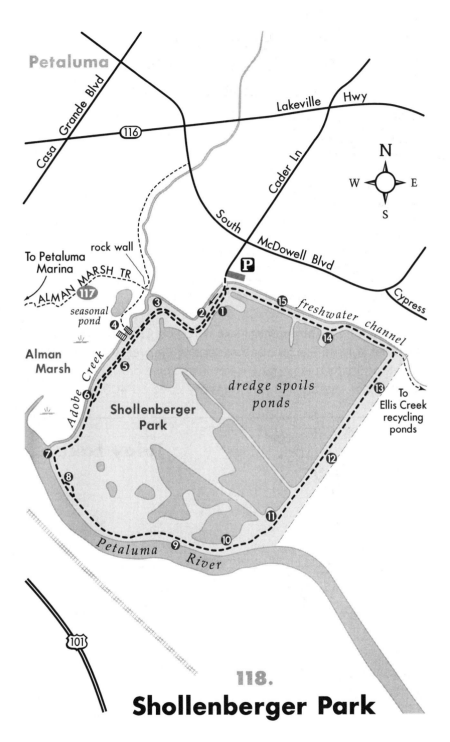

Petaluma

Casa Grande Blvd

Lakeville Hwy

116

Cader Ln

South McDowell Blvd

Cypress

N
W   E
S

To Petaluma Marina

rock wall

ALMAN MARSH TR

117

seasonal pond

Alman Marsh

Adobe Creek

Shollenberger Park

dredge spoils ponds

freshwater channel

To Ellis Creek recycling ponds

Petaluma River

101

118.
Shollenberger Park

119. Causeway Trail to Three Bridges Vista Point

TOLAY LAKE REGIONAL PARK

Day-Use Permit Orientation Required

Hiking distance: 5 miles round trip
Hiking time: 2.5 hours
Configuration: out-and-back
Elevation gain: 500 feet
Difficulty: moderate
Exposure: exposed grasslands
Dogs: allowed
Maps: U.S.G.S. Petaluma River and Sears Point
Tolay Lake Regional Park map

Tolay Lake is a freshwater lake that sits in a bowl-shaped basin bordered by low rolling hills between the Petaluma River and Sonoma Valley. The seasonal lake is fed by Cardoza Creek and 18 other springs. The lake bed fills during the wet winter months, but it is mostly a large freshwater marsh or a dry lake bed during the dry season. The lake originally covered 400 acres, but

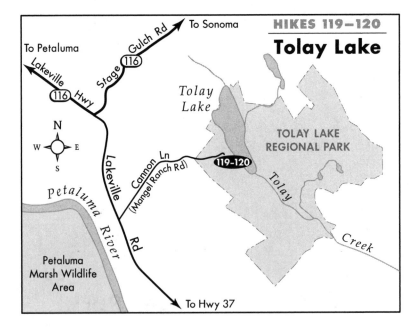

it is now a fraction of that size. In the 1850s, the natural dam that helped to create the lake was demolished, and the lake was drained for agricultural purposes.

The Tolay Basin is a significant site of ancient Native American settlements that date back nearly 10,000 years. The sacred site is associated with the belief in the lake's healing powers. It was a regional gathering place for tribes, including the Coast Miwok and Pomo, for the purpose of ceremonial healing.

Tolay Lake Regional Park was established adjacent to the lake. In addition to the lake, the 1,769-acre park contains wetlands, marshes, ponds, ephemeral creeks, grasslands, meadows, open rolling ridges, mature oak groves, and scattered eucalyptus trees.

This hike leads to the Three Bridges Vista Point atop a 750-foot ridge, where there are sweeping views of the Richmond—San Rafael Bridge, the Bay Bridge, and the Highway 37 overpass. The views also include downtown Petaluma, Mount Diablo, Mount Tamalpais, Mount Saint Helena, the Sonoma Range, San Pablo Bay, and the Petaluma River Basin. The route to the overlook follows the Causeway Trail along an earthen embankment that bisects Tolay Lake, then climbs up the ridge through an oak woodland.

Day-Use Permit

Access into Tolay Lake Regional Park is allowed through a day-use permit program. To receive the permit, a free one-hour class conducted by the ranger is mandatory. The orientation covers park history, permit procedures, and regulations. Permit holders may access the park from April through September on Fridays, Saturdays, and Sundays and October through March on Saturdays and Sundays.

WEBSITE:
http://parks.sonomacounty.ca.gov/Get_Outdoors/Parks/
Tolay_Lake_Regional_Park.aspx

EMAIL: tolaypermit@sonoma-county.org

To the trailhead

5869 CANNON LANE · PETALUMA   38.205398, -122.521390

Tolay Lake Regional Park is located halfway between downtown Petaluma and Highway 37, east of Lakeville Road (Highway 116).

FROM PETALUMA / HIGHWAY 101. Take Lakeville Highway (Highway 116) 7.8 miles south to Cannon Lane on the left. (En route, Lakeville Highway becomes Lakeville Road.) Turn left (east) on Cannon Lane and go 1.3 miles to the park entrance gate. After passing through the gate, continue 0.3 miles and curve right to the parking area by the historic farm buildings. A parking fee is required.

SONOMA. From Sonoma Plaza in downtown Sonoma, drive 1.8 miles south on Broadway (Highway 12) to Watmaugh Road and turn right (west). Continue 2.2 miles to Stage Gulch Road (Highway 116) and turn right. Go 4.9 miles on Stage Gulch Road to Lakeville Road. (At 2.6 miles, Stage Gulch Road turns off to the left, as Adobe Road veers off to the right.) Turn left on Lakeville Road. Drive 1.3 miles to Cannon Lane and turn left (east). Go 1.3 miles to the park entrance gate. After passing through the gate, continue 0.3 miles and curve right to the parking area by the historic farm buildings.

The hike

Walk east on the Causeway Trail, passing the Old Hay Barn on the left. Cross the causeway over Tolay Lake, which can merely be a wetland during the dry seasons. At the far east end of the lake, pass through a ranch gate by a junction with the Pond Trail on the right. Continue straight ahead toward the hills, skirting the edge of a vineyard to the base of the hill. Pass through another cattle gate and bend left. Gently gain elevation as the trail ascends clockwise up the mountain. Follow the border of the vineyard on the left and the natural open space parkland on the right. Enter the shade of an old oak forest. Leave the forest cover and follow the upper park boundary. Near the summit, the path levels out and curves right. Make the final short ascent to Three Bridges Vista Point, a circular bald knoll with sweeping vistas of the surrounding terrain. After taking in the views, return along the same route. ■

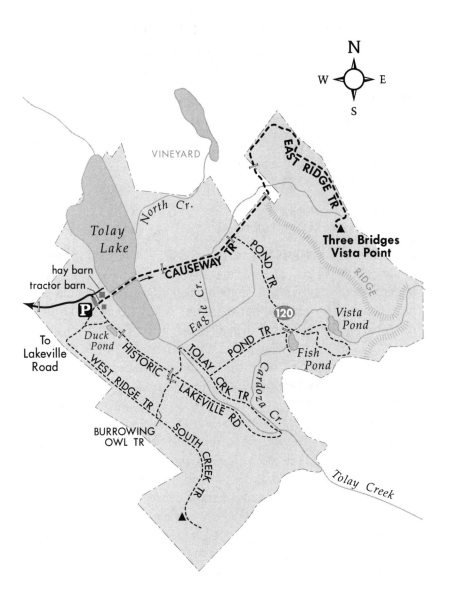

N
W · E
S

VINEYARD

North Cr.

Tolay
Lake

EAST RIDGE TR

**Three Bridges
Vista Point**

CAUSEWAY TR

POND TR

RIDGE

hay barn
tractor barn

P

120

Vista
Pond

To
Lakeville
Road

Duck
Pond

Eagle Cr.

POND TR

Cardoza Cr.

Fish
Pond

HISTORIC

TOLAY CRK TR

LAKEVILLE RD

WEST RIDGE TR

BURROWING
OWL TR

SOUTH CREEK TR

Tolay Creek

119.

Causeway Trail to
Three Bridges Vista Point

TOLAY LAKE REGIONAL PARK

120. Fish Pond—Vista Pond Loop
TOLAY LAKE REGIONAL PARK

Day-Use Permit Orientation Required

Hiking distance: 4.5-mile loop
Hiking time: 2.5 hours
Configuration: loop
Elevation gain: 150 feet
Difficulty: easy to slightly moderate
Exposure: exposed grasslands
Dogs: allowed
Maps: U.S.G.S. Petaluma River and Sears Point
　　　　Tolay Lake Regional Park map

Tolay Lake Regional Park is an expansive 1,769-acre park located in the southeast end of Petaluma. The Tolay Lake Basin is a valley confined by two north-south running ridges. It has a cultural history of human activity that spans nearly 10,000 years. Within the regional park are more than eight miles of hiking, biking, and equestrian paths with elevations ranging from 200 to 800 feet. All the trails originate from the park center farm buildings.

This hike follows seasonal Tolay Creek, the lake's outlet stream. Lined with riparian vegetation, the creek drains into the Napa— Sonoma Marsh before emptying into San Pablo Bay. The trail heads down the valley on the Historic Lakeville Road, a dirt road dating back to the mid-1800s. The hike then passes through open grassland to Fish Pond and Vista Pond, two man-made ponds primarily used as water sources for the cattle. The banks around Fish Pond are rich with vegetation, while only low grass surrounds Vista Pond. Both ponds are ideal sites for bird-watching. The return makes a large loop through the grassland basin, crossing Tolay Lake via an earthen causeway.

NOTE: Additional trail routes were in the development stage at the time of this publication. The acquisition of a large parcel of adjacent land is also in the park's future expansion plans.

Day-Use Permit

Access into Tolay Lake Regional Park is allowed through a day-use permit program. To receive the permit, a free one-hour class conducted by the ranger is mandatory. The orientation covers park history, permit procedures, and regulations. Permit holders may access the park from April through September on Fridays, Saturdays, and Sundays and October through March on Saturdays and Sundays.

WEBSITE:
http://parks.sonomacounty.ca.gov/Get_Outdoors/Parks/Tolay_Lake_Regional_Park.aspx

EMAIL: tolaypermit@sonoma-county.org

To the trailhead

5869 CANNON LANE · PETALUMA   38.205398, -122.521390

Tolay Lake Regional Park is located halfway between downtown Petaluma and Highway 37, east of Lakeville Road (Highway 116).

FROM PETALUMA/HIGHWAY 101. Take Lakeville Highway (Highway 116) 7.8 miles south to Cannon Lane on the left. (En route, Lakeville Highway becomes Lakeville Road.) Turn left (east) on Cannon Lane and go 1.3 miles to the park entrance gate. After passing through the gate, continue 0.3 miles and curve right to the parking area by the historic farm buildings. A parking fee is required.

SONOMA. From Sonoma Plaza in downtown Sonoma, drive 1.8 miles south on Broadway (Highway 12) to Watmaugh Road and turn right (west). Continue 2.2 miles to Stage Gulch Road (Highway 116) and turn right. Go 4.9 miles on Stage Gulch Road to Lakeville Road. (At 2.6 miles, Stage Gulch Road turns off to the left, as Adobe Road veers off to the right.) Turn left on Lakeville Road. Drive 1.3 miles to Cannon Lane and turn left (east). Go 1.3 miles to the park entrance gate. After passing through the gate, continue 0.3 miles and curve right to the parking area by the historic farm buildings.

The hike

Walk south on the Historic Lakeville Road, passing the farm animals and chicken coops on the right and the Tractor Barn on the left. Parallel the southern end of Tolay Lake, which is frequently a large freshwater marsh. Pass elevated Duck Pond on the right and pass through a cattle gate. Top a small rise with a view across the basin, then go through a second ranch gate. To the right, the Burrowing Owl Trail leads up to the West Ridge. To the left, the Tolay Creek Trail skirts the lower south end of Tolay Lake, with benches for bird observation. Stay on the Historic Lakeville Road. Walk parallel to seasonal Tolay Creek, lined with bay trees in an otherwise treeless landscape. At 1.2 miles, veer left onto the Tolay Creek Trail and cross the transient creek. Sharply bend left again, returning northwest through the open grasslands. Walk parallel to ephemeral Cardoza Creek. At 1.7 miles is a junction with the Pond Trail on the right. Bear right and follow the fence across the flat to a cattle gate.

Before going through the gate, detour right along the edge of Fish Pond. The short path skirts the west side of the pond. Return and pass through the gate. Immediately bear right on the Pond Trail to a posted Y-fork. Begin a short loop to the left, and head up the slope to an overlook on the west end of Vista Pond. From the rise is a view across the basin. Continue past the pond along the rolling hills forming a loop.

Return to the gate and continue straight ahead to the north. The Pond Trail ends at a gate with the Causeway Trail. The right fork leads up to Three Bridges Vista Point (Hike 119). Go through the gate to the left. Cross the causeway over Tolay Lake, completing the loop at the trailhead and ranch buildings. ■

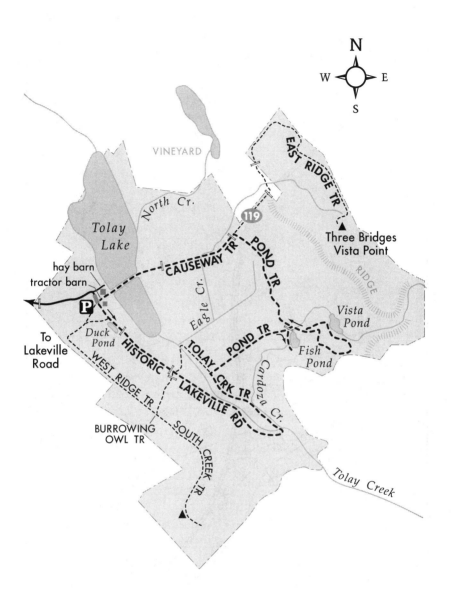

120.
Fish Pond and Vista Pond Loop
TOLAY LAKE REGIONAL PARK

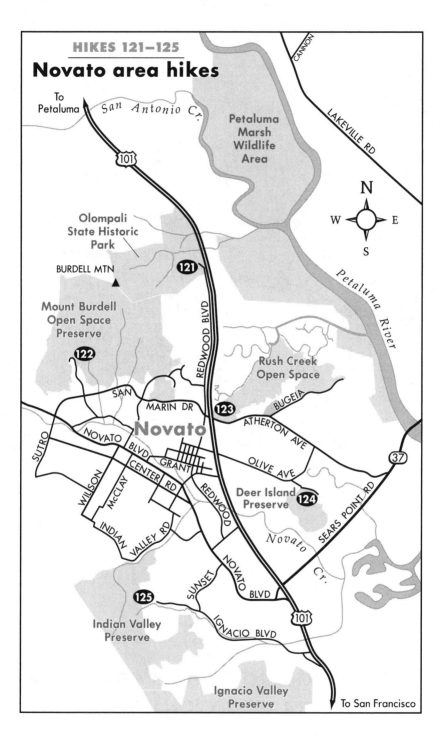

HIKES 121–125
Novato area hikes

To Petaluma

San Antonio Cr.

CANNON

LAKEVILLE RD

101

Petaluma Marsh Wildlife Area

Olompali State Historic Park

N
W — E
S

BURDELL MTN

121

Petaluma River

Mount Burdell Open Space Preserve

REDWOOD BLVD

122

Rush Creek Open Space

SAN

MARIN DR

123

BUGEIA

Novato

ATHERTON AVE

NOVATO BLVD

GRANT

OLIVE AVE

37

SUTRO

CENTER RD

WILSON

McCLAY

REDWOOD

Deer Island Preserve

124

SEARS POINT RD

INDIAN VALLEY RD

Novato Cr.

125

SUNSET

NOVATO BLVD

101

Indian Valley Preserve

IGNACIO BLVD

Ignacio Valley Preserve

To San Francisco

121. Olompali State Historic Park

Open Wednesday—Sunday · 9 a.m.—5 p.m.

Hiking distance: 2.7-mile loop
Hiking time: 2 hours
Configuration: loop
Elevation gain: 750 feet
Difficulty: easy to moderate
Exposure: shaded forest and open grassland
Dogs: not allowed
Maps: U.S.G.S. Petaluma River · Olompali State Historic Park map

Olompali State Historic Park is located a few miles north of Novato on the northeast slope of Burdell Mountain, facing San Antonio Creek and the Petaluma River Marsh Wildlife Area. The name comes from the Coast Miwok language meaning *southern village* or *southern people*. It was the site of Marin County's largest Miwok Indian village from about 500 A.D. and a major Miwok trading center.

The 700-acre park has a colorful and varied past. In the mid 1800s, Galen and Mary Burdell owned the land. They built an ornate 26-room mansion with a Victorian formal garden, brick-lined walkways, gazebos, exotic plants, fountains, and a lily pond. The Burdell mansion burned down in 1969, but the old adobe walls still remain. In the 1940s it was a Jesuit seminary. In 1966 it was home to the Grateful Dead band. A picture of the band relaxing on the Olompali hillside is on the back cover of their *American Beauty* album. In 1967 it was a commune for a hippy group known as "The Chosen Family." It became a state park in 1982.

This loop hike climbs the east-facing mountain slope, passing historic ranch buildings and an interpretive Miwok village, which was reconstructed with the assistance of Coast Miwok descendants. The path leads through rolling grasslands with majestic gnarled oaks and stream-fed ravines. The hike includes vistas of the coastal mountain ranges, the Petaluma River estuary, and San Pablo Bay. Olompali State Historic Park connects with the Mount Burdell Open Space Preserve at the ridge (Hike 122).

To the trailhead

NORTH END OF REDWOOD DR · NOVATO   38.151318, -122.571206

From Highway 101 in Petaluma, drive 10 miles south to the San Marin Drive/Atherton Avenue exit #463 at the north end of Novato. Turn right and immediately turn right again on Redwood Boulevard. Continue 2.8 miles to the trailhead parking lot. A parking fee is required.

The hike

This hike makes a loop along the lower slopes of Burdell Mountain and around the reconstructed Miwok village. The posted trailhead is at the far west end of the parking lot. Head up the grassy slope along a row of oak trees. Pass the historic Burdell Ranch buildings on the right to a posted junction. Begin the loop to the right, and cross the wooden bridge over a seasonal creek. Pass the Burdell Barns on the right, dating back to the 1880s, and follow the gravel road to the left. Meander through oaks to the site of the Coast Miwok village at 0.35 miles. Stroll through the village with interpretive panels, a roundhouse, a native plant garden, an acorn granary, and a redwood bark *kotcha* (dwelling).

Continue past the village through towering bay laurels, and parallel a stream in a deep ravine on the right. Enter a tree-shaded glen, passing an old ranch reservoir on the right, formed in the creek from a wooden spillway. Continue upstream on the south canyon wall. At 0.8 miles leave the stream and canyon on a switchback to the left. Weave through the oak forest, and cross a minor ridge to a posted junction at 1.1 mile. The Upper Mount Burdell Trail (the right fork) climbs 3.3 miles to the summit of Burdell Mountain and Mount Burdell Open Space Preserve, connecting to Hike 122.

Take the left fork on the Lower Mount Burdell Trail and traverse the mountain slope, overlooking the Petaluma River basin. Gently descend with the aid of a couple switchbacks, and enter an oak-studded grassland with overlooks of the Miwok Village and the Burdell Ranch. Complete the loop at the bridge and return to the right. ■

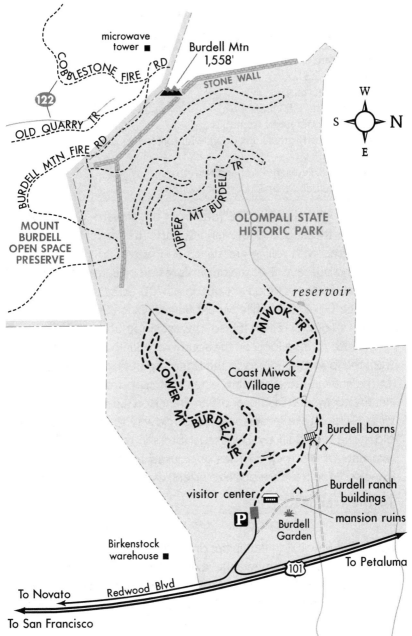

microwave tower ■

Burdell Mtn 1,558'

STONE WALL

COBBLESTONE FIRE RD.

122

OLD QUARRY TR.

BURDELL MTN FIRE RD.

UPPER MT BURDELL TR.

OLOMPALI STATE HISTORIC PARK

MOUNT BURDELL OPEN SPACE PRESERVE

reservoir

MIWOK TR

LOWER MT BURDELL TR

Coast Miwok Village

Burdell barns

visitor center

Burdell ranch buildings

mansion ruins

P

Burdell Garden

Birkenstock warehouse ■

To Novato

Redwood Blvd

 101

To Petaluma

To San Francisco

W N / S E (compass)

121.
Olompali State Historic Park

122. Burdell Mountain

MOUNT BURDELL OPEN SPACE PRESERVE

Hiking distance: 4.8-mile loop
Hiking time: 2.5 hours
Configuration: loop
Elevation gain: 1,150 feet
Difficulty: moderate to strenuous
Exposure: mostly grassy meadows with forested pockets
Dogs: allowed
Maps: U.S.G.S. Petaluma River and Novato
　　　 Mt. Burdell Open Space Preserve map

Burdell Mountain rises 1,558 feet from the Novato Valley floor on the northeast corner of Marin County. The serpentine slopes are covered with rolling grasslands and groves of live oak, bay laurel, and buckeye. Two major parks reside on Burdell Mountain: Olompali State Historic Park occupies 700 acres on the northeast face (Hike 121), while Mount Burdell Open Space Preserve occupies 1,600 acres on the southwest slope (this hike).

The hike forms a loop on the southwest flank of the mountain, from the lower meadows to the ridge separating the two parks. At the summit are sweeping vistas that span from Mount Saint Helena to Mount Diablo and San Francisco. En route, the hike visits Hidden Lake (a seasonal pond midway to the summit), an old stone wall built by Chinese laborers in the late 1800s, and remnants of old rock quarries once used for the streets in San Francisco. The trails are open to hikers, cyclists, and equestrians.

To the trailhead

NORTH END OF SAN ANDREAS DR · NOVATO　　　38.130062, –122.604261

From Highway 101 in Petaluma, drive 10 miles south to the San Marin Drive/Atherton Avenue exit #463 at the north end of Novato. Drive 2.2 miles west on San Marin Drive to San Andreas Drive and turn right. Continue 0.6 miles to the signed entrance gate. Park along San Andreas Drive.

The hike

From the trailhead gate and map board, begin the loop on the left fork. Climb up the San Andreas Fire Road through an oak savannah with California bay, passing the Little Tank Fire Road on the left. Pass through a cattle gate, and crest the hill to a large bowl-shaped meadow. Curve right and climb through the sloping meadow dotted with valley oak to a Y-fork with the Deer Camp Fire Road. Continue straight on the Middle Burdell Fire Road, with a view of Novato and the bay. Top the slope to the northwest edge of Hidden Lake and a junction at 1.5 miles. The right fork stays on the Middle Burdell Fire Road and eliminates 1.2 miles of the hike for a shorter and much easier loop.

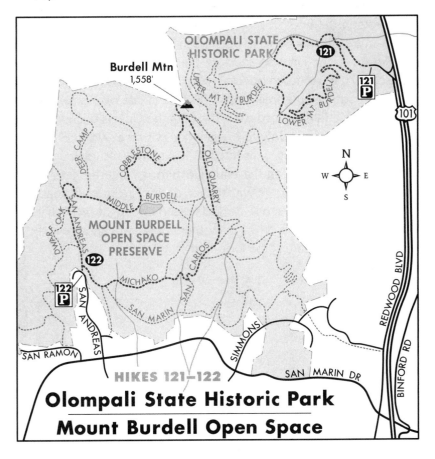

HIKES 121-122

Olompali State Historic Park
Mount Burdell Open Space

For this hike, bear left on the Cobblestone Fire Road to another Y-fork with the Deer Camp Fire Road at 1.9 miles. Veer to the right, staying on the Cobblestone Fire Road, and keep climbing toward the summit. The remains of a rock quarry site can be spotted on the right. At 2.5 miles, the trail tops out just below the ridge at a 5-way junction. The left fork leads to the microwave tower. The sharp right fork—the Old Quarry Trail—is the return route. The Burdell Mountain Fire Road heads southeast on the 90-degree right fork. It connects with the Upper Mount Burdell Trail in Olompali State Historic Park and descends on the northeast slope of the mountain.

Detour on the unmarked trail straight ahead about 200 yards to the rounded rock wall at the ridge and park boundary. This old stone wall, constructed without mortar, was built by Chinese laborers in the late 1800s. From the ridge are vistas across the Petaluma River Marshes and Upper San Pablo Bay.

Return to the junction and take the Old Quarry Trail. Steeply descend the stone-embedded path in the small canyon. Use careful footing—the trail drops 700 feet in just over a half mile and is littered with loose rock. The path then levels out and traverses a grassy meadow to a T-junction with the Middle Burdell Fire Road at 3.3 miles. Bear left for 100 yards, and pick up the posted Quarry Trail on the right. Go through a cattle gate and continue downhill. Merge with the San Carlos Fire Road and curve right. Weave down the oak-dotted hill and bear right on Michako Trail at 3.9 miles. Walk through another cattle gate and cross the rolling hills, completing the loop at the trailhead. ∎

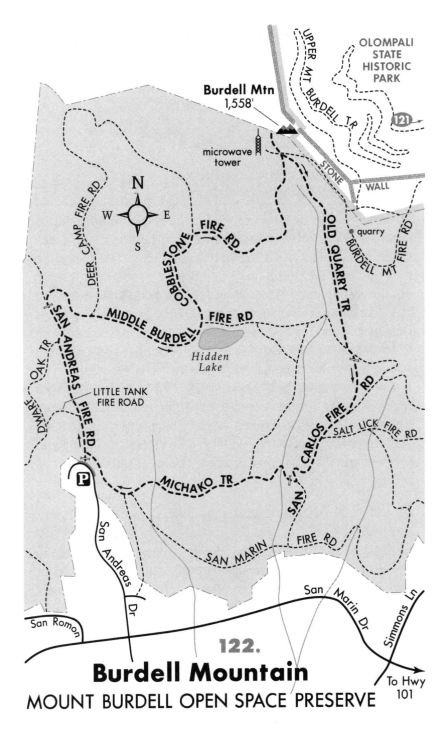

UPPER MT BURDELL TR

OLOMPALI
STATE
HISTORIC
PARK

Burdell Mtn
1,558'

121

microwave
tower

STONE

WALL

N
W E
S

quarry

COBBLESTONE FIRE RD

OLD QUARRY TR

BURDELL MT FIRE RD

DEER CAMP FIRE RD

MIDDLE BURDELL FIRE RD

Hidden Lake

SAN ANDREAS FIRE RD

DWARF OAK TR

LITTLE TANK FIRE ROAD

SAN CARLOS FIRE RD

SALT LICK FIRE RD

P

MICHAKO TR

SAN MARIN FIRE RD

San Andreas Dr

San Romon

San Marin Dr

Simmons Ln

122.
Burdell Mountain
MOUNT BURDELL OPEN SPACE PRESERVE

To Hwy 101

123. Rush Creek Open Space Preserve

Hiking distance: 5.5 miles round trip
Hiking time: 2.5 hours
Configuration: out-and-back
Elevation gain: 70 feet
Difficulty: easy to moderate
Exposure: forested hills and open wetlands
Dogs: allowed
Maps: U.S.G.S. Novato and Petaluma River
Rush Creek Open Space Preserve map

Stretching along the banks of the Petaluma River is a flat fertile region with coastal salt marshes and diked farmland. Rush Creek Open Space Preserve is adjacent to a vast wetland area along the Petaluma River and surrounded by oak woodlands. The preserve lies between Burdell Mountain and the Petaluma River delta. The 528-acre open space is a resting and nesting site for thousands of migrating and resident waterfowl. Within the preserve is Rush Creek Marsh; Pinheiro Ridge, a low 200-foot hill; and Cemetery Marsh, named for the adjacent Valley Memorial Park Cemetery.

The trail follows the Pinheiro Ridge Fire Road (an old ranch road) along the base of Pinheiro Ridge. The hike skirts the south edge of Rush Creek, then loops around Cemetery Marsh to Black John Slough, a unit of the Petaluma River Marsh. Throughout the hike are vistas of the expansive tidal wetlands and Burdell Mountain.

To the trailhead

BINFORD RD · NOVATO   38.118421, -122.564368

From Highway 101 in Petaluma, drive 10 miles south to the San Marin Drive/Atherton Avenue exit #463 at the north end of Novato. Turn left on Atherton Avenue, crossing over the freeway, and quickly turn left on Binford Road. Drive one block to the signed trailhead on the right. Park on the shoulder of the road.

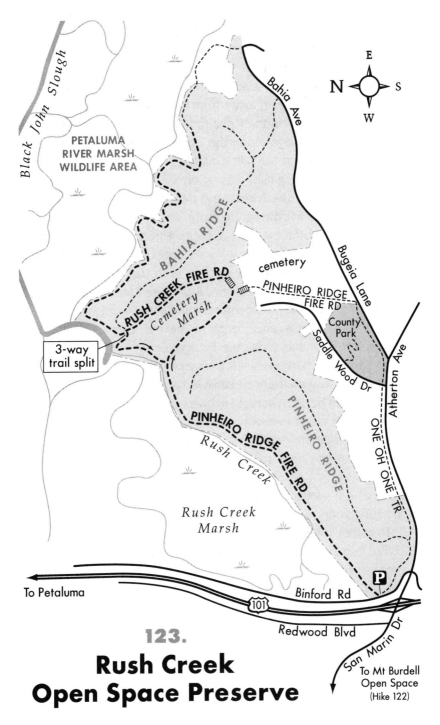

Black John Slough

PETALUMA
RIVER MARSH
WILDLIFE AREA

Bahia Ave

N E S W

BAHIA RIDGE

RUSH CREEK FIRE RD

Cemetery Marsh

cemetery

PINHEIRO RIDGE FIRE RD

Bugeia Lane

County Park

Saddle Wood Dr

Atherton Ave

3-way trail split

ONE OH ONE TR.

PINHEIRO RIDGE FIRE RD

PINHEIRO RIDGE

Rush Creek

Rush Creek Marsh

P

To Petaluma

101

Binford Rd

Redwood Blvd

San Marin Dr

To Mt Burdell
Open Space
(Hike 122)

123.
Rush Creek
Open Space Preserve

The hike

At the trailhead are two trails. The right fork follows Atherton Avenue and Bugeia Lane before curving north, away from the road and into the open space to Cemetery Marsh. To enter the quiet of the open space, away from the road, take the left fork. Walk straight ahead on the Pinheiro Ridge Fire Road. Follow the base of Pinheiro Ridge along the edge of the vast Rush Creek Marsh. Stroll through the hills covered with oak and bay trees. Curve over the rolling hills, staying on the edge of the wetland. Enter the shade of the forest, and descend to a junction at 1.3 miles. The left fork is the return route.

Begin the loop to the right, emerging from the forest to the open west edge of Cemetery Marsh. Continue to the south end of the brackish marsh and a junction with trail bridges in each direction at 1.9 miles. The Pinheiro Ridge Fire Road continues on the right fork, passing the cemetery and leading out of the preserve to Atherton Avenue, back to the trailhead. Stay straight on the left fork and cross the bridge. Curve left on the Rush Creek Fire Road, skirting the east edge of Cemetery Marsh on the fire road. Follow the base of Bahia Ridge along the cove. Burdell Mountain can be seen across Highway 101.

At 2.6 miles is a three-way trail split. The left fork is the return route. The right fork climbs through an oak and bay laurel forest to the ridge. Take the middle fork, rising gently up the hill and curving right. Stroll through the forest to Black John Slough and the vast wetlands. Follow the curving contours of the hills, choosing your own turn-around spot.

To return, head back to the three-way trail split at the north end of Cemetery Marsh. Take the lower fork to a berm. Bear left and cross the head of Cemetery Marsh on the narrow, raised trail, completing the loop. Return 1.3 miles to the trailhead on the Pinheiro Ridge Fire Road. ■

124. Deer Island Open Space Preserve

Hiking distance: 1.8 mile perimeter loop plus 0.8 mile across the ridge
Hiking time: 1 to 1.5 hours
Configuration: loop
Elevation gain: near level for loop; 200 feet for ridge
Difficulty: easy
Exposure: a mix of open grassland and shaded forest
Dogs: allowed
Maps: U.S.G.S. Novato
               Marin County Parks: Deer Island Open Space Preserve map

Deer Island isn't exactly an island. It is, rather, a 200-foot high hill that rises on the eastern edge of Novato and surrounded by seasonal wetlands. The 154-acre open space preserve lies within the extensive watershed of the Petaluma River Delta. Originally, Deer Island truly was an island, encircled by streams, marshes, wetlands, and the encroaching tides of San Pablo Bay. In the mid-1800s, dikes were built and waterways were drained for pastureland, altering the landscape.

This mini-refuge, where the hills meet the flood plain, is easily accessible and a popular get-away for local residents. A near-level trail loops around the perimeter of the preserve along the marsh's edge. From the perimeter loop are a couple of short detours to overlooks. The trail leads through open grassland, pockets of California bay laurel, eucalyptus, and buckeye. A second trail climbs to the grassy ridge and follows the spine amid a mixed oak savannah. The ridge trail connects with the loop trail on each end.

To the trailhead

DEER ISLAND LANE · NOVATO   38.102261, -122.538949

From Highway 101, at the north end of Novato, take the Atherton Avenue/San Marin Drive exit. Drive 1.7 miles east on Atherton Avenue to Olive Avenue and turn right (south). Continue 0.7 miles to Deer Island Lane and turn left. Go 0.2 miles to the trailhead parking area on the right.

The hike

Walk up the slope 25 yards past the trailhead entrance to a signed Y-fork. The DeBorba Trail veers left to the ridge. For now, continue straight on the Deer Island Loop Trail. Walk above the marshes of Novato Creek to a junction with the Russel Antonio Trail on the right. Detour right and climb 0.1 mile to a 90-foot knoll with 360-degree panoramas amid scattered oaks and an electric tower.

Back on the loop trail, weave along the contours of the hills, passing in and out of shaded oak groves. Traverse the hillside, overlooking two water treatment ponds (one with six islands) and a distant view of Mount Diablo. After looping around the southern end of Deer Island, head north, passing the east end of the DeBorba Trail. Wind along the hillside path, viewing Simmonds Slough and the wetlands below. At the north end of the loop, stroll through the shade of a bay laurel forest and complete the loop at the trailhead.

To extend the hike, walk 25 yards up the path again to the 0.8 mile-long DeBorba Trail. Veer left, heading up the slope at an easy to moderate grade. The open ridge offers views across San Pablo Bay to the Benicia Bridge. Follow the ridge south to views of Mount Tamalpais. At the far south end of the ridge, curve left and duck into the dense oak forest, descending to the Deer Island Loop Trail. ■

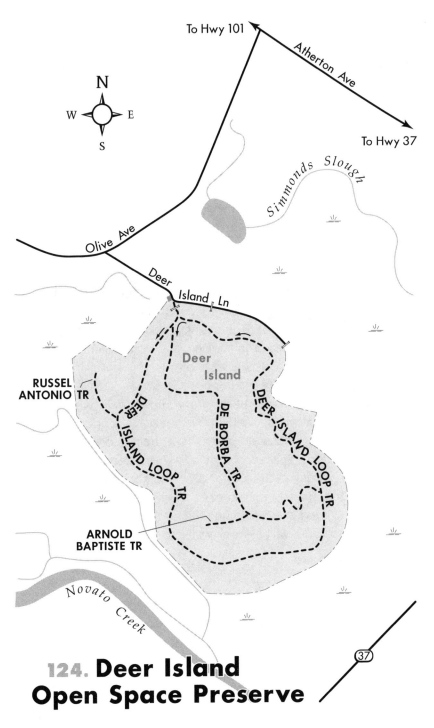

N
W E
S

To Hwy 101

Atherton Ave

To Hwy 37

Simmonds Slough

Olive Ave

Deer Island Ln

Deer Island

RUSSEL ANTONIO TR

DEER ISLAND LOOP TR

DE BORBA TR

DEER ISLAND LOOP TR

ARNOLD BAPTISTE TR

Novato Creek

37

124. Deer Island Open Space Preserve

125. Indian Valley Open Space Preserve

Hiking distance: 3.8-mile loop
Hiking time: 2.5 hours
Configuration: loop
Elevation gain: 600 feet
Difficulty: moderate
Exposure: mostly forested
Dogs: allowed
Maps: U.S.G.S. Novato
Marin County Parks: Indian Valley Open Space Preserve map

Indian Valley Open Space Preserve stretches over 885 acres on the forested eastern slopes of Big Rock Ridge at the west end of Ignacio Valley in Novato. The parkland lies adjacent to the Indian Valley campus of the College of Marin. A seasonal creek flows through Indian Valley near the center of the reserve. A mosaic of crisscrossing dirt roads and single-track trails form a web of looping routes. The hiking, biking, and equestrian trails wind through the hills in shaded forests of oak, bay laurel, madrones, buckeye, and manzanita.

This hike forms a loop utilizing a group of trails weaving up drainages and canyons, climbing over deeply wooded hills and traversing grassy mountain slopes. The trail leads to Pacheco Pond, built for the Pacheco Ranch in 1947 as a dependable water source for grazing cattle. Cattails line the scenic pond in a forested setting. The trail continues to a seasonal 20-foot cataract in a creek-carved channel. During the wet season, the cascading stream drops off a vertical rock wall into the pool below.

To the trailhead

1800 IGNACIO BLVD · NOVATO   38.076872, -122.581523

From Highway 101 in Novato, take the Ignacio Boulevard exit. Drive 2.5 miles west, passing through the College of Marin campus, to the parking lot. Park in the lot at the west end. A parking fee is required.

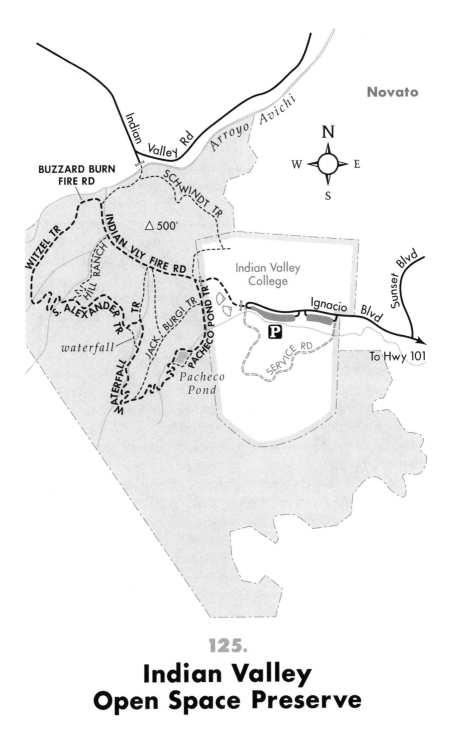

125.

Indian Valley
Open Space Preserve

The hike

From the far west end of the parking lot, take the asphalt path past the ballfields. At 0.2 miles, leave the developed park behind and enter the open space preserve at a trail gate. Just past the gate is a junction. Begin the 3.4-mile loop to the left on the Pacheco Pond Trail. Climb the short, steep hill, passing the Jack Burgi Trail on the right. Descend and curve right to a signed fork with the Waterfall Trail. Veer left, climbing the slope to Pacheco Pond. Loop around the east and south sides of the pond, where the two paths rejoin.

Continue up canyon, zigzagging up the forested hillside with the aid of twelve switchbacks. Pass the upper south end of the Jack Burgi Trail atop a ridge at one mile. Stay on the Waterfall Trail, and zigzag down the hill on five more switchbacks. Follow the drainage downstream, crossing the seasonal stream a few times to a Y-fork with the Susan Alexander Trail on the left. Stay to the right and cross the drainage above the ephemeral waterfall. Just beyond the falls, veer left on the connector trail to the Susan Alexander Trail, then go to the right on the main trail. Steadily climb through the shade of the oak, madrone, and bay laurel forest. Atop the steep slope, drop down again. Traverse the mountain on a hillside perch to a posted trail split with the Hill Ranch Trail on the right at just under two miles. (The right fork will form a shorter loop.)

Stay left, now on the Witzel Trail, and continue veering right at a posted bend. Head north on a steady downhill grade as the Witzel Trail becomes the Buzzard Burn Fire Road. The dirt road ends at a T-junction with the Indian Valley Fire Road. The left fork leads to the Indian Valley Road trailhead at the north end of the preserve. Go to the right on the wide dirt road. Follow the tree-lined valley floor at a near-level grade, walking parallel to seasonal Arroyo Avichi on the right. Pass the lower (north) junctions with the Hill Ranch Trail and the Waterfall Trail. Complete the loop at the gate by the Pacheco Pond Trail. Return 0.2 miles, passing the ball fields back to the trailhead parking lot. ■

Laguna de Santa Rosa Foundation

900 Sanford Road · Santa Rosa, CA 95401
(707) 572-9277
www.lagunadesantarosa.org

This non-profit foundation is the only agency that focuses exclusively on the Laguna de Santa Rosa watershed. Their invaluable work aims to permanently preserve, protect, restore, and enhance the 10,000-acre watershed. To find out more about their organization and their learning center, or to get involved, be a volunteer, a docent, attend regularly scheduled docent-led hikes, or to make a tax-deductible donation, call or visit their website.

The Laguna de Santa Rosa Foundation is instrumental in the creation and maintenance of Hikes 63—66, 68—69 and 77.

Stewards of the Coast and Redwoods

P.O. Box 2 · Duncan Mills, CA 95430
(707) 869-9177
www.stewardscr.org

This non-profit environmental organization works in partnership with the California Department of Parks and Recreation in the Russian River Sector. They provide the public with environmental stewardship programs, including educational and interpretive programs and resource management projects. They provide volunteers in the parks; sponsor interpretive talks; organize naturalist-led hikes, bike rides, and kayak trips; support land acquisition; and upgrade and build interpretive facilities. They have regularly scheduled docent-led hikes. Their focus is in Armstrong Redwoods State Natural Reserve, Austin Creek State Recreation Area, Sonoma Coast State Park and Beach, and the Willow Creek Watershed. To find our more or to be a volunteer, a docent, make a tax-deductible donation, or just enjoy one of their activities, call or visit their website.

Stewards of the Coast and Redwoods is connected with Hikes 30, 33 and 45—48.

DAY HIKE BOOKS

These books may be purchased at your local bookstore or outdoor shop. Or, order them directly from the distributor:

National Book Network

800-462-6420

Day Hikes Around Napa Valley

Napa Valley is a beautiful, verdant basin framed by mountain ranges that run parallel to the wide valley bottom. Thousands of acres of public greenspace lie interspersed amongst the region's world-renown wineries. This comprehensive collection of 88 day hikes provides access to the many trails through the valley, across mountain ranges, alongside bays and rivers, and through cool forests.

288 pages • 88 hikes • 1st Edition 2008

Day Hikes Around Monterey and Carmel

Monterey County in Central California is home to a hundred miles of picture-perfect coastline, from Monterey Bay to the rugged Big Sur oceanfront. Mountains backdrop the coast, separating the coastline from the rich agricultural land. Carmel and other quaint communities dot a landscape that is abundant with green valleys, woodlands, beaches, parks, and calm bays along the scalloped Pacific coast.

384 pages • 127 hikes • 2nd Edition 2013

Day Hikes In Yosemite National Park

Yosemite is one of the world's most loved national parks. These 80 hikes include all of Yosemite's well-known attractions, plus many other hiking options to out-of-the-way destinations and unique vistas. Highlights include incredible waterfalls, the granite monoliths of Yosemite Valley, alpine meadows, giant sequoia groves, and unforgettable views from perspectives that are only accessible from the trails.

208 pages • 80 hikes • 3rd Edition 2009

INDEX

ADRIENNE METTER

About the Author

Since 1991, Robert Stone has been writer, photographer, and publisher of Day Hike Books. He is a Los Angeles Times Best Selling Author and an award-winning journalist of Rocky Mountain Outdoor Writers and Photographers, the Outdoor Writers Association of California, the Northwest Outdoor Writers Association, the Outdoor Writers Association of America, and the Bay Area Travel Writers.

Robert has hiked every trail in the Day Hike Book series. With 20 hiking guides in the series, many in their fourth and fifth editions, he has hiked thousands of miles of trails throughout the western United States. When Robert is not hiking, he researches, writes, and maps the hikes before returning to the trails. He spends summers in the Rocky Mountains of Montana and winters on the California Central Coast.